SORCERER HUNTERS™

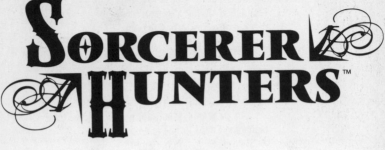

BOOK 1

BY SATORU AKAHORI
& RAY OMISHI

TOKYOPOP®

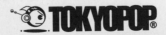

HAMBURG // LONDON // LOS ANGELES // TOKYO

Sorcerer Hunters Vol. 1
Story by Satoru Akahori
Art by Ray Omishi

Translation - Anita Sengupta
Retouch and Lettering - Jose Macasocol, Jr.
Production Artist - Vincente Rivera, Jr.
Cover Design - Gary Schum

Editor - Lillian Diaz-Przybyl
Digital Imaging Manager - Chris Buford
Pre-Press Manager - Antonio DePietro
Production Managers - Jennifer Miller and Mutsumi Miyazaki
Art Director - Matt Alford
Managing Editor - Jill Freshney
VP of Production - Ron Klamert
Editor-in-Chief - Mike Kiley
President and C.O.O. - John Parker
Publisher and C.E.O. - Stuart Levy

A 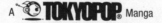 Manga

TOKYOPOP Inc.
5900 Wilshire Blvd. Suite 2000
Los Angeles, CA 90036

E-mail: info@TOKYOPOP.com
Come visit us online at www.TOKYOPOP.com

ISBN: 1-59532-494-1

First TOKYOPOP® printing: March 2005
10 9 8 7 6 5 4 3 2 1
Printed in the USA

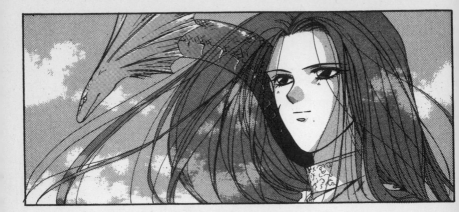

THE WAY PEOPLE ADDRESS EACH OTHER IN JAPANESE TELLS THE LISTENER (OR READER) A LOT ABOUT THEIR RELATIONSHIPS. FOR EXAMPLE, RIN CALLS KOH, "ONII-CHAN," WHICH LITERALLY MEANS "OLDER BROTHER," BUT IS A FAIRLY POLITE AND DEFERENTIAL TERM, ALTHOUGH ATTACHING "-CHAN" ADDS A BIT OF FEMININE CUTENESS. SIMILARLY, MARRON CALLS CARROT "NII-SAN," WHICH IS THE SAME TERM, BUT WITH THE HONORIFIC "O" AT THE BEGINNING DROPPED--HE HAS A LOT OF RESPECT FOR HIS DEAR BROTHER, BUT THEY'RE ALSO A LITTLE CLOSER. TIRA CALLS MARRON, "MARRON-CHAN," A TERM THAT SHOWS AFFECTION, BUT MIGHT BE OFFENSIVE TO AN ADULT MAN, UNLESS IT CAME FROM A CHILDHOOD FRIEND. ON THE OTHER HAND, SHE USES "-SAN" WITH CARROT, WHICH IS A MORE POLITE ADDRESS, MORE OR LESS EQUIVALENT TO "MISS" OR "MR." I GUESS SHE'S STILL A LITTLE SHY AROUND HIM.

THE SUFFIX "-SAMA" SHOWS UP IN THIS VOLUME AS WELL. "-SAMA" IS ONE OF THE HIGHEST HONORIFICS, USED WHEN BEING PARTICULARLY POLITE. OF COURSE, IF YOU USE "-SAMA" WHEN REFERRING TO YOURSELF, WHAT COMES ACROSS INSTEAD IS IMPRESSIVE ARROGANCE! *KI O TSUKE, NE!*

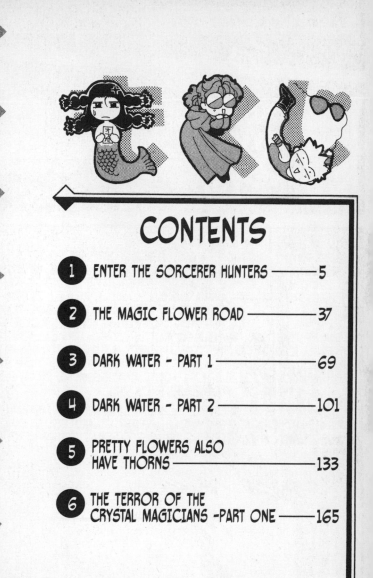

CONTENTS

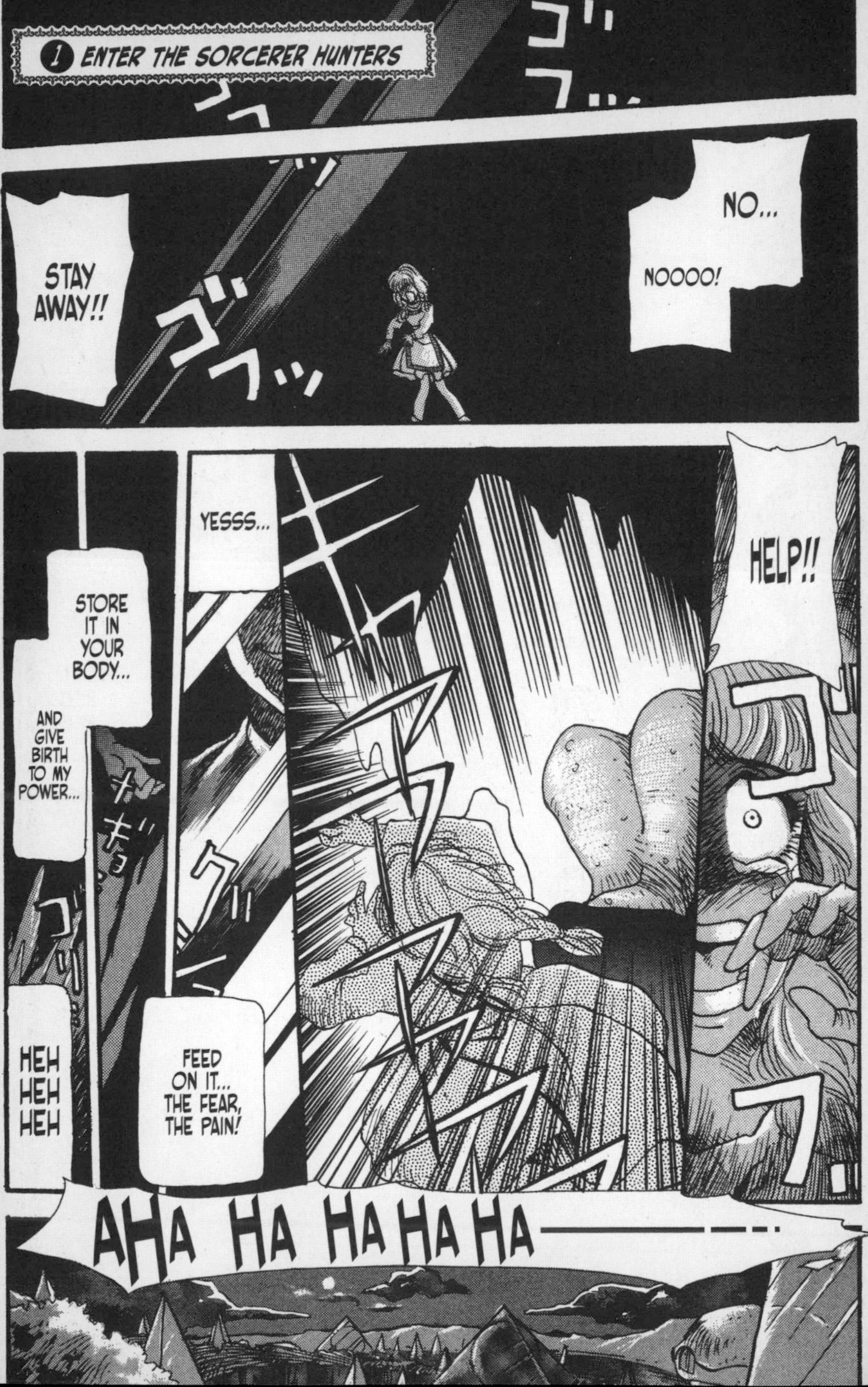
1 ENTER THE SORCERER HUNTERS
NO...
NOOOO!
STAY AWAY!!
HELP!!
YESSS...
STORE IT IN YOUR BODY...
AND GIVE BIRTH TO MY POWER...
FEED ON IT... THE FEAR, THE PAIN!
HEH HEH HEH
AHA HA HA HA HA HA———

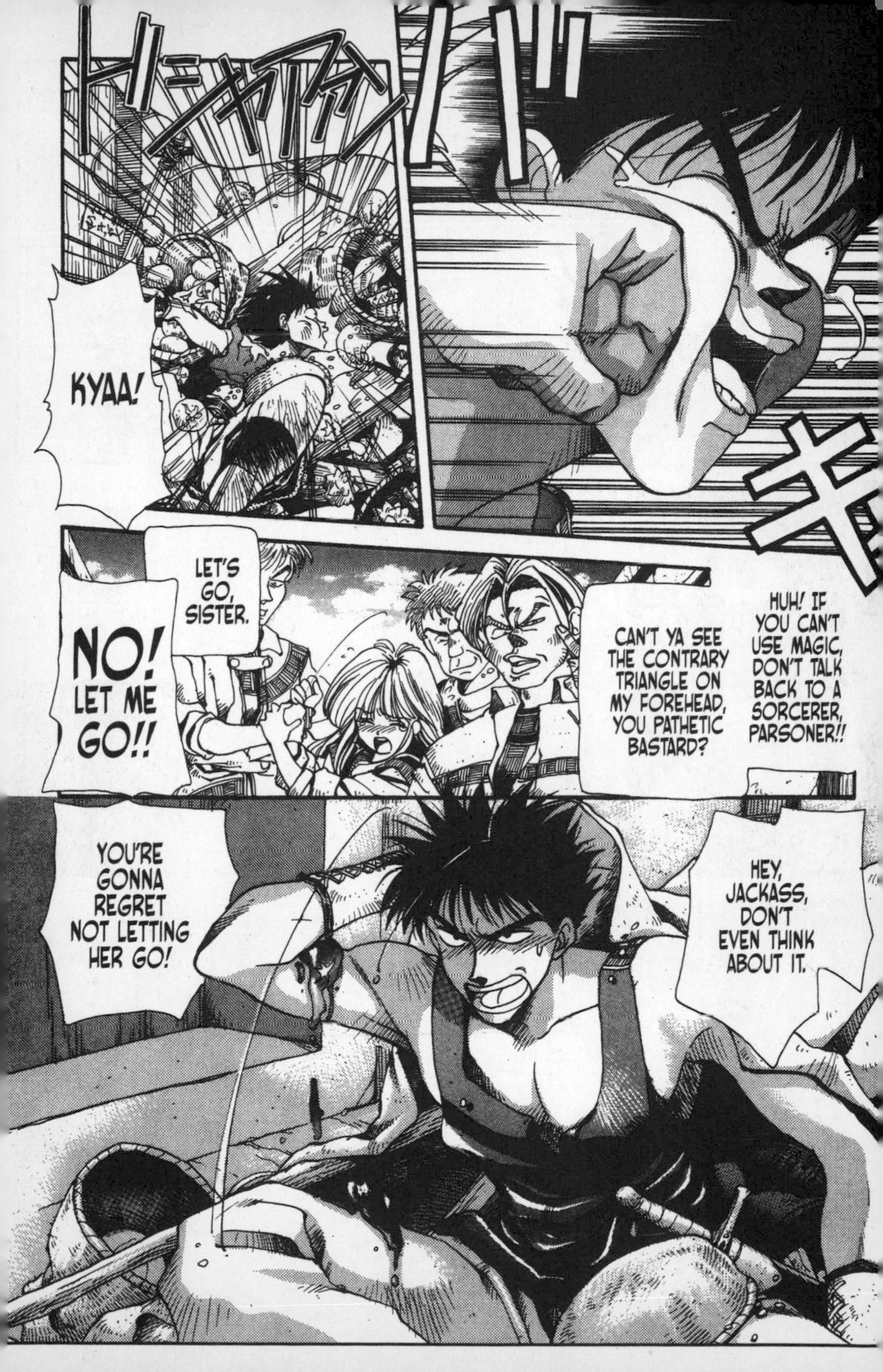
KYAA!
HUH! IF YOU CAN'T USE MAGIC, DON'T TALK BACK TO A SORCERER, PARSONER!!
CAN'T YA SEE THE CONTRARY TRIANGLE ON MY FOREHEAD, YOU PATHETIC BASTARD?
LET'S GO, SISTER.
NO! LET ME GO!!
HEY, JACKASS, DON'T EVEN THINK ABOUT IT.
YOU'RE GONNA REGRET NOT LETTING HER GO!

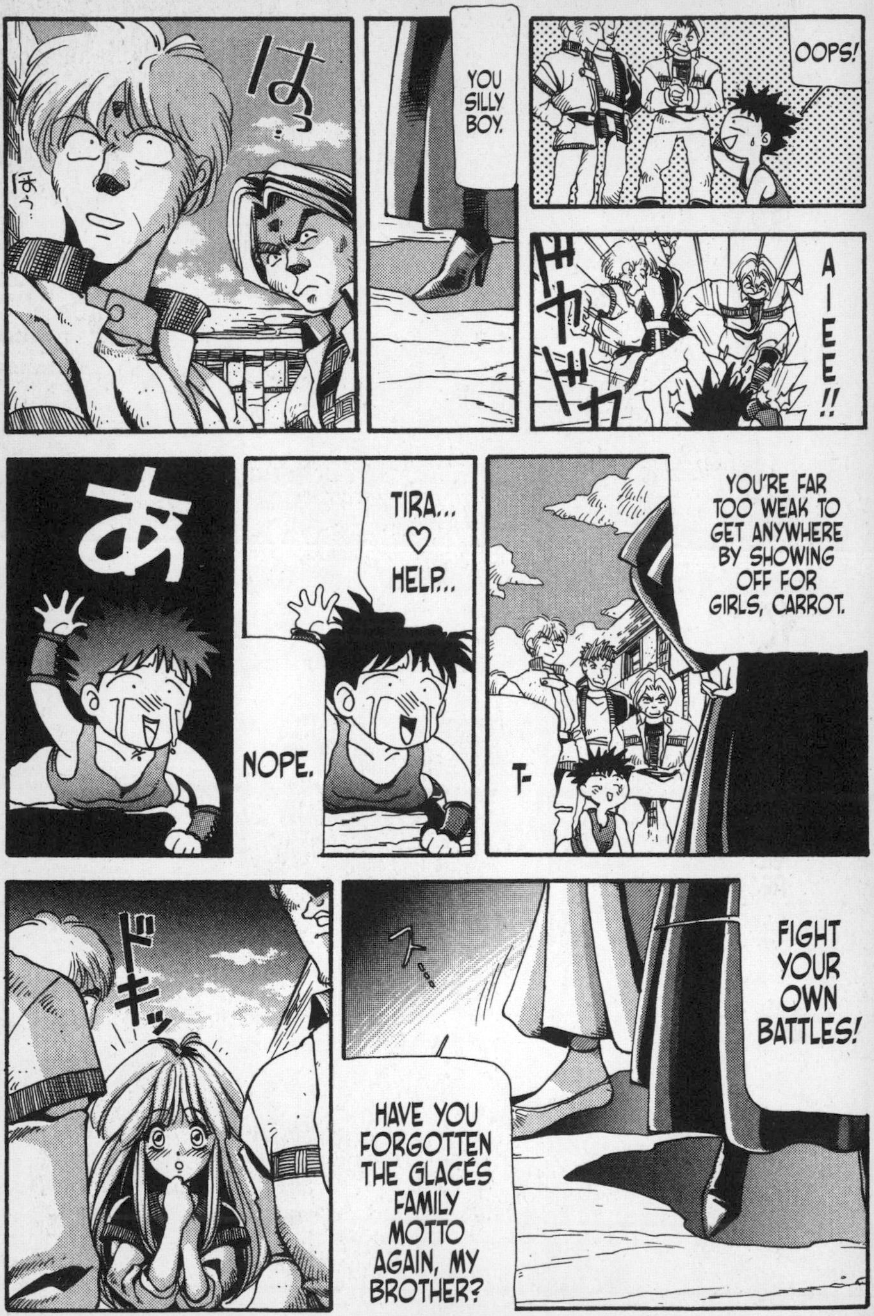
OOPS!
AIEE!!
YOU SILLY BOY.
はっ
YOU'RE FAR TOO WEAK TO GET ANYWHERE BY SHOWING OFF FOR GIRLS, CARROT.
T-
TIRA... ♡ HELP...
NOPE.
あ
FIGHT YOUR OWN BATTLES!
HAVE YOU FORGOTTEN THE GLACÉS FAMILY MOTTO AGAIN, MY BROTHER?
ドキッ

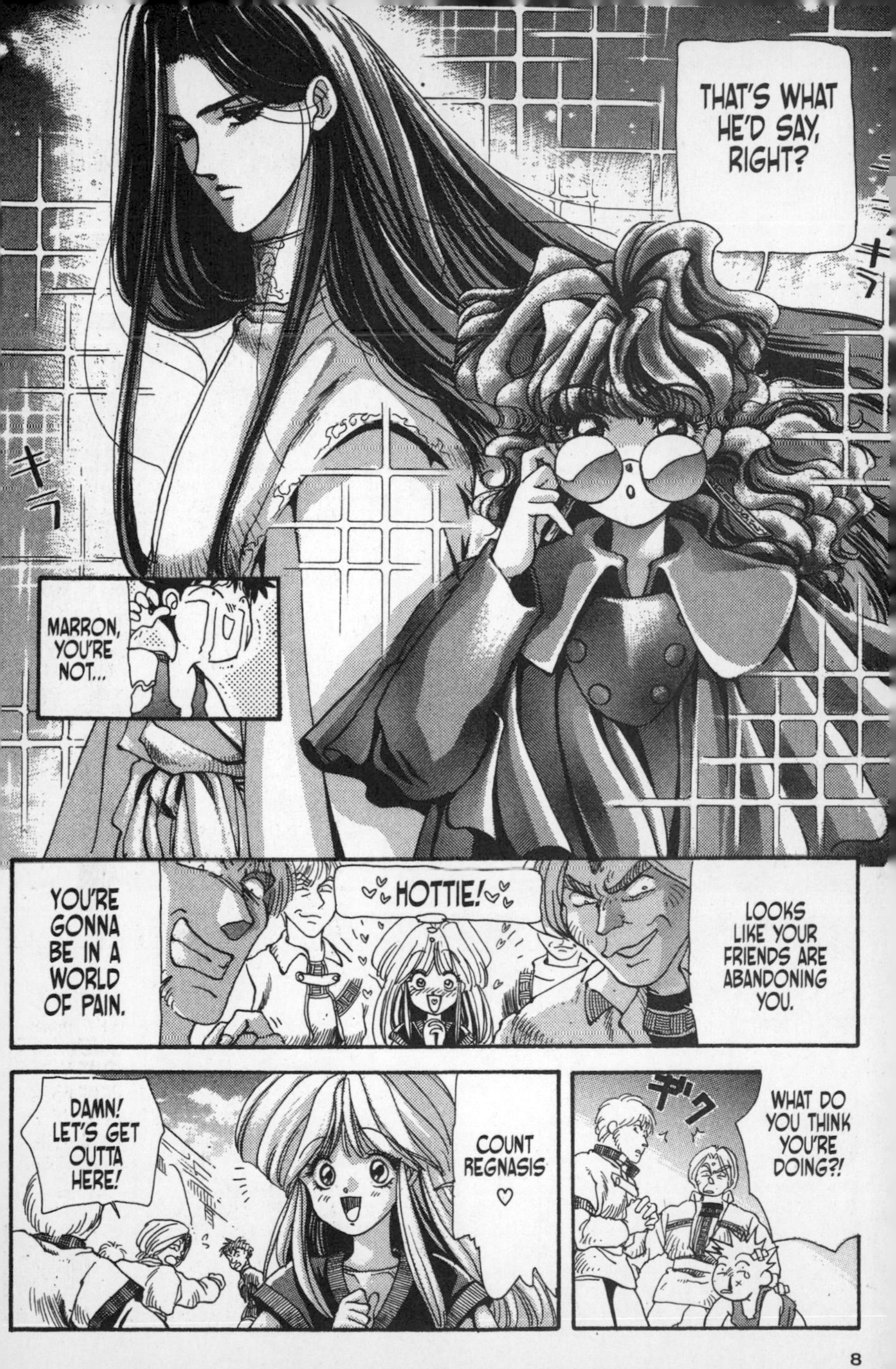
THAT'S WHAT HE'D SAY, RIGHT?
MARRON, YOU'RE NOT...
LOOKS LIKE YOUR FRIENDS ARE ABANDONING YOU.
HOTTIE!
YOU'RE GONNA BE IN A WORLD OF PAIN.
WHAT DO YOU THINK YOU'RE DOING?!
COUNT REGNASIS ♡
DAMN! LET'S GET OUTTA HERE!

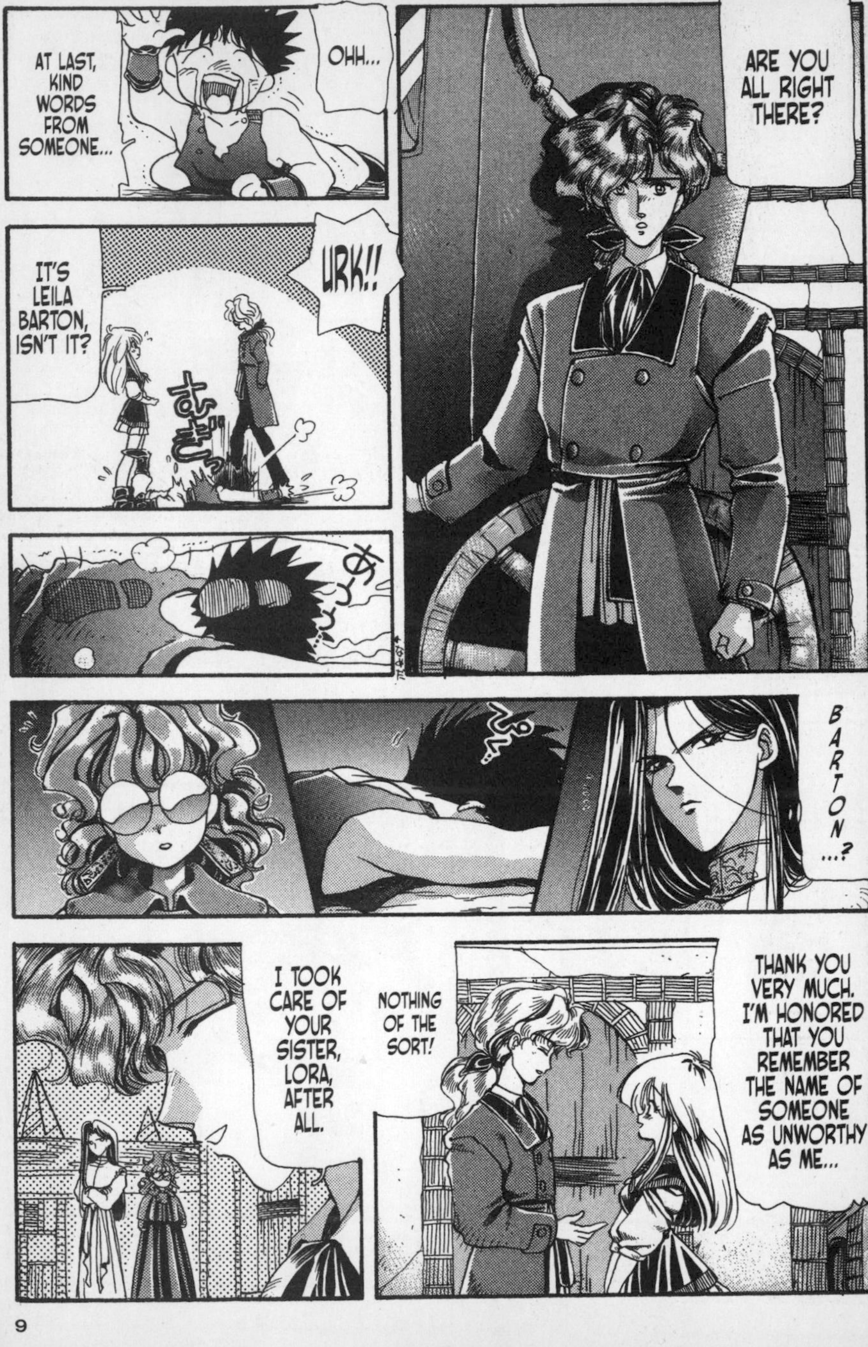
ARE YOU ALL RIGHT THERE?
OHH...
AT LAST, KIND WORDS FROM SOMEONE...
URK!!
IT'S LEILA BARTON, ISN'T IT?
BARTON...?
THANK YOU VERY MUCH. I'M HONORED THAT YOU REMEMBER THE NAME OF SOMEONE AS UNWORTHY AS ME...
NOTHING OF THE SORT!
I TOOK CARE OF YOUR SISTER, LORA, AFTER ALL.

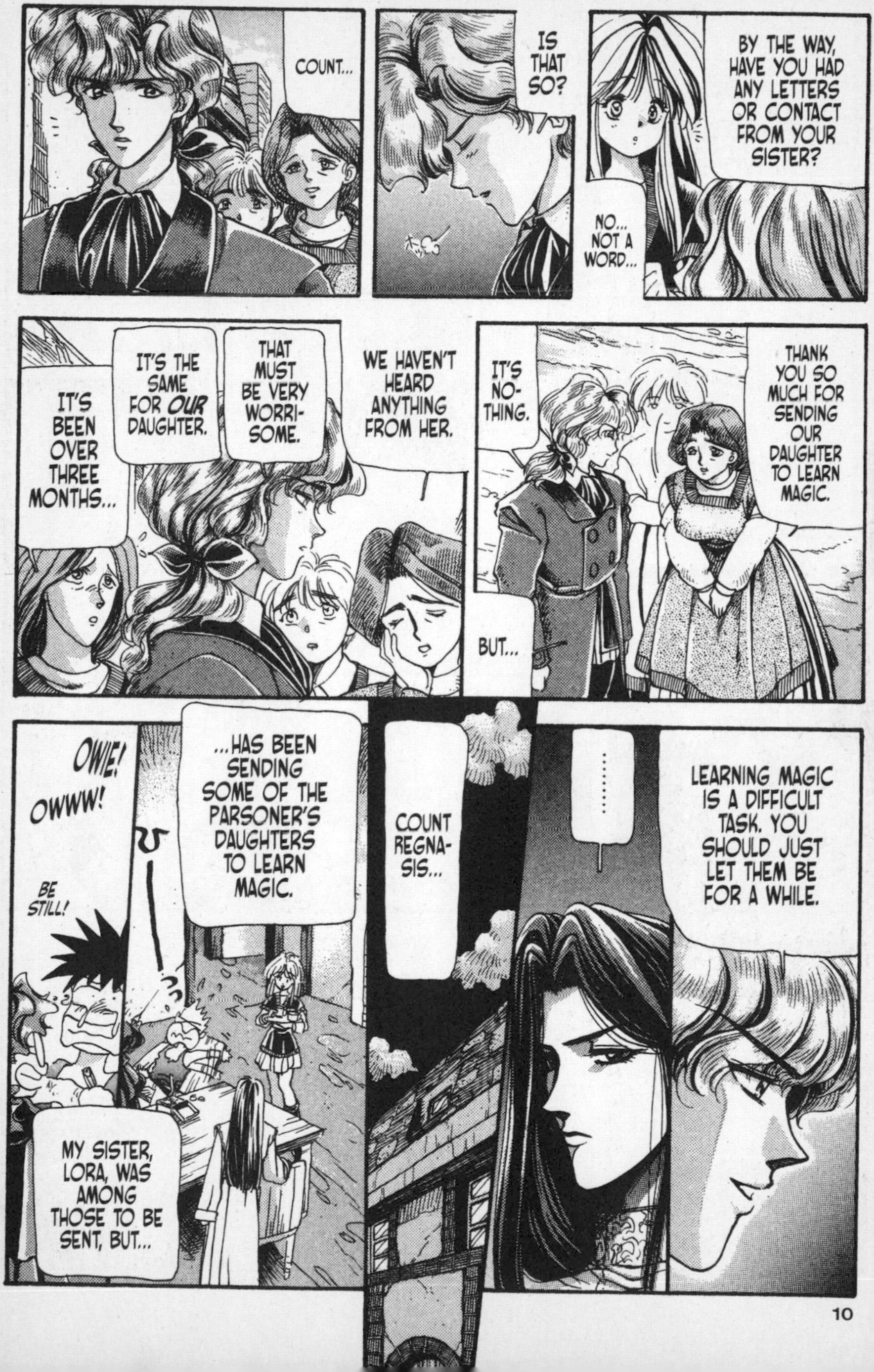
BY THE WAY, HAVE YOU HAD ANY LETTERS OR CONTACT FROM YOUR SISTER?
NO... NOT A WORD...
IS THAT SO?
COUNT...
THANK YOU SO MUCH FOR SENDING OUR DAUGHTER TO LEARN MAGIC.
IT'S NO-THING.
BUT...
WE HAVEN'T HEARD ANYTHING FROM HER.
THAT MUST BE VERY WORRI-SOME.
IT'S THE SAME FOR OUR DAUGHTER.
IT'S BEEN OVER THREE MONTHS...
LEARNING MAGIC IS A DIFFICULT TASK. YOU SHOULD JUST LET THEM BE FOR A WHILE.
......
COUNT REGNA-SIS...
...HAS BEEN SENDING SOME OF THE PARSONER'S DAUGHTERS TO LEARN MAGIC.
OWIE!
OWWW!
BE STILL!
MY SISTER, LORA, WAS AMONG THOSE TO BE SENT, BUT...

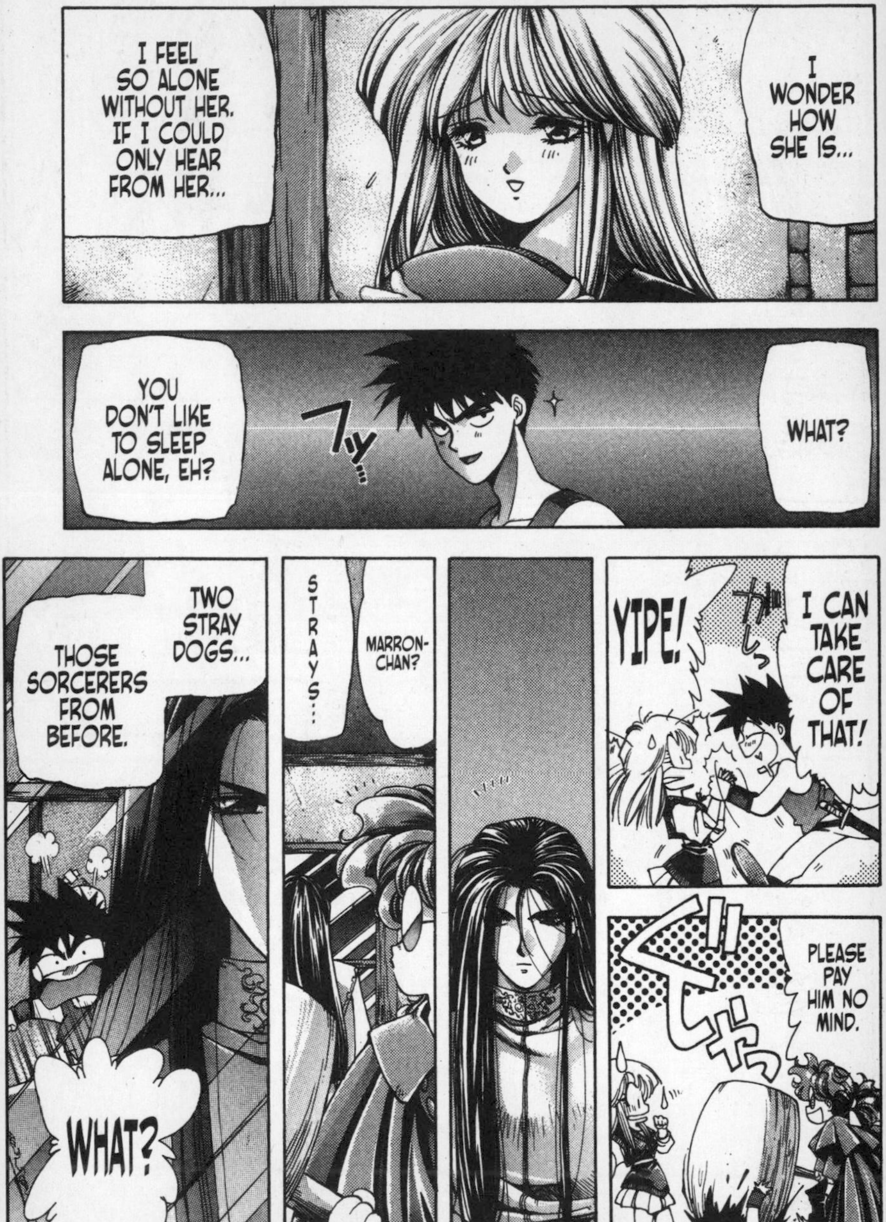

I WONDER HOW SHE IS...
I FEEL SO ALONE WITHOUT HER. IF I COULD ONLY HEAR FROM HER...
WHAT?
YOU DON'T LIKE TO SLEEP ALONE, EH?
I CAN TAKE CARE OF THAT!
YIPE!
PLEASE PAY HIM NO MIND.
MARRON-CHAN?
STRAYS...
TWO STRAY DOGS...
THOSE SORCERERS FROM BEFORE.
WHAT?

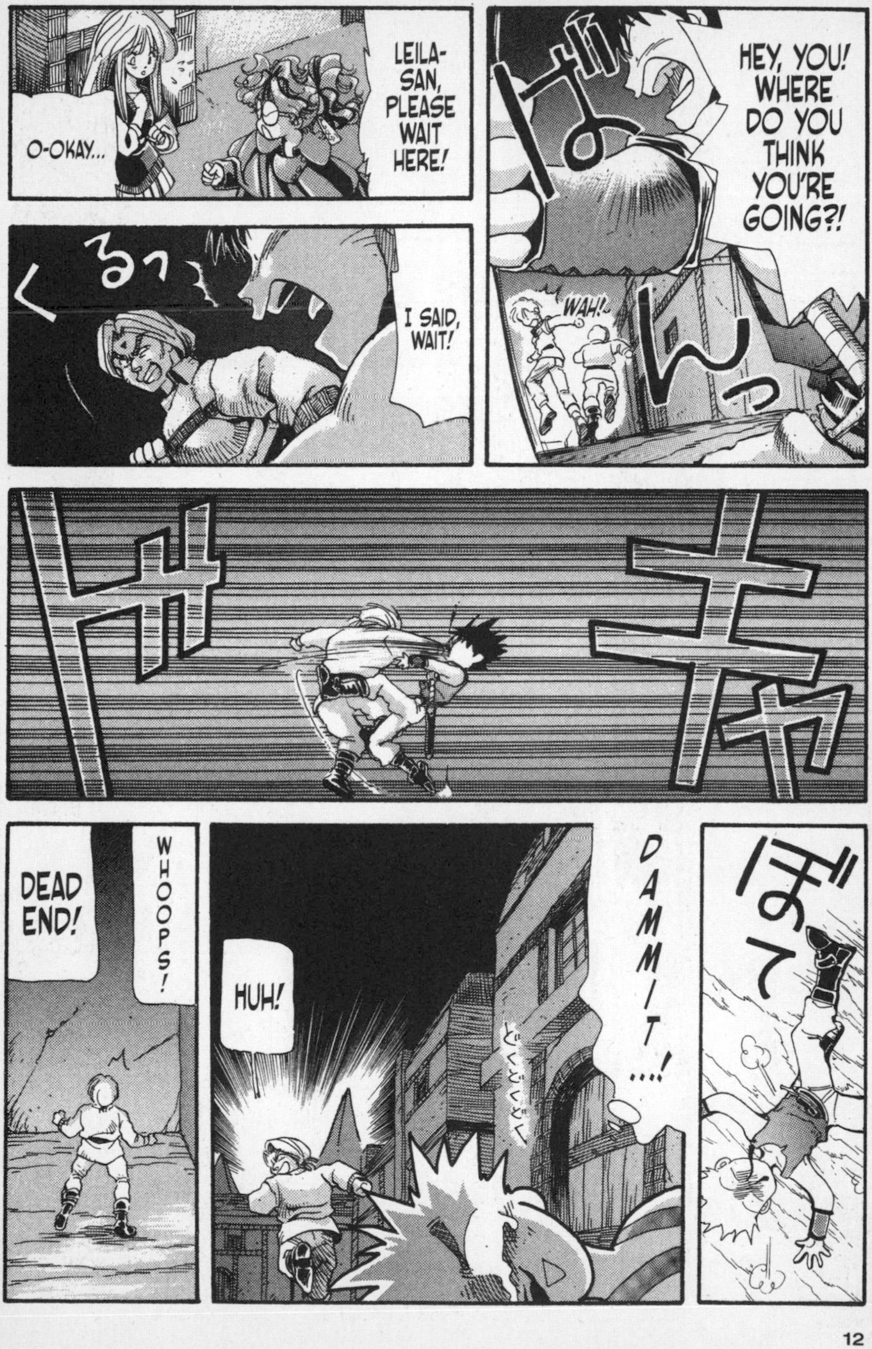
HEY, YOU! WHERE DO YOU THINK YOU'RE GOING?!
WAH!
LEILA-SAN, PLEASE WAIT HERE!
O-OKAY...
I SAID, WAIT!
ぼて
DAMMIT...!
HUH!
WHOOPS!
DEAD END!

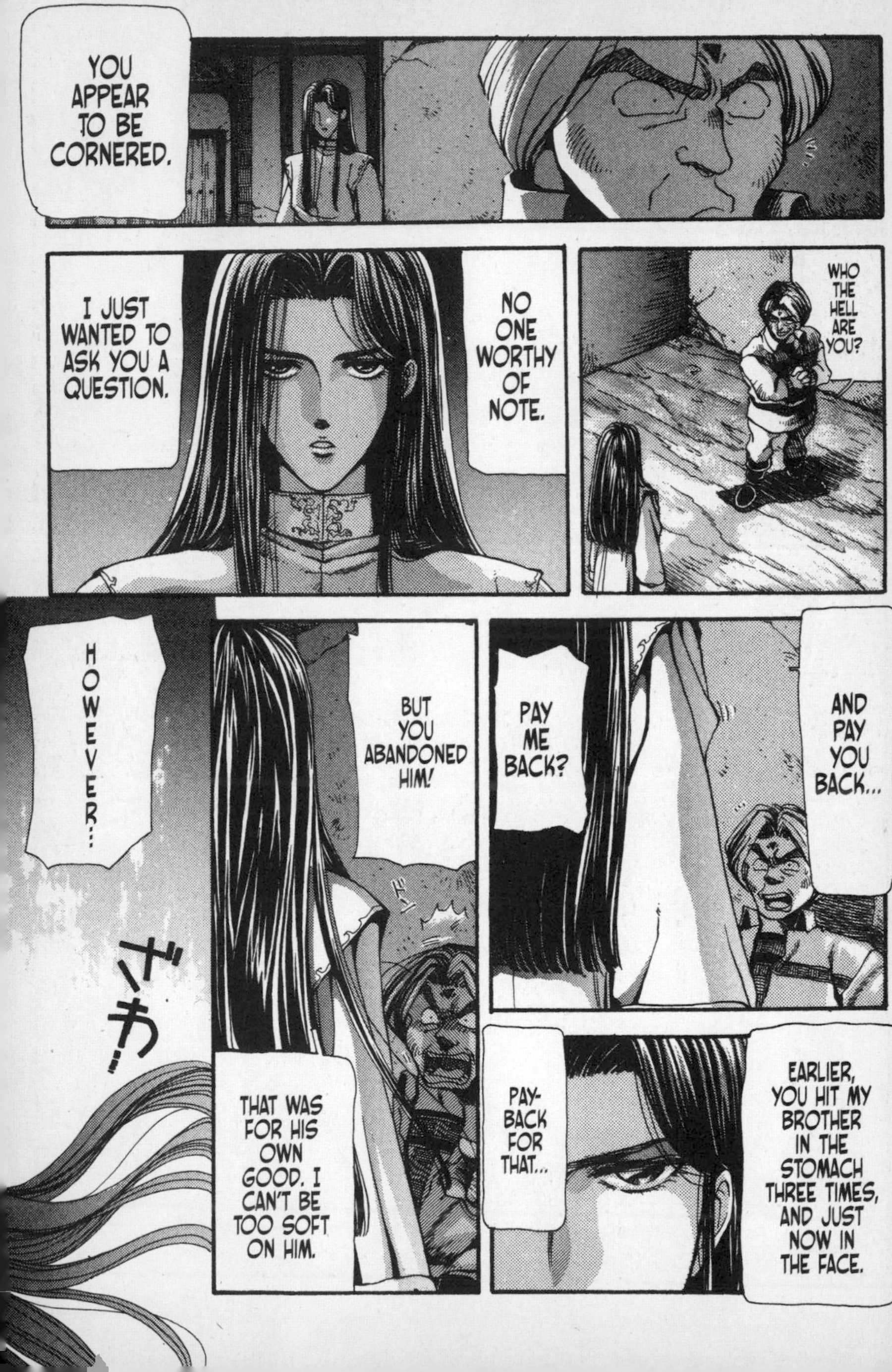
YOU APPEAR TO BE CORNERED.
WHO THE HELL ARE YOU?
NO ONE WORTHY OF NOTE.
I JUST WANTED TO ASK YOU A QUESTION.
AND PAY YOU BACK...
PAY ME BACK?
EARLIER, YOU HIT MY BROTHER IN THE STOMACH THREE TIMES, AND JUST NOW IN THE FACE.
PAY-BACK FOR THAT...
BUT YOU ABANDONED HIM!
THAT WAS FOR HIS OWN GOOD. I CAN'T BE TOO SOFT ON HIM.
HOWEVER...

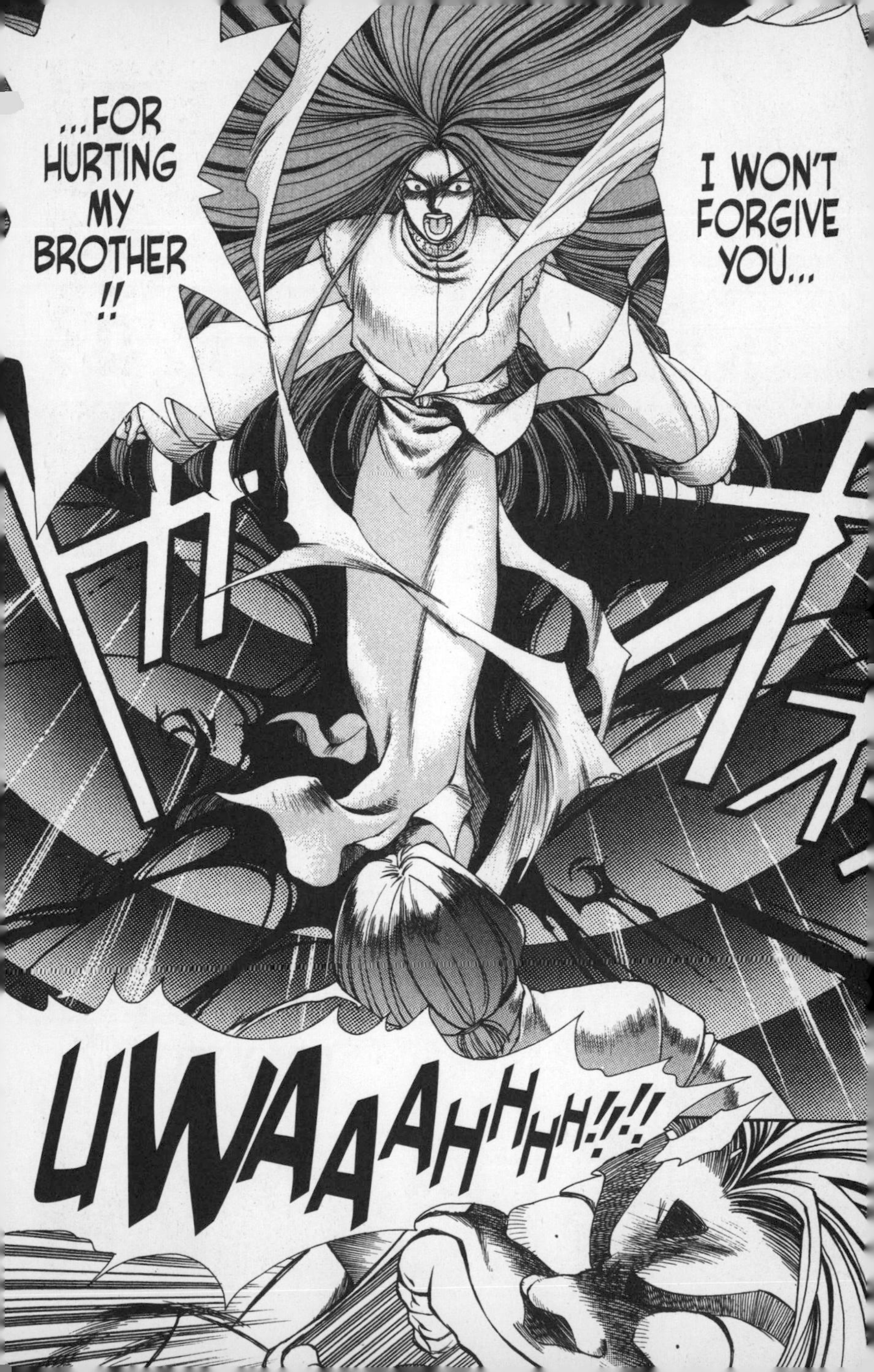
I WON'T FORGIVE YOU...
...FOR HURTING MY BROTHER!!
UWAAAAHHHH!!!!

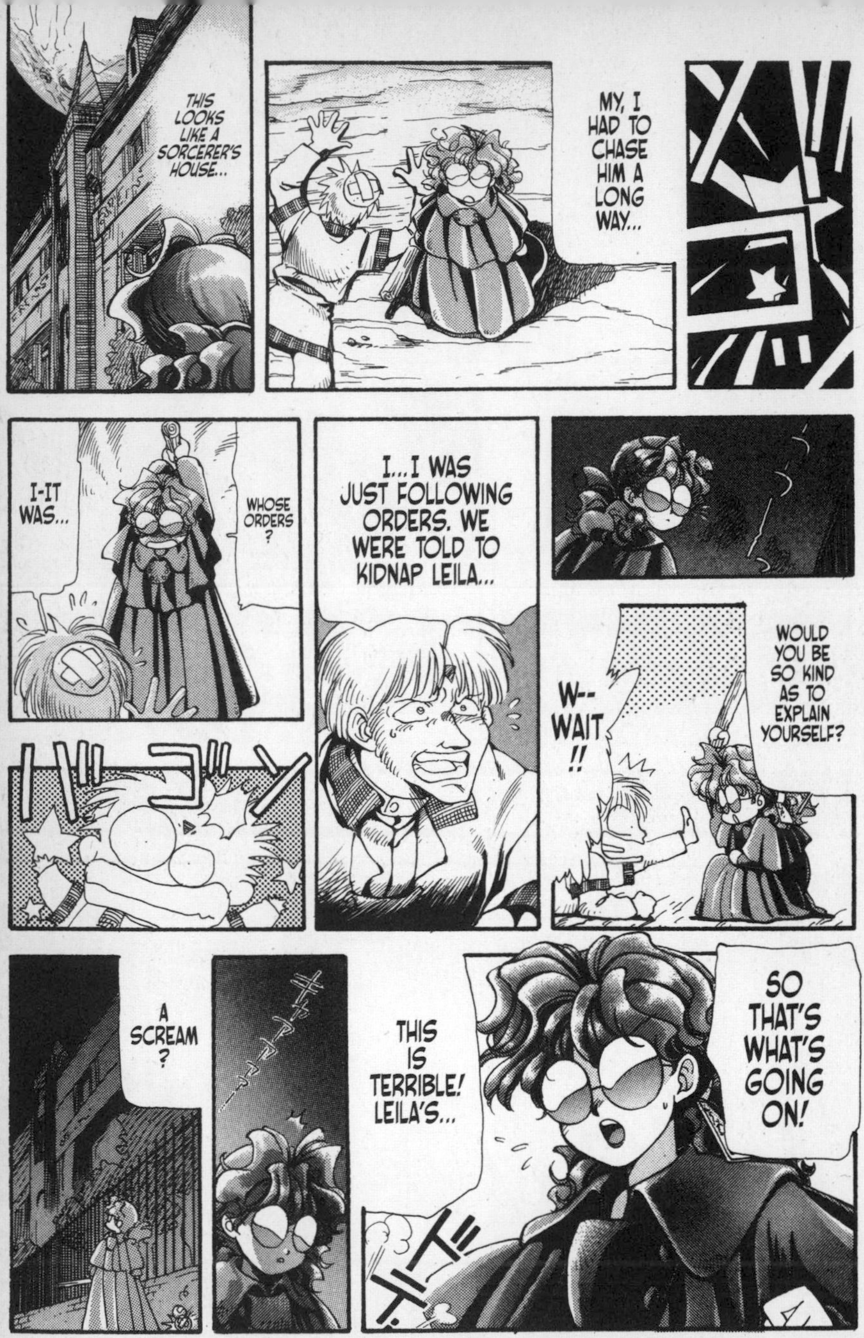
MY, I HAD TO CHASE HIM A LONG WAY...
THIS LOOKS LIKE A SORCERER'S HOUSE...
WOULD YOU BE SO KIND AS TO EXPLAIN YOURSELF?
W-- WAIT !!
I...I WAS JUST FOLLOWING ORDERS. WE WERE TOLD TO KIDNAP LEILA...
WHOSE ORDERS ?
I-IT WAS...
SO THAT'S WHAT'S GOING ON!
THIS IS TERRIBLE! LEILA'S...
A SCREAM ?

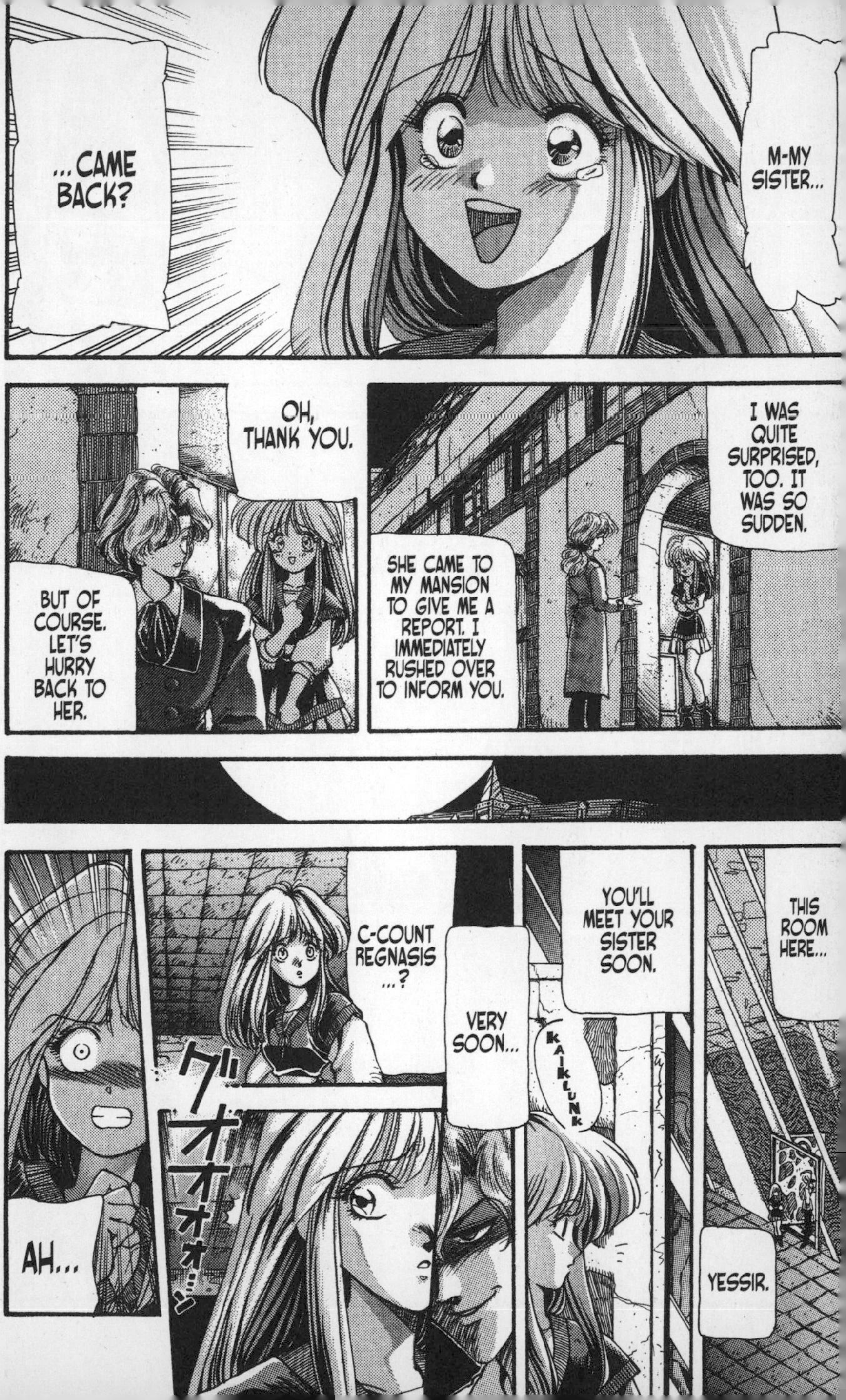
M-MY SISTER...
...CAME BACK?
I WAS QUITE SURPRISED, TOO. IT WAS SO SUDDEN.
SHE CAME TO MY MANSION TO GIVE ME A REPORT. I IMMEDIATELY RUSHED OVER TO INFORM YOU.
OH, THANK YOU.
BUT OF COURSE. LET'S HURRY BACK TO HER.
THIS ROOM HERE...
YESSIR.
YOU'LL MEET YOUR SISTER SOON.
KAIKLUNK
VERY SOON...
C-COUNT REGNASIS ...?
グオオオオ…ン
AH...

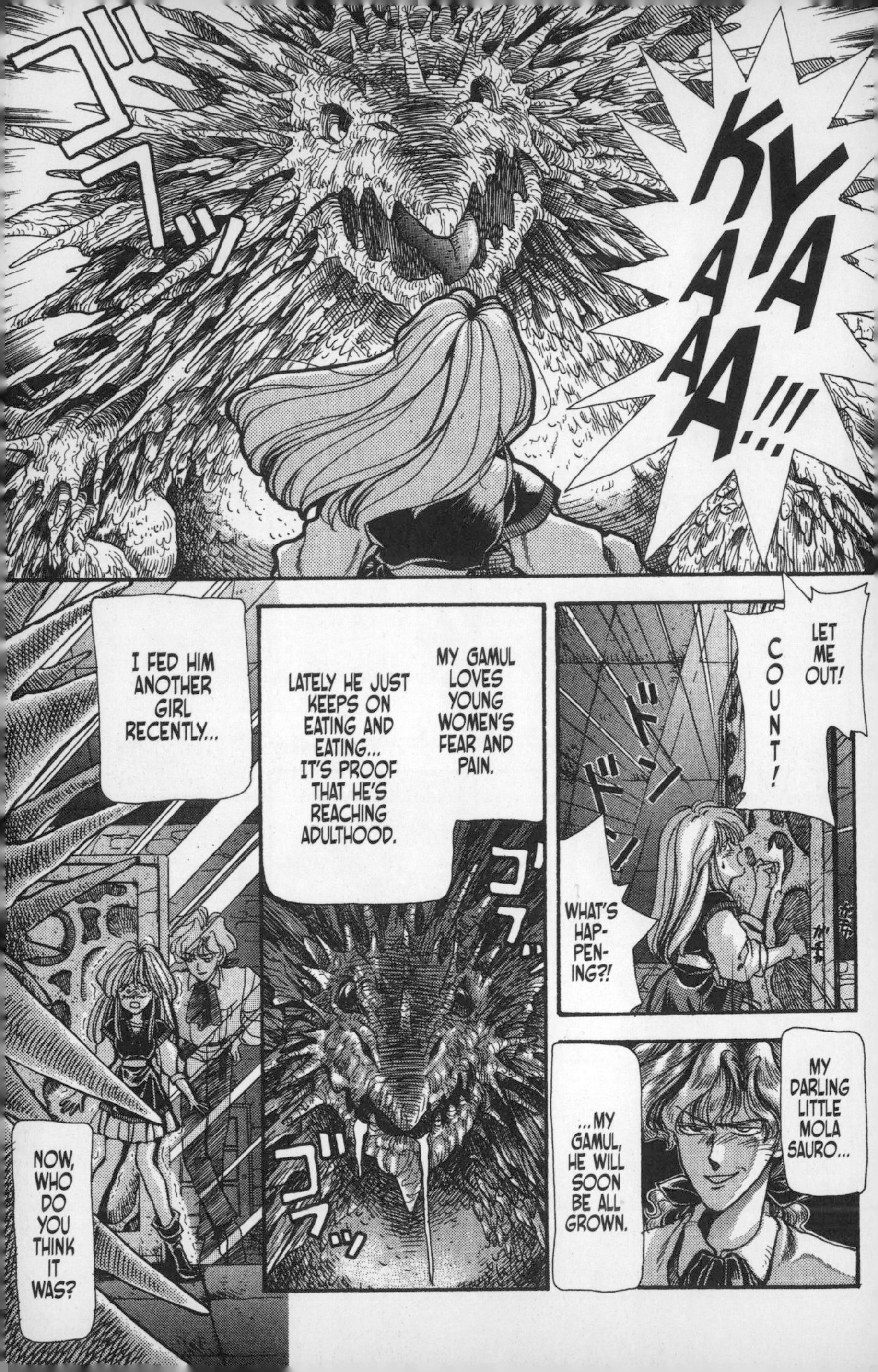

KYAAAA!!!
LET ME OUT!
COUNT!
WHAT'S HAP-PEN-ING?!
MY DARLING LITTLE MOLA SAURO...
...MY GAMUL, HE WILL SOON BE ALL GROWN.
MY GAMUL LOVES YOUNG WOMEN'S FEAR AND PAIN.
LATELY HE JUST KEEPS ON EATING AND EATING... IT'S PROOF THAT HE'S REACHING ADULTHOOD.
I FED HIM ANOTHER GIRL RECENTLY...
NOW, WHO DO YOU THINK IT WAS?

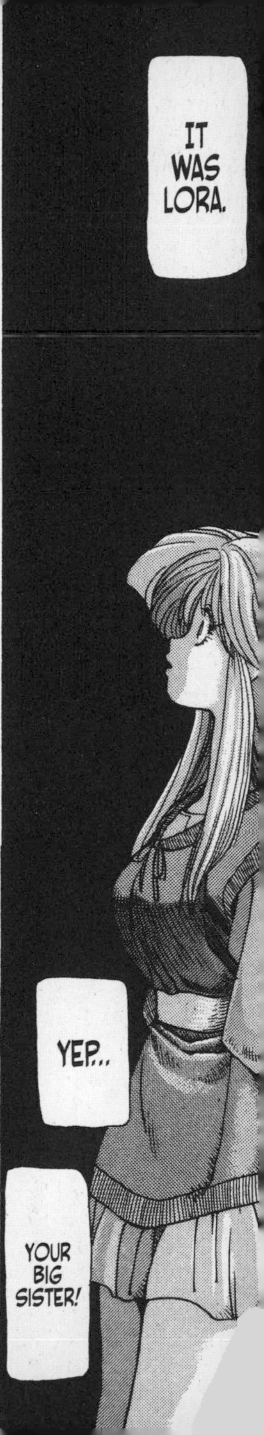
IT WAS LORA.
YEP...
YOUR BIG SISTER!

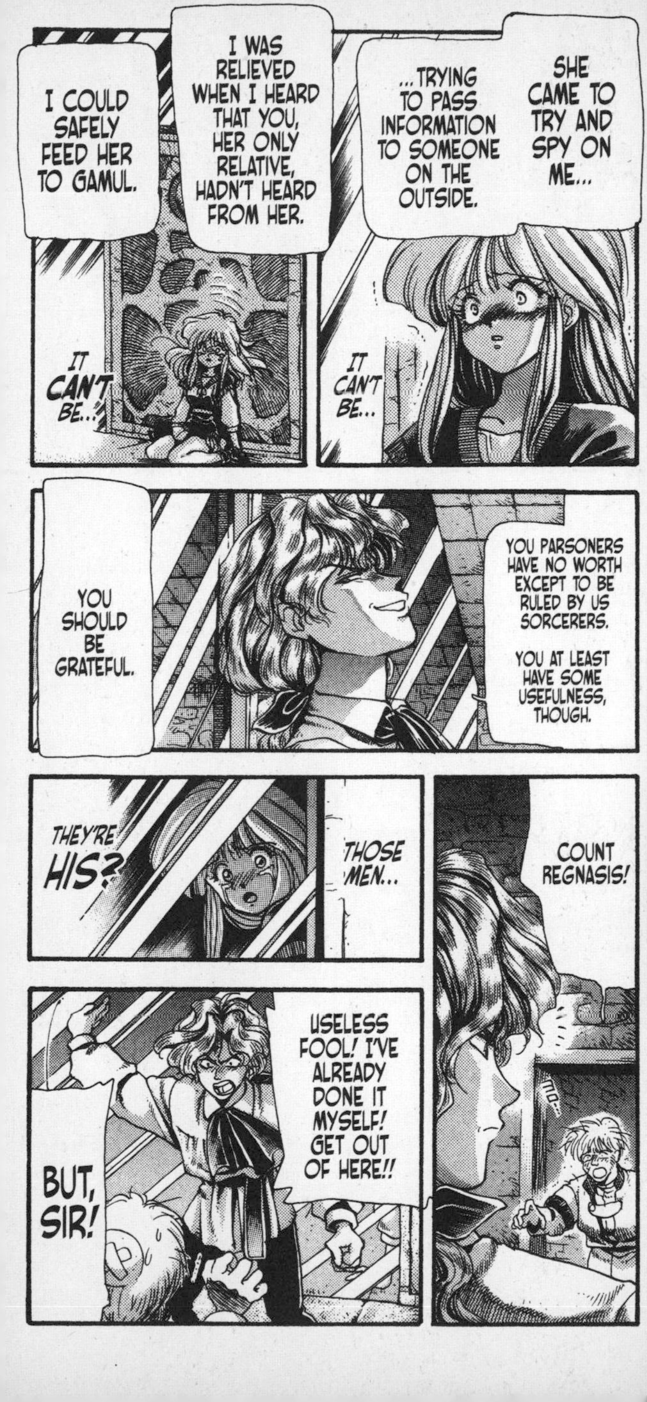
SHE CAME TO TRY AND SPY ON ME...
...TRYING TO PASS INFORMATION TO SOMEONE ON THE OUTSIDE.
IT CAN'T BE...
I WAS RELIEVED WHEN I HEARD THAT YOU, HER ONLY RELATIVE, HADN'T HEARD FROM HER.
I COULD SAFELY FEED HER TO GAMUL.
IT CAN'T BE...
YOU PARSONERS HAVE NO WORTH EXCEPT TO BE RULED BY US SORCERERS.
YOU AT LEAST HAVE SOME USEFULNESS, THOUGH.
YOU SHOULD BE GRATEFUL.
COUNT REGNASIS!
THOSE MEN...
THEY'RE HIS?
USELESS FOOL! I'VE ALREADY DONE IT MYSELF! GET OUT OF HERE!!
BUT, SIR!

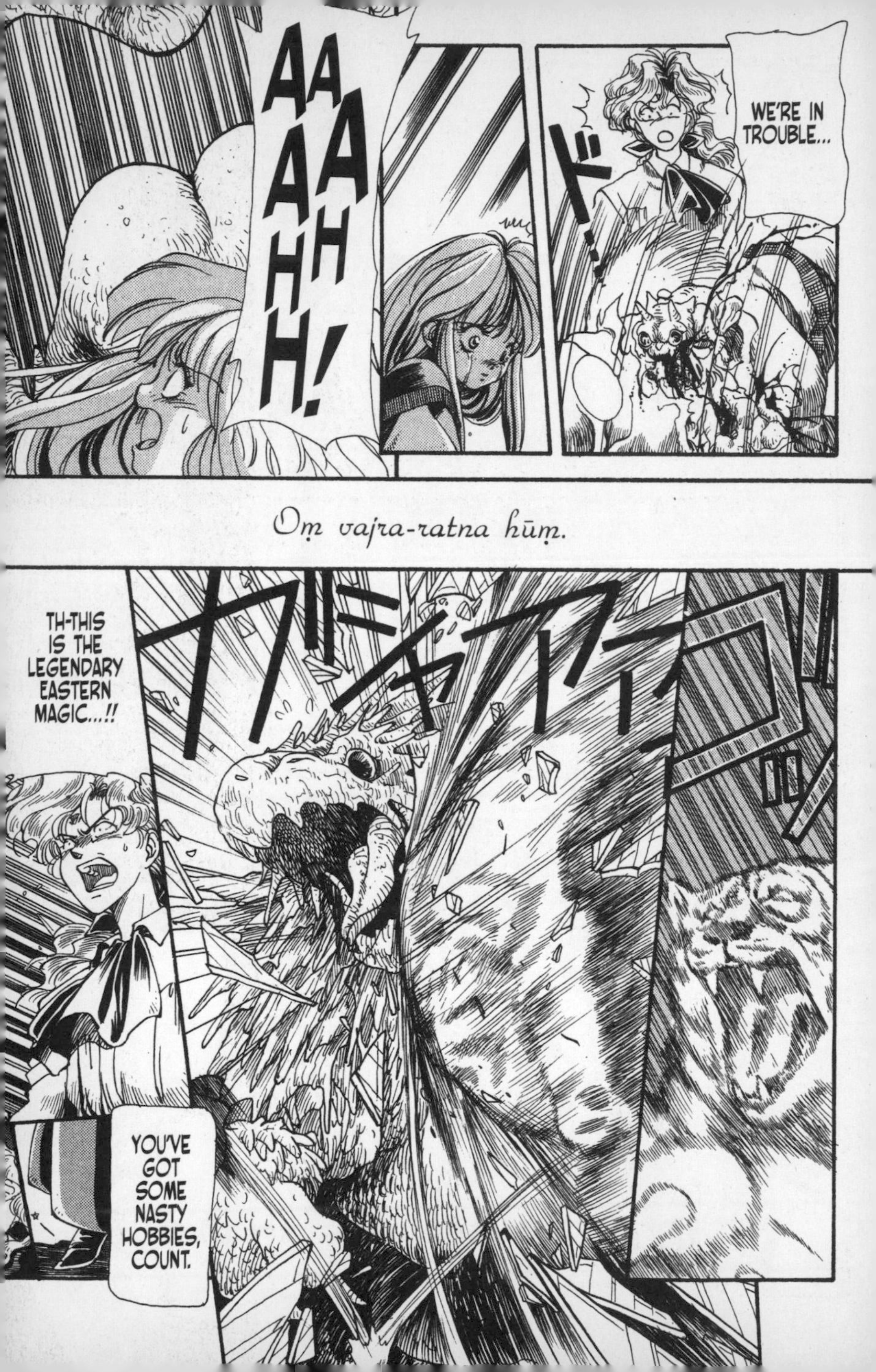
WE'RE IN TROUBLE...
ド
AAAAHHH!
Oṃ vajra-ratna hūṃ.
TH-THIS IS THE LEGENDARY EASTERN MAGIC...!!
YOU'VE GOT SOME NASTY HOBBIES, COUNT.

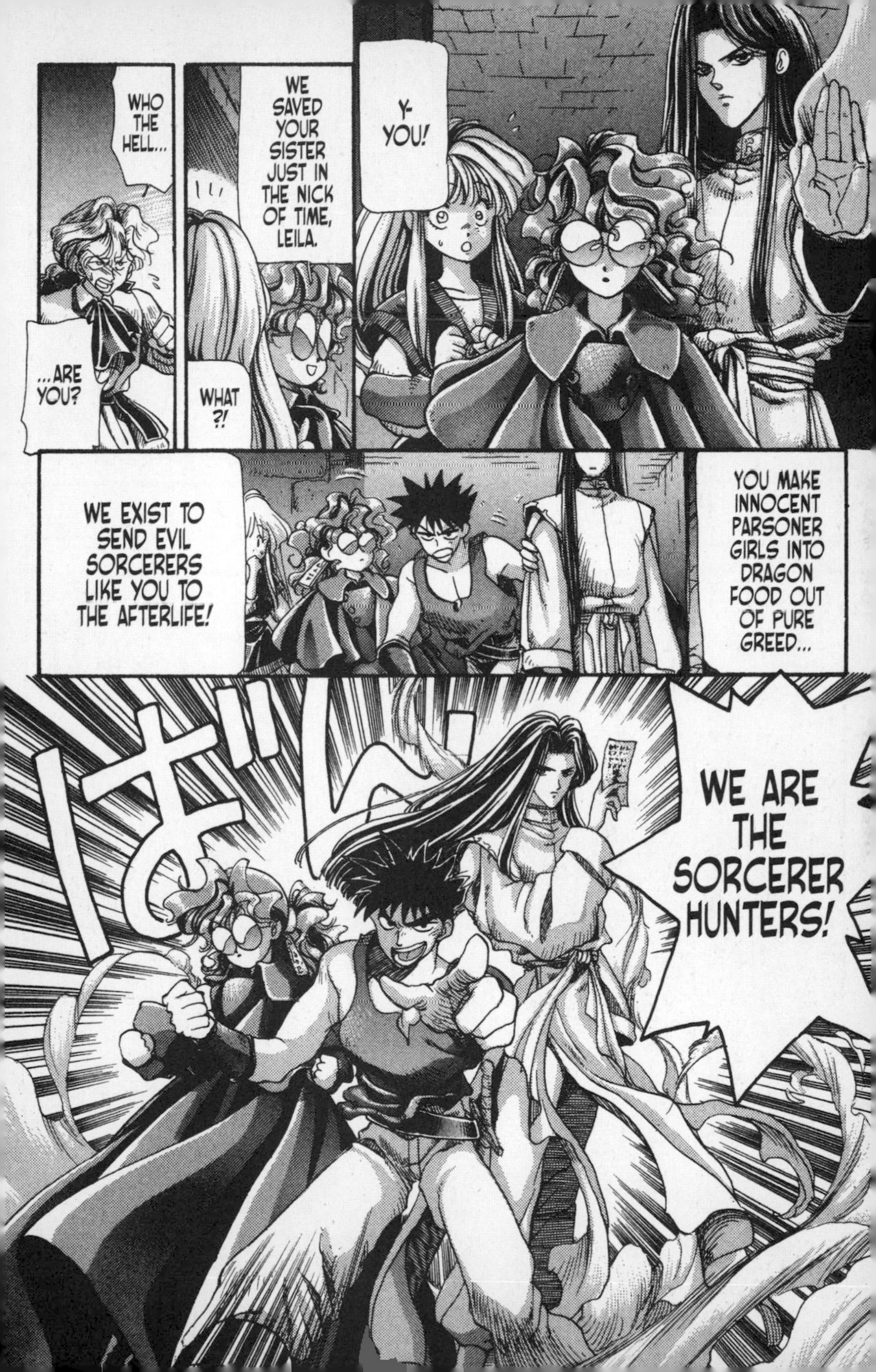
Y-
YOU!
WE SAVED YOUR SISTER JUST IN THE NICK OF TIME, LEILA.
WHAT ?!
WHO THE HELL...
...ARE YOU?
YOU MAKE INNOCENT PARSONER GIRLS INTO DRAGON FOOD OUT OF PURE GREED...
WE EXIST TO SEND EVIL SORCERERS LIKE YOU TO THE AFTERLIFE!
WE ARE THE SORCERER HUNTERS!

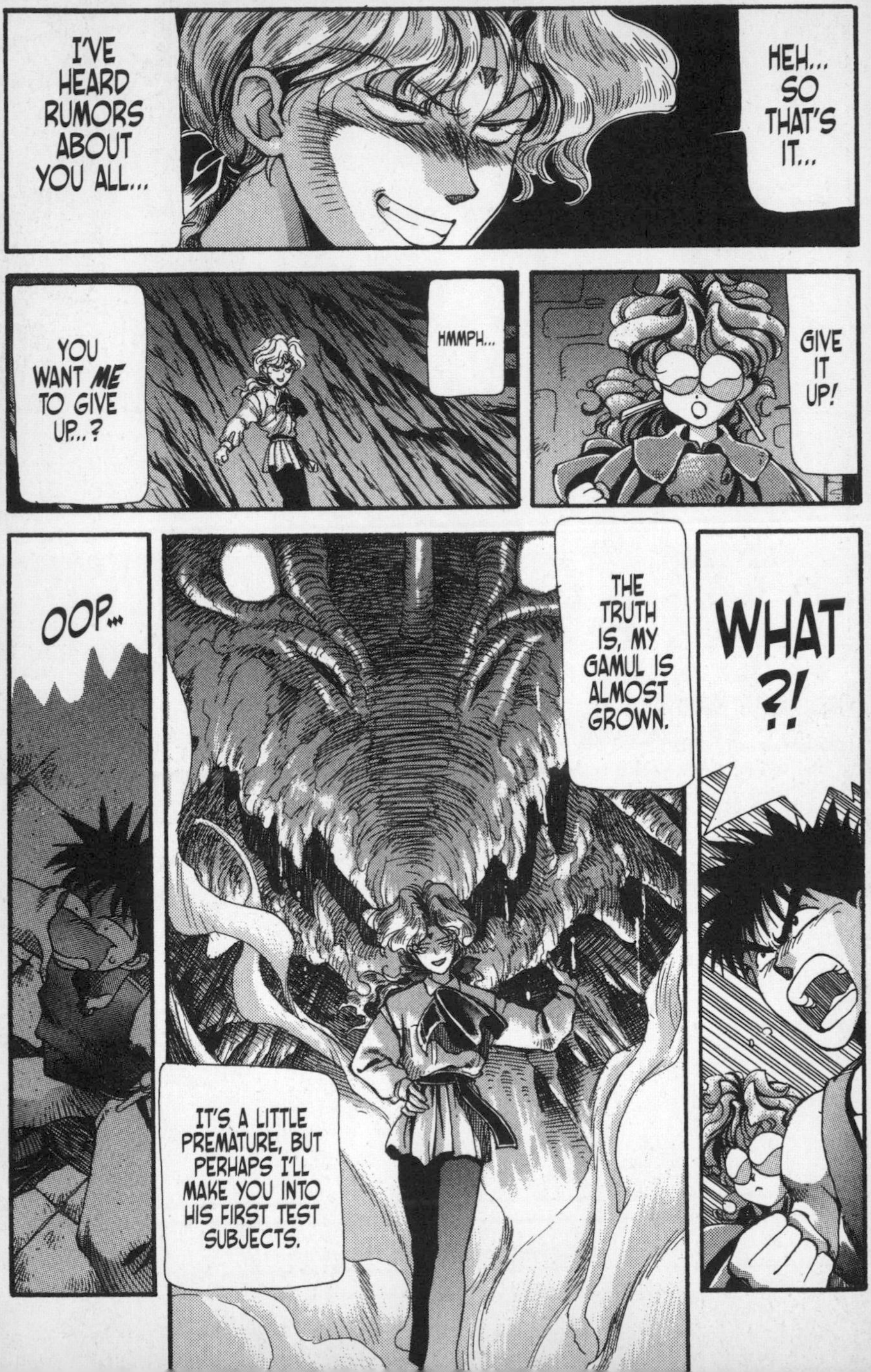
HEH... SO THAT'S IT...
I'VE HEARD RUMORS ABOUT YOU ALL...
GIVE IT UP!
HMMPH...
YOU WANT *ME* TO GIVE UP...?
WHAT?!
THE TRUTH IS, MY GAMUL IS ALMOST GROWN.
IT'S A LITTLE PREMATURE, BUT PERHAPS I'LL MAKE YOU INTO HIS FIRST TEST SUBJECTS.
OOP...

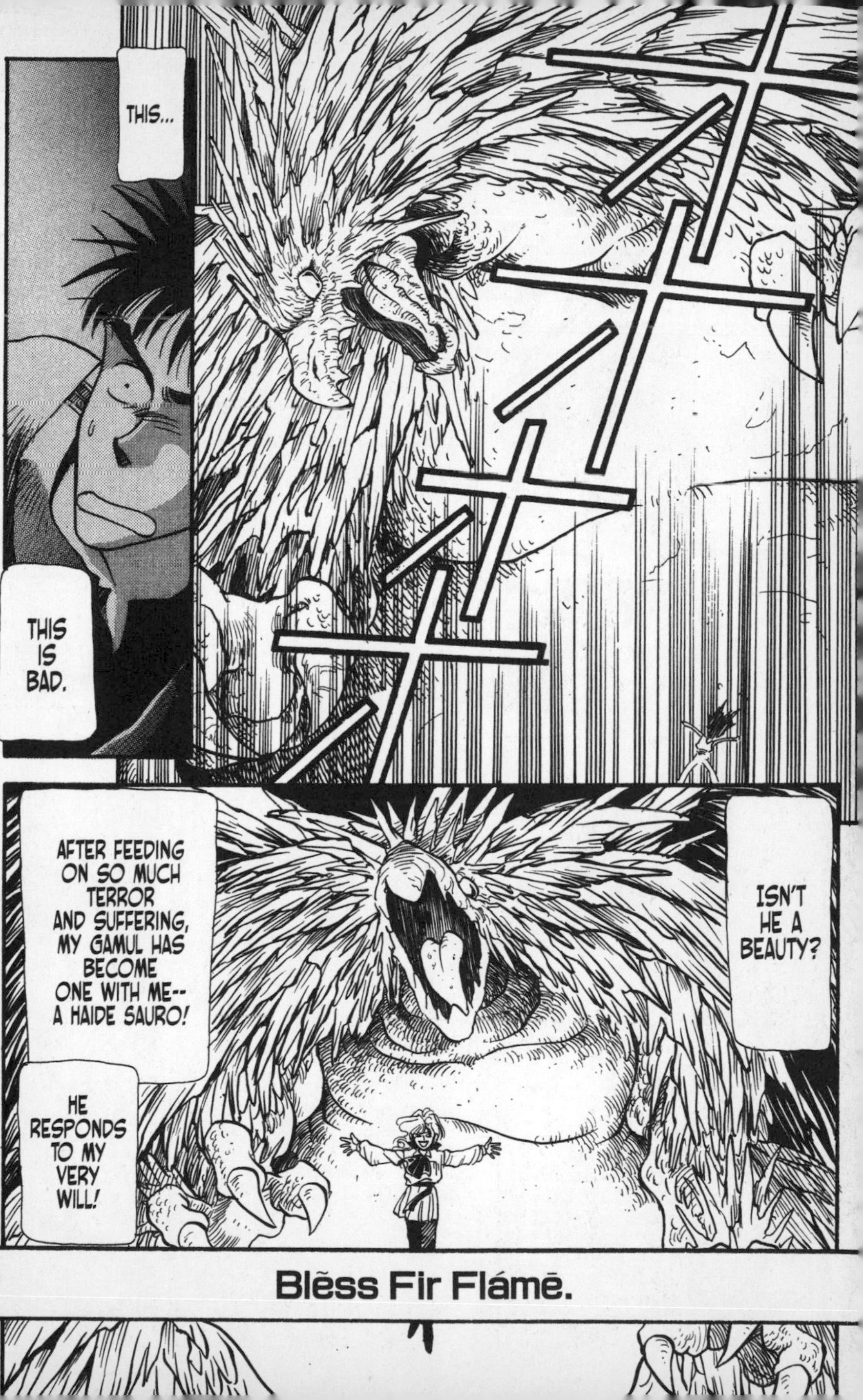
THIS...
THIS IS BAD.
ISN'T HE A BEAUTY?
AFTER FEEDING ON SO MUCH TERROR AND SUFFERING, MY GAMUL HAS BECOME ONE WITH ME-- A HAIDE SAURO!
HE RESPONDS TO MY VERY WILL!
Blĕss Fir Flámĕ.

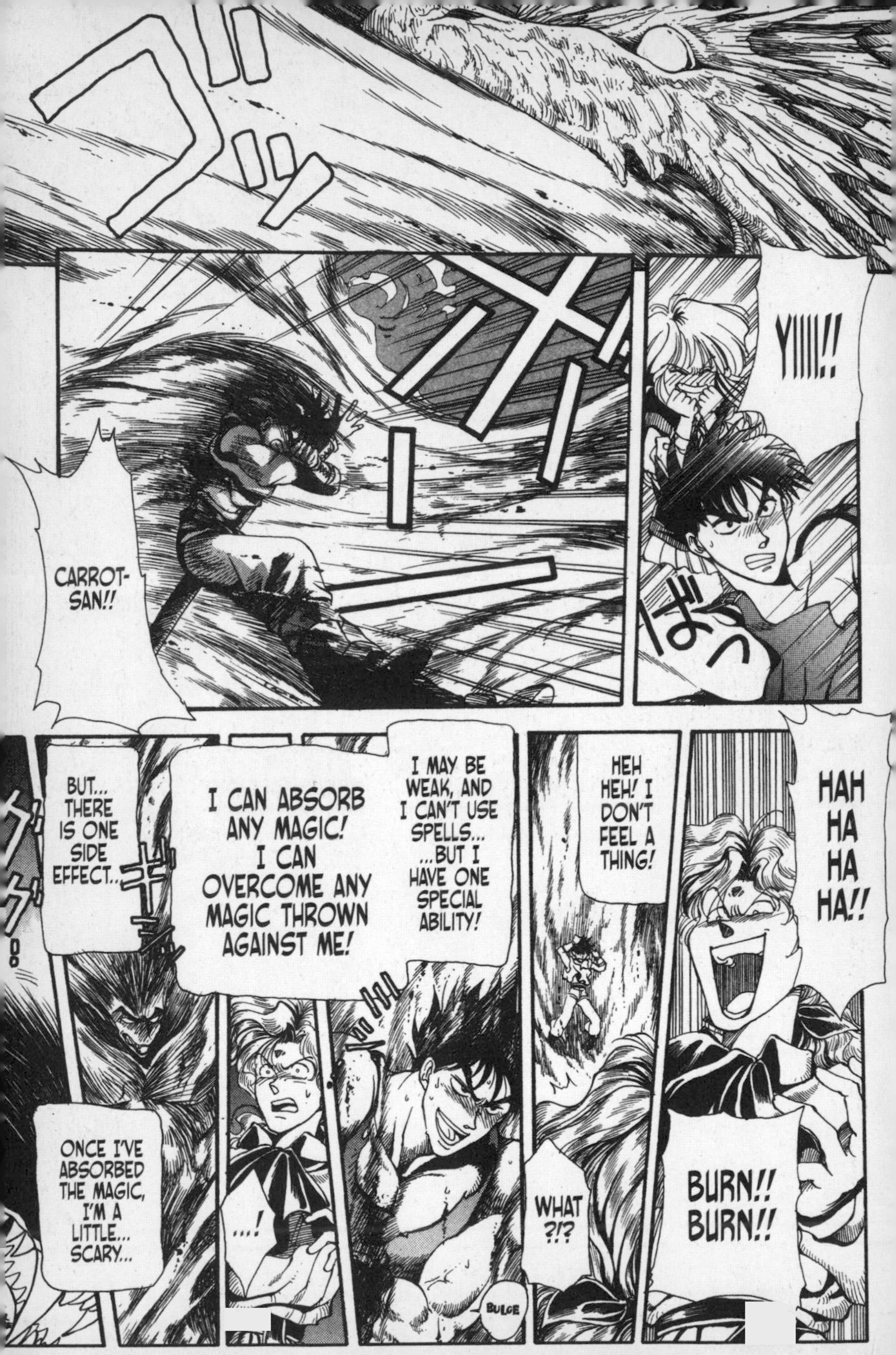
YIIII!!
CARROT-SAN!!
HAH HA HA HA!!
BURN!! BURN!!
HEH HEH! I DON'T FEEL A THING!
WHAT ?!?
I MAY BE WEAK, AND I CAN'T USE SPELLS... ...BUT I HAVE ONE SPECIAL ABILITY!
BULGE
I CAN ABSORB ANY MAGIC! I CAN OVERCOME ANY MAGIC THROWN AGAINST ME!
...!
BUT... THERE IS ONE SIDE EFFECT...
ONCE I'VE ABSORBED THE MAGIC, I'M A LITTLE... SCARY...

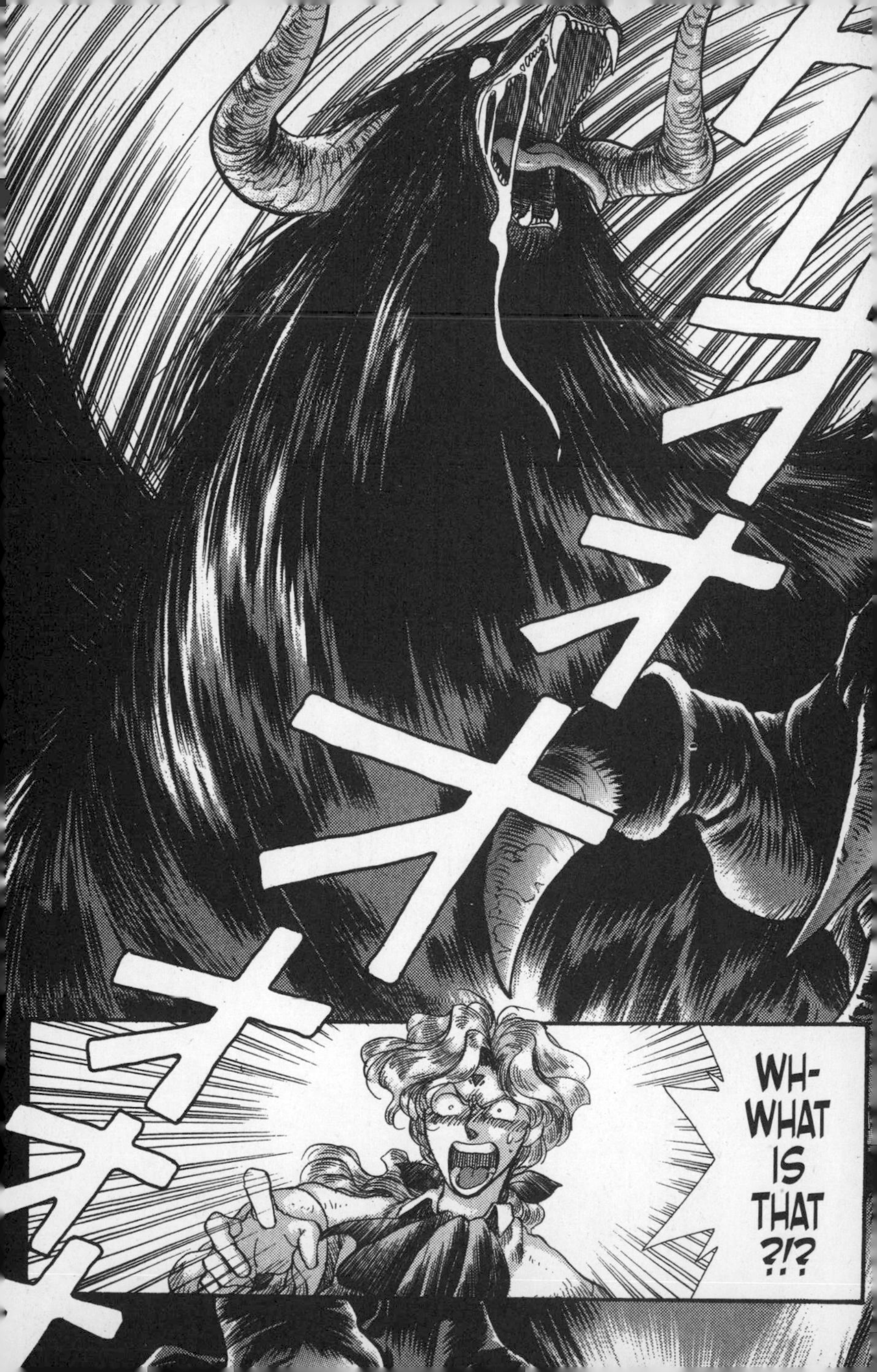
WH-WHAT IS THAT?!?

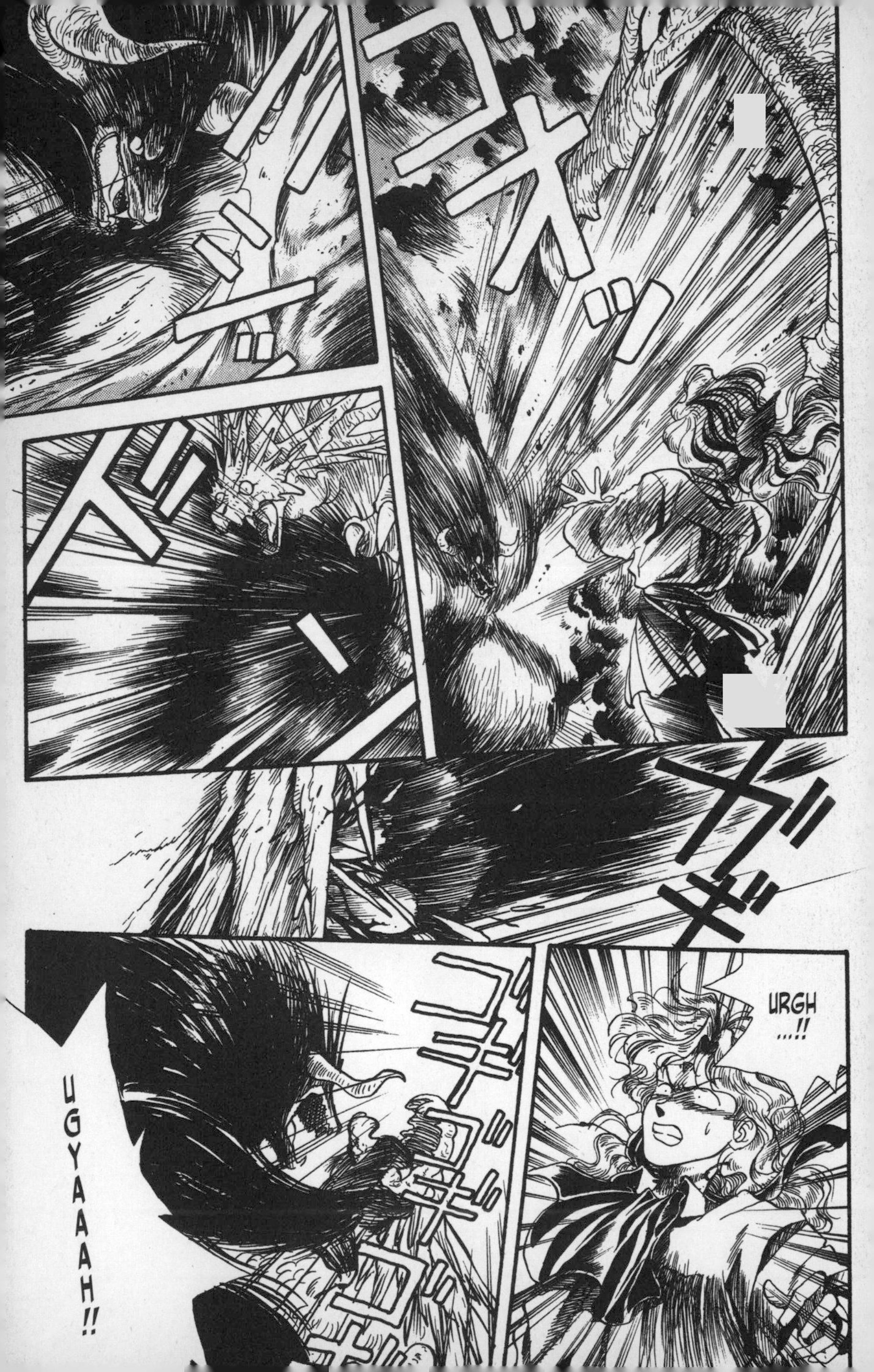
URGH ...!!
UGYAAAH!!

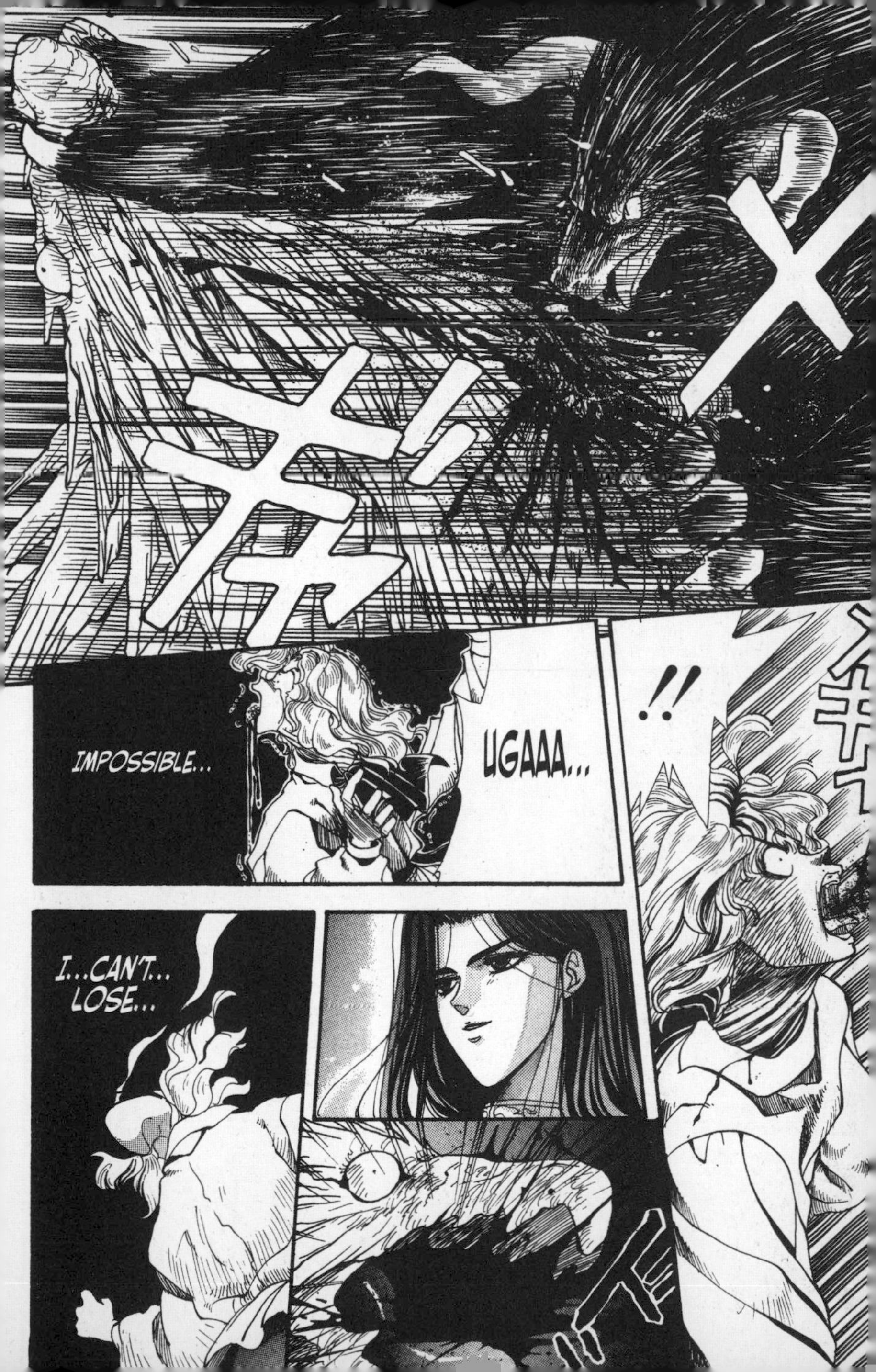
!!
UGAAA...
IMPOSSIBLE...
I...CAN'T... LOSE...

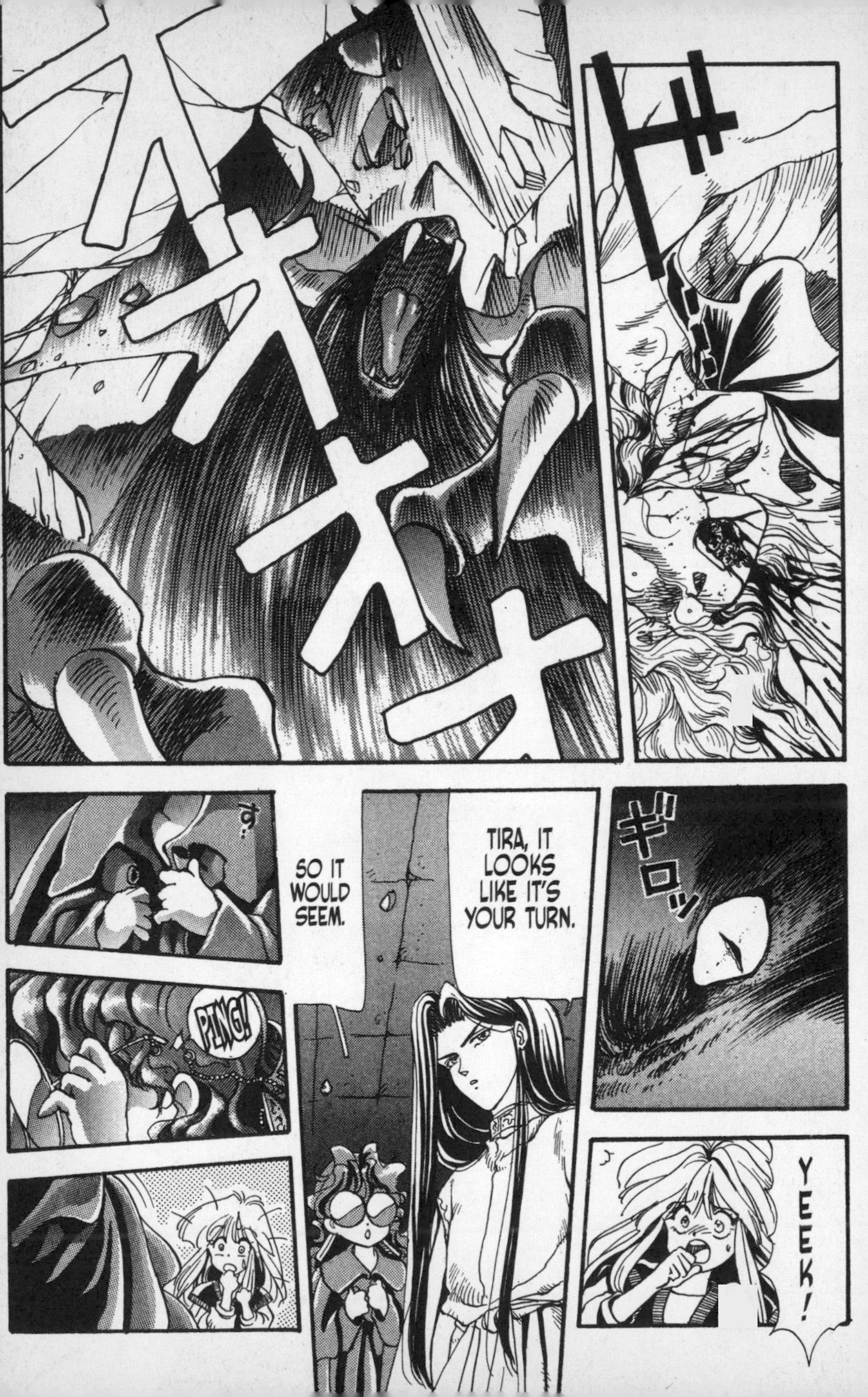

ギロッ
TIRA, IT LOOKS LIKE IT'S YOUR TURN.
SO IT WOULD SEEM.
す..
PING!
YEEK!

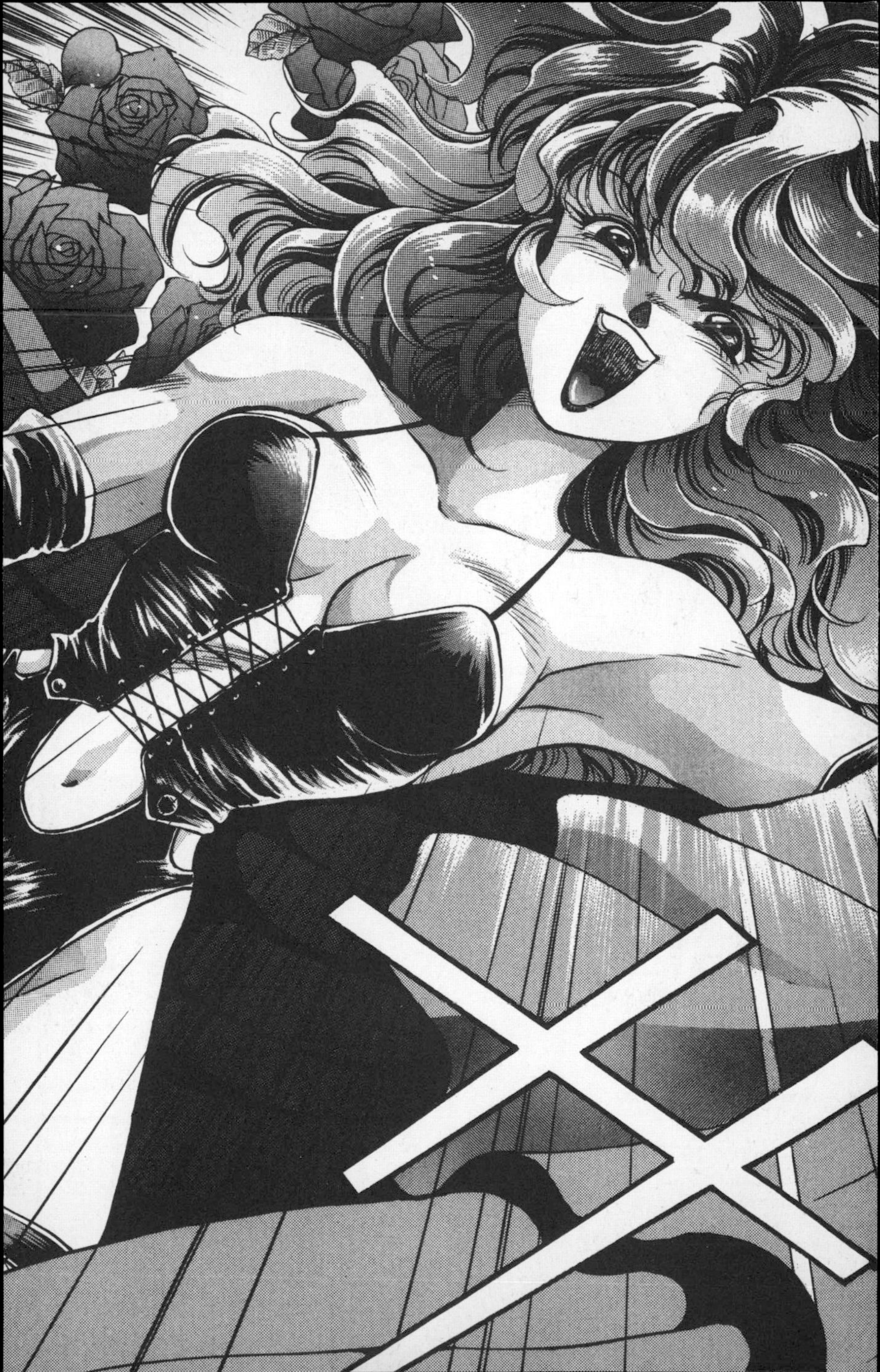

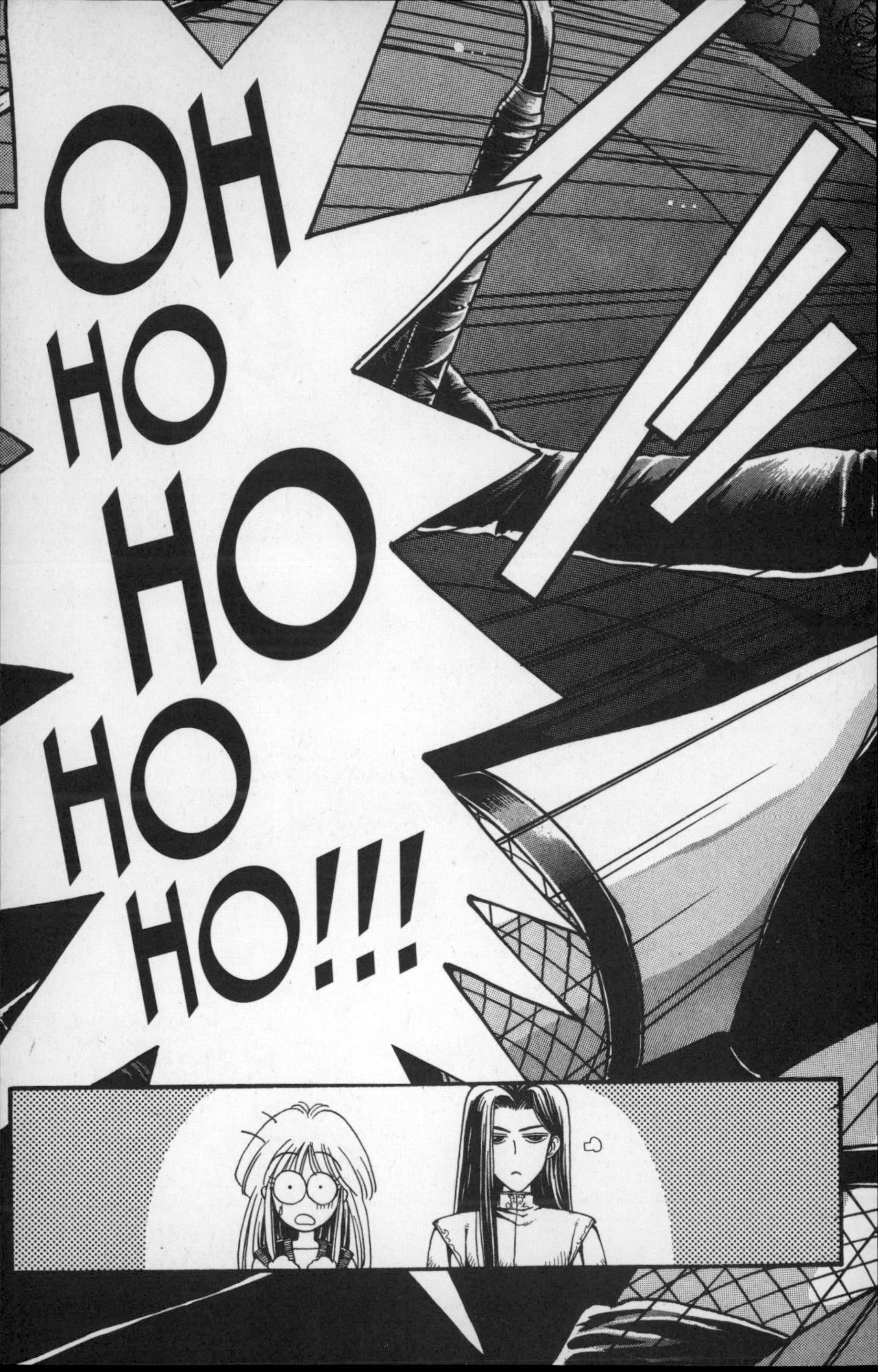
OH HO HO HO HO!!!

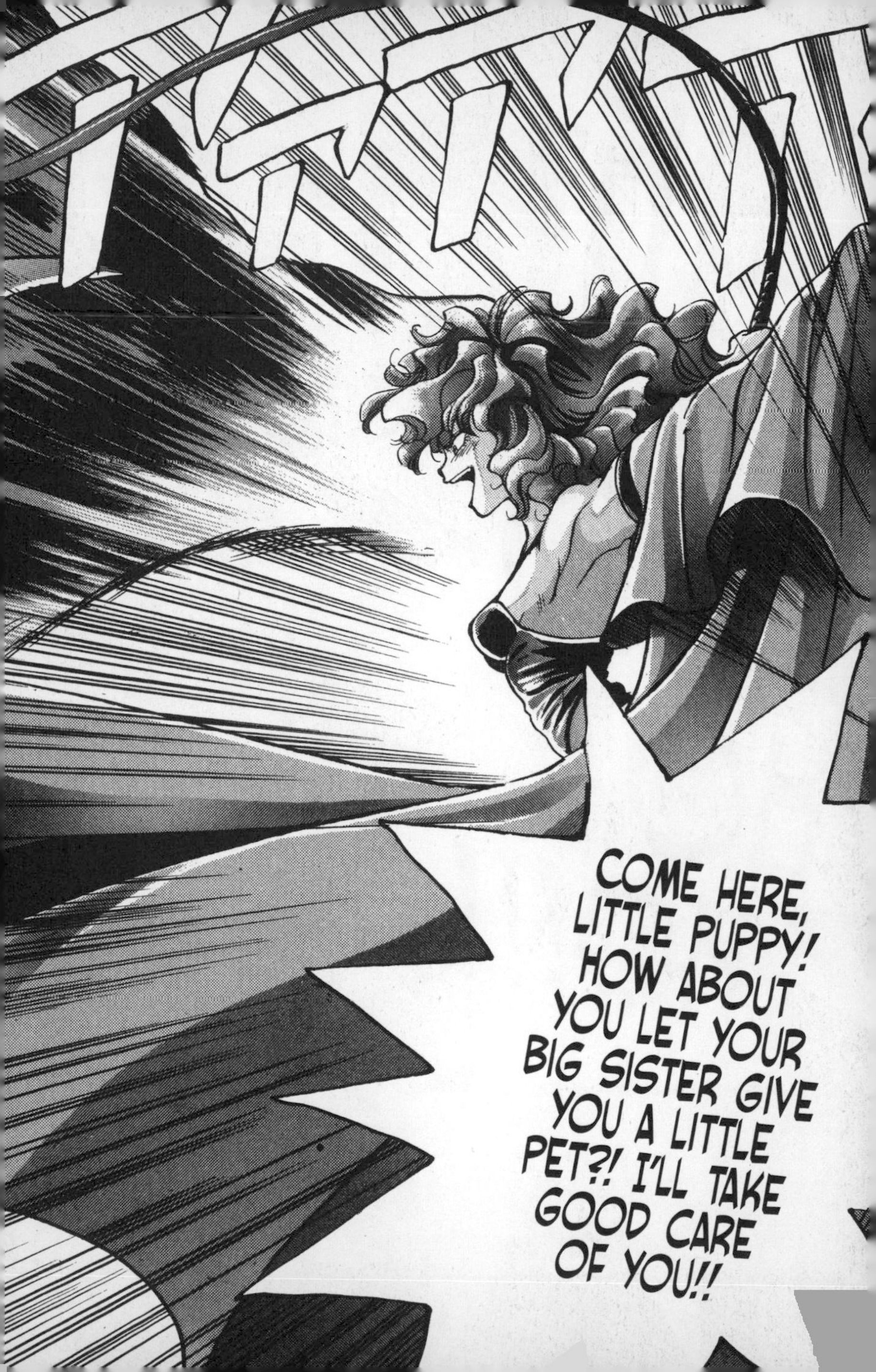
COME HERE, LITTLE PUPPY! HOW ABOUT YOU LET YOUR BIG SISTER GIVE YOU A LITTLE PET?! I'LL TAKE GOOD CARE OF YOU!!

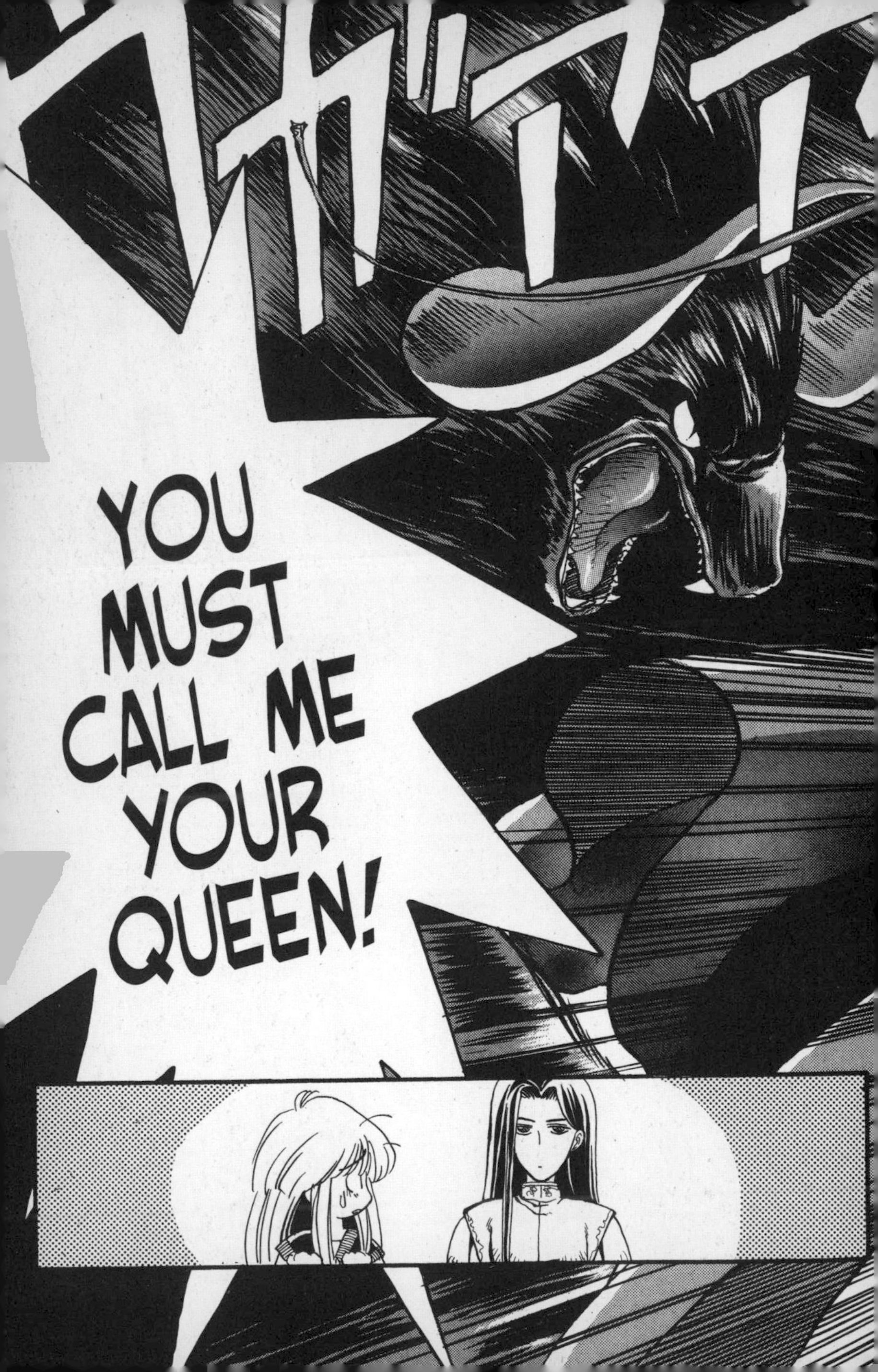
YOU MUST CALL ME YOUR QUEEN!

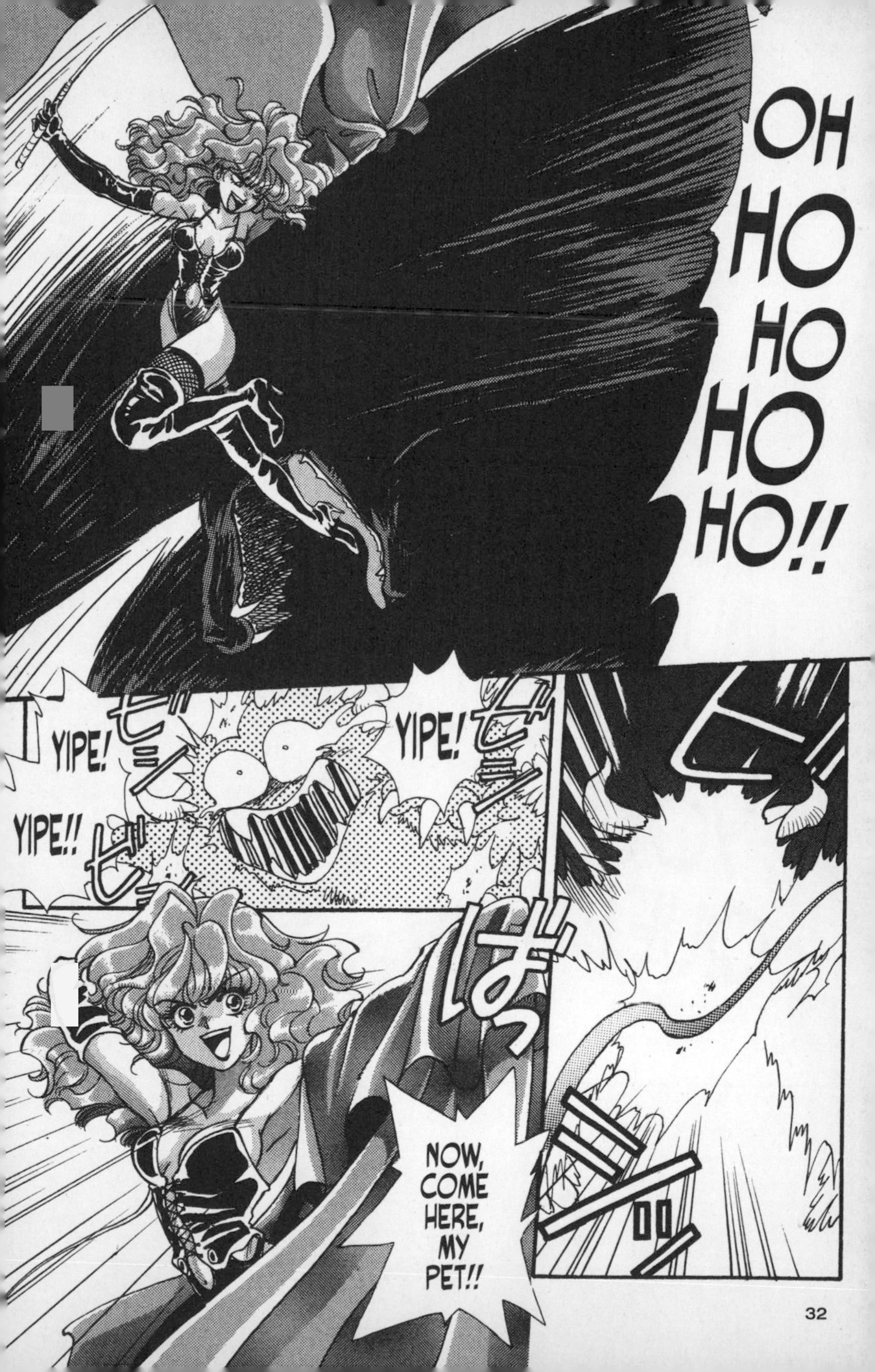
OH HO HO HO HO!!
YIPE!
YIPE!
YIPE!!
ばっ
NOW, COME HERE, MY PET!!

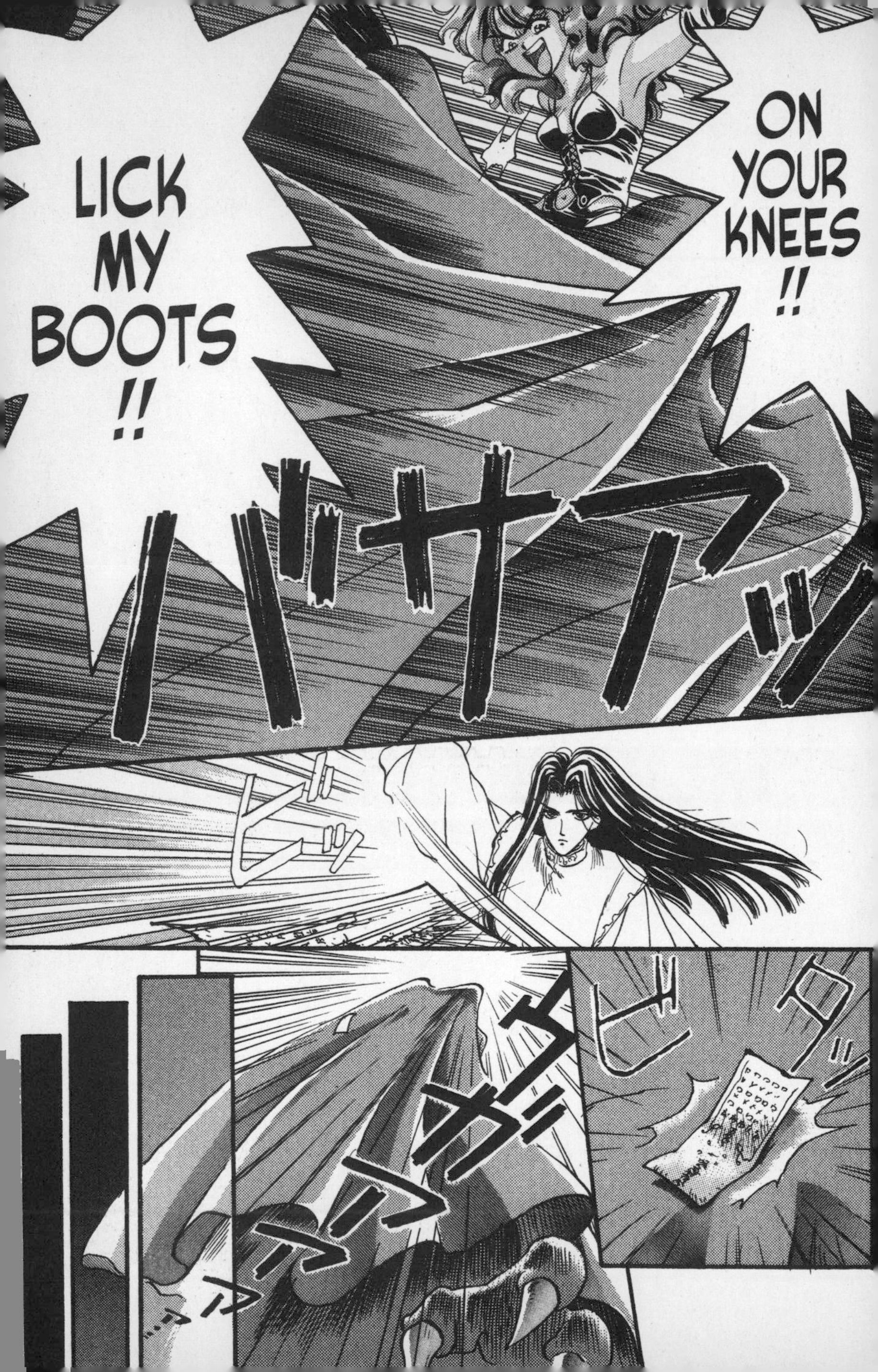
ON YOUR KNEES!!
LICK MY BOOTS!!
バサアッ
ビッ
ダッ

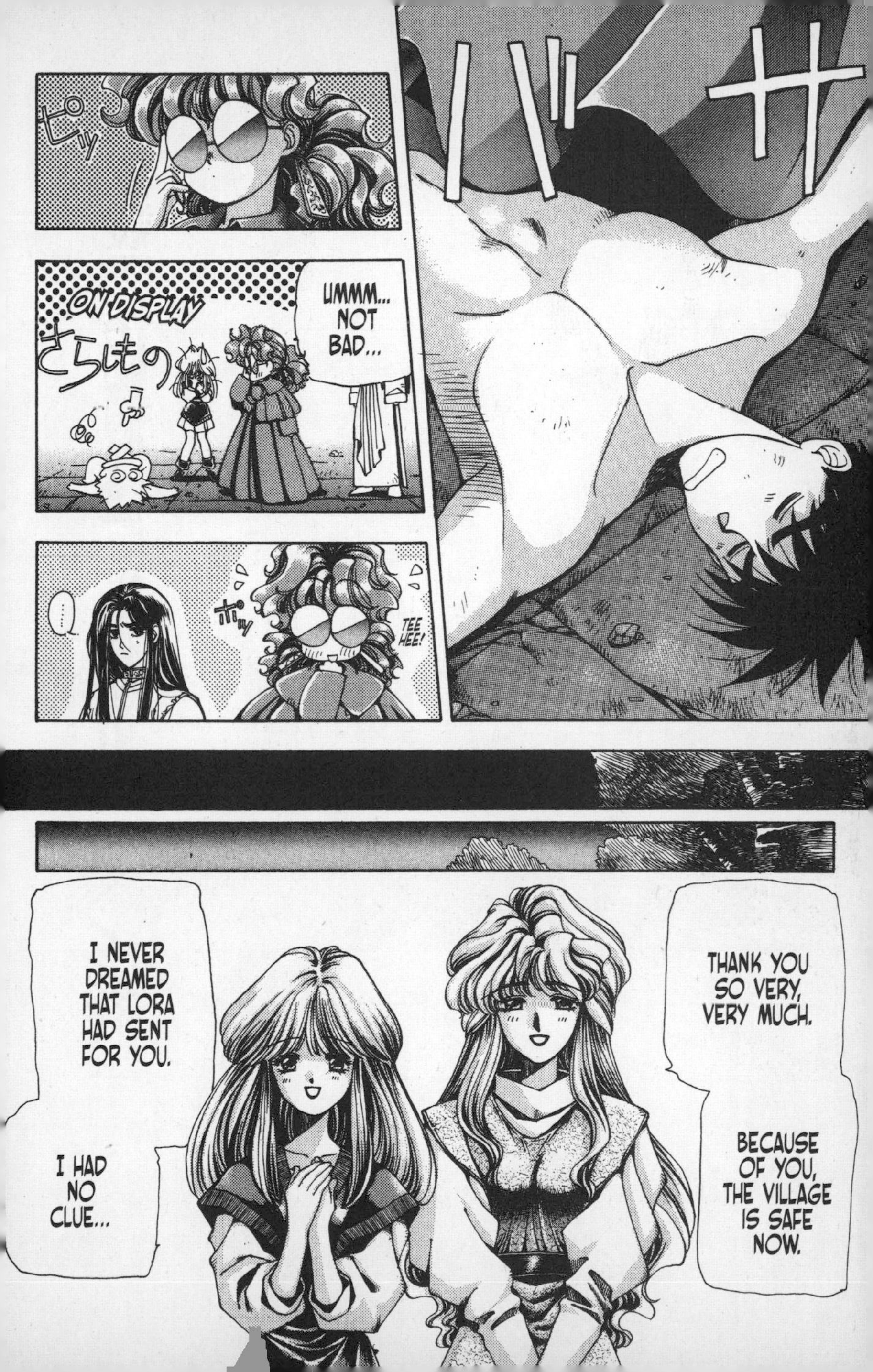
ピッ
ON DISPLAY
さらしもの
UMMM... NOT BAD...
...
ポッ
TEE HEE!
THANK YOU SO VERY, VERY MUCH.
BECAUSE OF YOU, THE VILLAGE IS SAFE NOW.
I NEVER DREAMED THAT LORA HAD SENT FOR YOU.
I HAD NO CLUE...

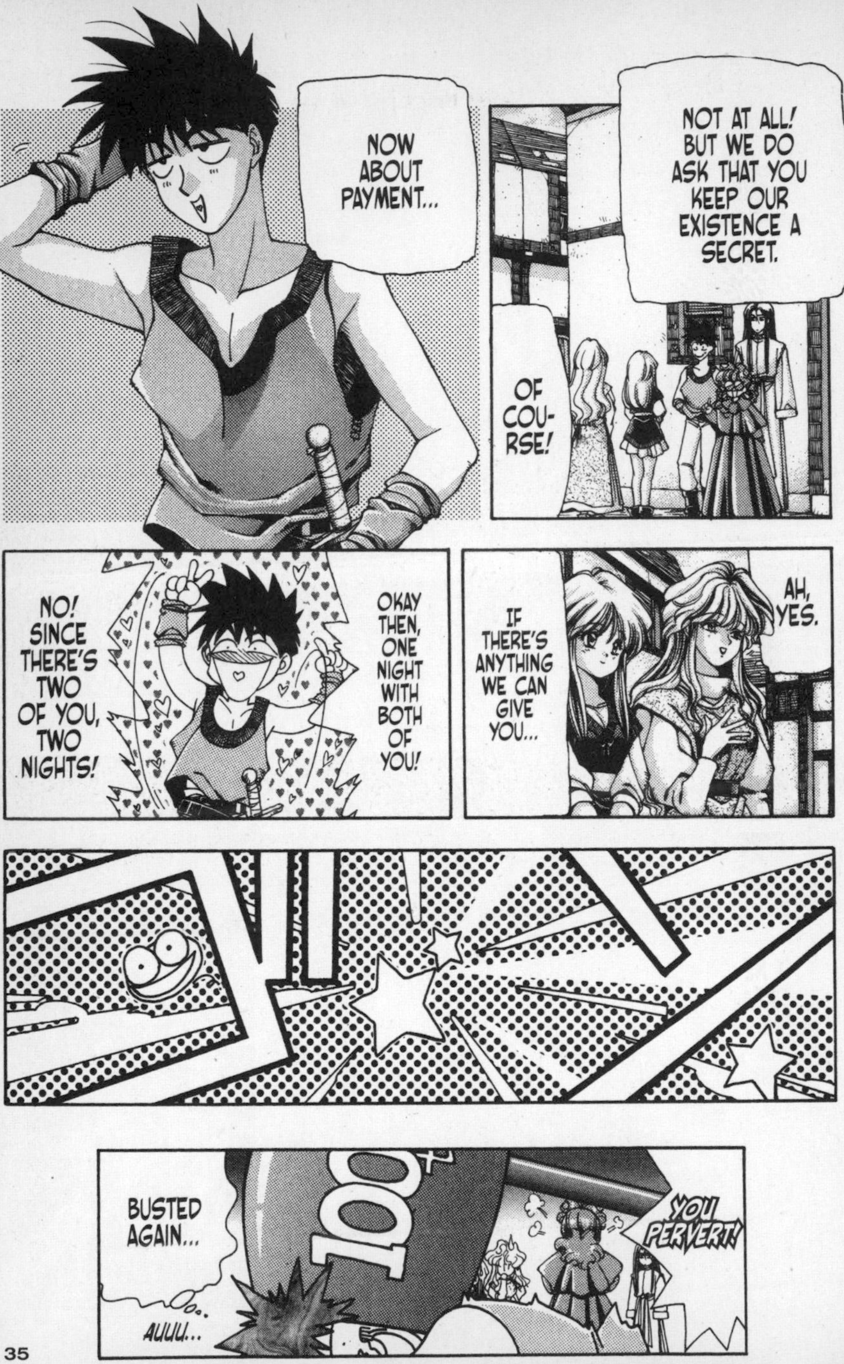
NOT AT ALL! BUT WE DO ASK THAT YOU KEEP OUR EXISTENCE A SECRET.
OF COURSE!
NOW ABOUT PAYMENT...
AH, YES.
IF THERE'S ANYTHING WE CAN GIVE YOU...
OKAY THEN, ONE NIGHT WITH BOTH OF YOU!
NO! SINCE THERE'S TWO OF YOU, TWO NIGHTS!
YOU PERVERT!
BUSTED AGAIN...
AUUU...

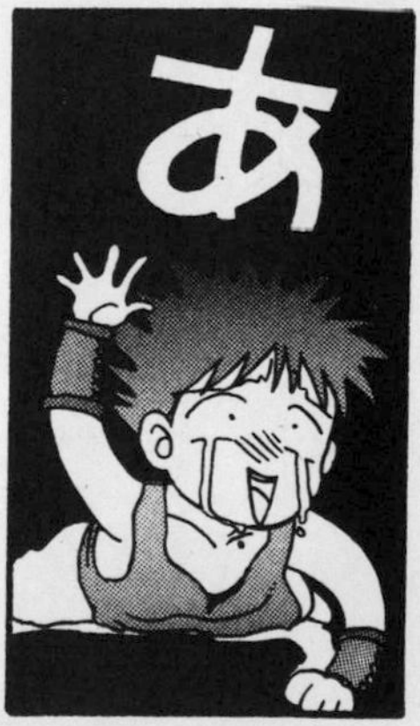
あ

♡ー

オホホホホホーッ

2 THE MAGIC FLOWER ROAD

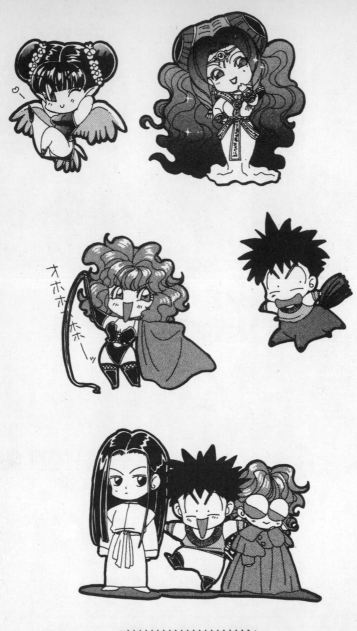

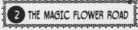

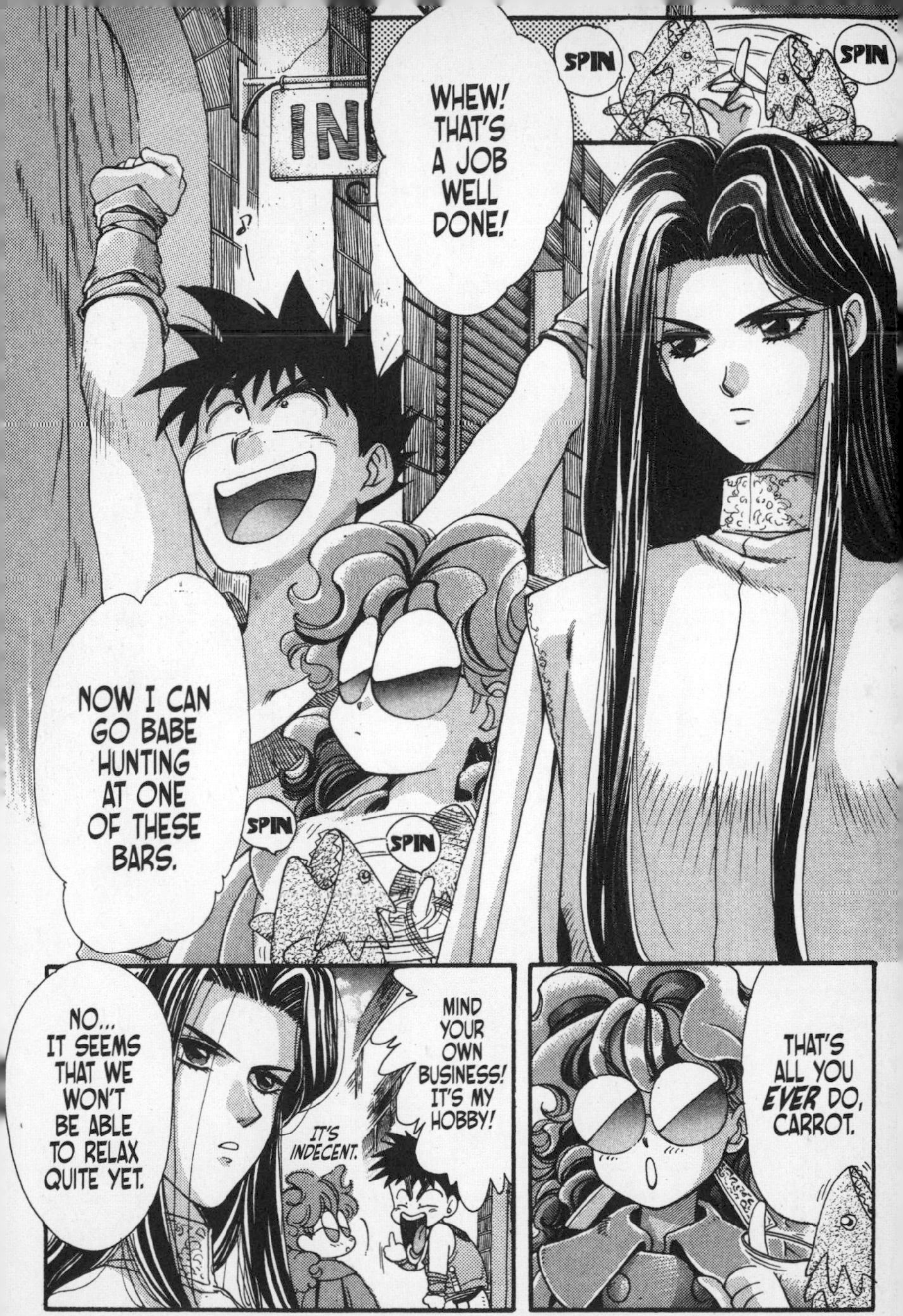
SPIN
SPIN
WHEW! THAT'S A JOB WELL DONE!
IN
NOW I CAN GO BABE HUNTING AT ONE OF THESE BARS.
SPIN
SPIN
THAT'S ALL YOU ***EVER*** DO, CARROT.
MIND YOUR OWN BUSINESS! IT'S MY HOBBY!
IT'S INDECENT.
NO... IT SEEMS THAT WE WON'T BE ABLE TO RELAX QUITE YET.

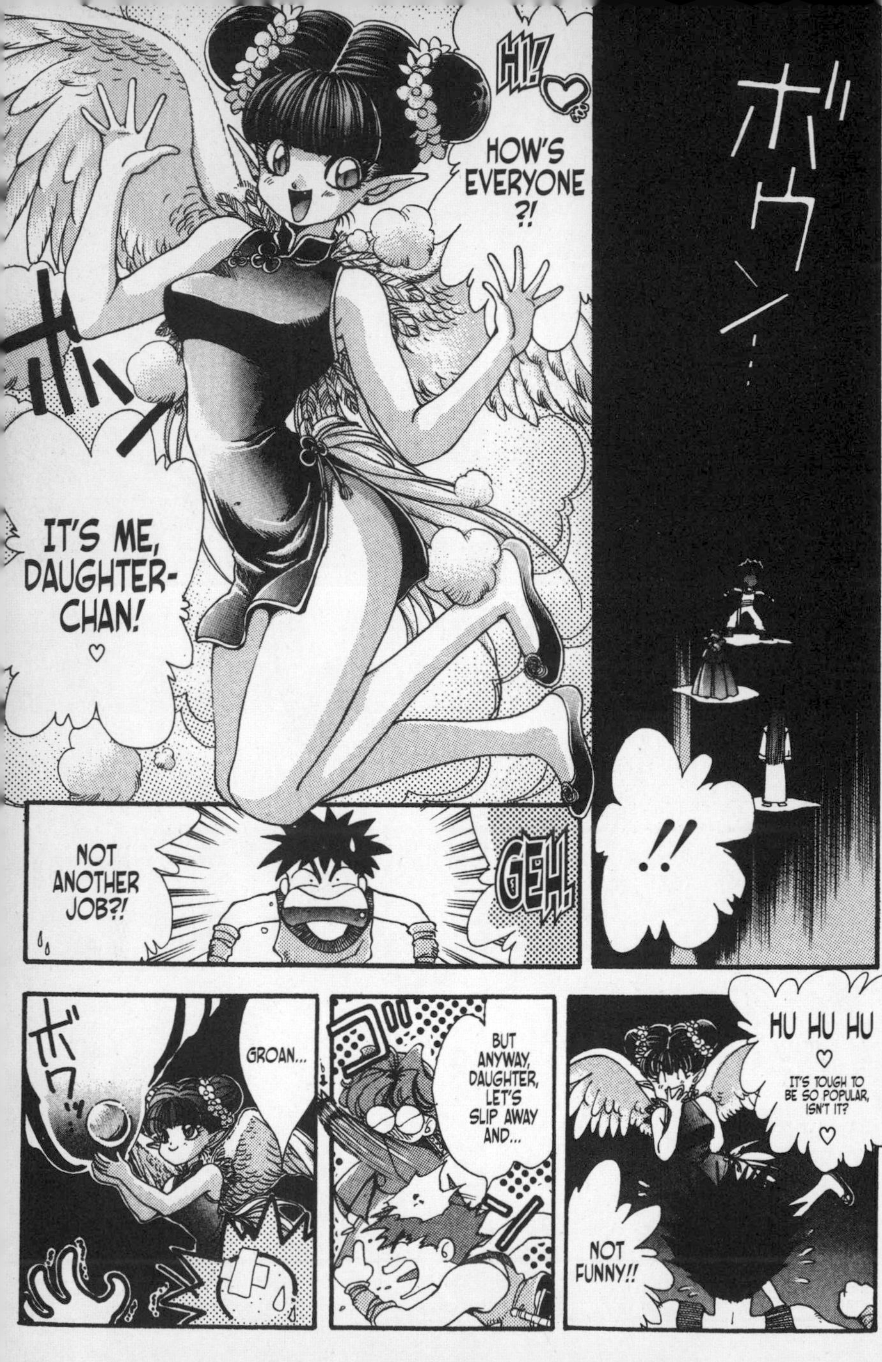
!!
HI! ♥
HOW'S EVERYONE ?!
IT'S ME, DAUGHTER-CHAN! ♡
NOT ANOTHER JOB?!
GEH
HU HU HU ♡
IT'S TOUGH TO BE SO POPULAR, ISN'T IT? ♡
NOT FUNNY!!
BUT ANYWAY, DAUGHTER, LET'S SLIP AWAY AND...
GROAN...

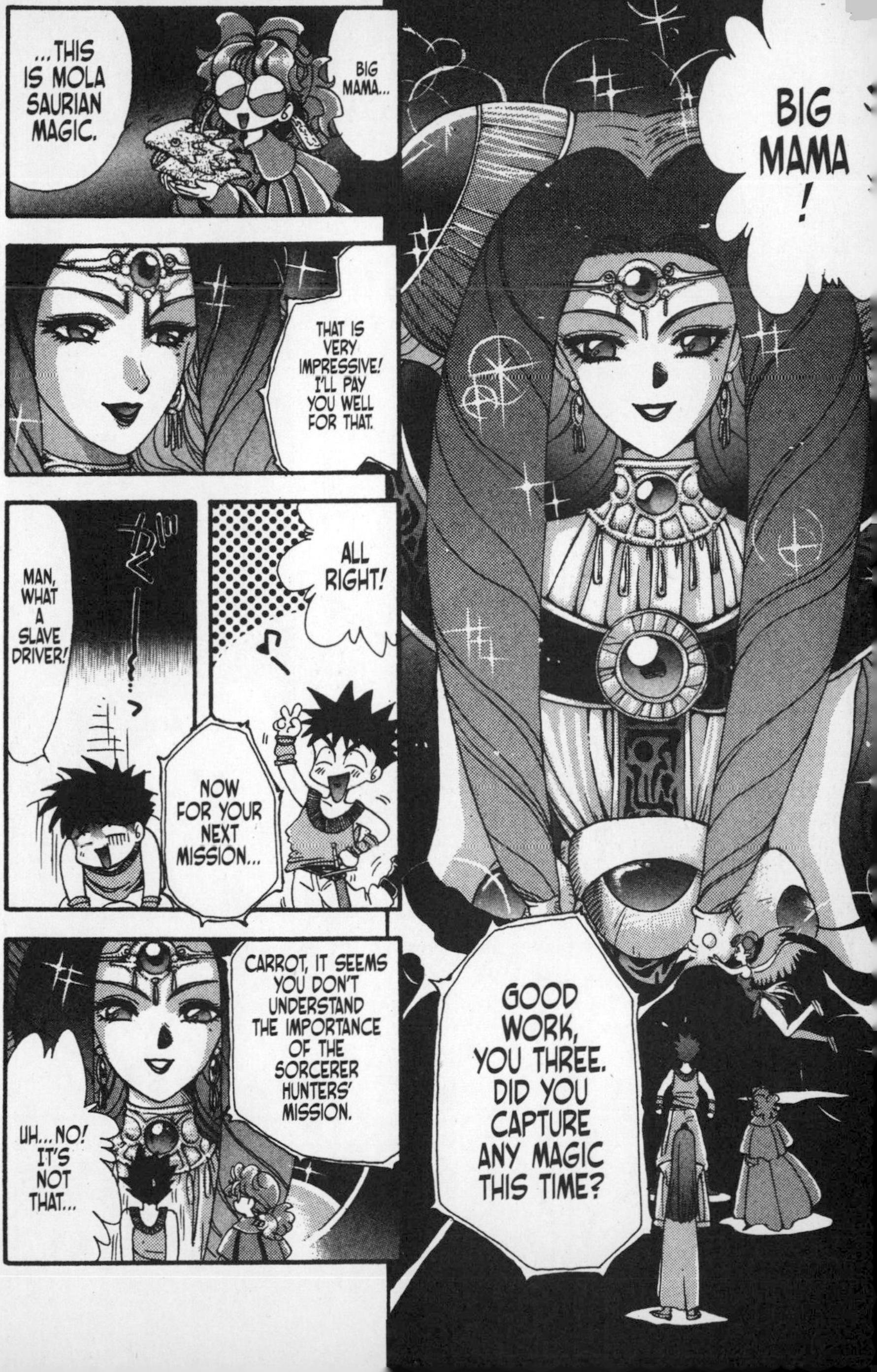
BIG MAMA!
GOOD WORK, YOU THREE. DID YOU CAPTURE ANY MAGIC THIS TIME?
BIG MAMA...
...THIS IS MOLA SAURIAN MAGIC.
THAT IS VERY IMPRESSIVE! I'LL PAY YOU WELL FOR THAT.
ALL RIGHT!
NOW FOR YOUR NEXT MISSION...
MAN, WHAT A SLAVE DRIVER!
CARROT, IT SEEMS YOU DON'T UNDERSTAND THE IMPORTANCE OF THE SORCERER HUNTERS' MISSION.
UH...NO! IT'S NOT THAT...

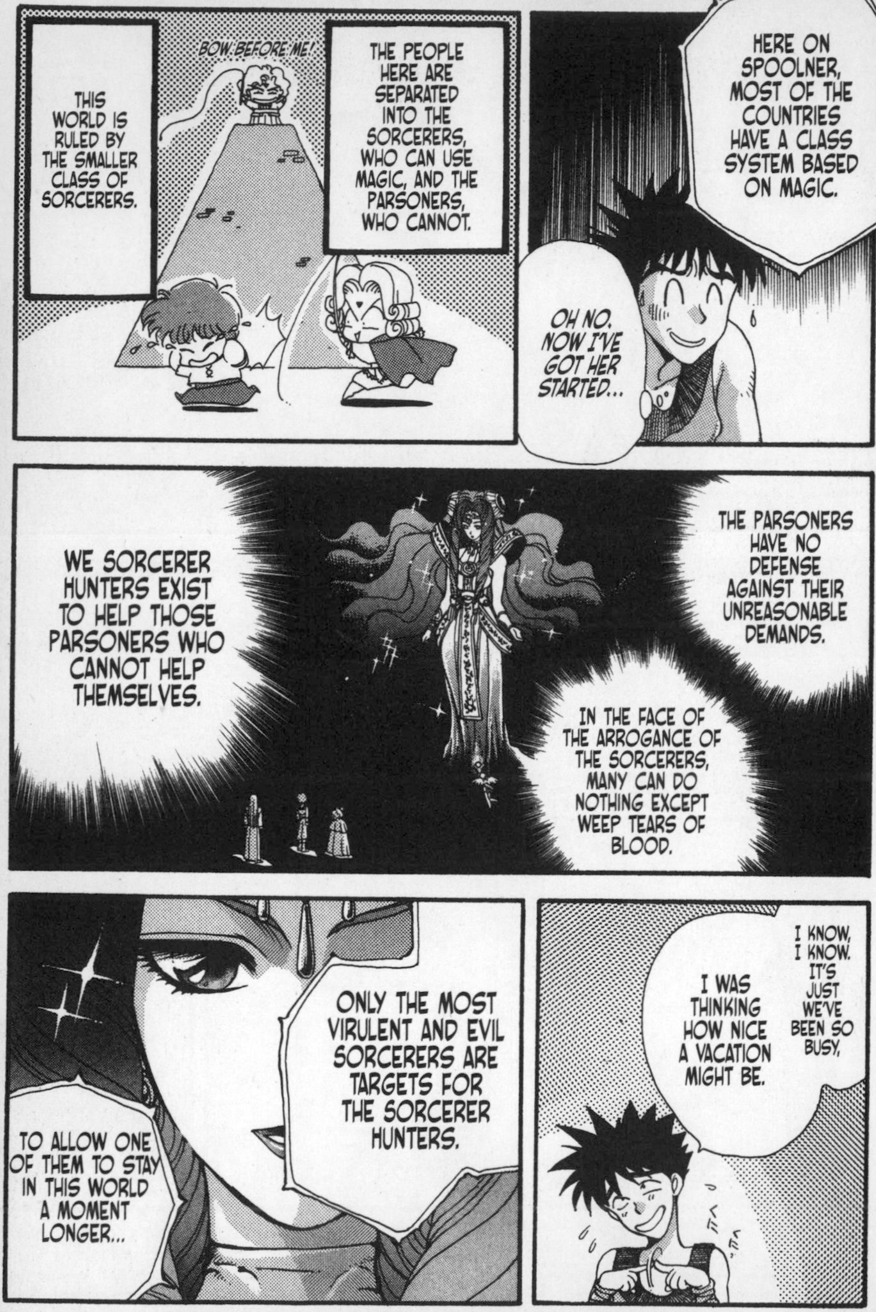
HERE ON SPOOLNER, MOST OF THE COUNTRIES HAVE A CLASS SYSTEM BASED ON MAGIC.
OH NO. NOW I'VE GOT HER STARTED...
THE PEOPLE HERE ARE SEPARATED INTO THE SORCERERS, WHO CAN USE MAGIC, AND THE PARSONERS, WHO CANNOT.
BOW BEFORE ME!
THIS WORLD IS RULED BY THE SMALLER CLASS OF SORCERERS.
THE PARSONERS HAVE NO DEFENSE AGAINST THEIR UNREASONABLE DEMANDS.
IN THE FACE OF THE ARROGANCE OF THE SORCERERS, MANY CAN DO NOTHING EXCEPT WEEP TEARS OF BLOOD.
WE SORCERER HUNTERS EXIST TO HELP THOSE PARSONERS WHO CANNOT HELP THEMSELVES.
I KNOW, I KNOW. IT'S JUST WE'VE BEEN SO BUSY,
I WAS THINKING HOW NICE A VACATION MIGHT BE.
ONLY THE MOST VIRULENT AND EVIL SORCERERS ARE TARGETS FOR THE SORCERER HUNTERS.
TO ALLOW ONE OF THEM TO STAY IN THIS WORLD A MOMENT LONGER...

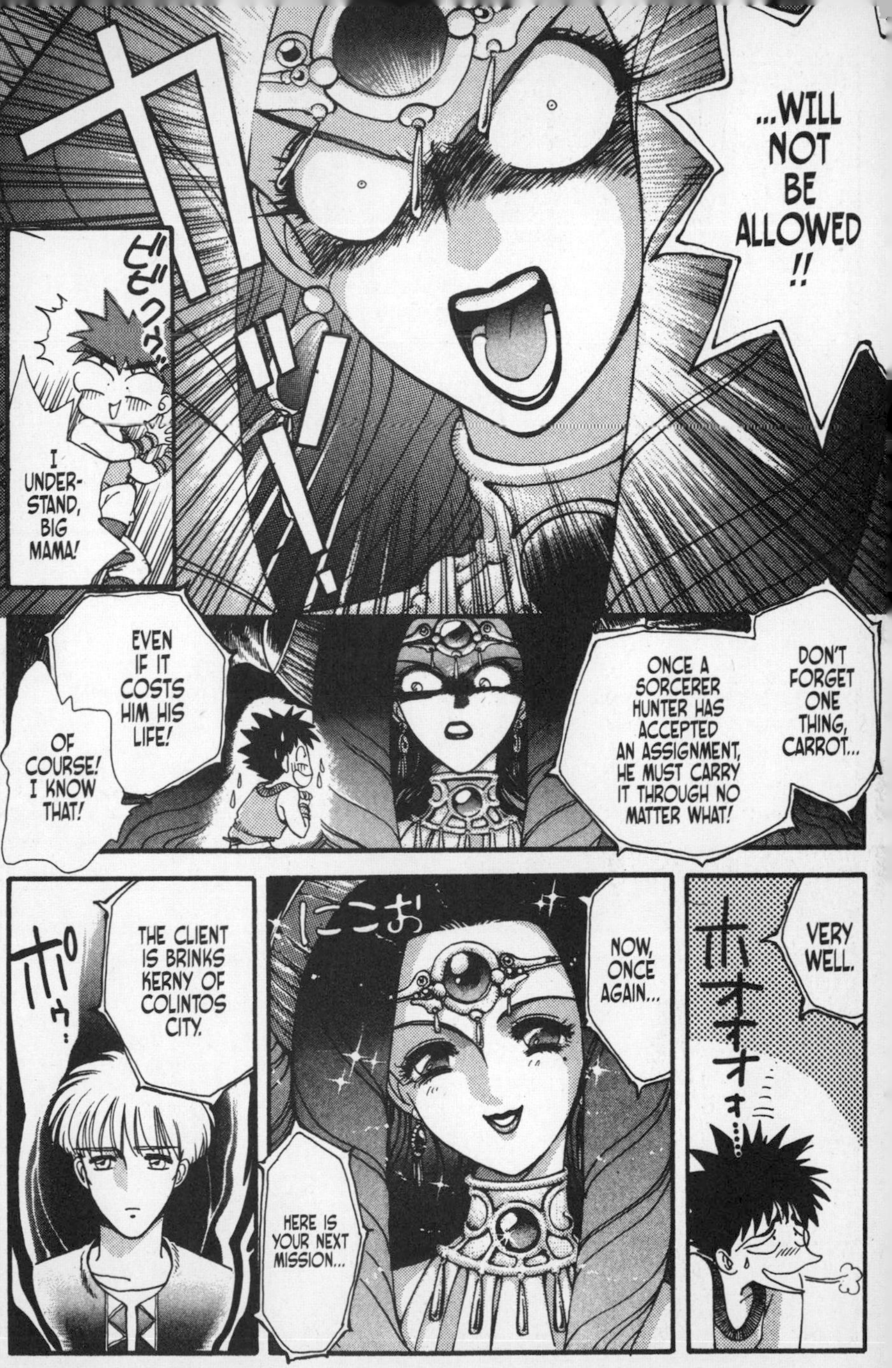
...WILL NOT BE ALLOWED!!
I UNDER-STAND, BIG MAMA!
DON'T FORGET ONE THING, CARROT...
ONCE A SORCERER HUNTER HAS ACCEPTED AN ASSIGNMENT, HE MUST CARRY IT THROUGH NO MATTER WHAT!
EVEN IF IT COSTS HIM HIS LIFE!
OF COURSE! I KNOW THAT!
VERY WELL.
NOW, ONCE AGAIN...
HERE IS YOUR NEXT MISSION...
THE CLIENT IS BRINKS KERNY OF COLINTOS CITY.

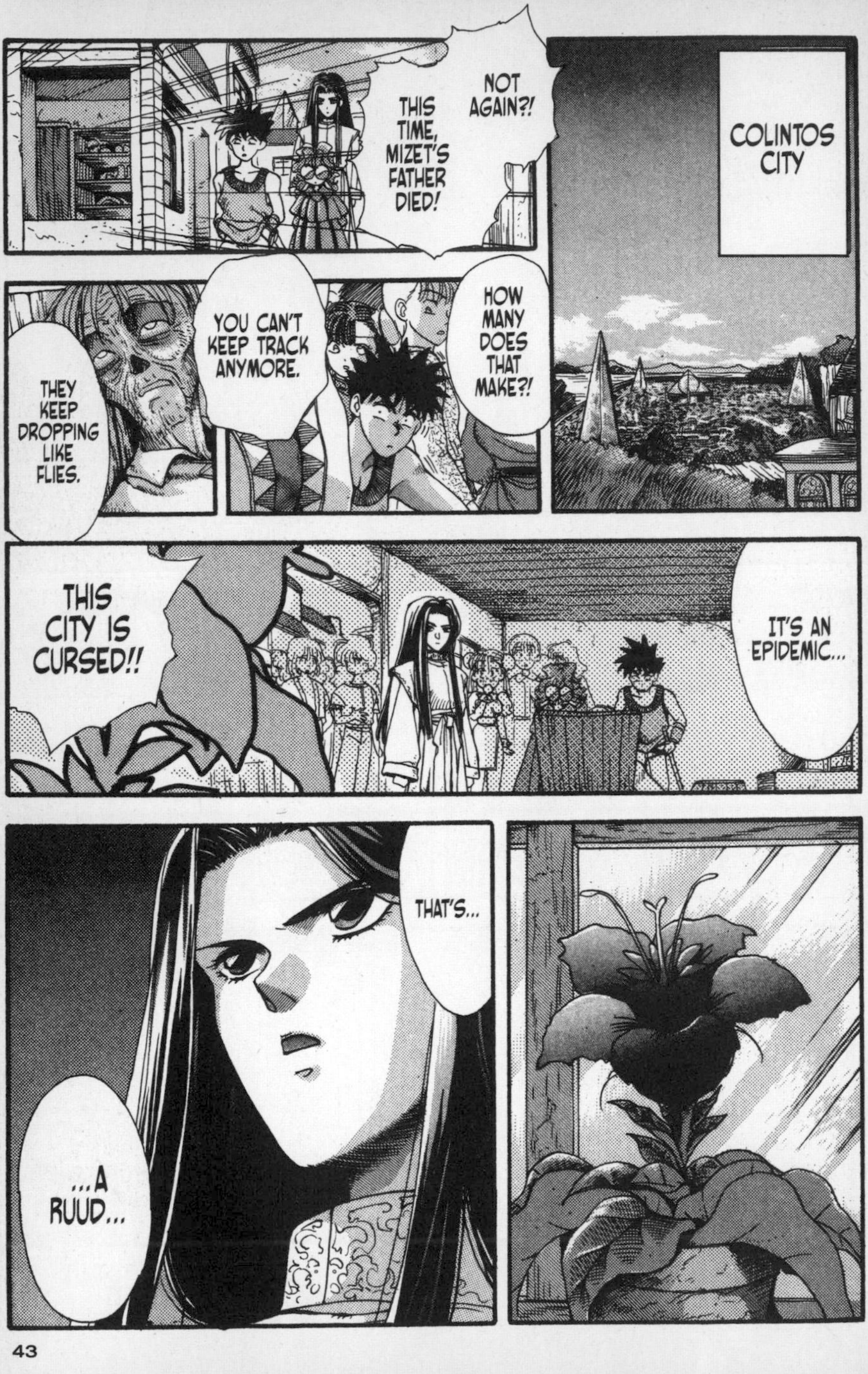
COLINTOS CITY
NOT AGAIN?!
THIS TIME, MIZET'S FATHER DIED!
HOW MANY DOES THAT MAKE?!
YOU CAN'T KEEP TRACK ANYMORE.
THEY KEEP DROPPING LIKE FLIES.
IT'S AN EPIDEMIC...
THIS CITY IS CURSED!!
THAT'S...
...A RUUD...

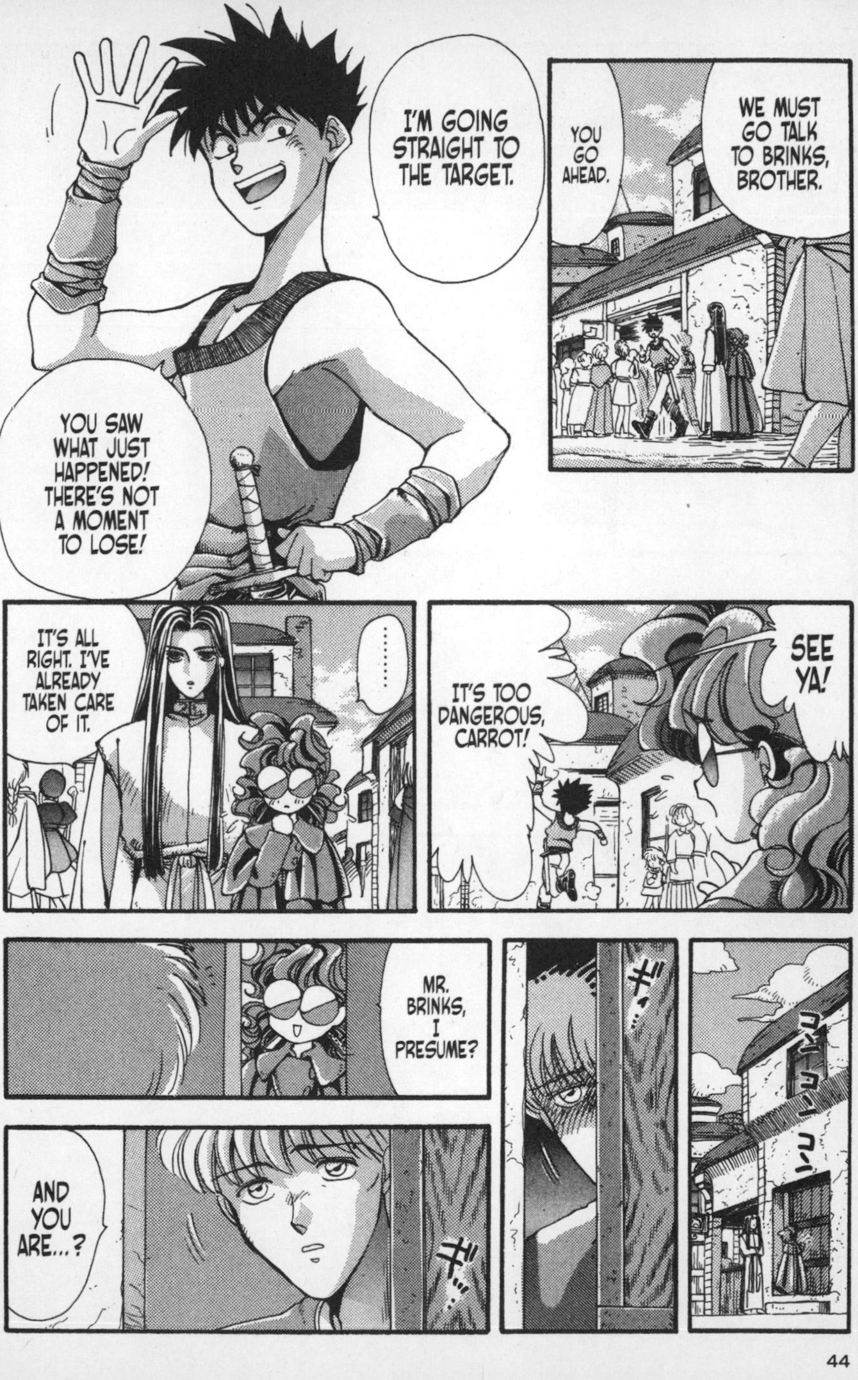
WE MUST GO TALK TO BRINKS, BROTHER.
YOU GO AHEAD.
I'M GOING STRAIGHT TO THE TARGET.
YOU SAW WHAT JUST HAPPENED! THERE'S NOT A MOMENT TO LOSE!
SEE YA!
IT'S TOO DANGEROUS, CARROT!
......
IT'S ALL RIGHT. I'VE ALREADY TAKEN CARE OF IT.
コンコン
ギ…
ギ…
MR. BRINKS, I PRESUME?
AND YOU ARE...?

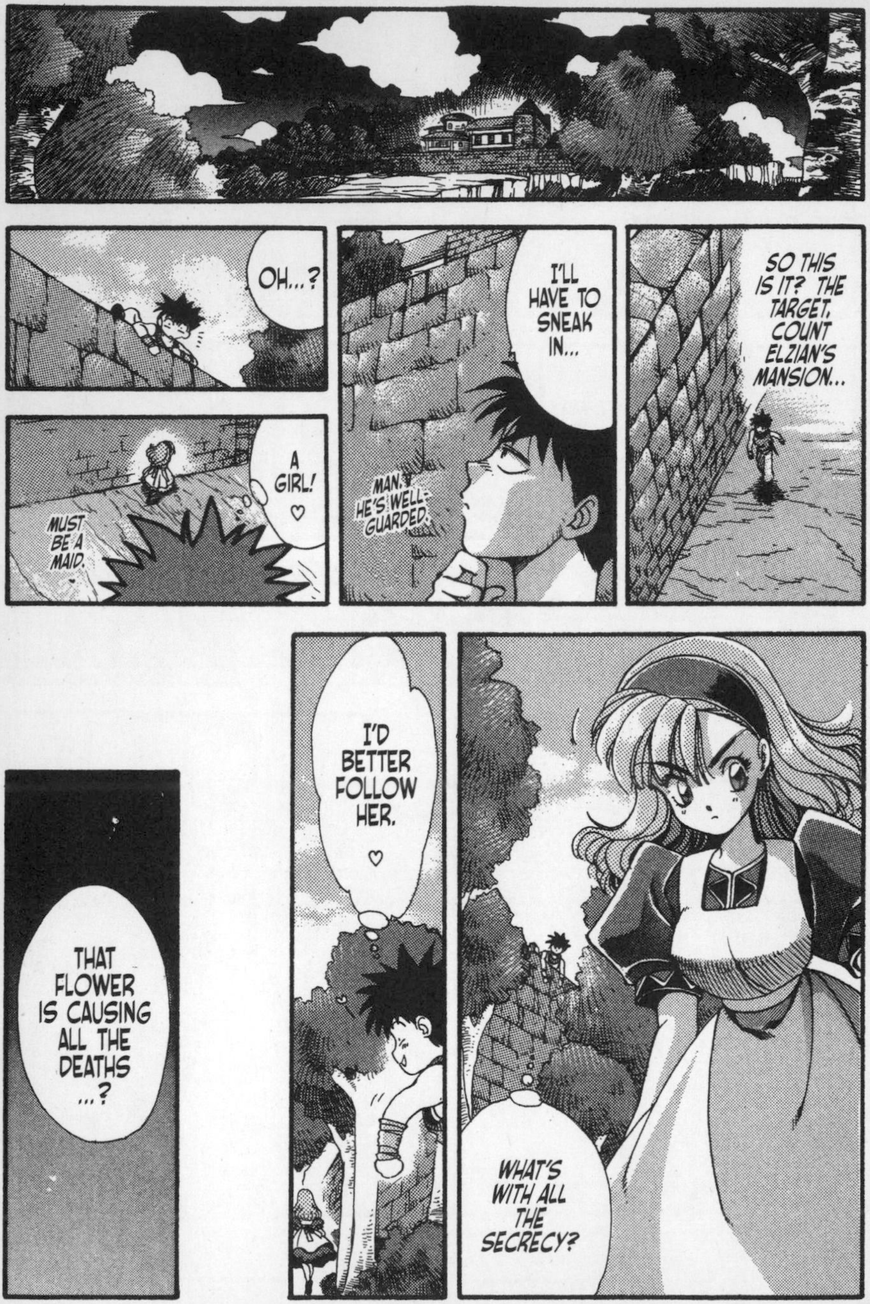
SO THIS IS IT? THE TARGET, COUNT ELZIAN'S MANSION...
I'LL HAVE TO SNEAK IN...
MAN. HE'S WELL-GUARDED.
OH...?
A GIRL! ♡
MUST BE A MAID.
WHAT'S WITH ALL THE SECRECY?
I'D BETTER FOLLOW HER. ♡
THAT FLOWER IS CAUSING ALL THE DEATHS ...?

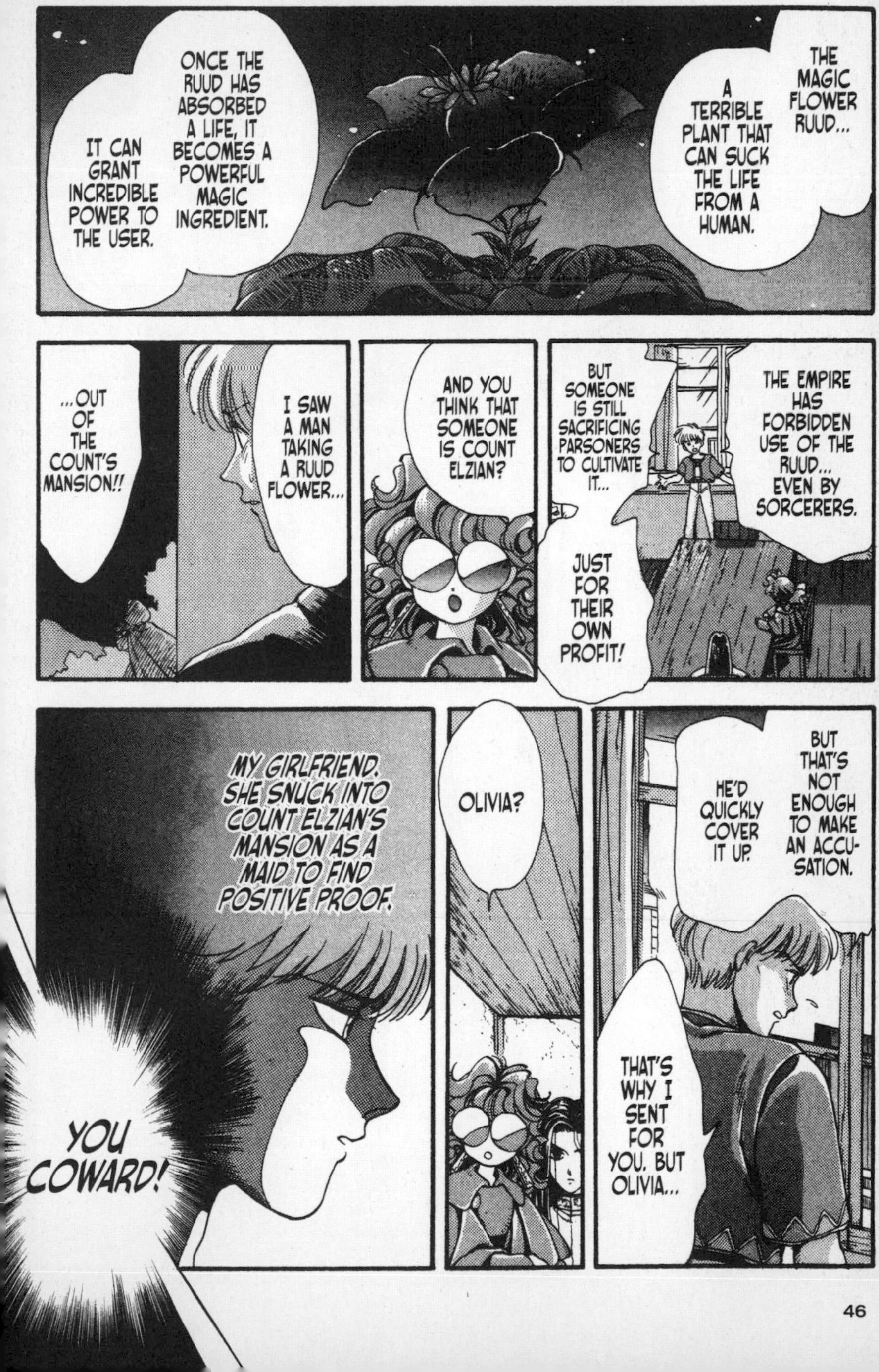
THE MAGIC FLOWER RUUD...
A TERRIBLE PLANT THAT CAN SUCK THE LIFE FROM A HUMAN.
ONCE THE RUUD HAS ABSORBED A LIFE, IT BECOMES A POWERFUL MAGIC INGREDIENT.
IT CAN GRANT INCREDIBLE POWER TO THE USER.
THE EMPIRE HAS FORBIDDEN USE OF THE RUUD... EVEN BY SORCERERS.
BUT SOMEONE IS STILL SACRIFICING PARSONERS TO CULTIVATE IT...
JUST FOR THEIR OWN PROFIT!
AND YOU THINK THAT SOMEONE IS COUNT ELZIAN?
I SAW A MAN TAKING A RUUD FLOWER...
...OUT OF THE COUNT'S MANSION!!
BUT THAT'S NOT ENOUGH TO MAKE AN ACCU-SATION.
HE'D QUICKLY COVER IT UP.
THAT'S WHY I SENT FOR YOU. BUT OLIVIA...
OLIVIA?
MY GIRLFRIEND. SHE SNUCK INTO COUNT ELZIAN'S MANSION AS A MAID TO FIND POSITIVE PROOF.
YOU COWARD!

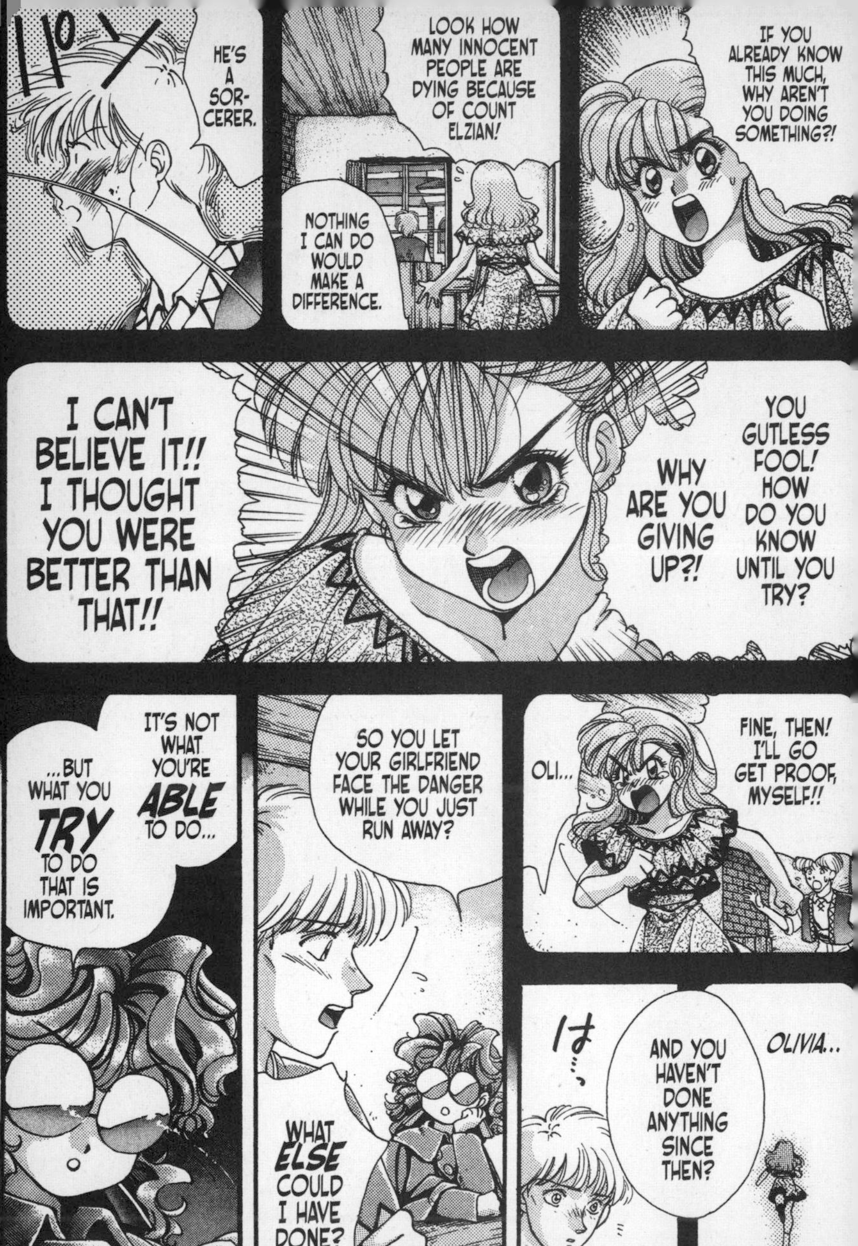
IF YOU ALREADY KNOW THIS MUCH, WHY AREN'T YOU DOING SOMETHING?!
LOOK HOW MANY INNOCENT PEOPLE ARE DYING BECAUSE OF COUNT ELZIAN!
NOTHING I CAN DO WOULD MAKE A DIFFERENCE.
HE'S A SOR-CERER.
YOU GUTLESS FOOL! HOW DO YOU KNOW UNTIL YOU TRY?
WHY ARE YOU GIVING UP?!
I CAN'T BELIEVE IT!! I THOUGHT YOU WERE BETTER THAN THAT!!
FINE, THEN! I'LL GO GET PROOF, MYSELF!!
OLI...
OLIVIA...
AND YOU HAVEN'T DONE ANYTHING SINCE THEN?
は...
SO YOU LET YOUR GIRLFRIEND FACE THE DANGER WHILE YOU JUST RUN AWAY?
WHAT ELSE COULD I HAVE DONE?
IT'S NOT WHAT YOU'RE ABLE TO DO...
...BUT WHAT YOU TRY TO DO THAT IS IMPORTANT.

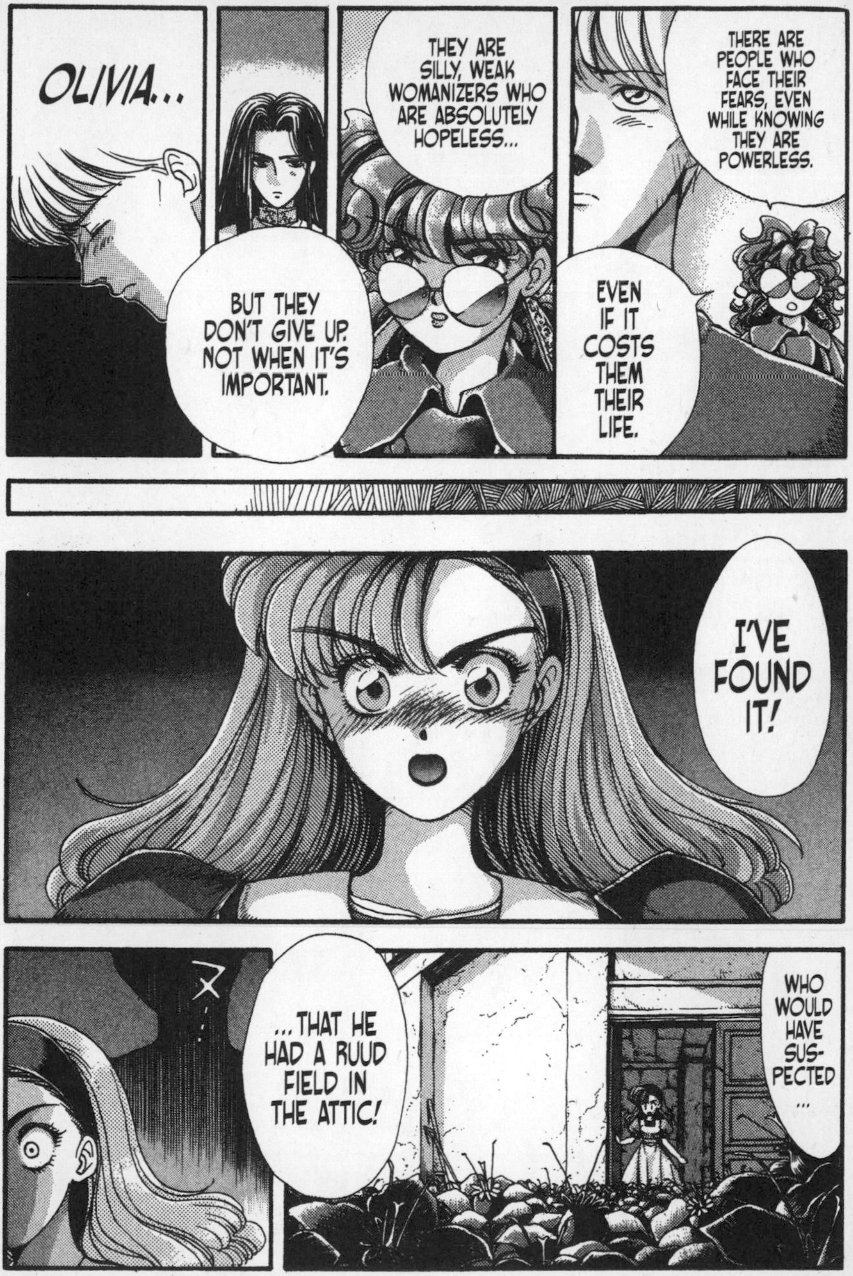
THERE ARE PEOPLE WHO FACE THEIR FEARS, EVEN WHILE KNOWING THEY ARE POWERLESS.
EVEN IF IT COSTS THEM THEIR LIFE.
THEY ARE SILLY, WEAK WOMANIZERS WHO ARE ABSOLUTELY HOPELESS...
BUT THEY DON'T GIVE UP. NOT WHEN IT'S IMPORTANT.
OLIVIA...
I'VE FOUND IT!
WHO WOULD HAVE SUS-PECTED...
...THAT HE HAD A RUUD FIELD IN THE ATTIC!

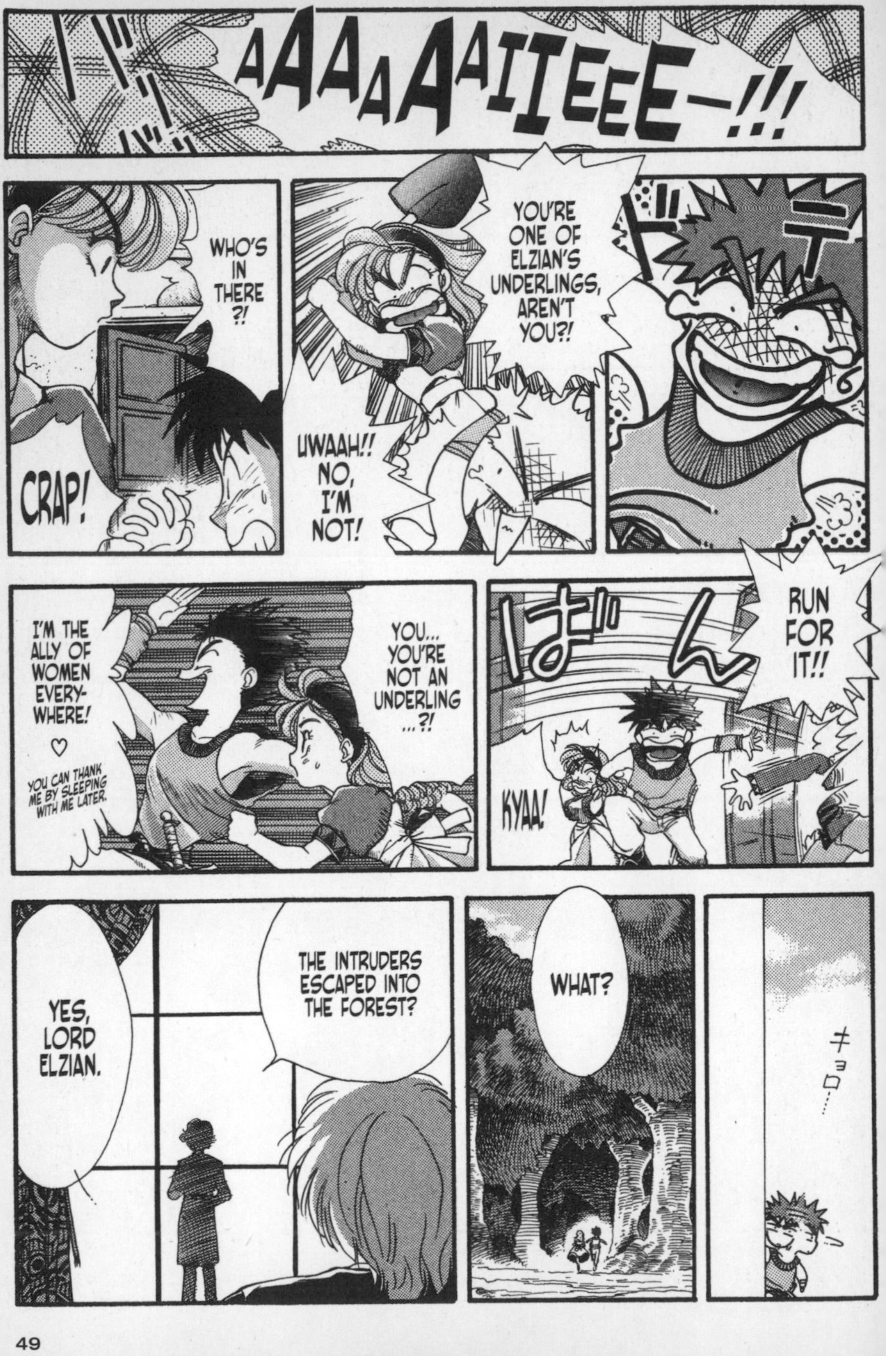
AAAAAAIEEE—!!!
ドテ
YOU'RE ONE OF ELZIAN'S UNDERLINGS, AREN'T YOU?!
UWAAH!! NO, I'M NOT!
WHO'S IN THERE ?!
CRAP!
ばん
RUN FOR IT!!
KYAA!
YOU... YOU'RE NOT AN UNDERLING ...?!
I'M THE ALLY OF WOMEN EVERY-WHERE! ♡
YOU CAN THANK ME BY SLEEPING WITH ME LATER.
キョロ…
WHAT?
THE INTRUDERS ESCAPED INTO THE FOREST?
YES, LORD ELZIAN.

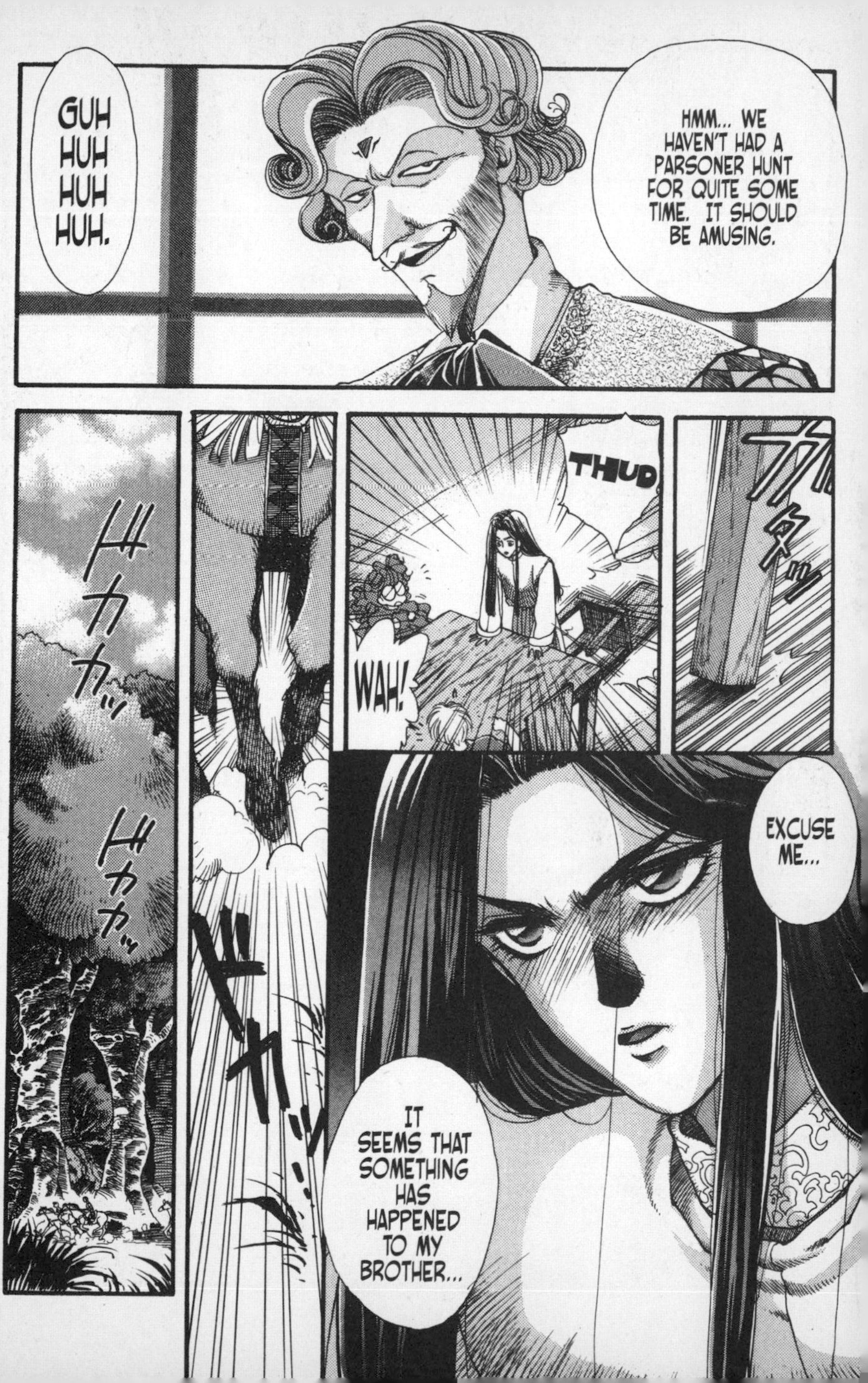
HMM... WE HAVEN'T HAD A PARSONER HUNT FOR QUITE SOME TIME. IT SHOULD BE AMUSING.
GUH HUH HUH HUH.
THUD
WAH!
EXCUSE ME...
IT SEEMS THAT SOMETHING HAS HAPPENED TO MY BROTHER...

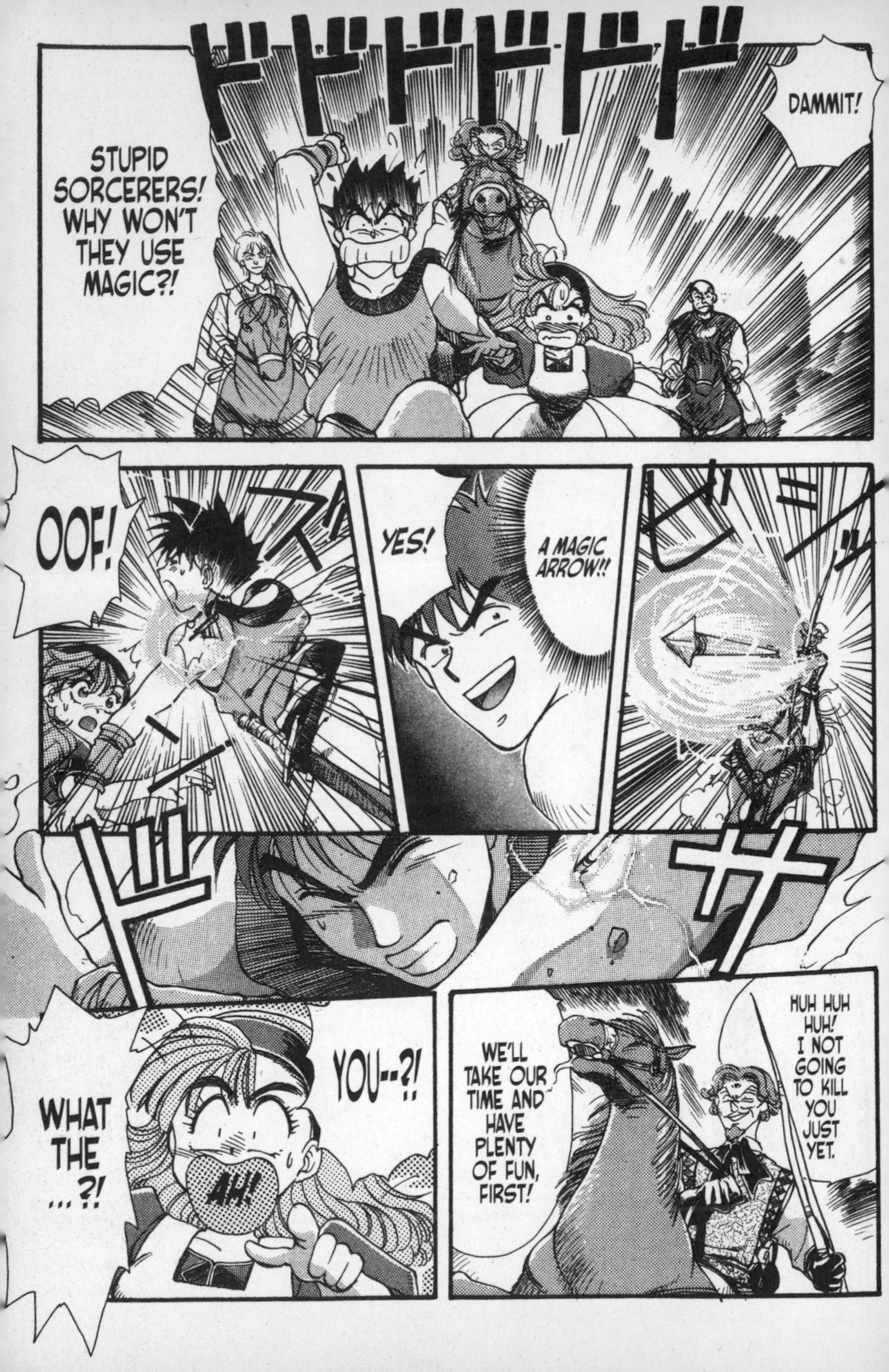
DAMMIT!
STUPID SORCERERS! WHY WON'T THEY USE MAGIC?!
A MAGIC ARROW!!
YES!
OOF!
HUH HUH HUH! I NOT GOING TO KILL YOU JUST YET.
WE'LL TAKE OUR TIME AND HAVE PLENTY OF FUN, FIRST!
YOU--?!
AH!
WHAT THE ...?!

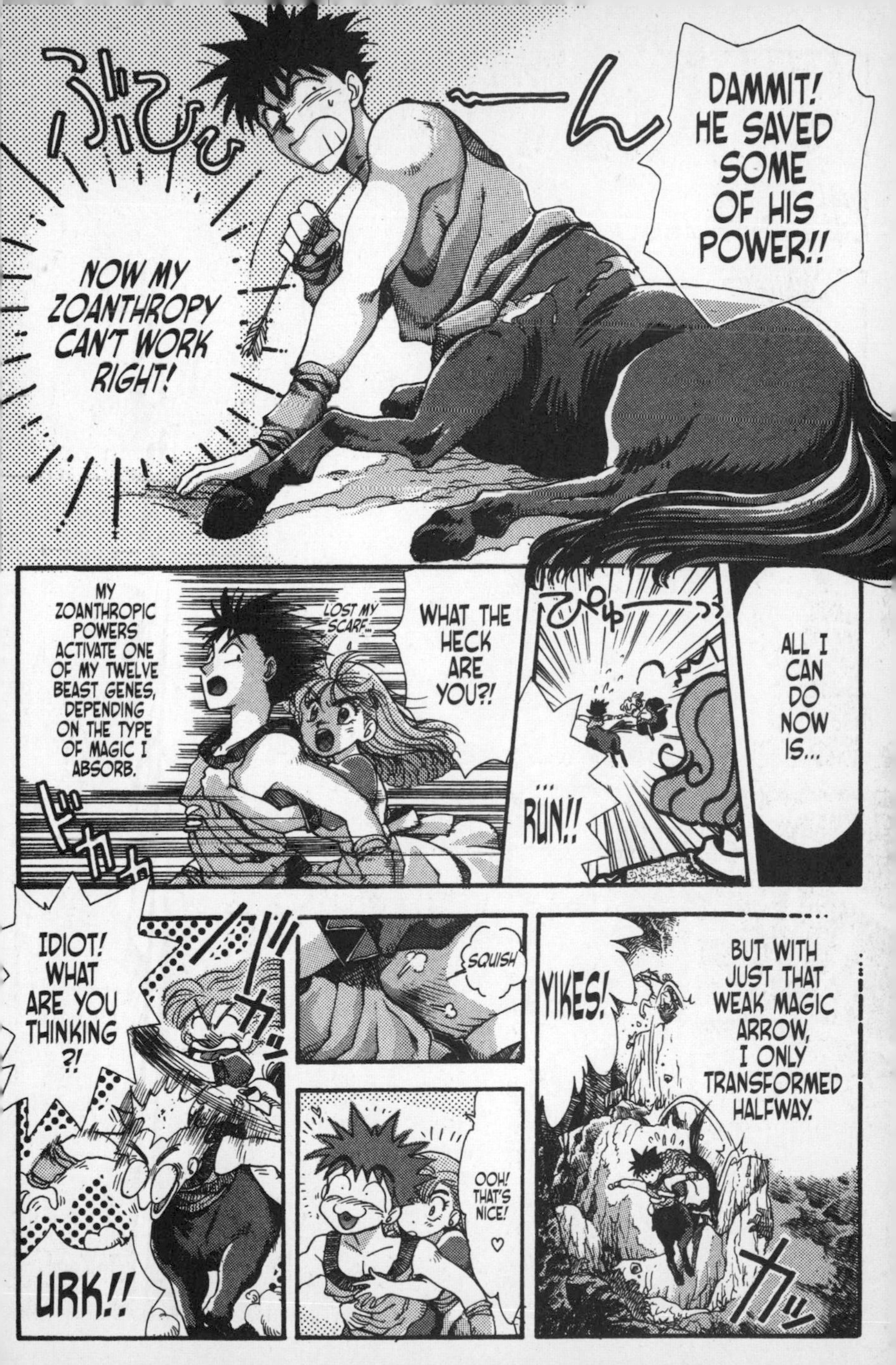
DAMMIT! HE SAVED SOME OF HIS POWER!!
NOW MY ZOANTHROPY CAN'T WORK RIGHT!
ALL I CAN DO NOW IS...
RUN!!
WHAT THE HECK ARE YOU?!
LOST MY SCARF...
MY ZOANTHROPIC POWERS ACTIVATE ONE OF MY TWELVE BEAST GENES, DEPENDING ON THE TYPE OF MAGIC I ABSORB.
BUT WITH JUST THAT WEAK MAGIC ARROW, I ONLY TRANSFORMED HALFWAY.
YIKES!
SQUISH
OOH! THAT'S NICE! ♡
IDIOT! WHAT ARE YOU THINKING?!
URK!!

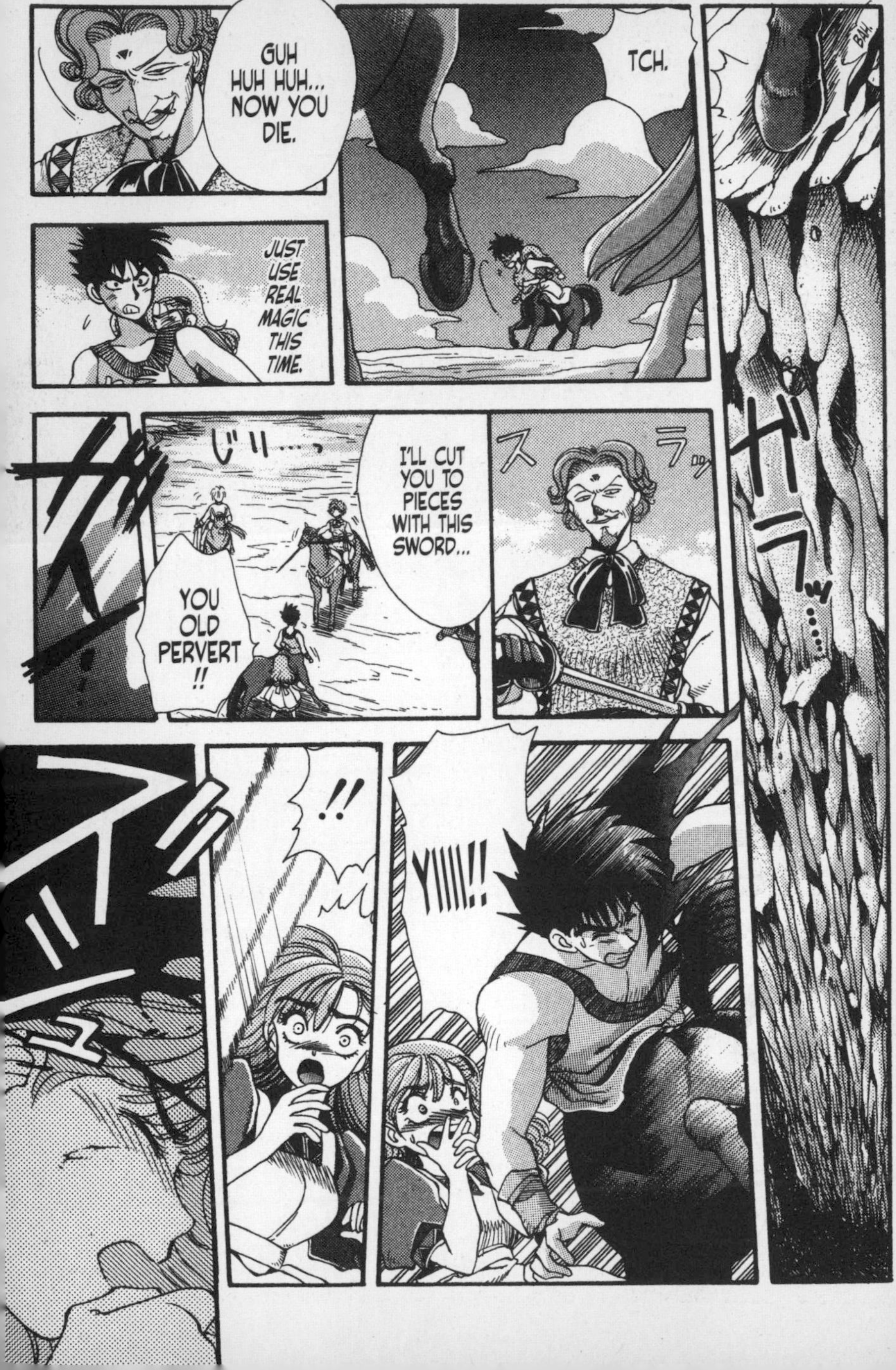
BAH.
ガラッ……
TCH.
GUH HUH HUH... NOW YOU DIE.
JUST USE REAL MAGIC THIS TIME.
スラッ
I'LL CUT YOU TO PIECES WITH THIS SWORD...
YOU OLD PERVERT !!
じり…
YIIII!!
!!

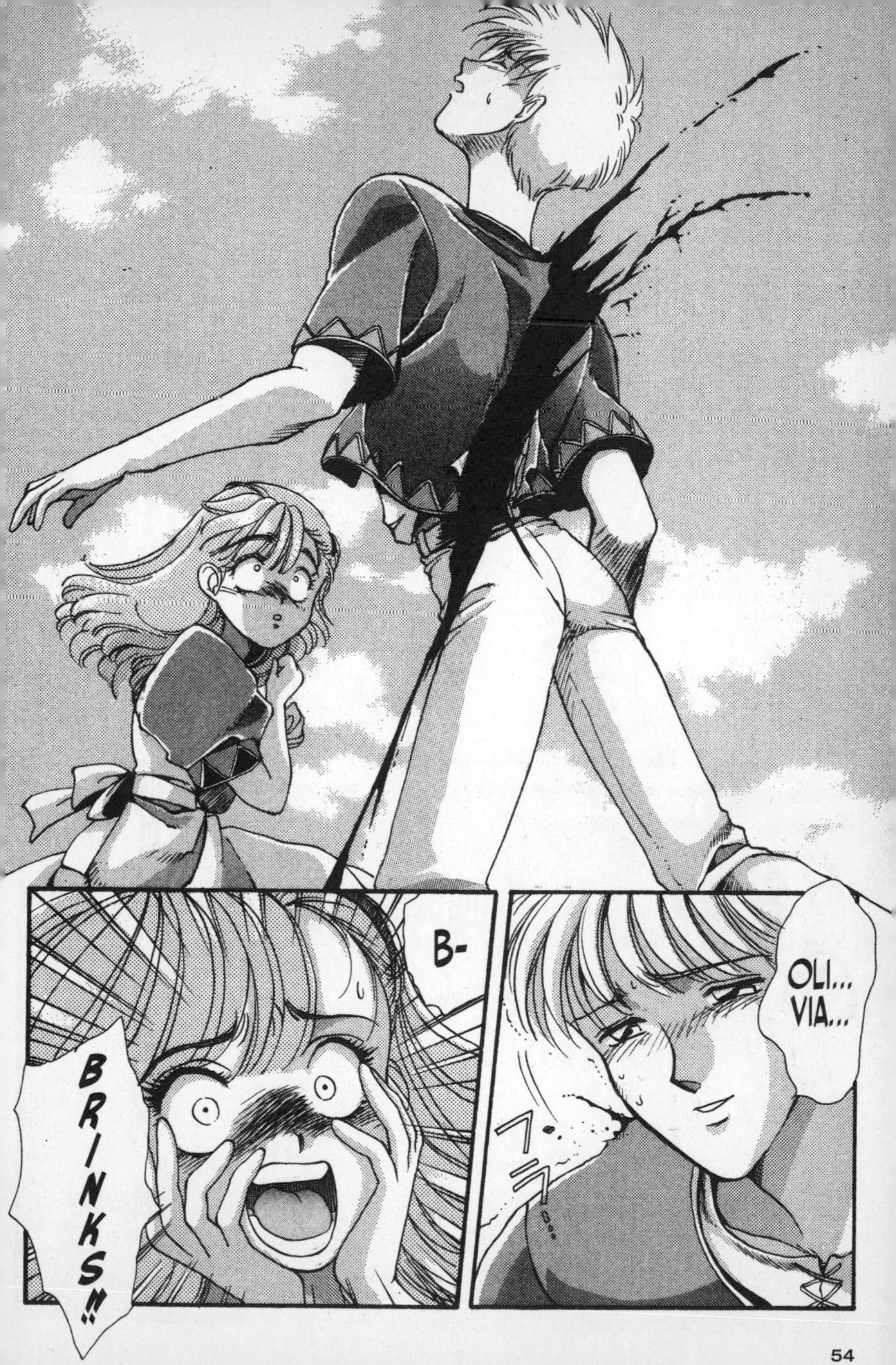
OLI... VIA...
B-
BRINKS!!

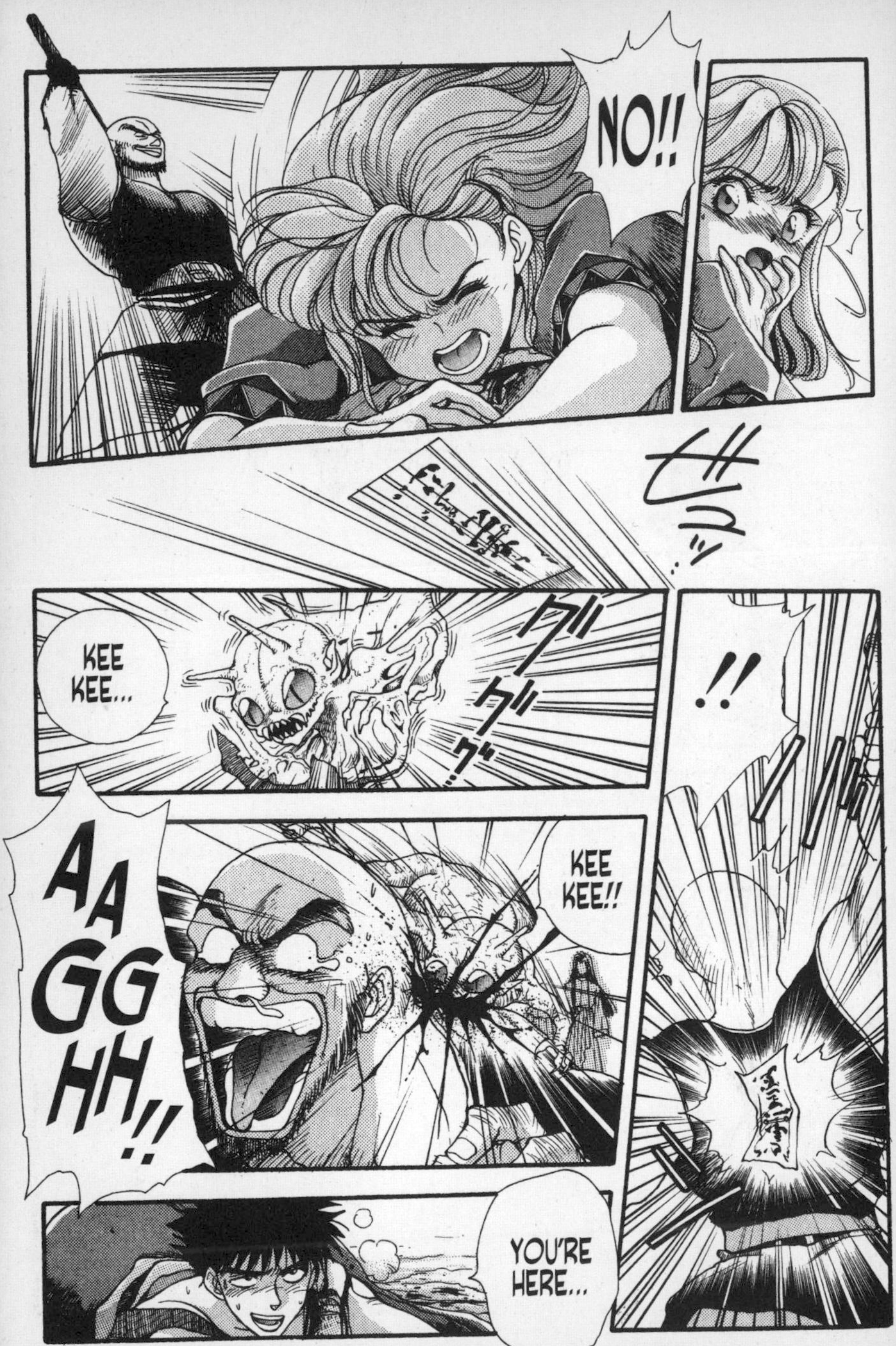
NO!!
!!
KEE KEE...
KEE KEE!!
AAGGHH!!
YOU'RE HERE...

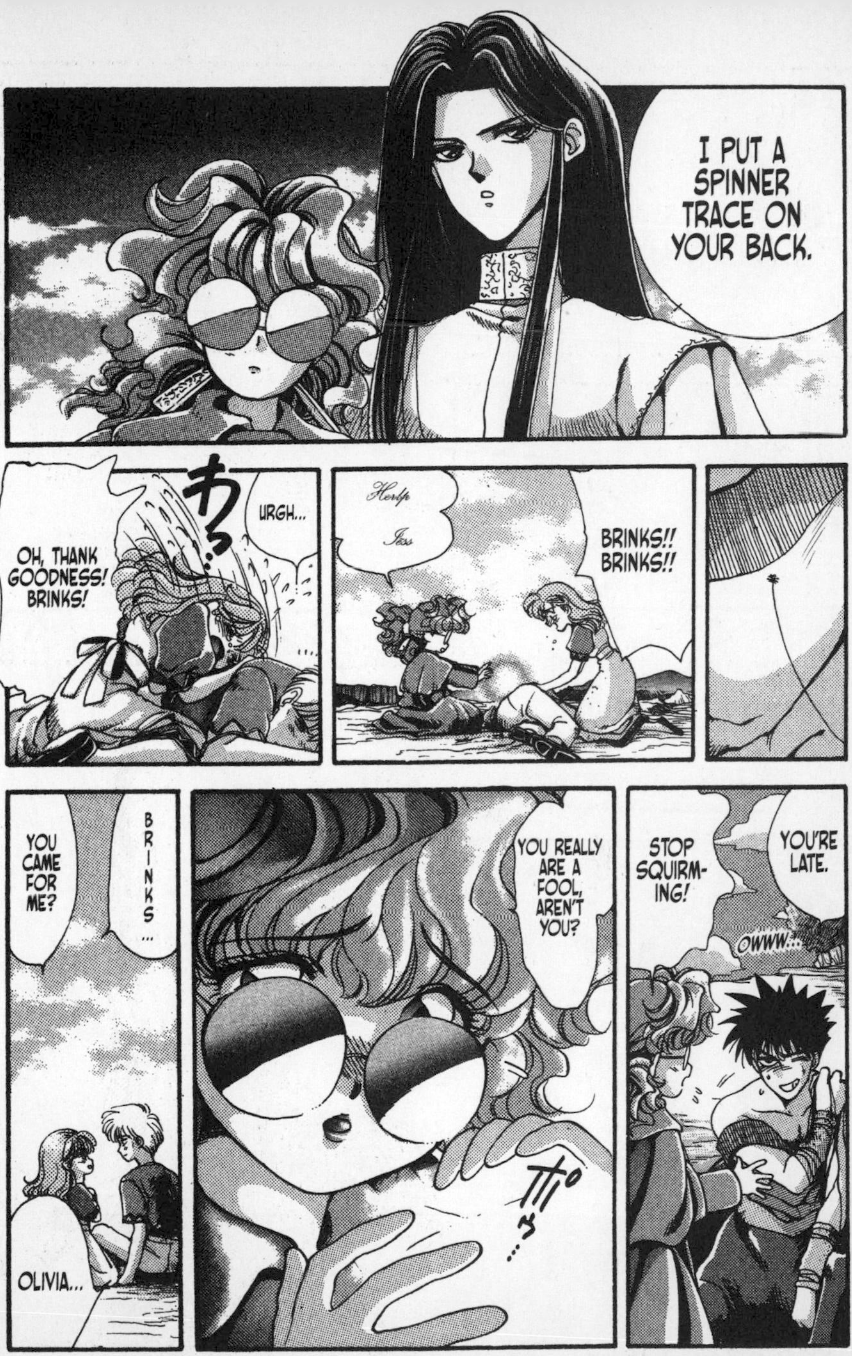
I PUT A SPINNER TRACE ON YOUR BACK.
BRINKS!! BRINKS!!
URGH...
OH, THANK GOODNESS! BRINKS!
YOU'RE LATE.
STOP SQUIRMING!
OWWW...
YOU REALLY ARE A FOOL, AREN'T YOU?
BRINKS...
YOU CAME FOR ME?
OLIVIA...

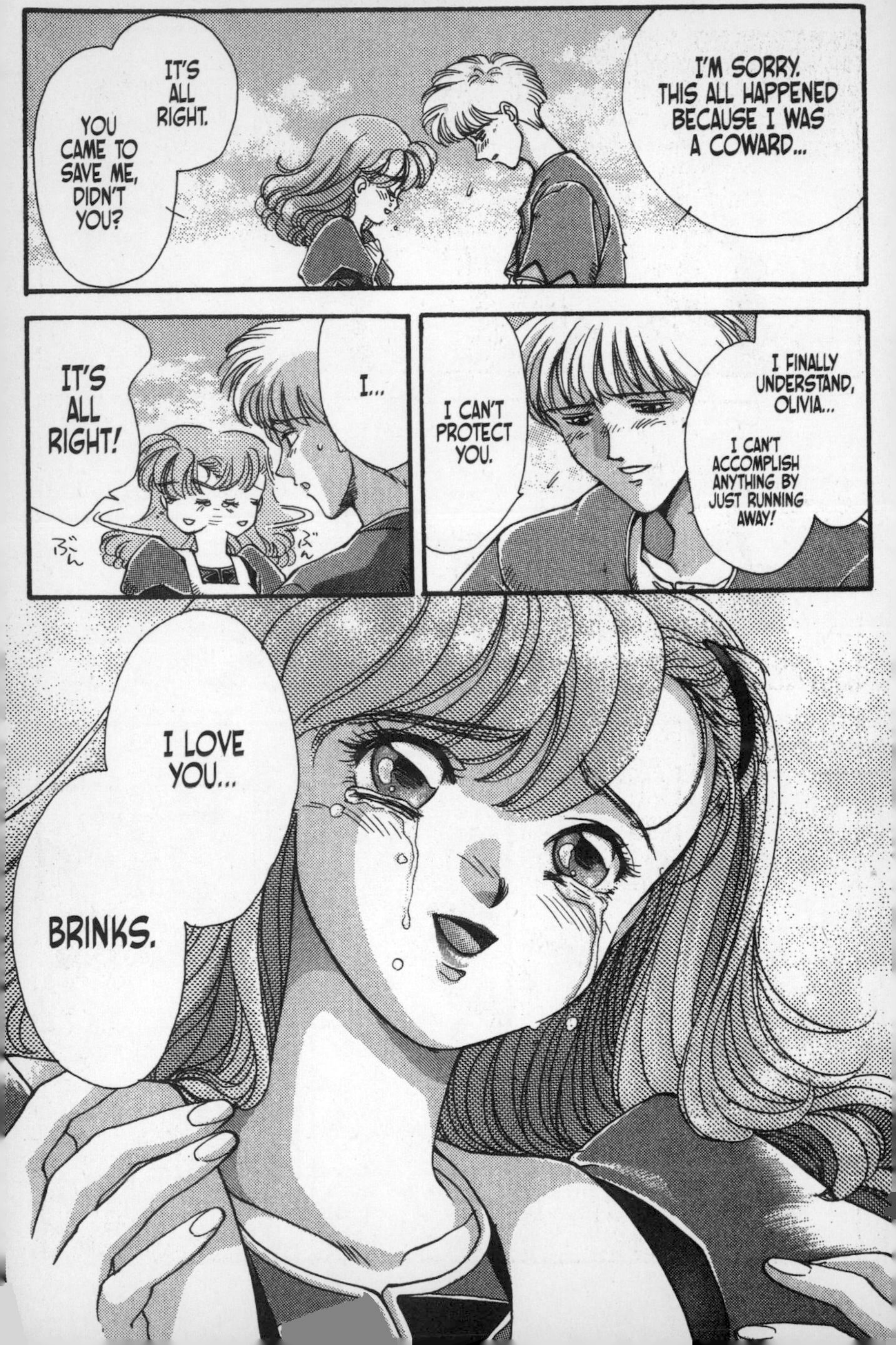
I'M SORRY. THIS ALL HAPPENED BECAUSE I WAS A COWARD...
IT'S ALL RIGHT.
YOU CAME TO SAVE ME, DIDN'T YOU?
I FINALLY UNDERSTAND, OLIVIA...
I CAN'T ACCOMPLISH ANYTHING BY JUST RUNNING AWAY!
I CAN'T PROTECT YOU.
I...
IT'S ALL RIGHT!
ぶん
ぶん
I LOVE YOU...
BRINKS.

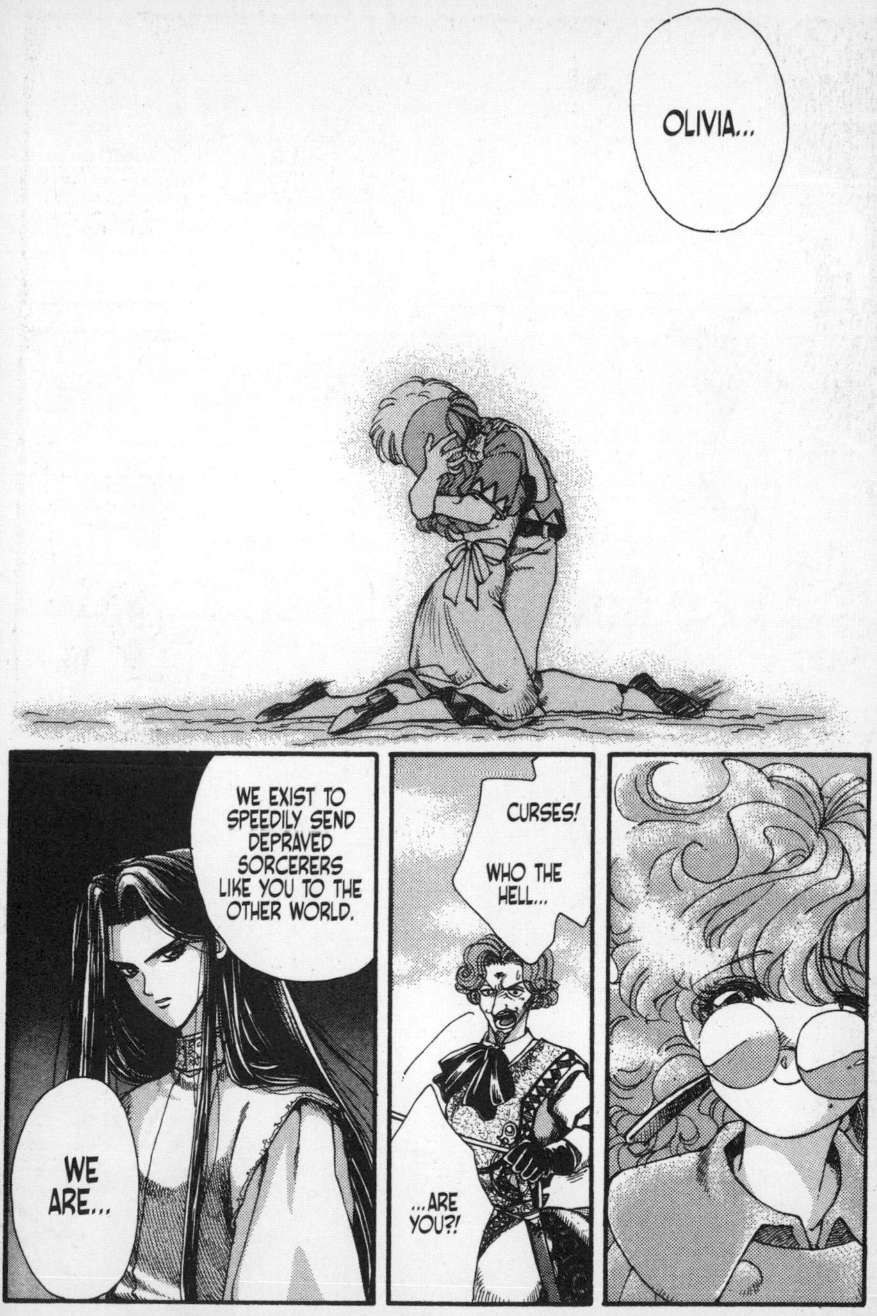
OLIVIA...
CURSES!
WHO THE HELL...
...ARE YOU?!
WE EXIST TO SPEEDILY SEND DEPRAVED SORCERERS LIKE YOU TO THE OTHER WORLD.
WE ARE...

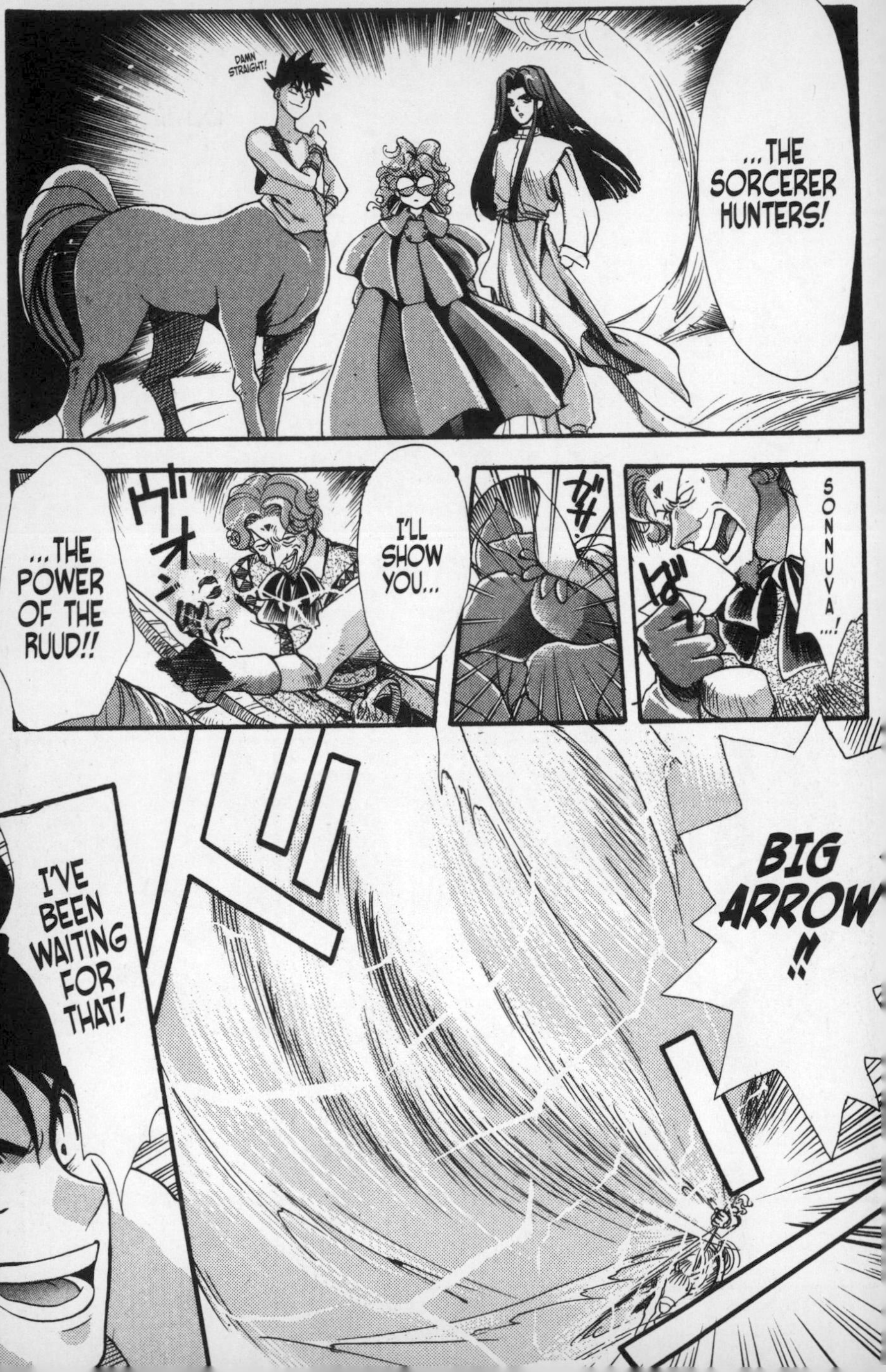
...THE SORCERER HUNTERS!
DAMN STRAIGHT!
SONNUVA...!
I'LL SHOW YOU...
...THE POWER OF THE RUUD!!
BIG ARROW!!
I'VE BEEN WAITING FOR THAT!

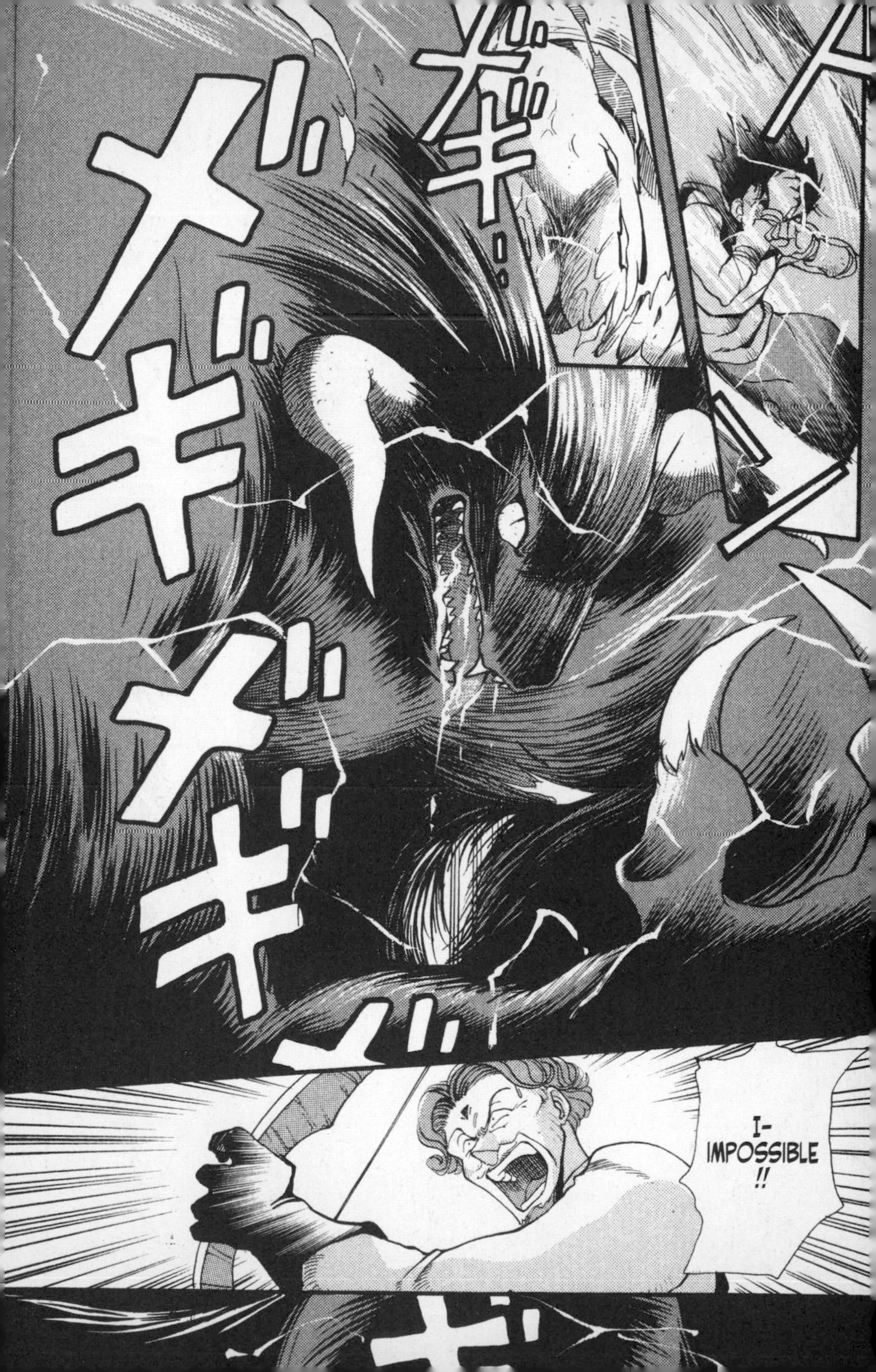
I- IMPOSSIBLE !!

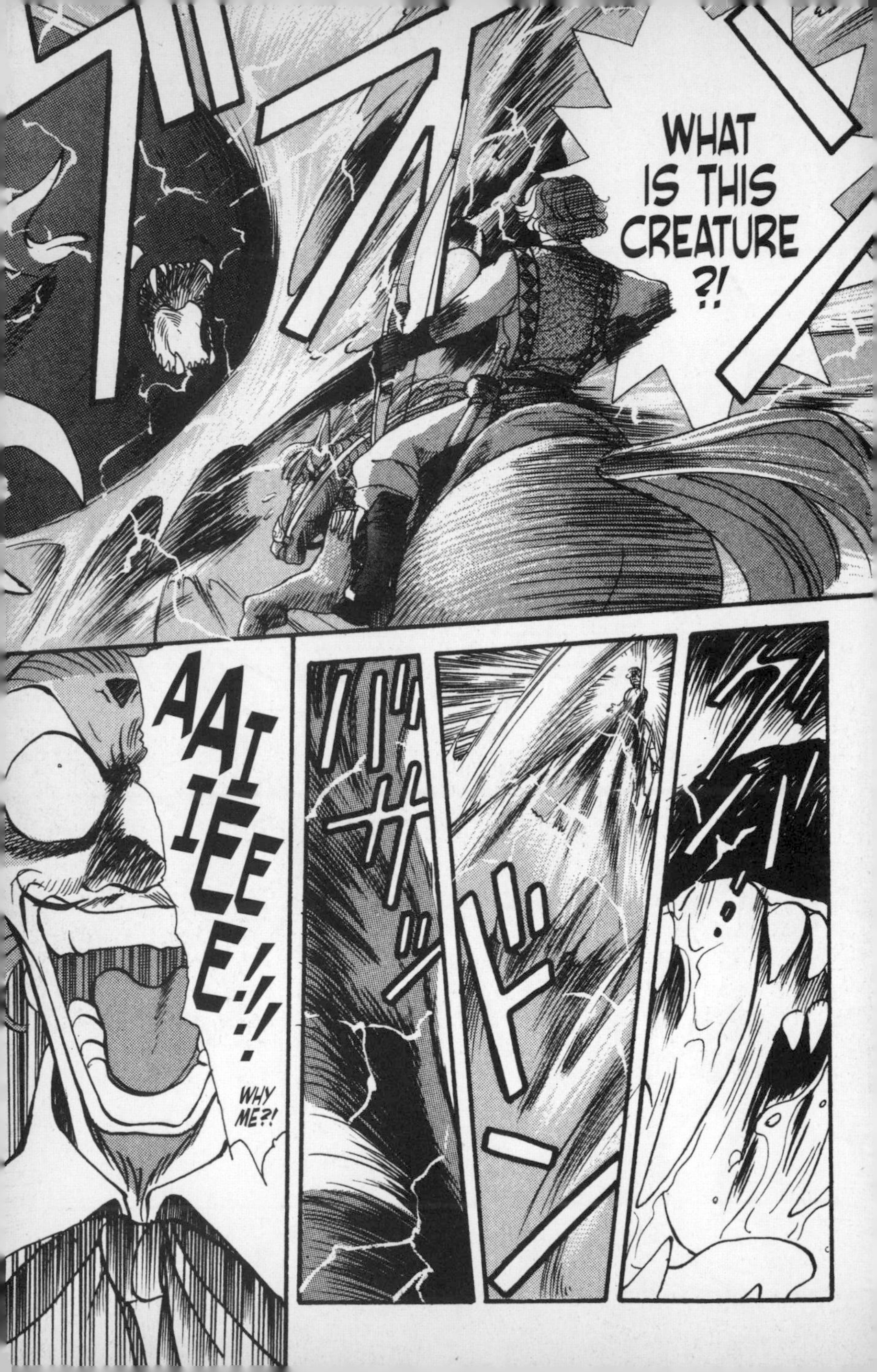

WHAT IS THIS CREATURE ?!
AAIIEEEE!!!
WHY ME?!

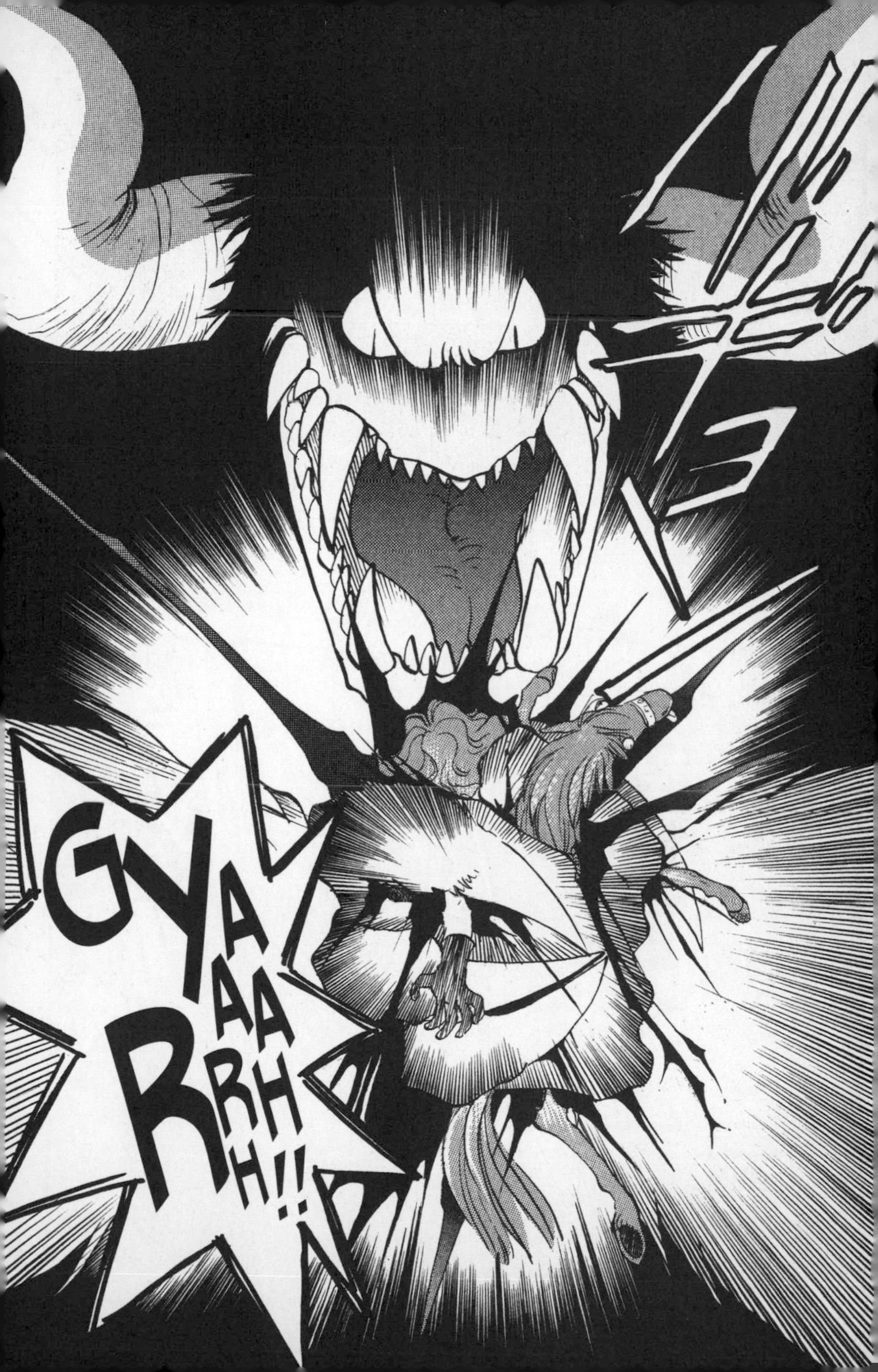
GYAAARRHH!!

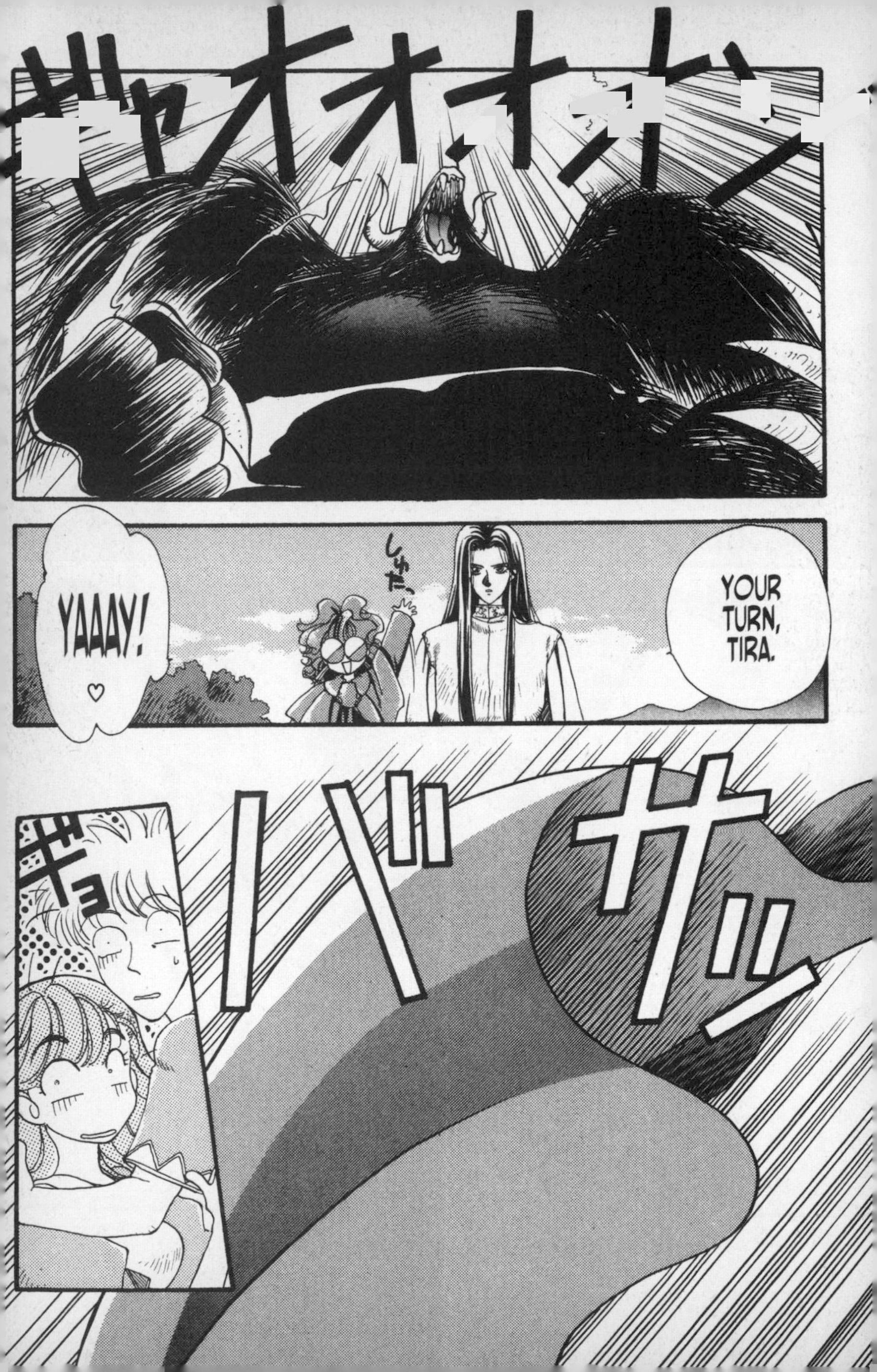
ギャオオオン
YOUR TURN, TIRA.
しゅた、
YAAAY! ♡
バザッ
ギョ

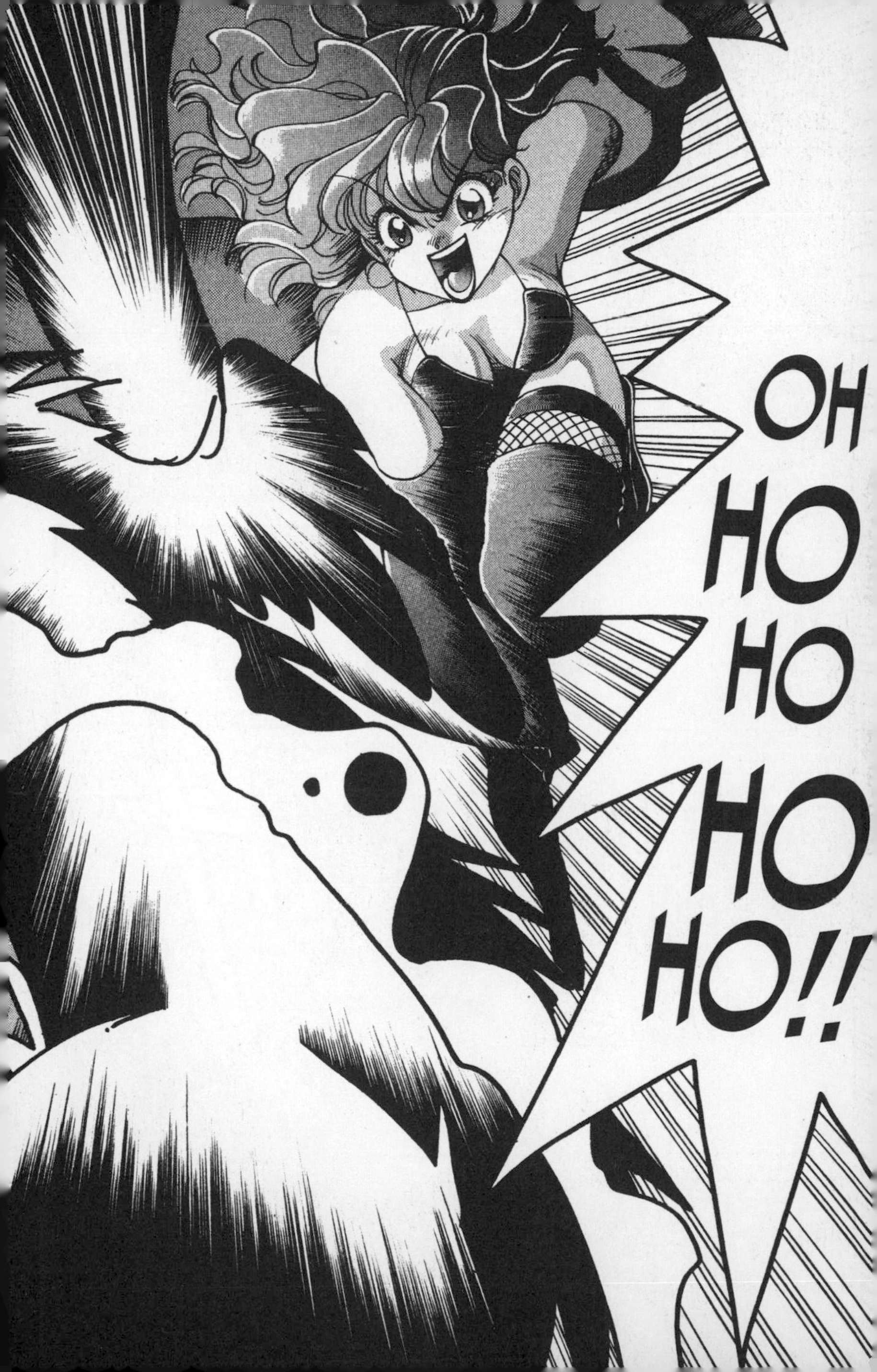
OH HO HO HO HO!!

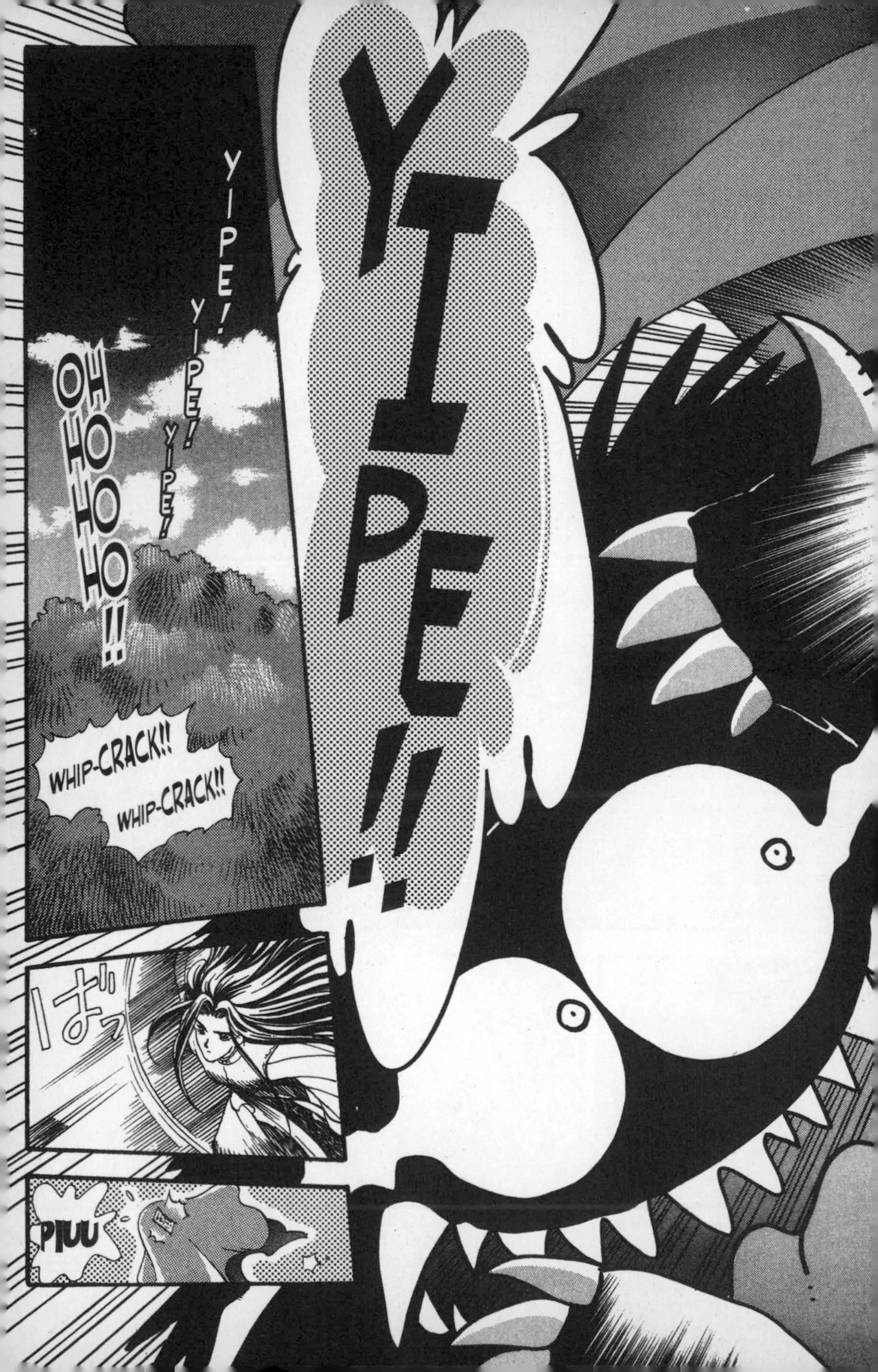
YIPE!!
YIPE!
YIPE!
YIPE!
OHOHOHO!!
WHIP-CRACK!!
WHIP-CRACK!!
ばっ
PIUU

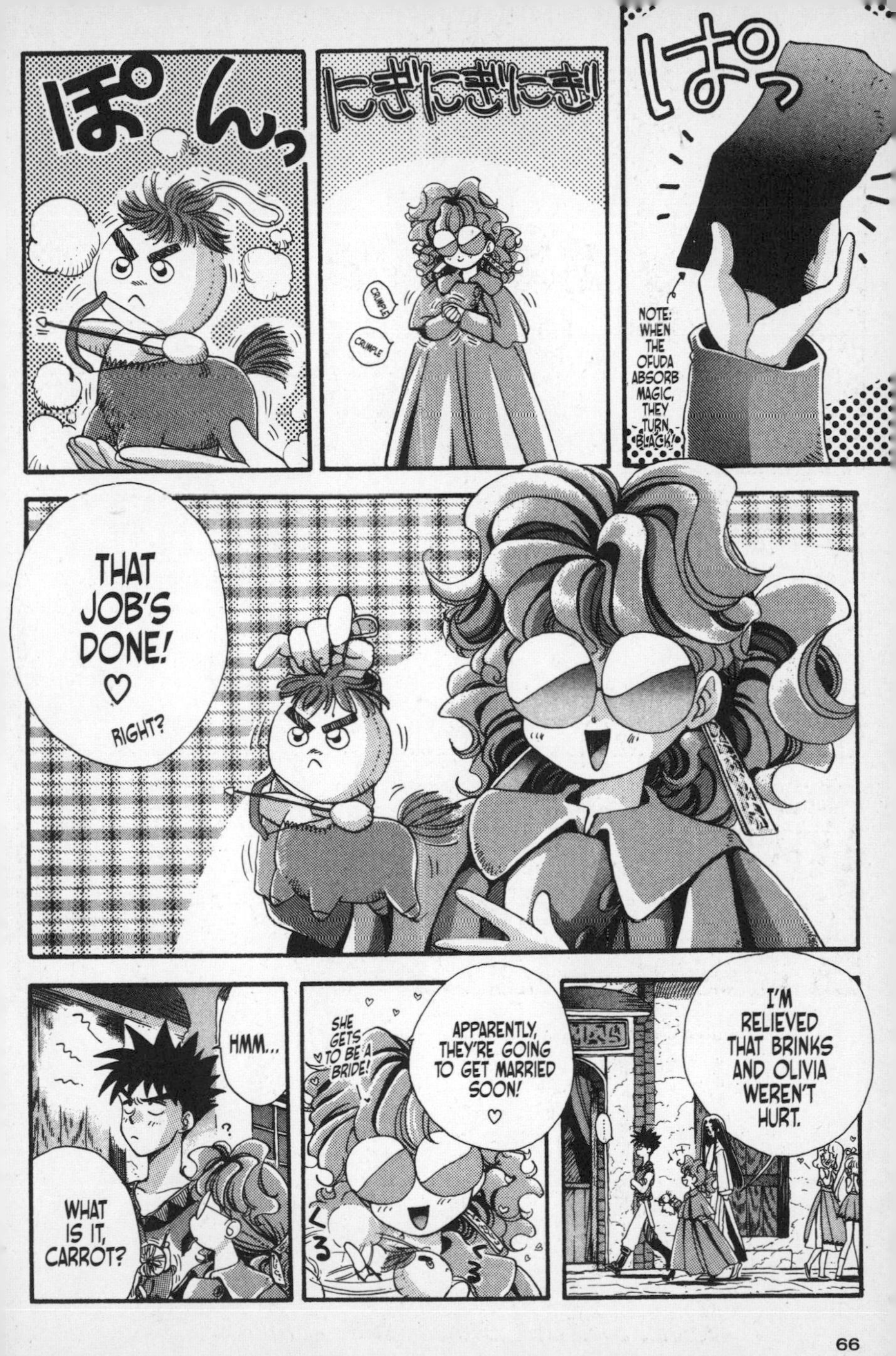
ぱっ
NOTE: WHEN THE OFUDA ABSORB MAGIC, THEY TURN BLACK!
にぎにぎにぎ
CRUMPLE
CRUMPLE
ぽんっ
THAT JOB'S DONE! ♡ RIGHT?
I'M RELIEVED THAT BRINKS AND OLIVIA WEREN'T HURT.
...
APPARENTLY, THEY'RE GOING TO GET MARRIED SOON! ♡
SHE GETS TO BE A BRIDE!
くる
くる
HMM...
?
WHAT IS IT, CARROT?

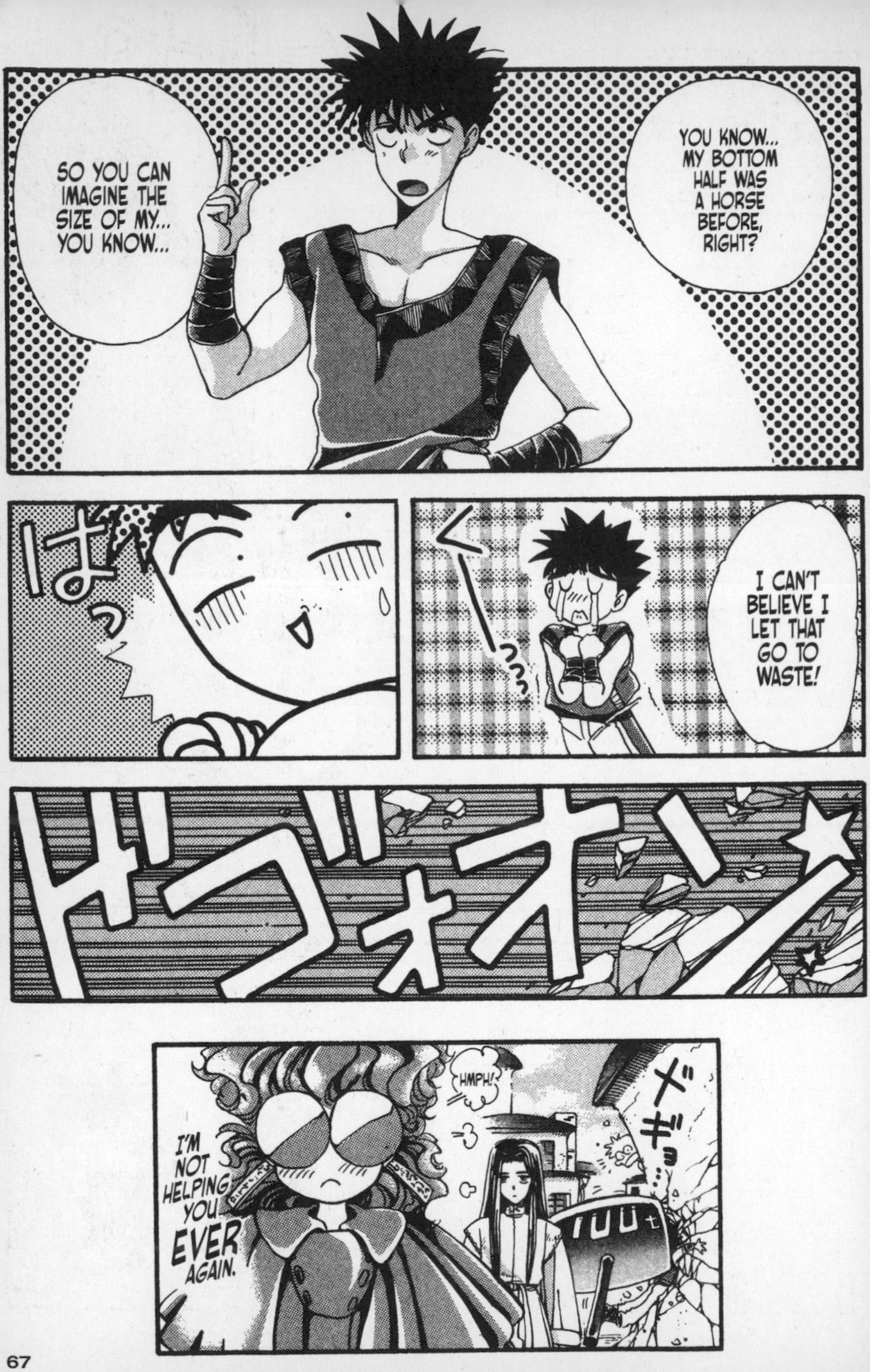
YOU KNOW... MY BOTTOM HALF WAS A HORSE BEFORE, RIGHT?
SO YOU CAN IMAGINE THE SIZE OF MY... YOU KNOW...
くーっ
I CAN'T BELIEVE I LET THAT GO TO WASTE!
はっ
ドヴォオン☆
メギョ...
HMPH!
100t
I'M NOT HELPING YOU EVER AGAIN.

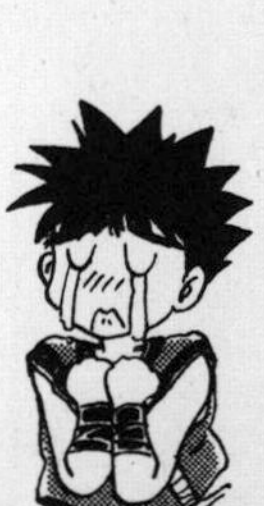

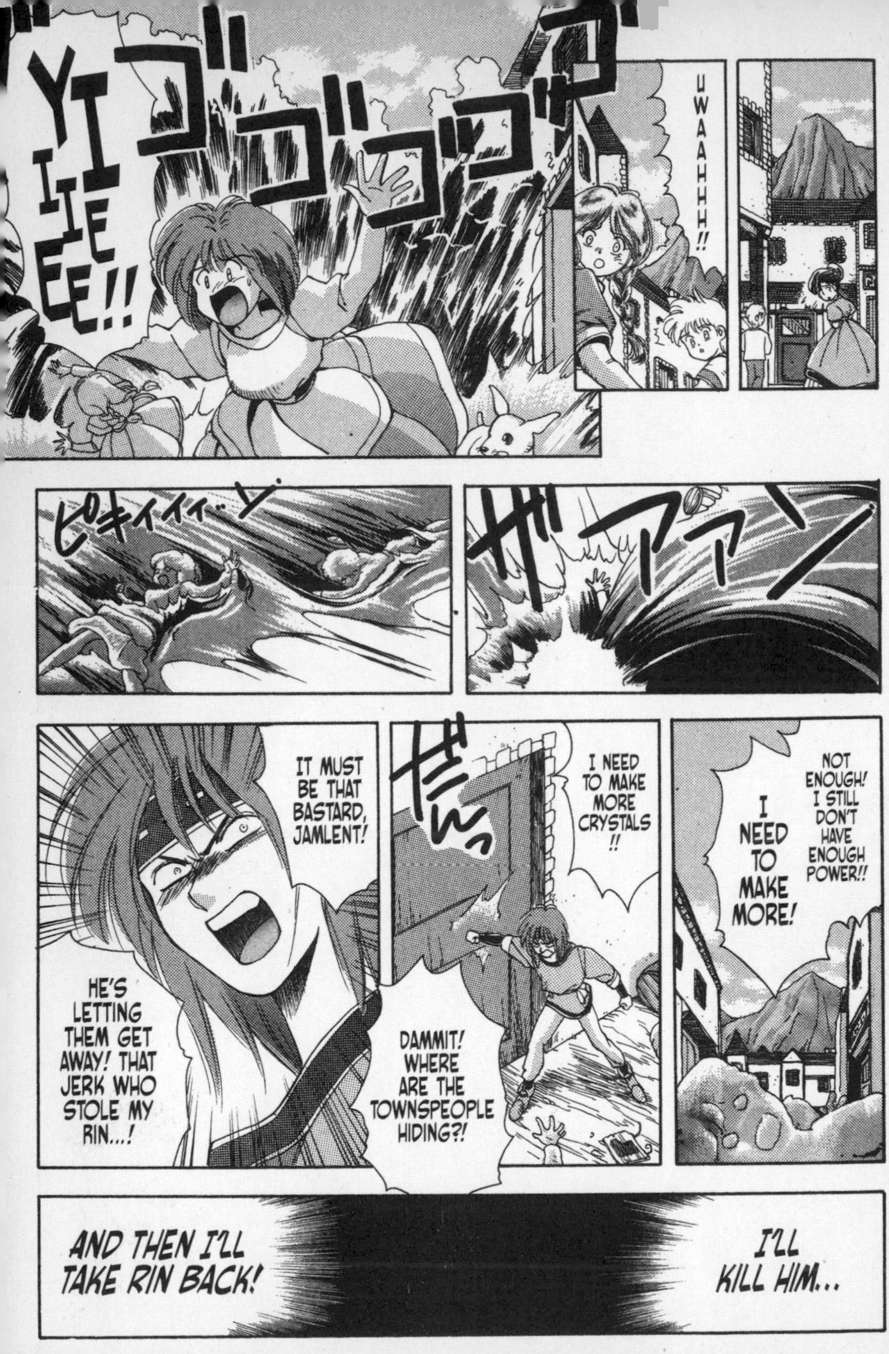
UWAAHHH!!
YIIEEEE!!
NOT ENOUGH! I STILL DON'T HAVE ENOUGH POWER!!
I NEED TO MAKE MORE!
I NEED TO MAKE MORE CRYSTALS!!
DAMMIT! WHERE ARE THE TOWNSPEOPLE HIDING?!
IT MUST BE THAT BASTARD, JAMLENT!
HE'S LETTING THEM GET AWAY! THAT JERK WHO STOLE MY RIN...!
I'LL KILL HIM...
AND THEN I'LL TAKE RIN BACK!

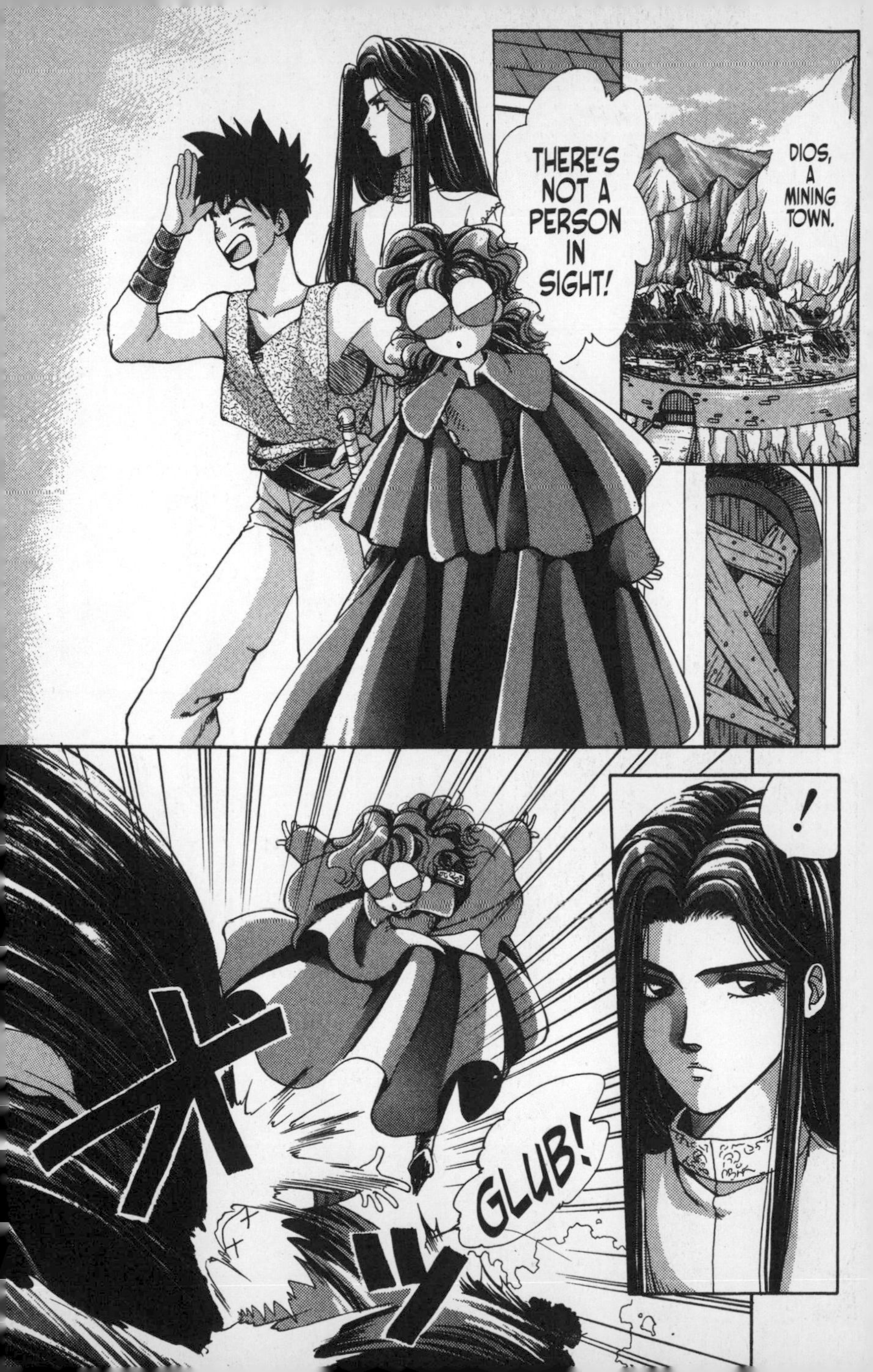
DIOS, A MINING TOWN.
THERE'S NOT A PERSON IN SIGHT!
!
GLUB!

3 DARK WATER - PART 1

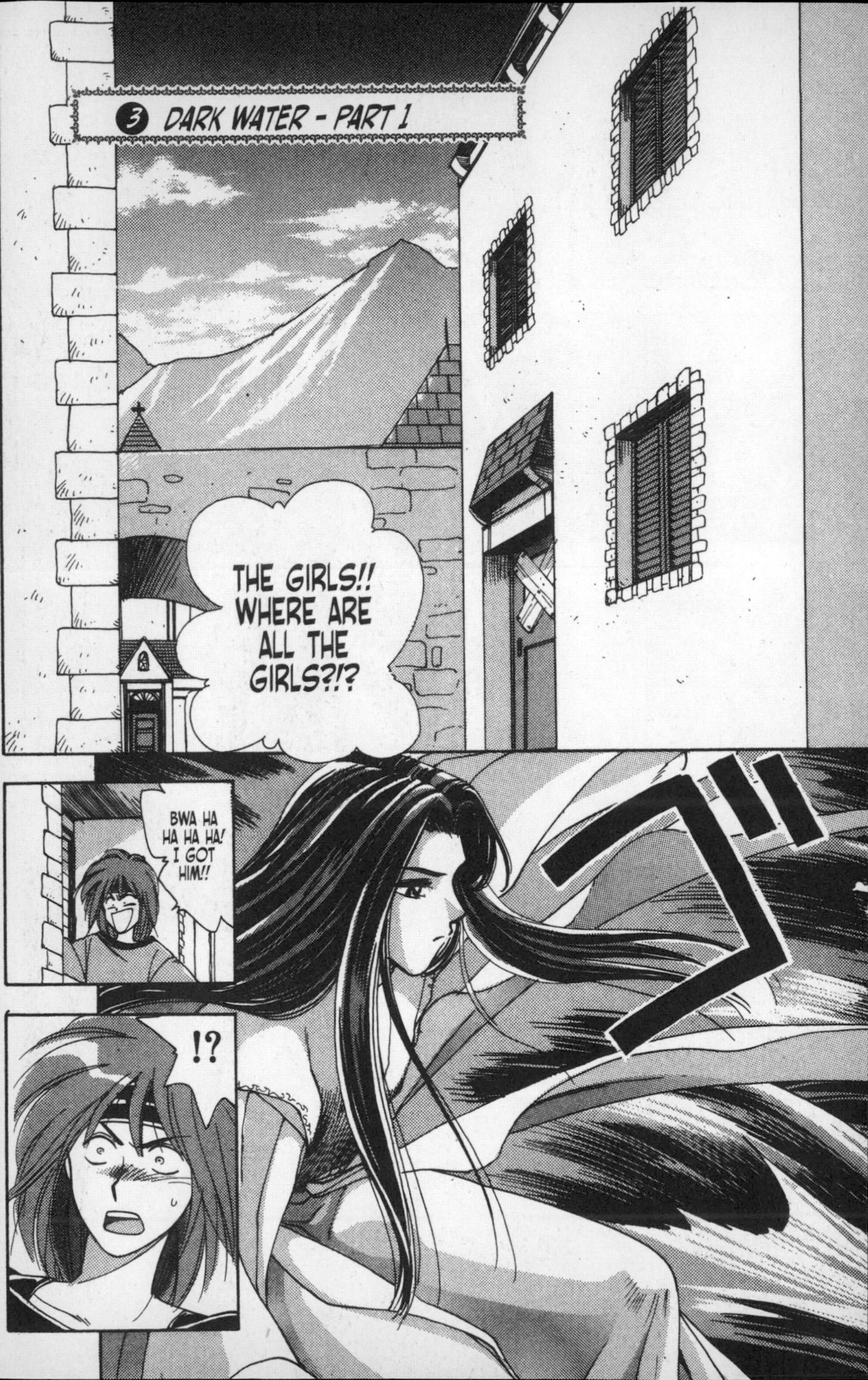
THE GIRLS!! WHERE ARE ALL THE GIRLS?!?
BWA HA HA HA HA! I GOT HIM!!
!?

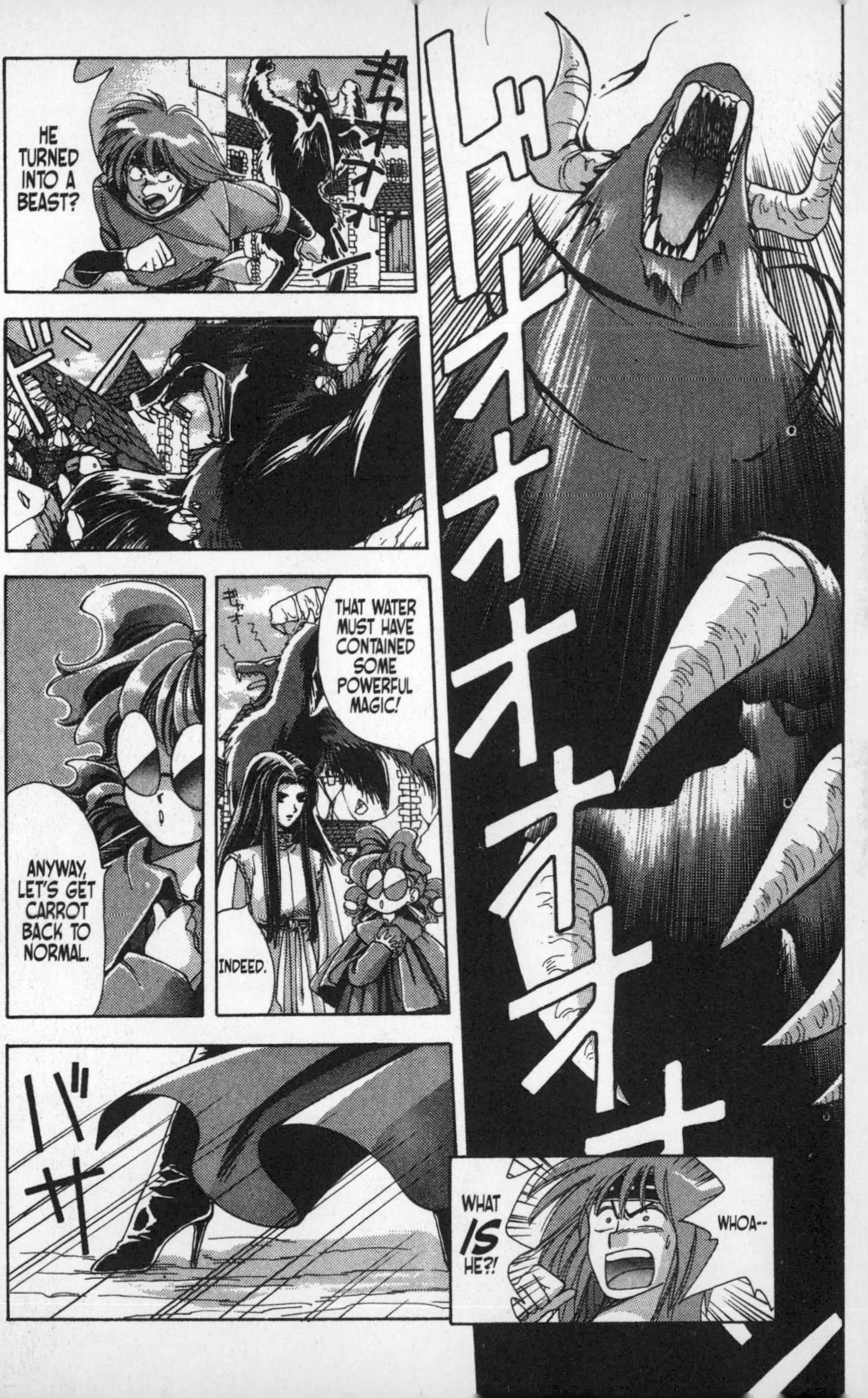
WHOA--
WHAT IS HE?!
HE TURNED INTO A BEAST?
THAT WATER MUST HAVE CONTAINED SOME POWERFUL MAGIC!
INDEED.
ANYWAY, LET'S GET CARROT BACK TO NORMAL.
バサ

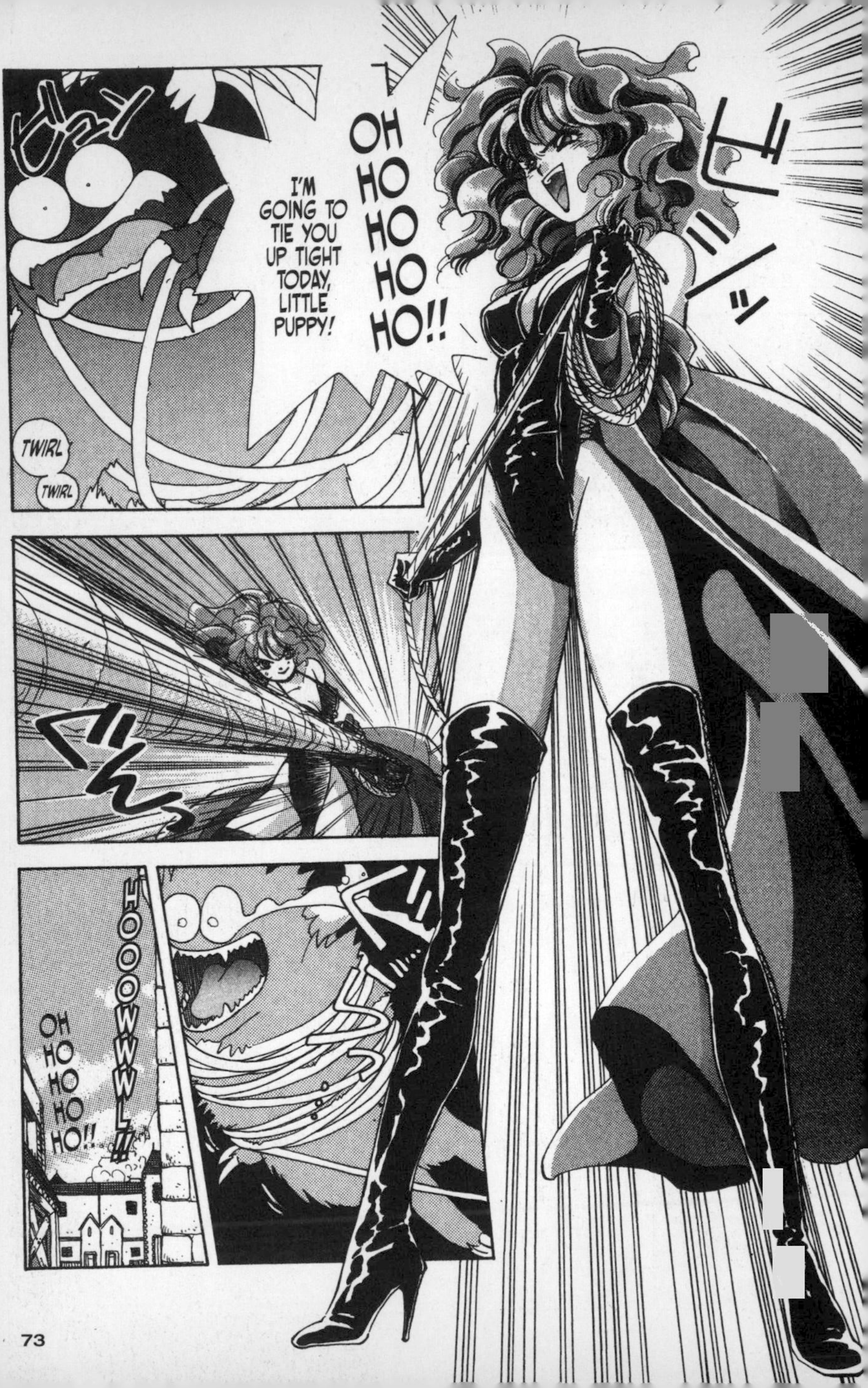
OH HO HO HO HO!!
I'M GOING TO TIE YOU UP TIGHT TODAY, LITTLE PUPPY!
TWIRL
TWIRL
HOOOOWWWL!!!
OH HO HO HO HO!!

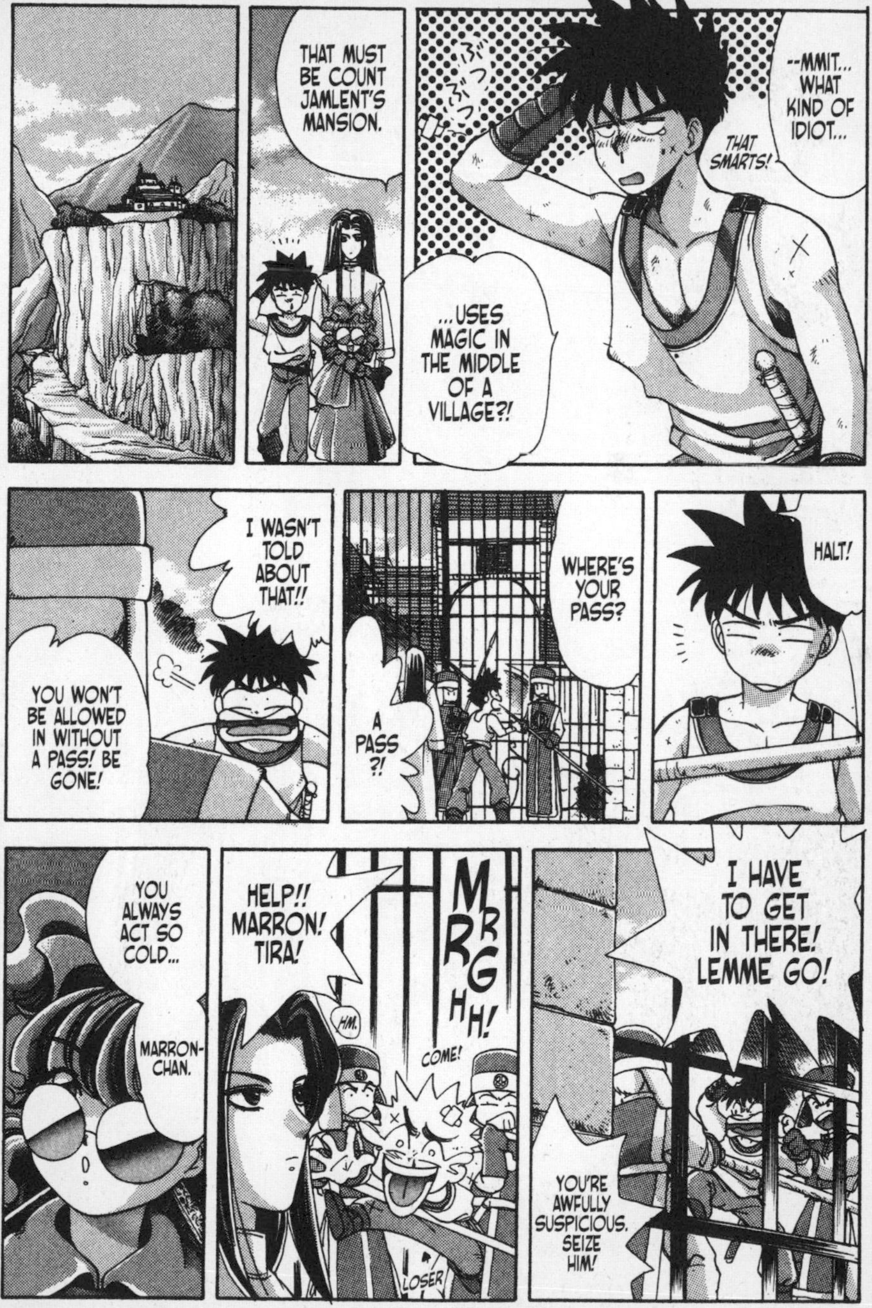
--MMIT... WHAT KIND OF IDIOT...
THAT SMARTS!
ぶつぶつ
...USES MAGIC IN THE MIDDLE OF A VILLAGE?!
THAT MUST BE COUNT JAMLENT'S MANSION.
HALT!
WHERE'S YOUR PASS?
A PASS?!
I WASN'T TOLD ABOUT THAT!!
YOU WON'T BE ALLOWED IN WITHOUT A PASS! BE GONE!
I HAVE TO GET IN THERE! LEMME GO!
YOU'RE AWFULLY SUSPICIOUS. SEIZE HIM!
HELP!! MARRON! TIRA!
MRRGHH!
HM.
COME!
LOSER
YOU ALWAYS ACT SO COLD...
MARRON-CHAN.

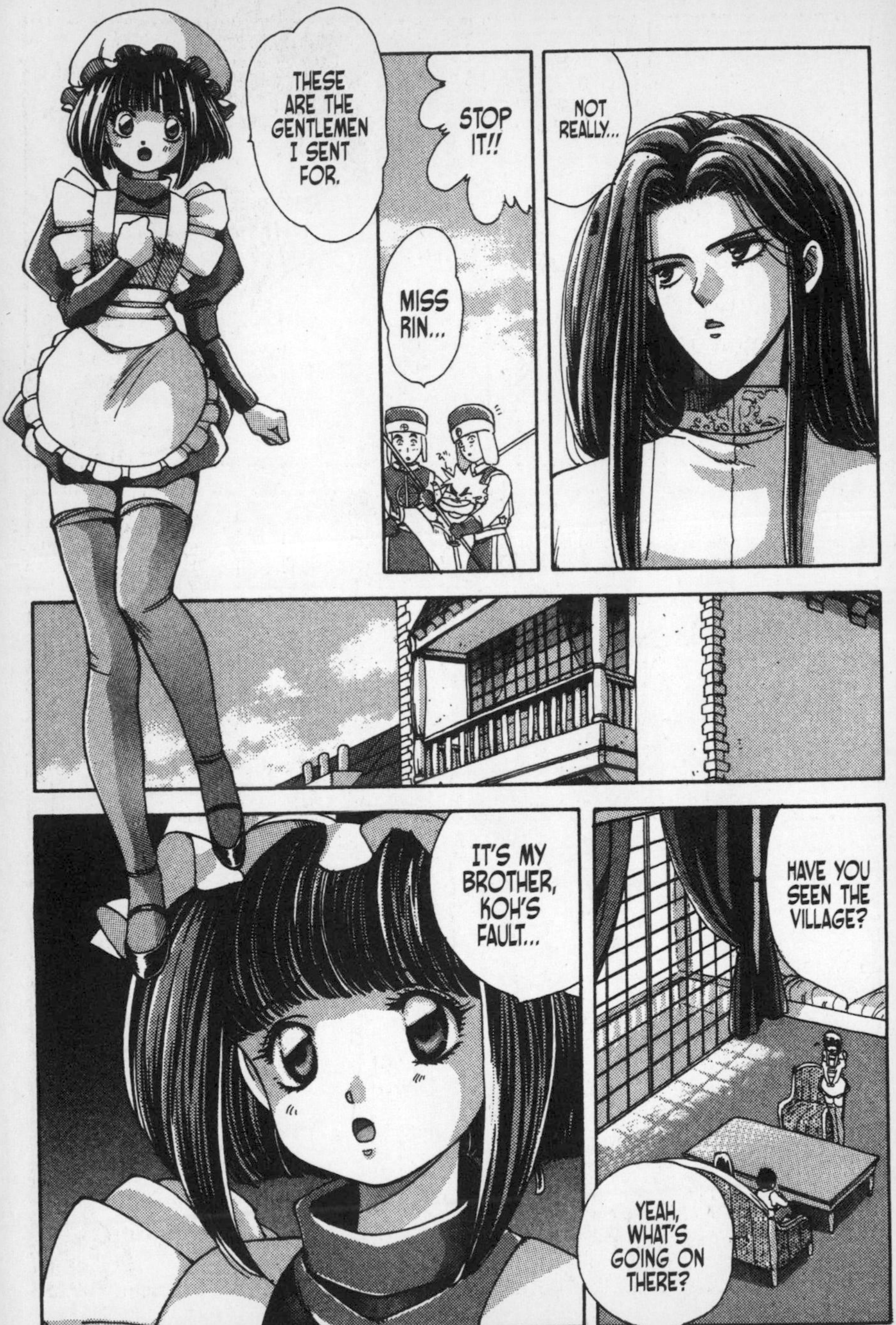
NOT REALLY...
STOP IT!!
MISS RIN...
THESE ARE THE GENTLEMEN I SENT FOR.
HAVE YOU SEEN THE VILLAGE?
YEAH, WHAT'S GOING ON THERE?
IT'S MY BROTHER, KOH'S FAULT...

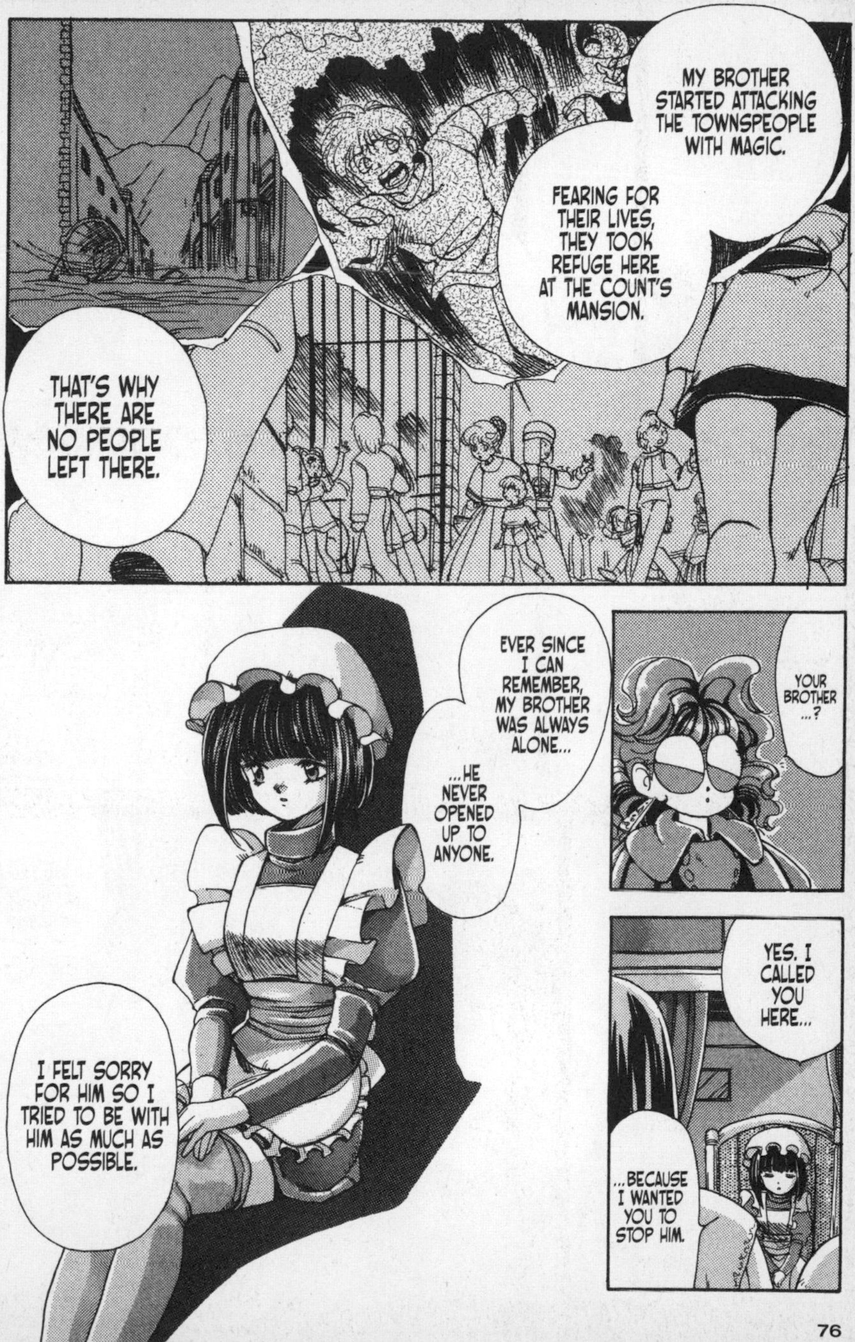
MY BROTHER STARTED ATTACKING THE TOWNSPEOPLE WITH MAGIC.
FEARING FOR THEIR LIVES, THEY TOOK REFUGE HERE AT THE COUNT'S MANSION.
THAT'S WHY THERE ARE NO PEOPLE LEFT THERE.
YOUR BROTHER ...?
YES. I CALLED YOU HERE...
...BECAUSE I WANTED YOU TO STOP HIM.
EVER SINCE I CAN REMEMBER, MY BROTHER WAS ALWAYS ALONE...
...HE NEVER OPENED UP TO ANYONE.
I FELT SORRY FOR HIM SO I TRIED TO BE WITH HIM AS MUCH AS POSSIBLE.

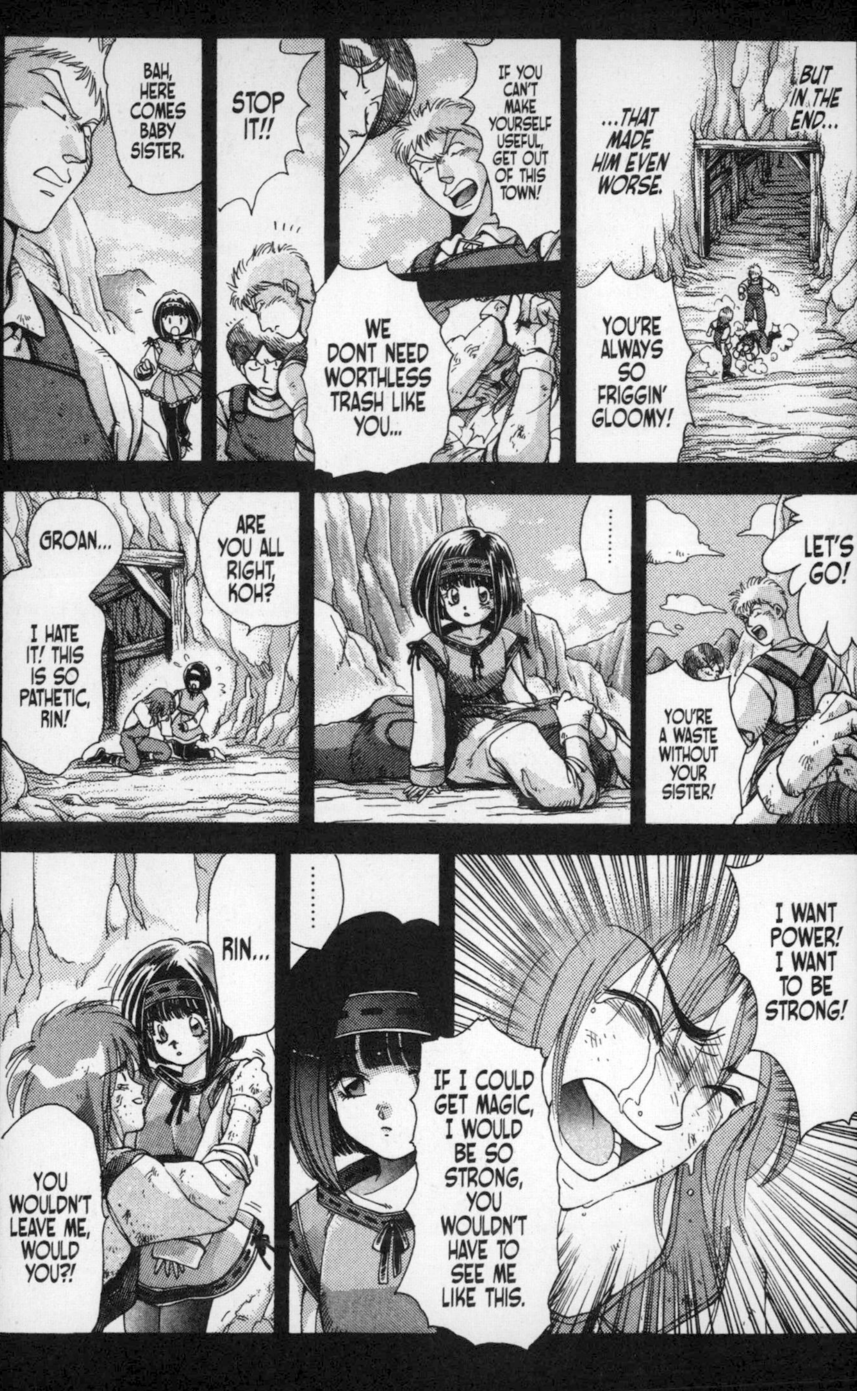
BUT IN THE END...
...THAT MADE HIM EVEN WORSE.
YOU'RE ALWAYS SO FRIGGIN' GLOOMY!
IF YOU CAN'T MAKE YOURSELF USEFUL, GET OUT OF THIS TOWN!
WE DONT NEED WORTHLESS TRASH LIKE YOU...
STOP IT!!
BAH, HERE COMES BABY SISTER.
LET'S GO!
YOU'RE A WASTE WITHOUT YOUR SISTER!
......
ARE YOU ALL RIGHT, KOH?
GROAN...
I HATE IT! THIS IS SO PATHETIC, RIN!
I WANT POWER! I WANT TO BE STRONG!
......
IF I COULD GET MAGIC, I WOULD BE SO STRONG, YOU WOULDN'T HAVE TO SEE ME LIKE THIS.
RIN...
YOU WOULDN'T LEAVE ME, WOULD YOU?!

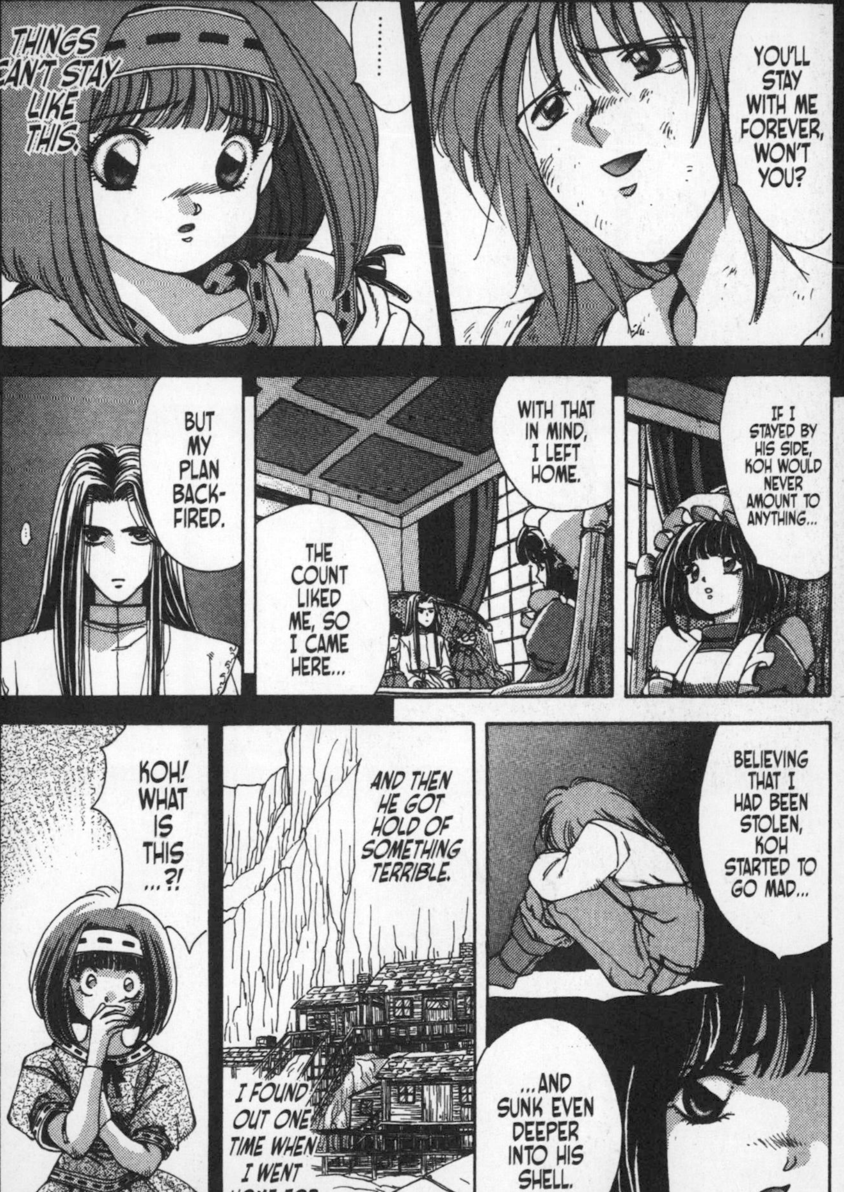
YOU'LL STAY WITH ME FOREVER, WON'T YOU?
......
THINGS CAN'T STAY LIKE THIS.
IF I STAYED BY HIS SIDE, KOH WOULD NEVER AMOUNT TO ANYTHING...
WITH THAT IN MIND, I LEFT HOME.
THE COUNT LIKED ME, SO I CAME HERE...
BUT MY PLAN BACK-FIRED.
...
BELIEVING THAT I HAD BEEN STOLEN, KOH STARTED TO GO MAD...
...AND SUNK EVEN DEEPER INTO HIS SHELL.
AND THEN HE GOT HOLD OF SOMETHING TERRIBLE.
I FOUND OUT ONE TIME WHEN I WENT HOME FOR A VISIT...
KOH! WHAT IS THIS ...?!

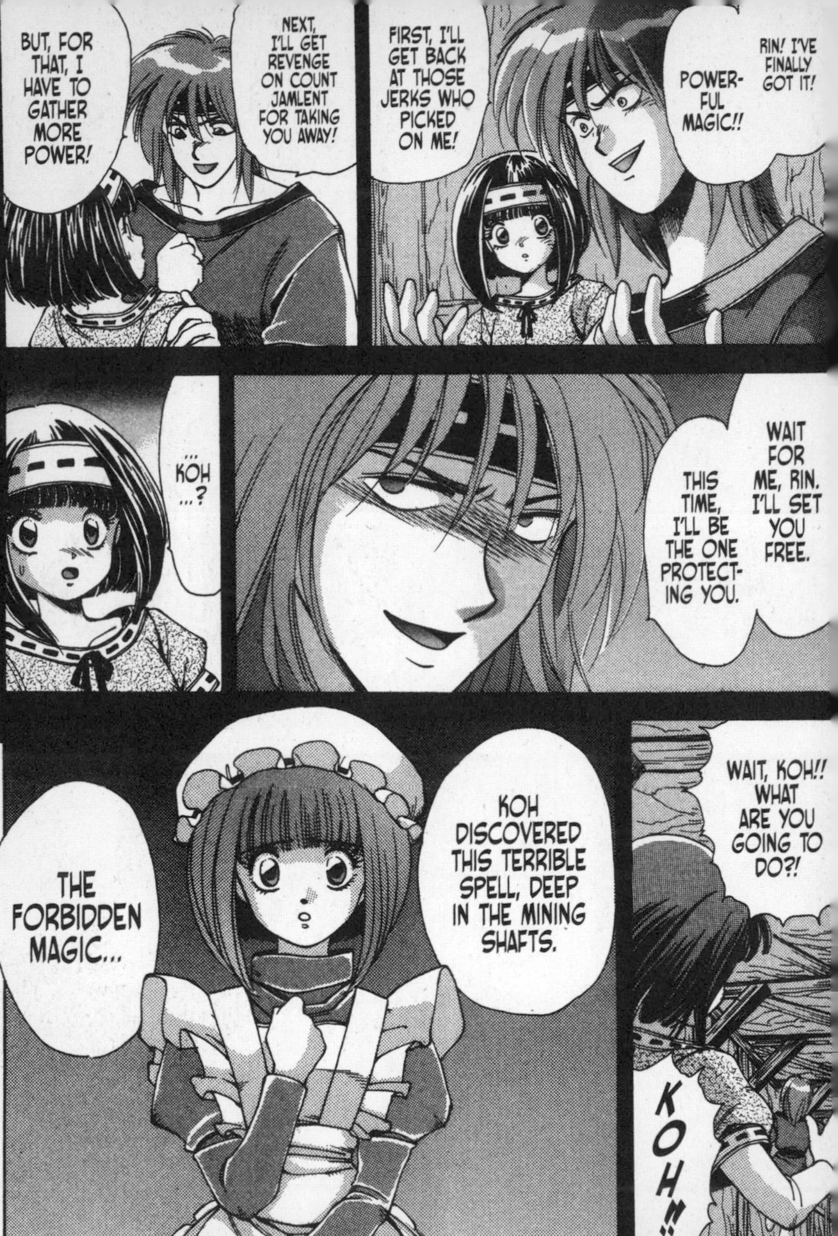
RIN! I'VE FINALLY GOT IT!
POWERFUL MAGIC!!
FIRST, I'LL GET BACK AT THOSE JERKS WHO PICKED ON ME!
NEXT, I'LL GET REVENGE ON COUNT JAMLENT FOR TAKING YOU AWAY!
BUT, FOR THAT, I HAVE TO GATHER MORE POWER!
WAIT FOR ME, RIN. I'LL SET YOU FREE.
THIS TIME, I'LL BE THE ONE PROTECTING YOU.
...KOH...?
WAIT, KOH!! WHAT ARE YOU GOING TO DO?!
KOH!!
KOH DISCOVERED THIS TERRIBLE SPELL, DEEP IN THE MINING SHAFTS.
THE FORBIDDEN MAGIC...

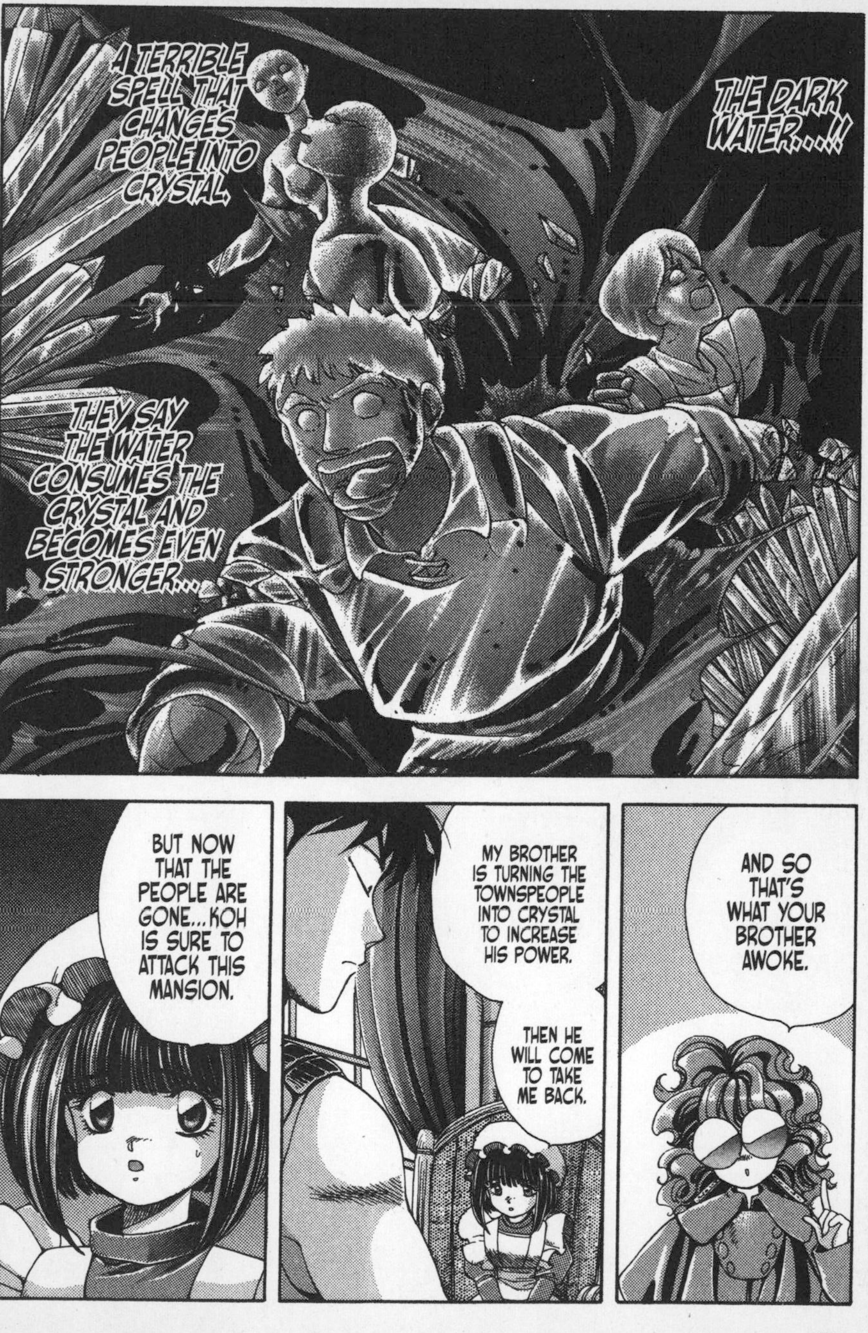
THE DARK WATER...!!
A TERRIBLE SPELL THAT CHANGES PEOPLE INTO CRYSTAL.
THEY SAY THE WATER CONSUMES THE CRYSTAL AND BECOMES EVEN STRONGER...
AND SO THAT'S WHAT YOUR BROTHER AWOKE.
MY BROTHER IS TURNING THE TOWNSPEOPLE INTO CRYSTAL TO INCREASE HIS POWER.
THEN HE WILL COME TO TAKE ME BACK.
BUT NOW THAT THE PEOPLE ARE GONE...KOH IS SURE TO ATTACK THIS MANSION.

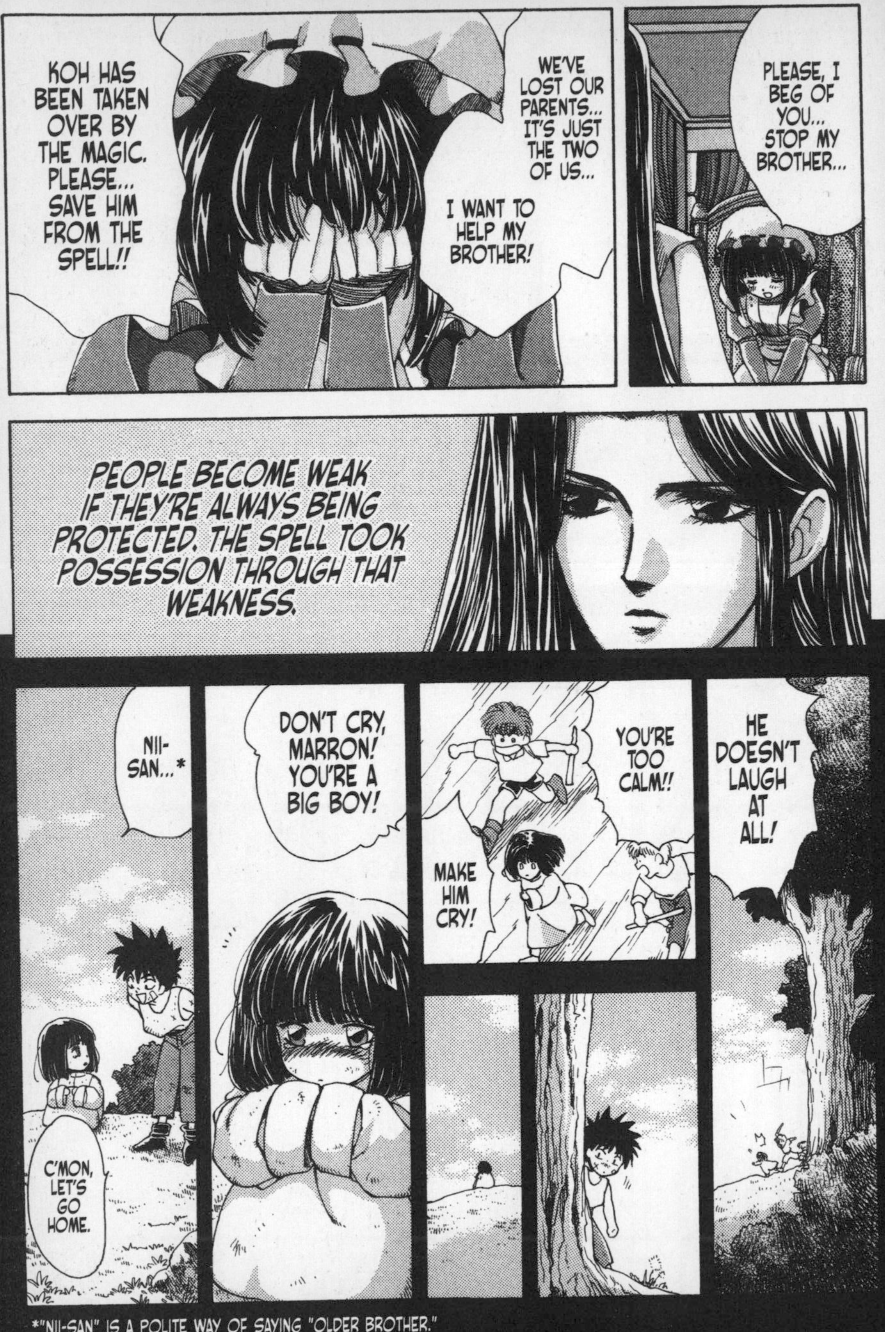
PLEASE, I BEG OF YOU... STOP MY BROTHER...
WE'VE LOST OUR PARENTS... IT'S JUST THE TWO OF US...
I WANT TO HELP MY BROTHER!
KOH HAS BEEN TAKEN OVER BY THE MAGIC. PLEASE... SAVE HIM FROM THE SPELL!!
PEOPLE BECOME WEAK IF THEY'RE ALWAYS BEING PROTECTED. THE SPELL TOOK POSSESSION THROUGH THAT WEAKNESS.
HE DOESN'T LAUGH AT ALL!
YOU'RE TOO CALM!!
MAKE HIM CRY!
DON'T CRY, MARRON! YOU'RE A BIG BOY!
NII-SAN...*
C'MON, LET'S GO HOME.

*"NII-SAN" IS A POLITE WAY OF SAYING "OLDER BROTHER."

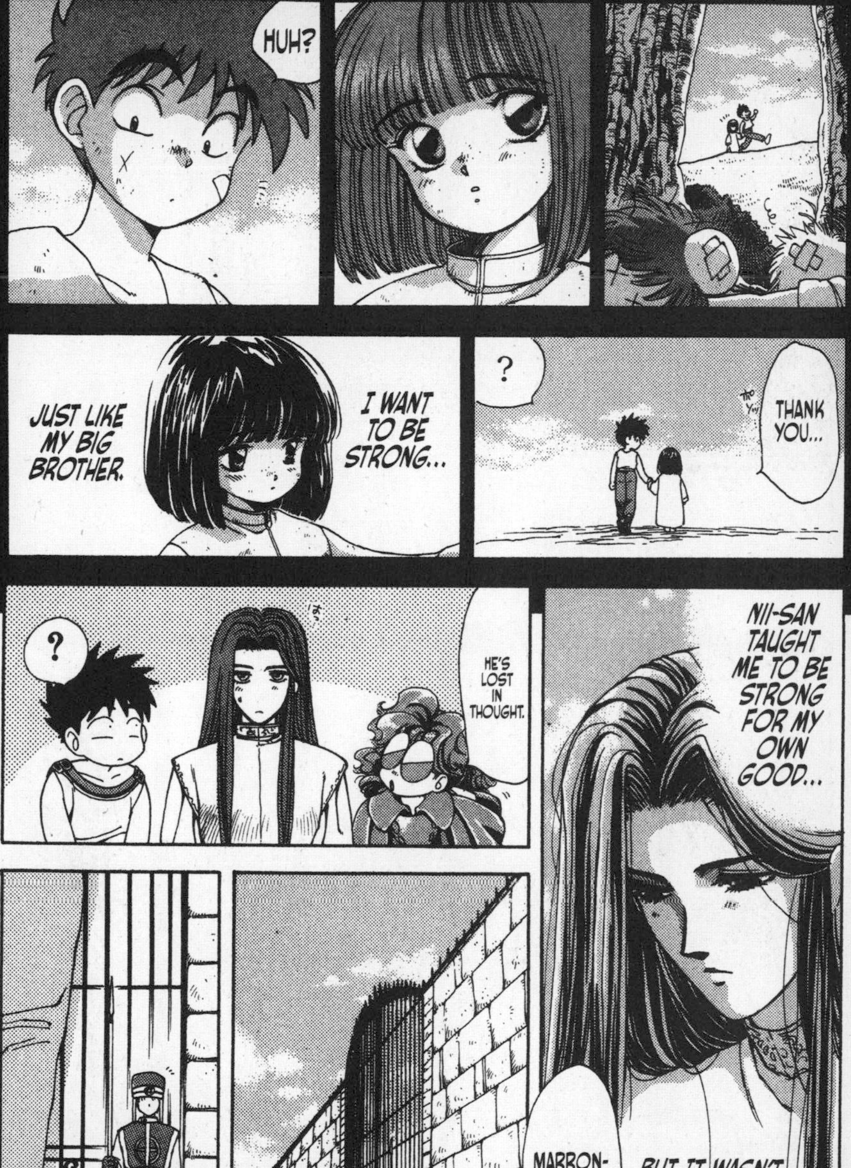
HUH?
THANK YOU...
?
I WANT TO BE STRONG...
JUST LIKE MY BIG BROTHER.
NII-SAN TAUGHT ME TO BE STRONG FOR MY OWN GOOD...
BUT IT WASN'T JUST FOR MYSELF THAT...
MARRON-CHAN?
HE'S LOST IN THOUGHT.
?

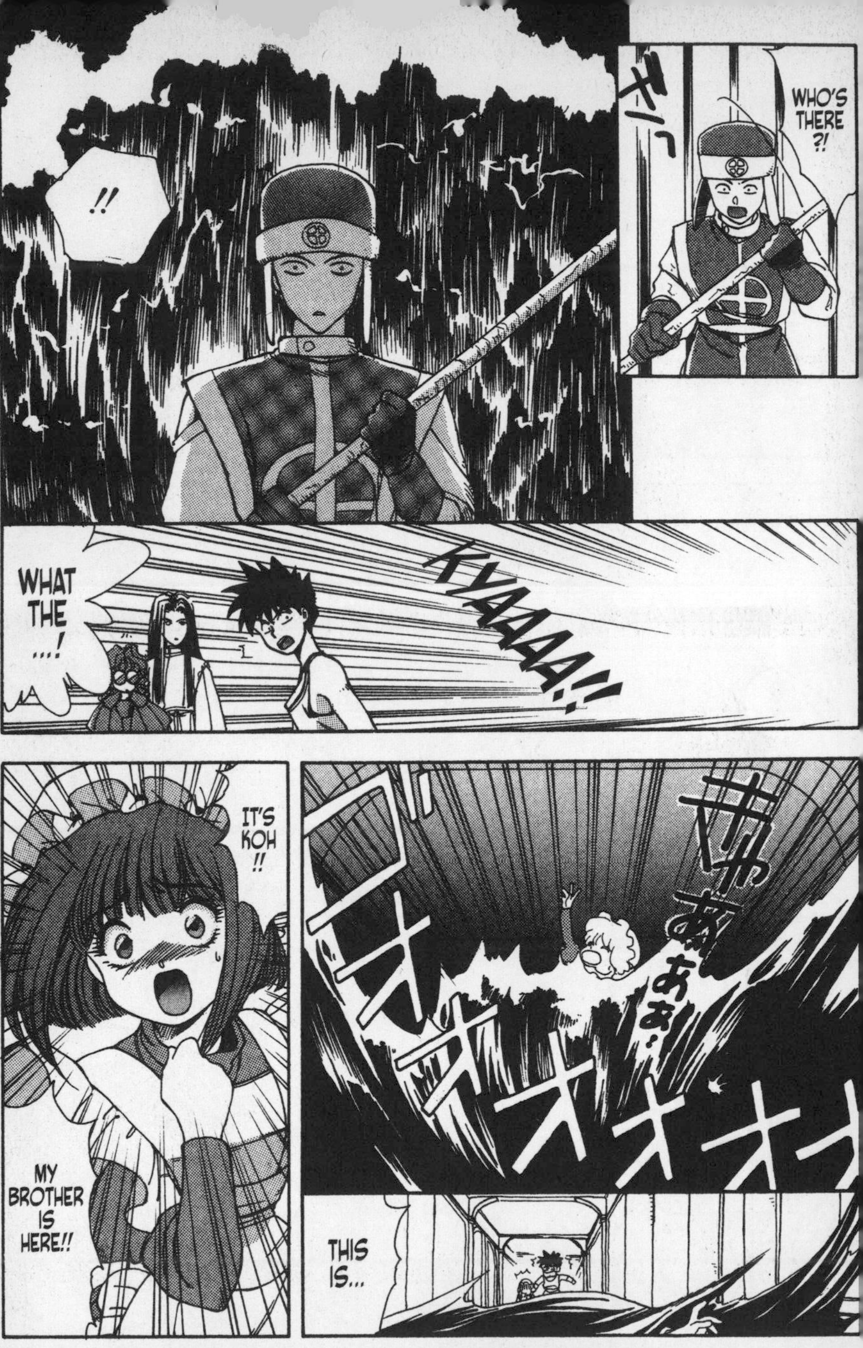
WHO'S THERE ?!
!!
KYAAAA!!
WHAT THE ...!
きゃあああ
THIS IS...
IT'S KOH !!
MY BROTHER IS HERE!!

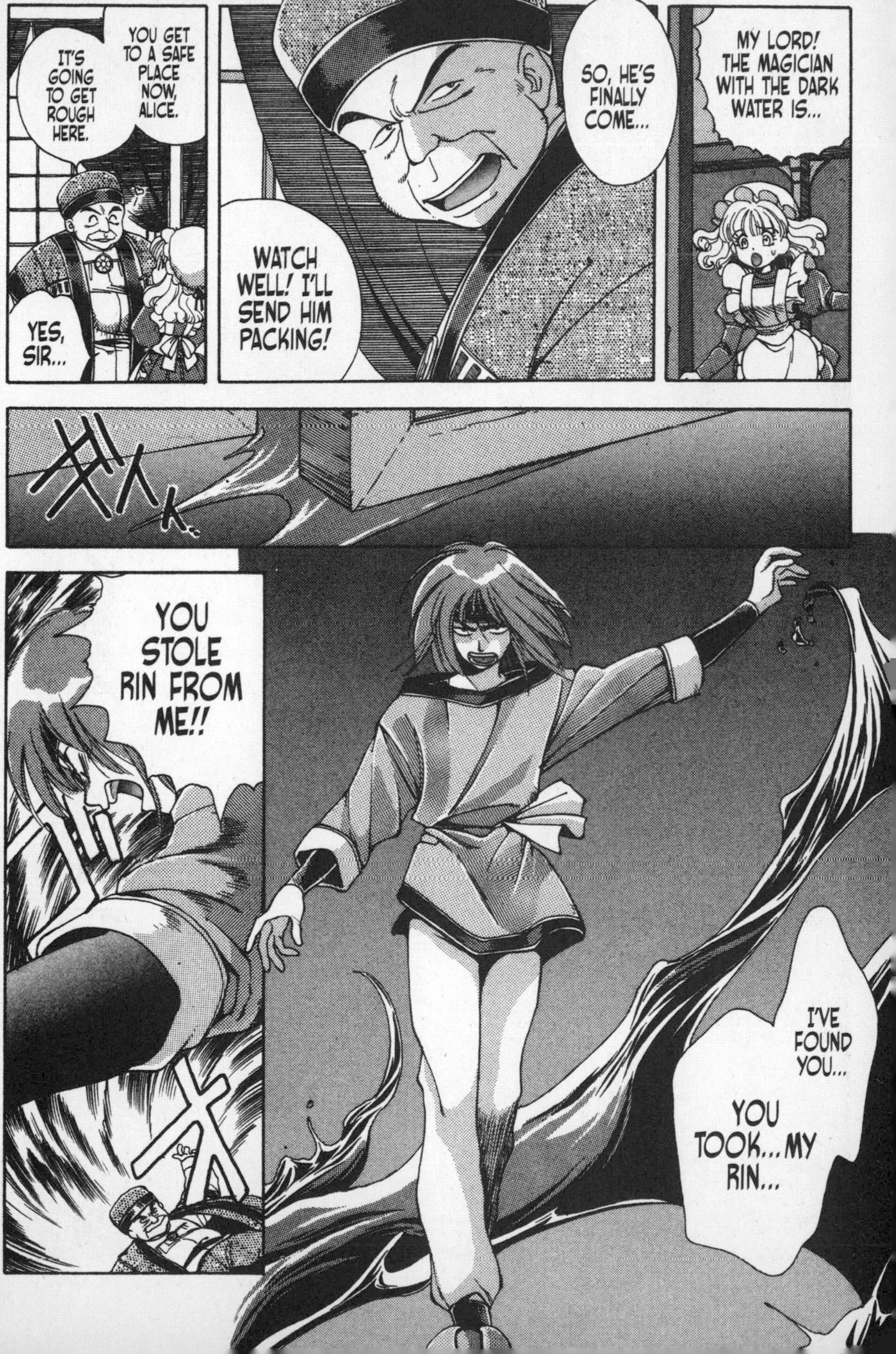
MY LORD! THE MAGICIAN WITH THE DARK WATER IS...
SO, HE'S FINALLY COME...
WATCH WELL! I'LL SEND HIM PACKING!
YOU GET TO A SAFE PLACE NOW, ALICE.
IT'S GOING TO GET ROUGH HERE.
YES, SIR...
I'VE FOUND YOU...
YOU TOOK...MY RIN...
YOU STOLE RIN FROM ME!!

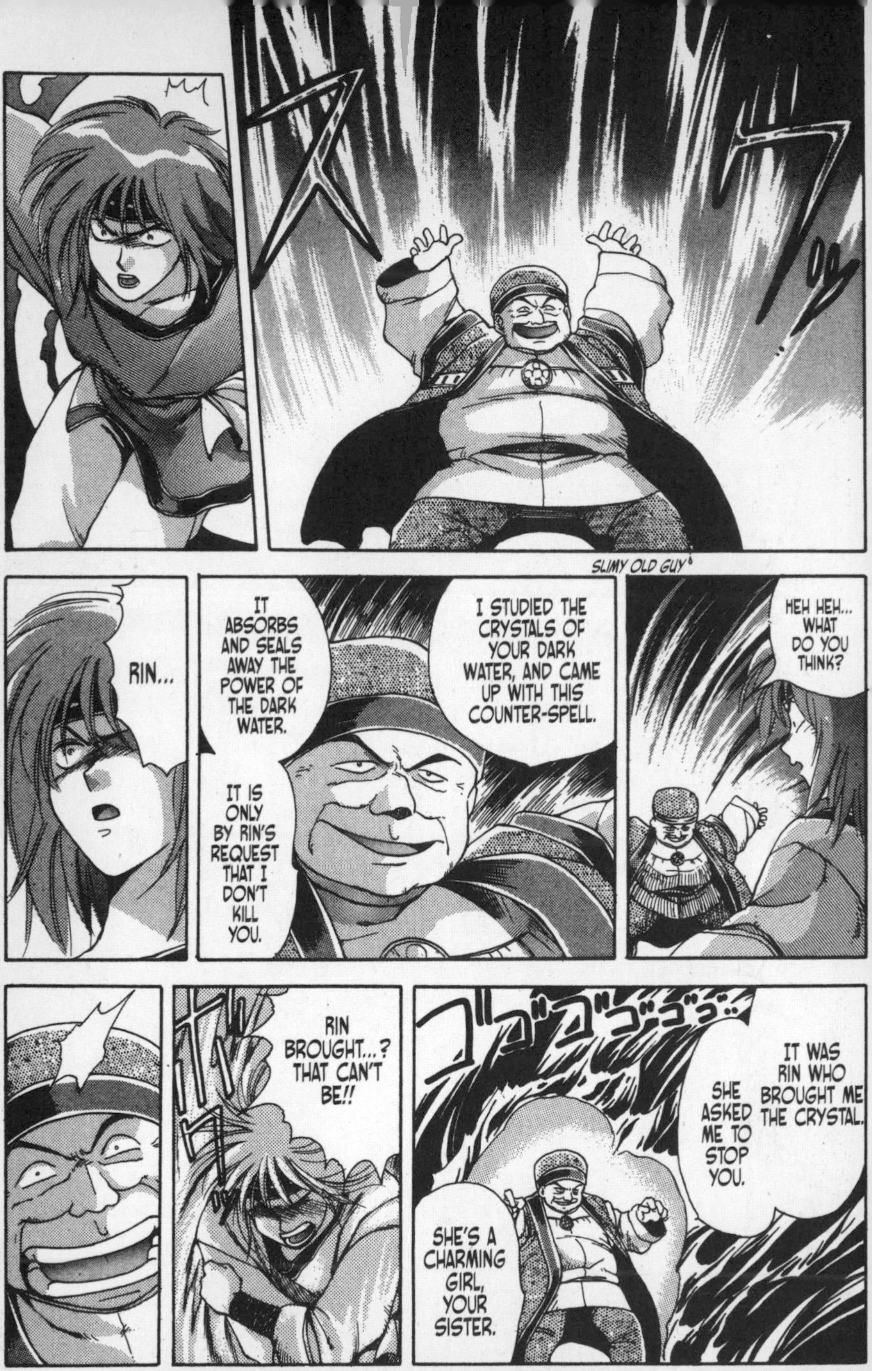
SLIMY OLD GUY
HEH HEH... WHAT DO YOU THINK?
I STUDIED THE CRYSTALS OF YOUR DARK WATER, AND CAME UP WITH THIS COUNTER-SPELL.
IT ABSORBS AND SEALS AWAY THE POWER OF THE DARK WATER.
IT IS ONLY BY RIN'S REQUEST THAT I DON'T KILL YOU.
RIN...
IT WAS RIN WHO BROUGHT ME THE CRYSTAL.
SHE ASKED ME TO STOP YOU.
SHE'S A CHARMING GIRL, YOUR SISTER.
RIN BROUGHT...? THAT CAN'T BE!!

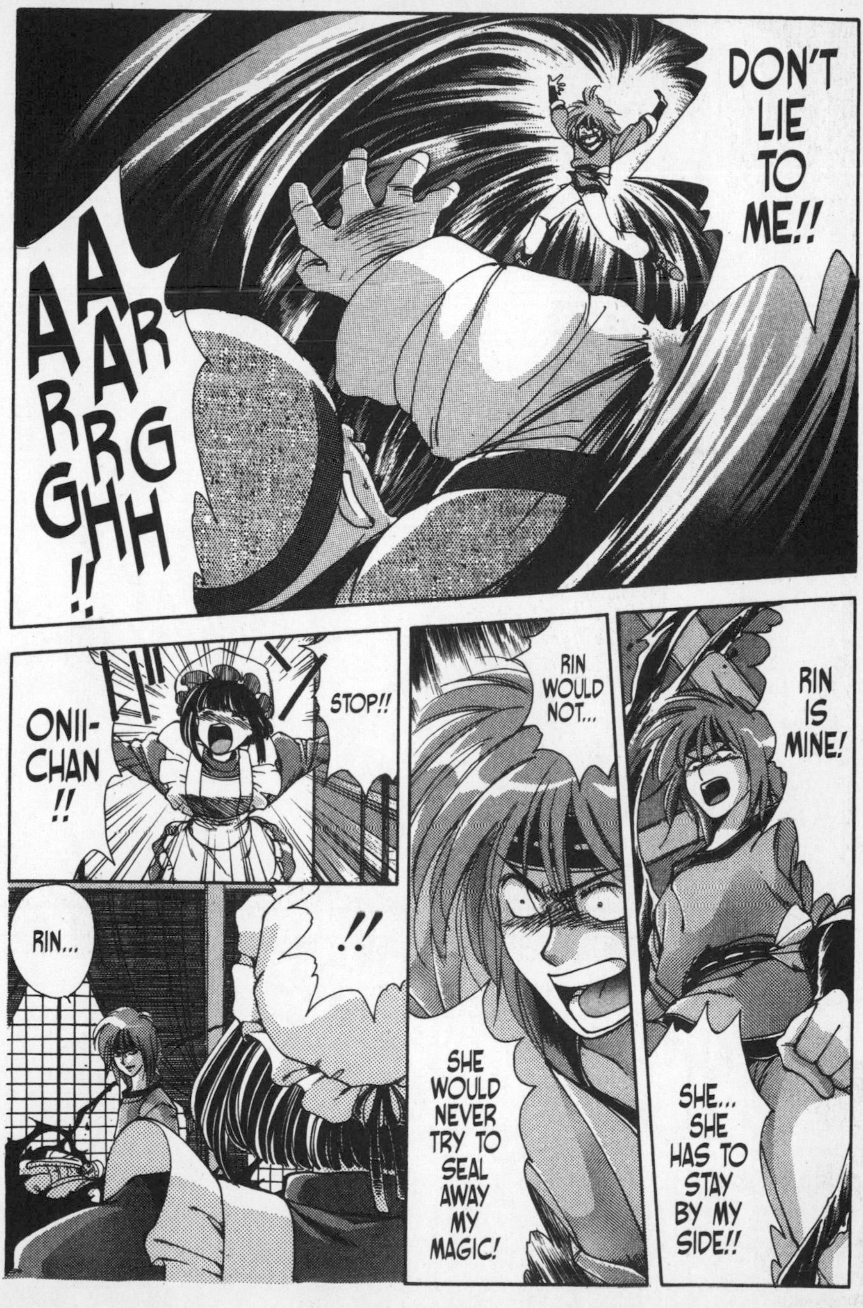
DON'T LIE TO ME!!
AAARRRGGHH!!
RIN IS MINE!
SHE... SHE HAS TO STAY BY MY SIDE!!
RIN WOULD NOT...
SHE WOULD NEVER TRY TO SEAL AWAY MY MAGIC!
STOP!!
ONII-CHAN!!
!!
RIN...

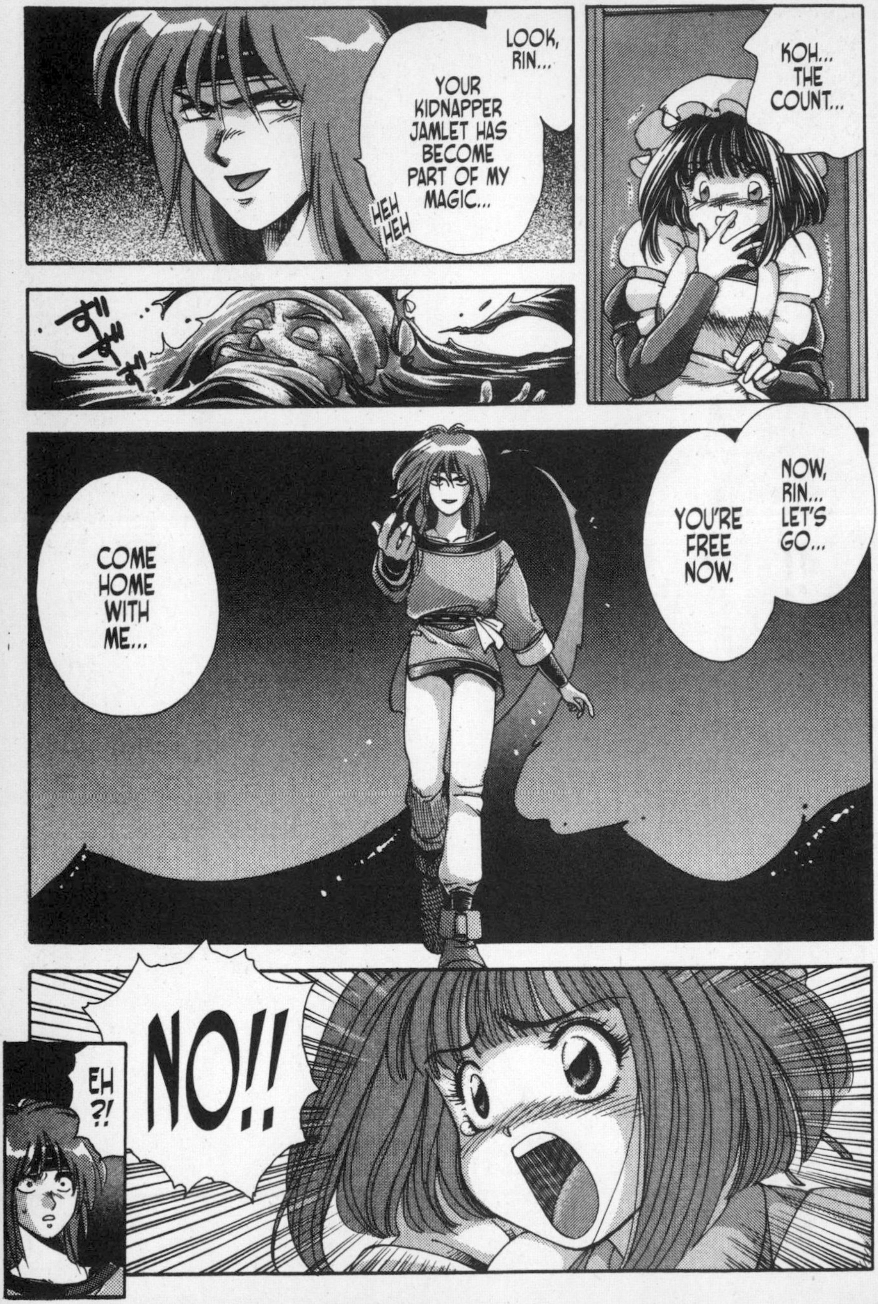
KOH... THE COUNT...
LOOK, RIN...
YOUR KIDNAPPER JAMLET HAS BECOME PART OF MY MAGIC...
HEH HEH
ずずず
NOW, RIN... LET'S GO...
YOU'RE FREE NOW.
COME HOME WITH ME...
NO!!
EH?!

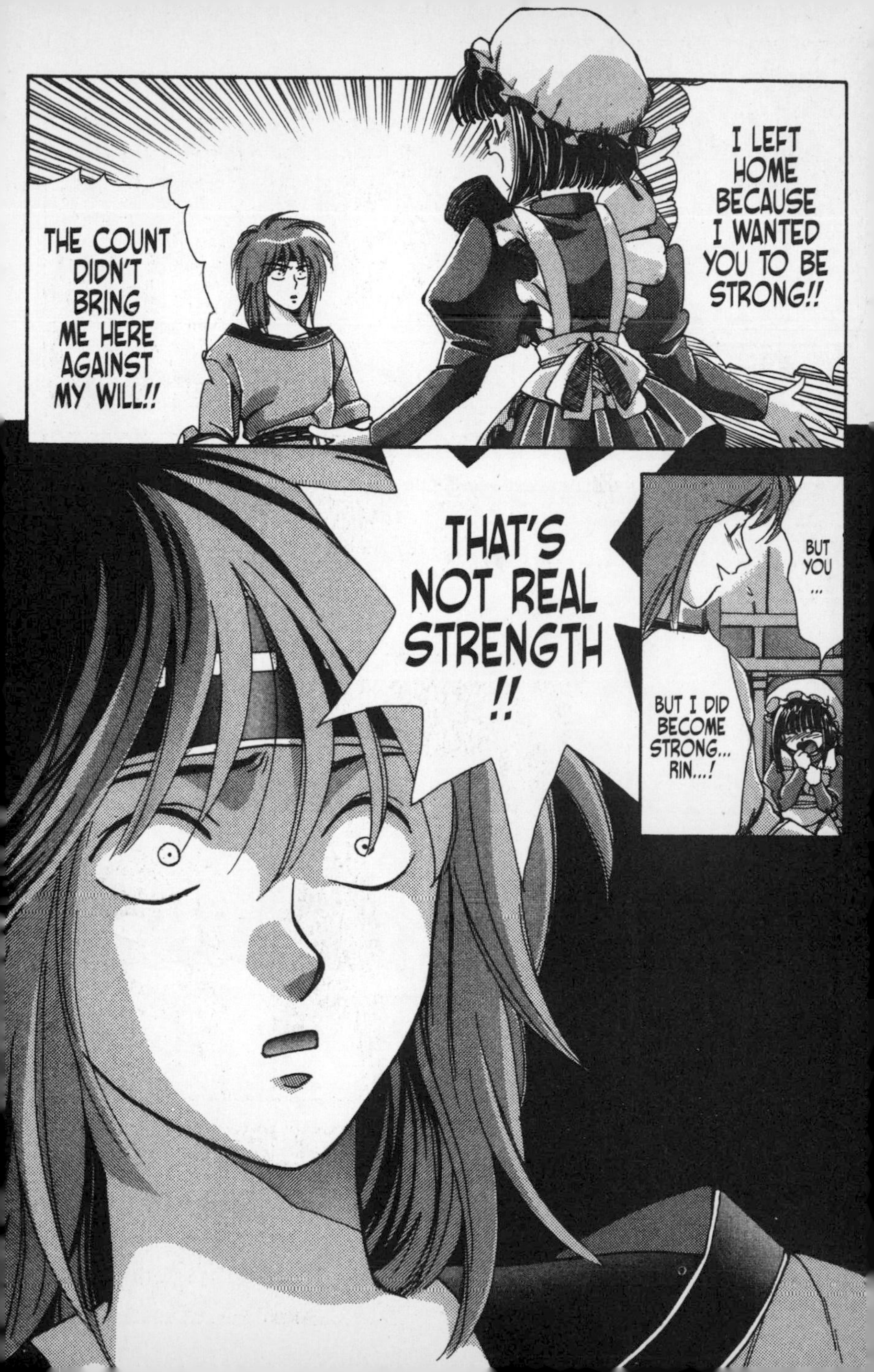
I LEFT HOME BECAUSE I WANTED YOU TO BE STRONG!!
THE COUNT DIDN'T BRING ME HERE AGAINST MY WILL!!
THAT'S NOT REAL STRENGTH!!
BUT YOU ...
BUT I DID BECOME STRONG... RIN...!

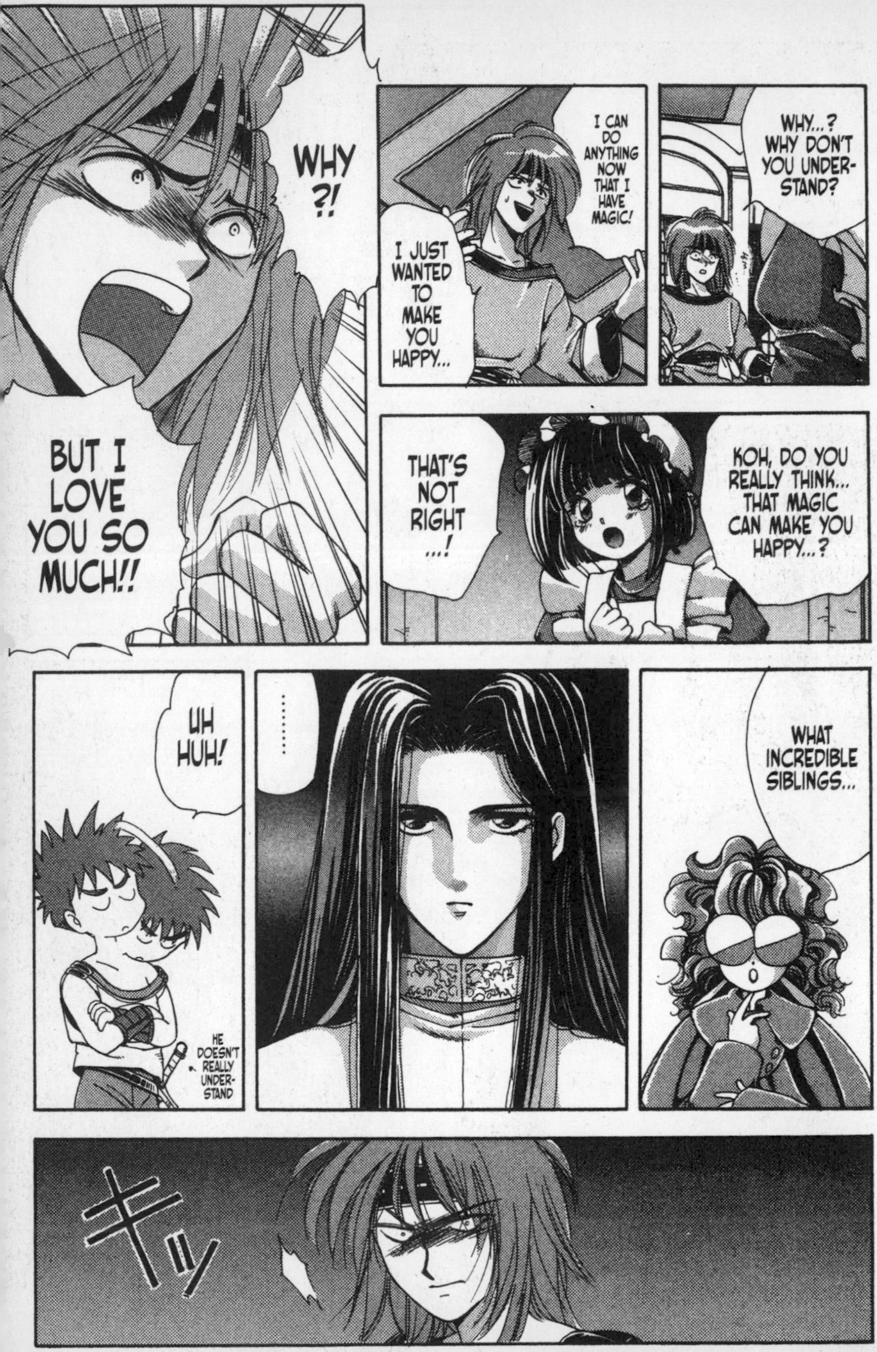
WHY...? WHY DON'T YOU UNDER-STAND?
I CAN DO ANYTHING NOW THAT I HAVE MAGIC!
I JUST WANTED TO MAKE YOU HAPPY...
KOH, DO YOU REALLY THINK... THAT MAGIC CAN MAKE YOU HAPPY...?
THAT'S NOT RIGHT ...!
WHY ?!
BUT I LOVE YOU SO MUCH!!
WHAT INCREDIBLE SIBLINGS...
....
UH HUH!
HE DOESN'T REALLY UNDER-STAND
キッ

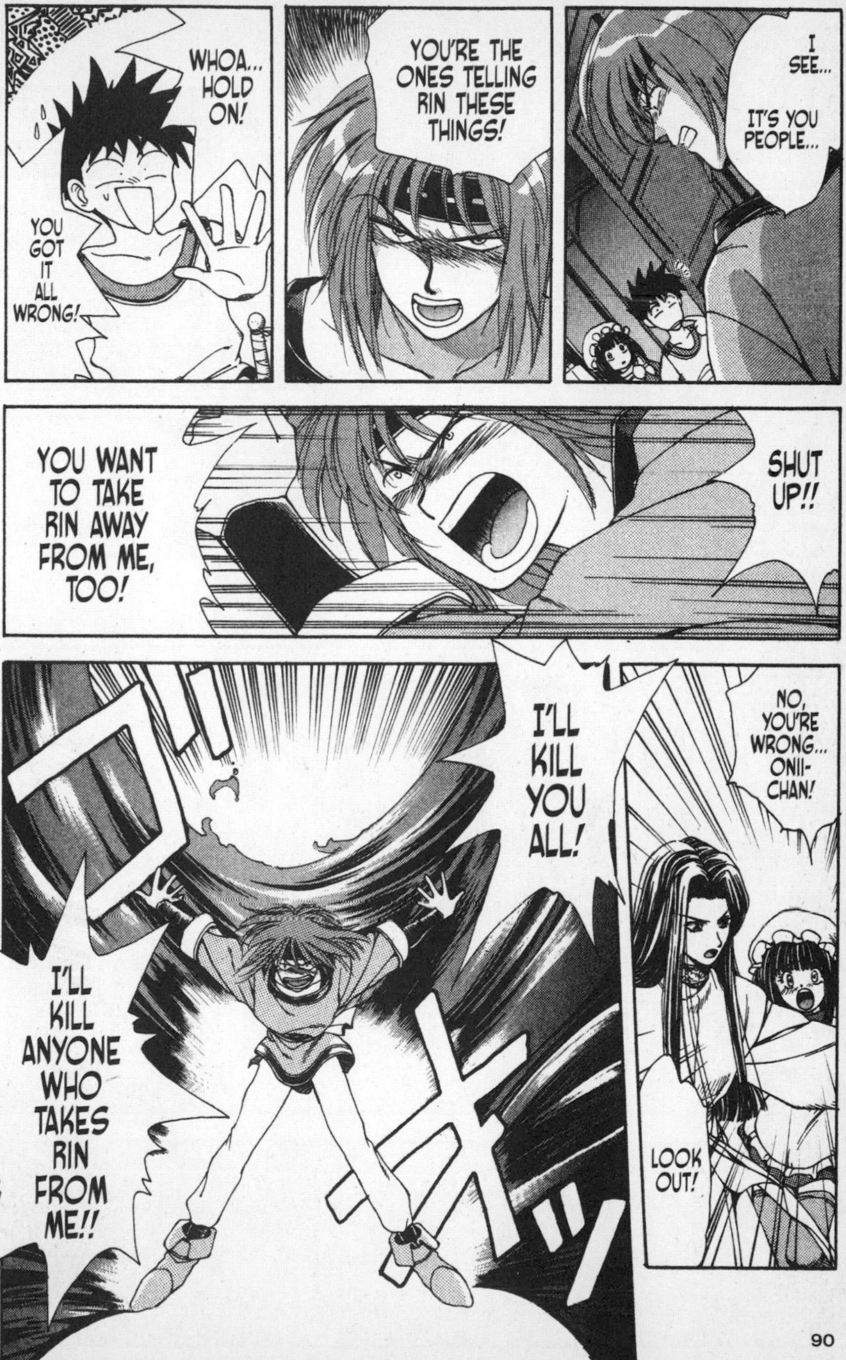
I SEE...
IT'S YOU PEOPLE...
YOU'RE THE ONES TELLING RIN THESE THINGS!
WHOA... HOLD ON!
YOU GOT IT ALL WRONG!
SHUT UP!!
YOU WANT TO TAKE RIN AWAY FROM ME, TOO!
NO, YOU'RE WRONG... ONII-CHAN!
LOOK OUT!
I'LL KILL YOU ALL!
I'LL KILL ANYONE WHO TAKES RIN FROM ME!!

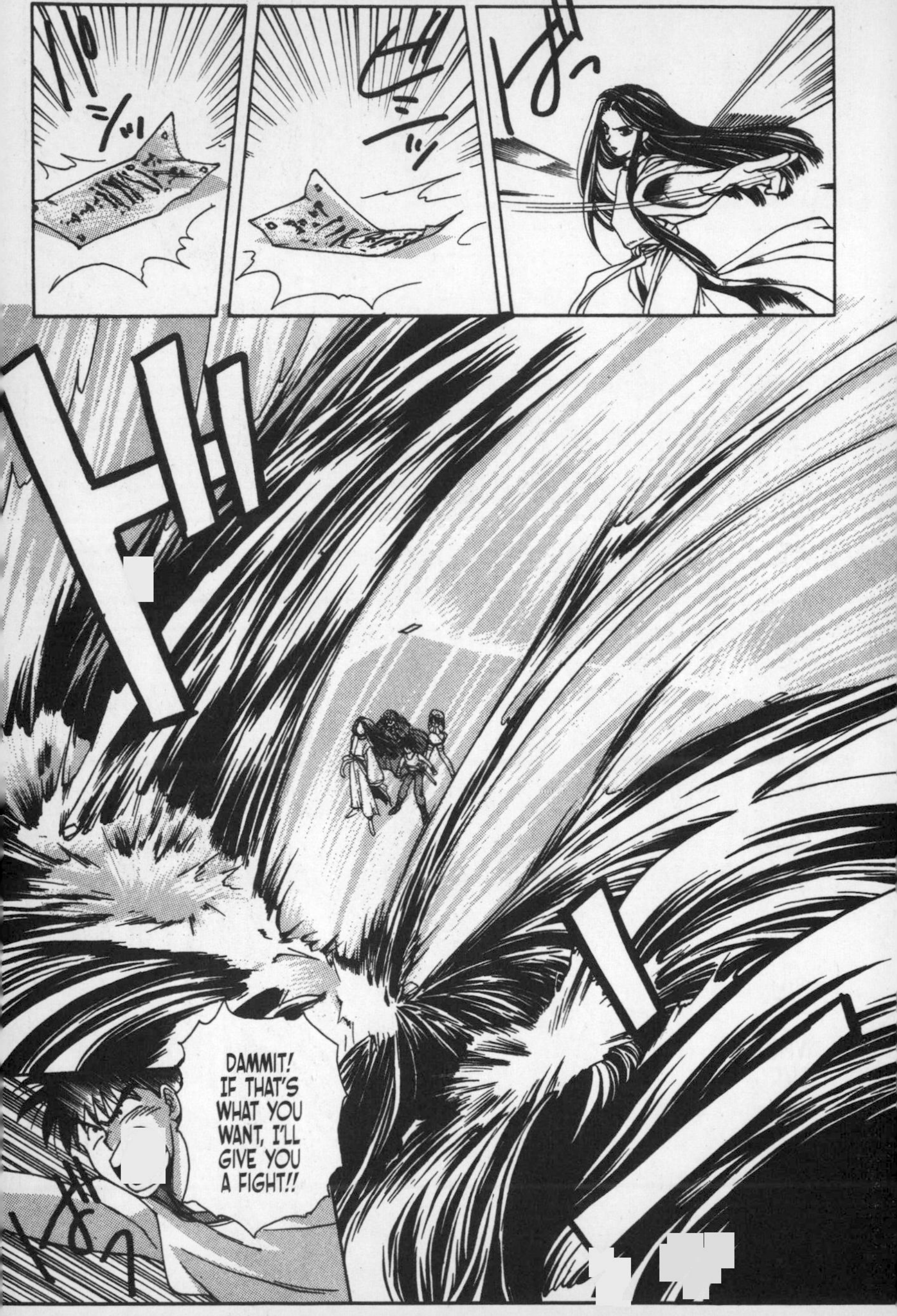
DAMMIT! IF THAT'S WHAT YOU WANT, I'LL GIVE YOU A FIGHT!!

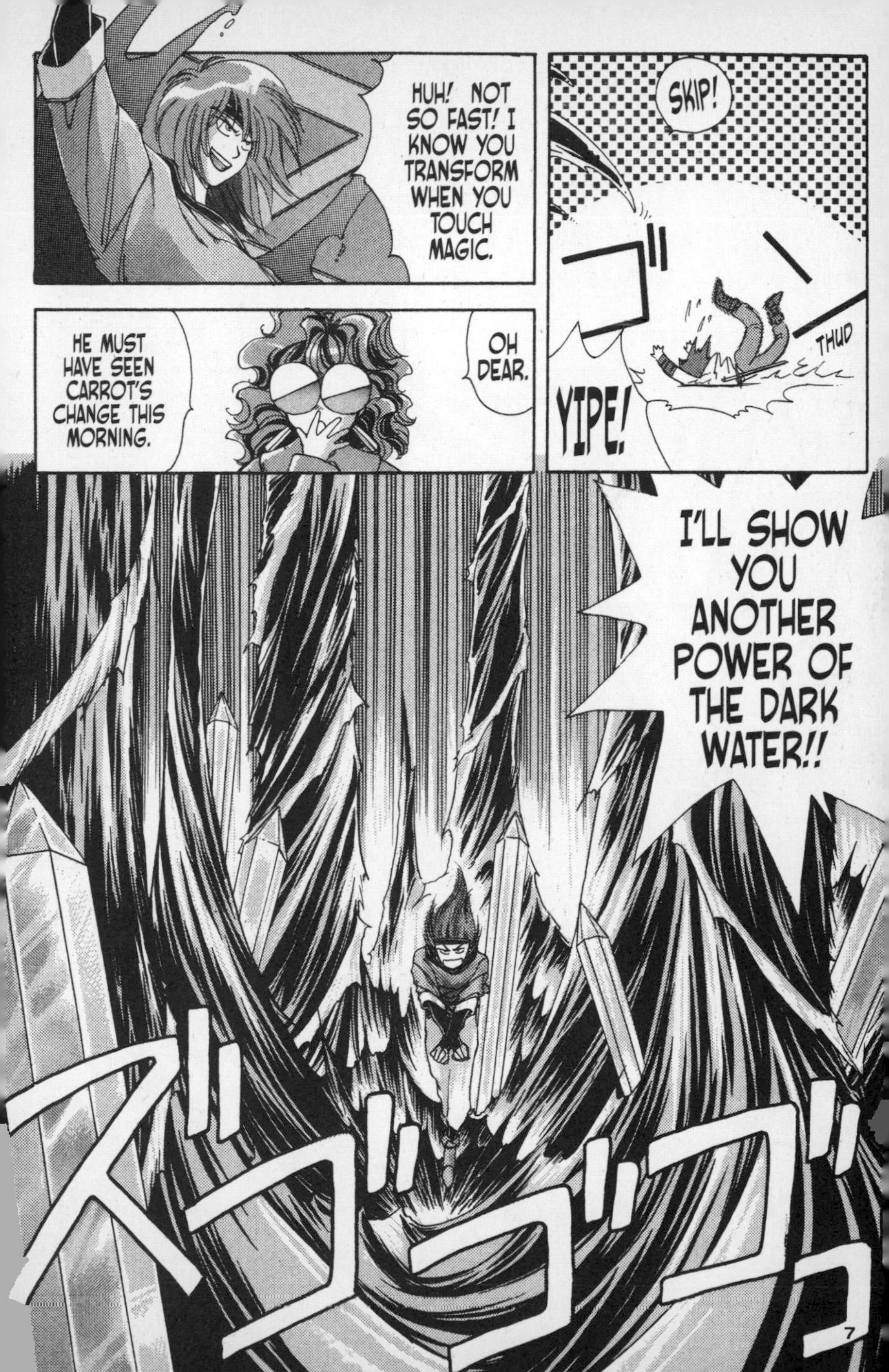
SKIP!
YIPE!
THUD
HUH! NOT SO FAST! I KNOW YOU TRANSFORM WHEN YOU TOUCH MAGIC.
OH DEAR.
HE MUST HAVE SEEN CARROT'S CHANGE THIS MORNING.
I'LL SHOW YOU ANOTHER POWER OF THE DARK WATER!!

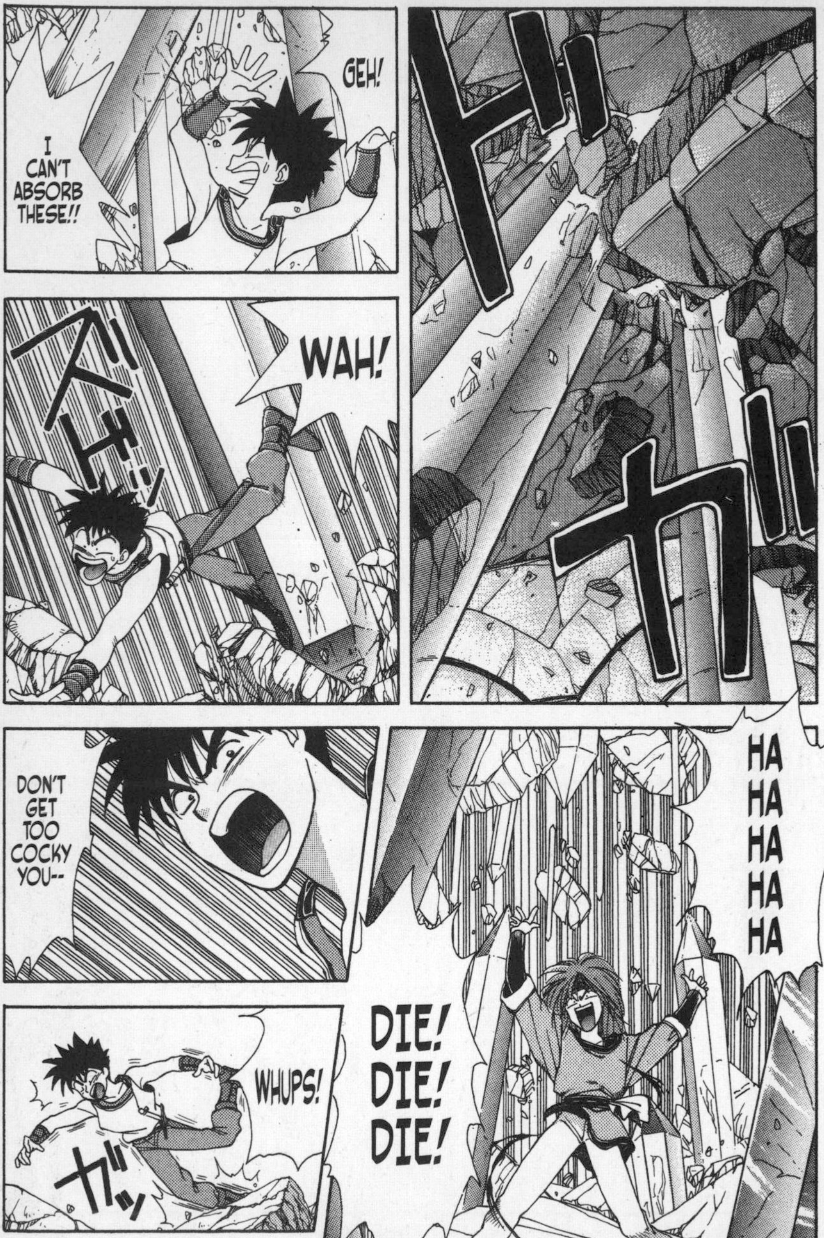
GEH!
I CAN'T ABSORB THESE!!
WAH!
HA HA HA HA HA HA
DIE! DIE! DIE!
DON'T GET TOO COCKY YOU--
WHUPS!

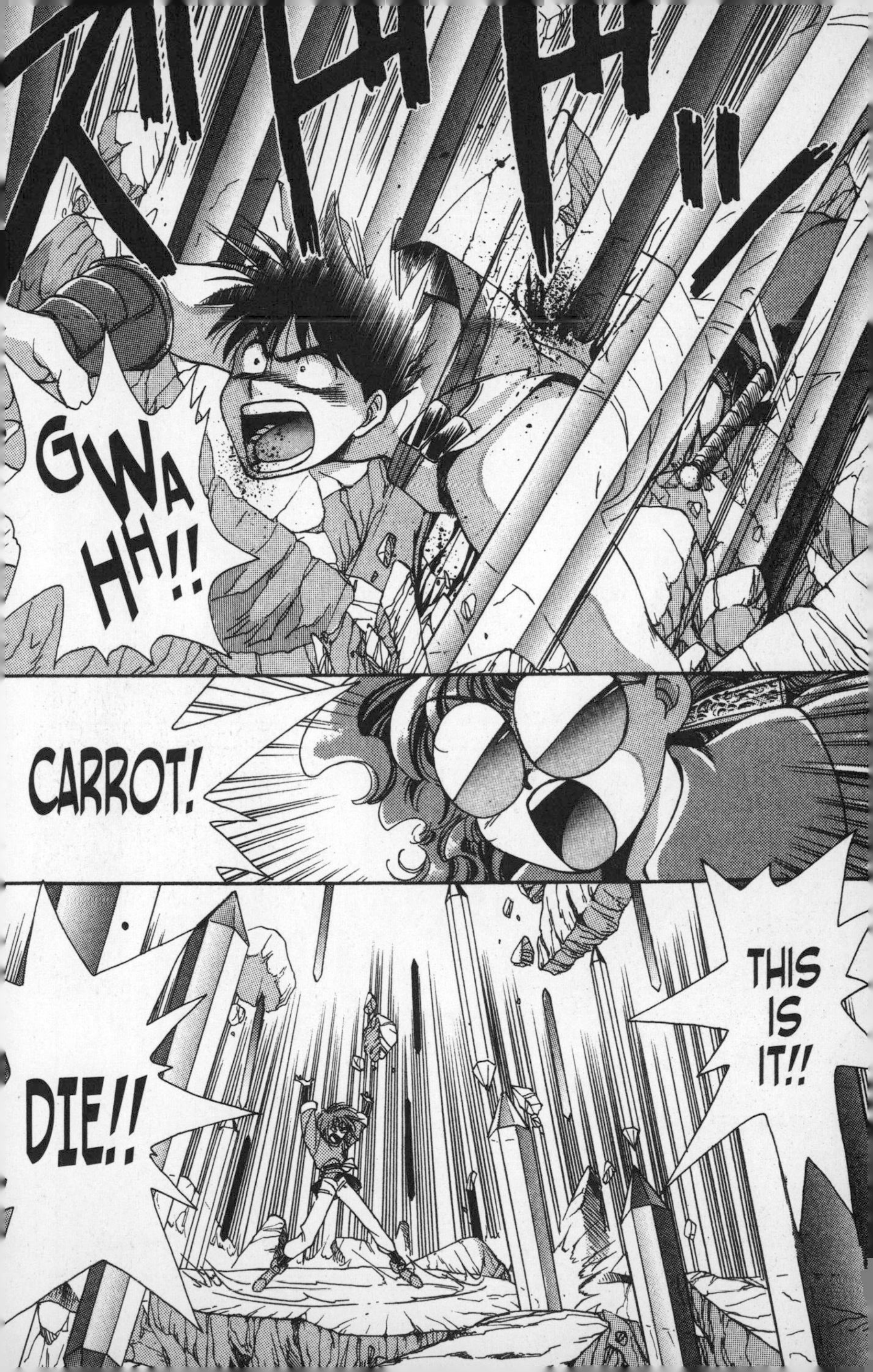
GWAHH!!
CARROT!
THIS IS IT!!
DIE!!

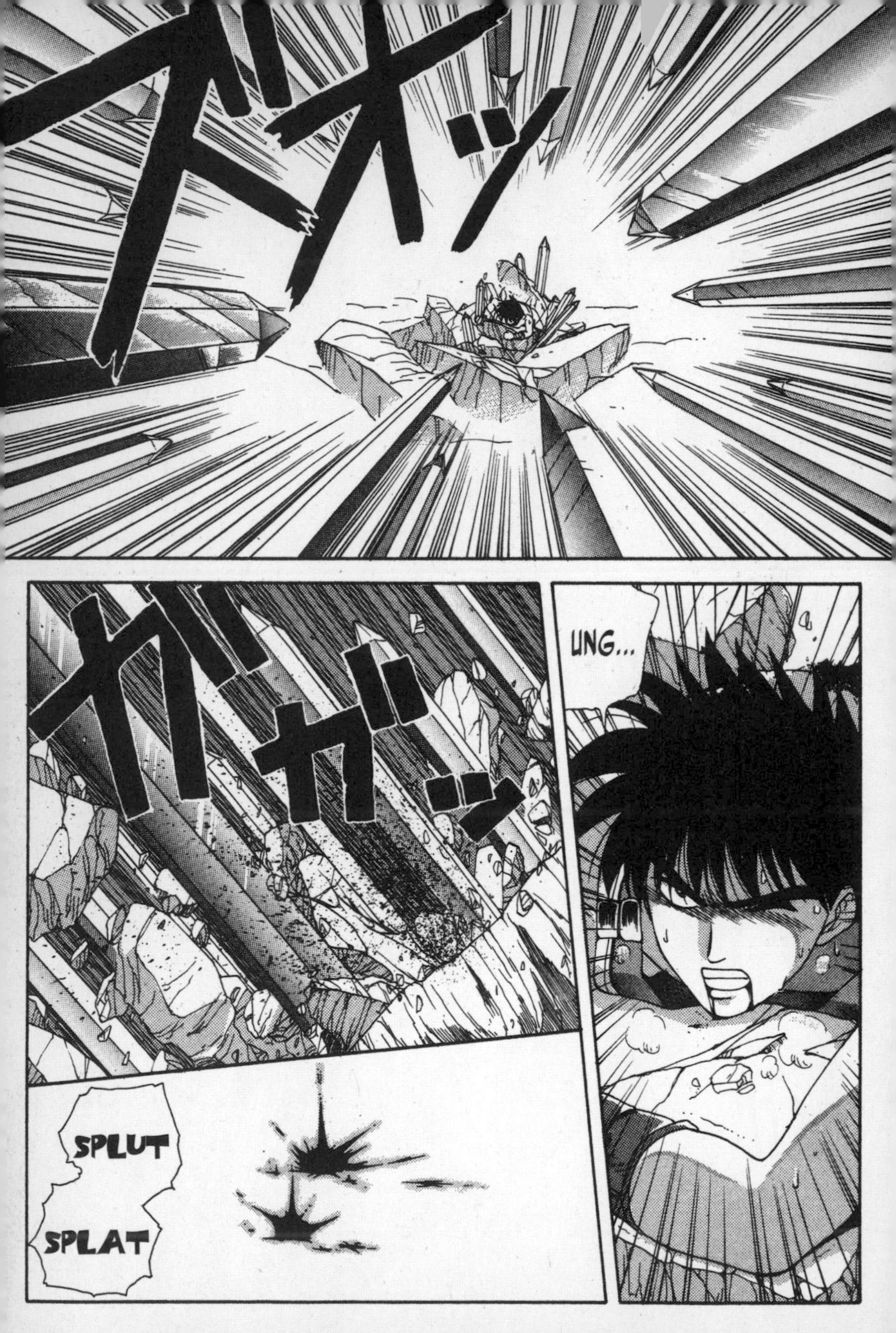
ズオッ
UNG...
SPLUT
SPLAT

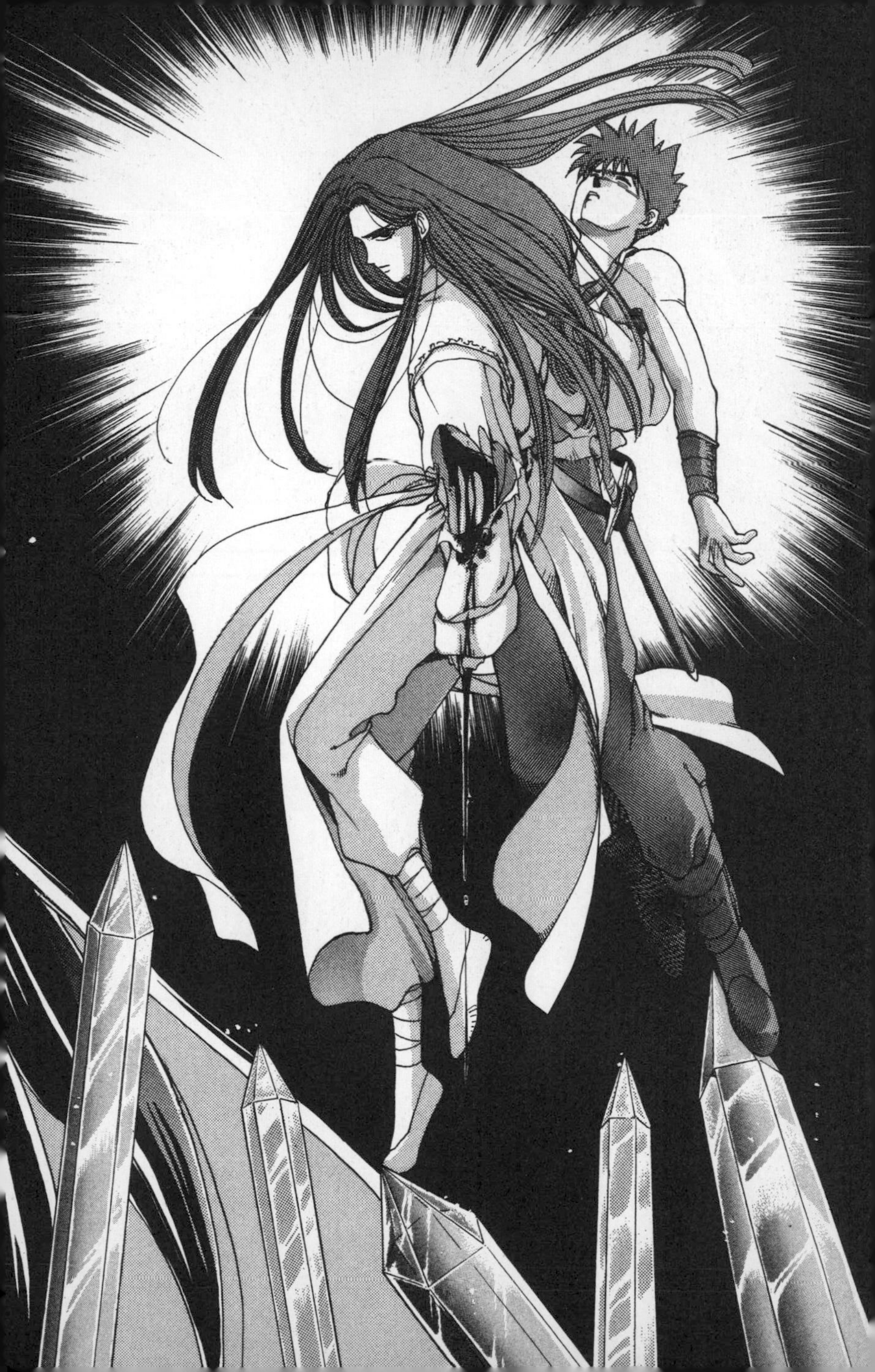

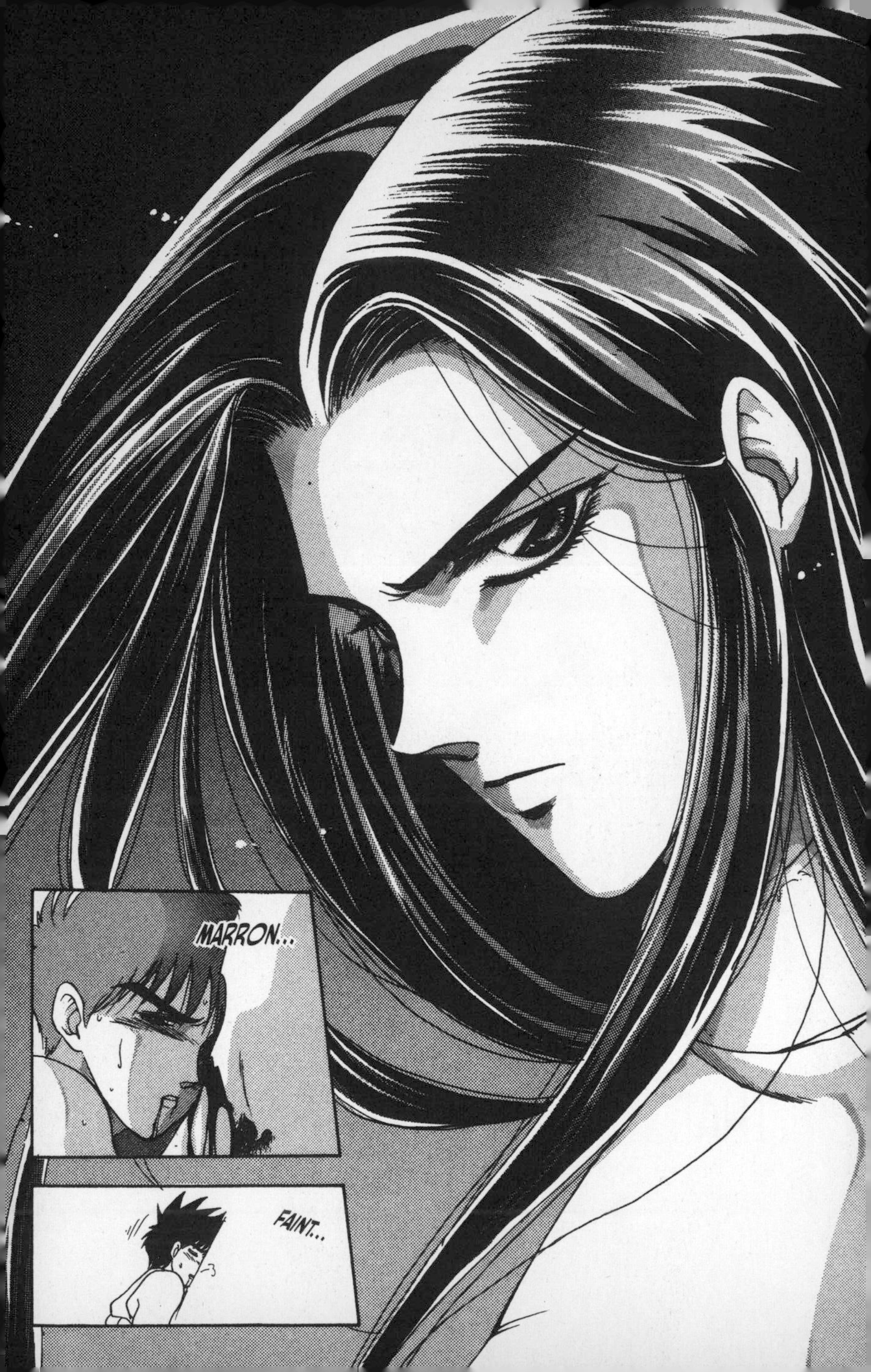
MARRON...
FAINT...

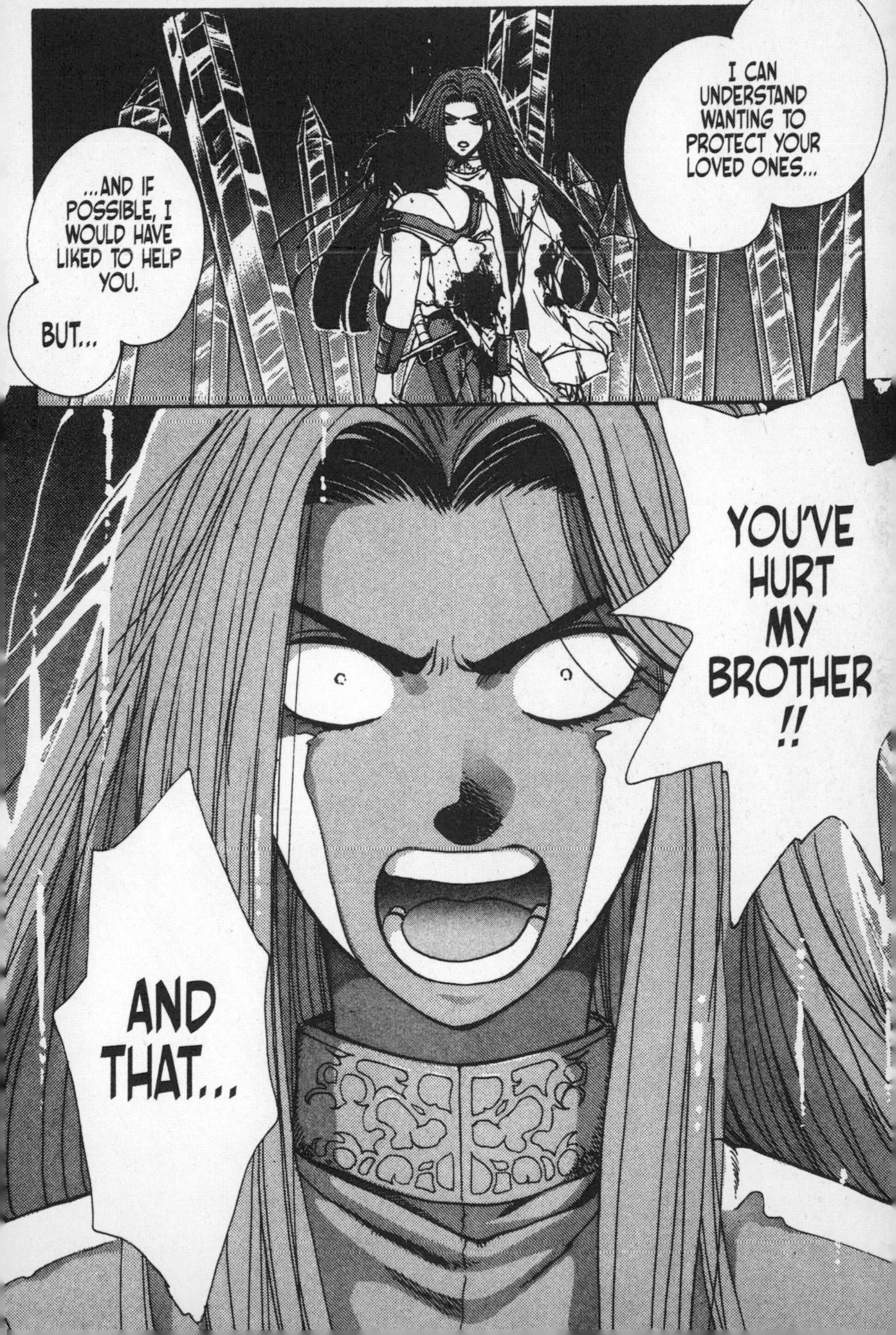
I CAN UNDERSTAND WANTING TO PROTECT YOUR LOVED ONES...
...AND IF POSSIBLE, I WOULD HAVE LIKED TO HELP YOU.
BUT...
YOU'VE HURT MY BROTHER !!
AND THAT...

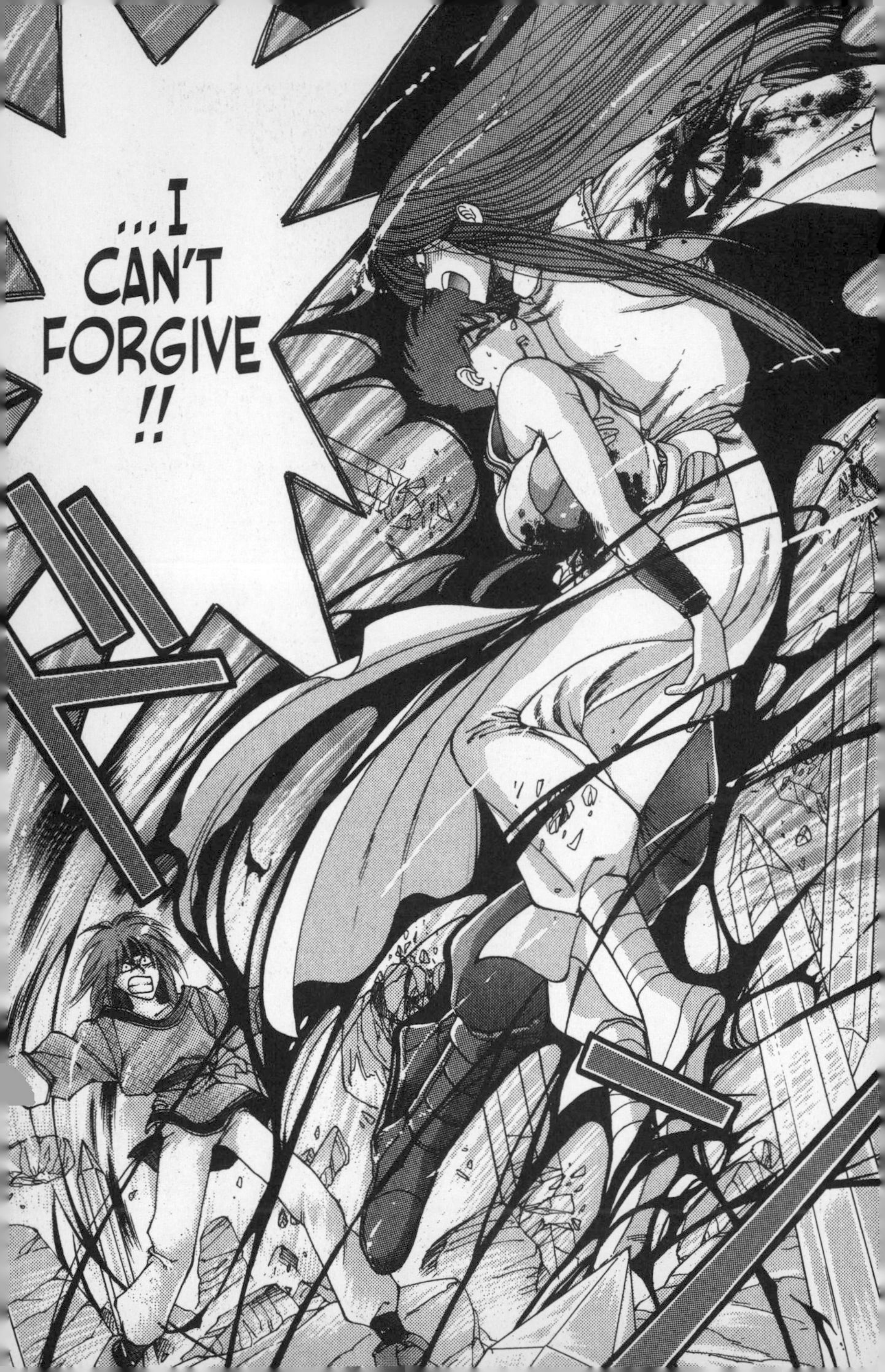
...I CAN'T FORGIVE!!

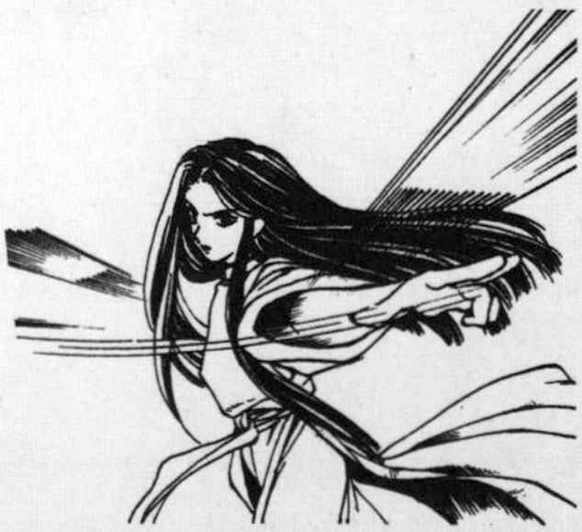

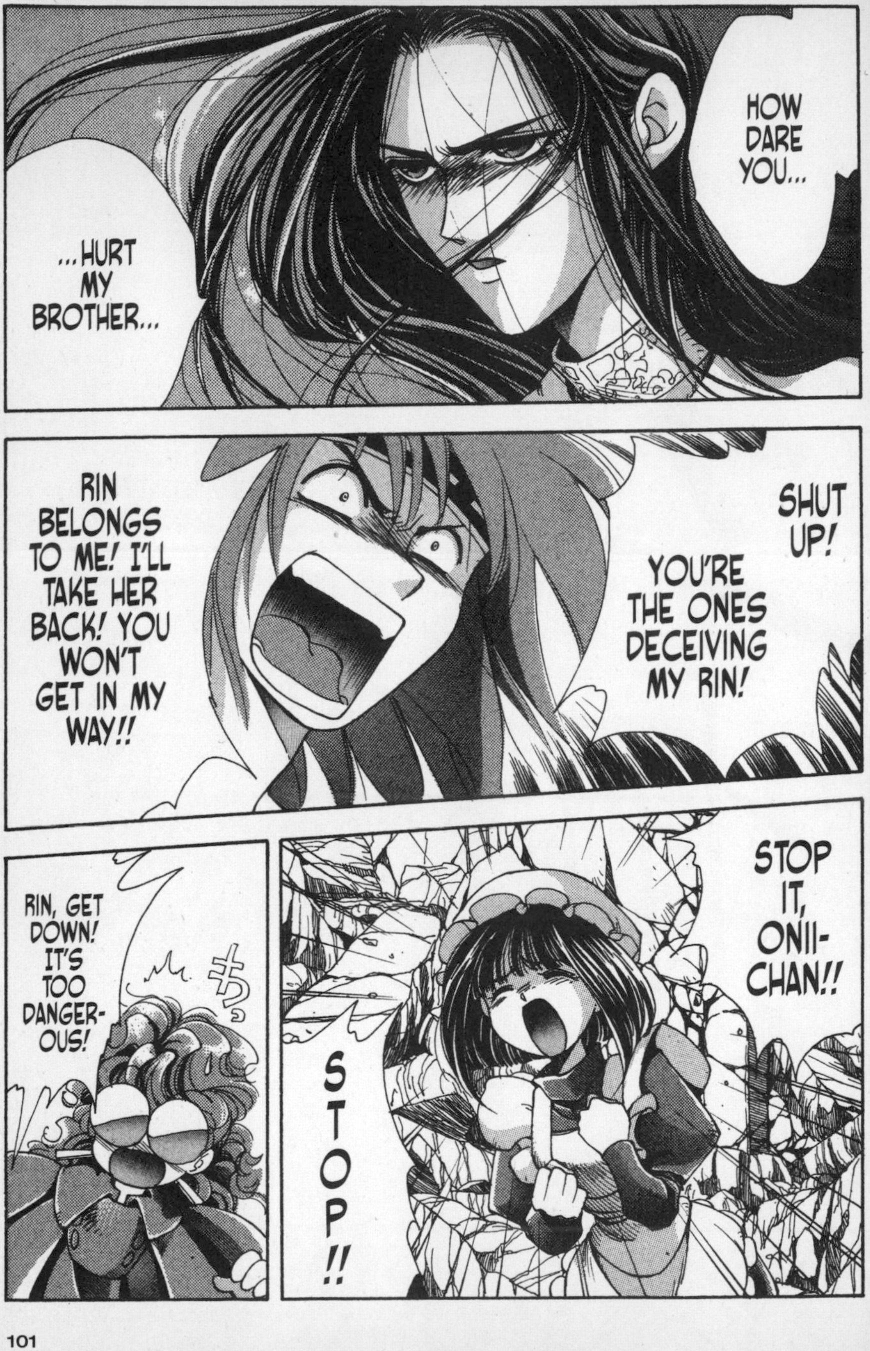

HOW DARE YOU...
...HURT MY BROTHER...
SHUT UP!
YOU'RE THE ONES DECEIVING MY RIN!
RIN BELONGS TO ME! I'LL TAKE HER BACK! YOU WON'T GET IN MY WAY!!
STOP IT, ONII-CHAN!!
STOP!!
RIN, GET DOWN! IT'S TOO DANGER-OUS!
わっ

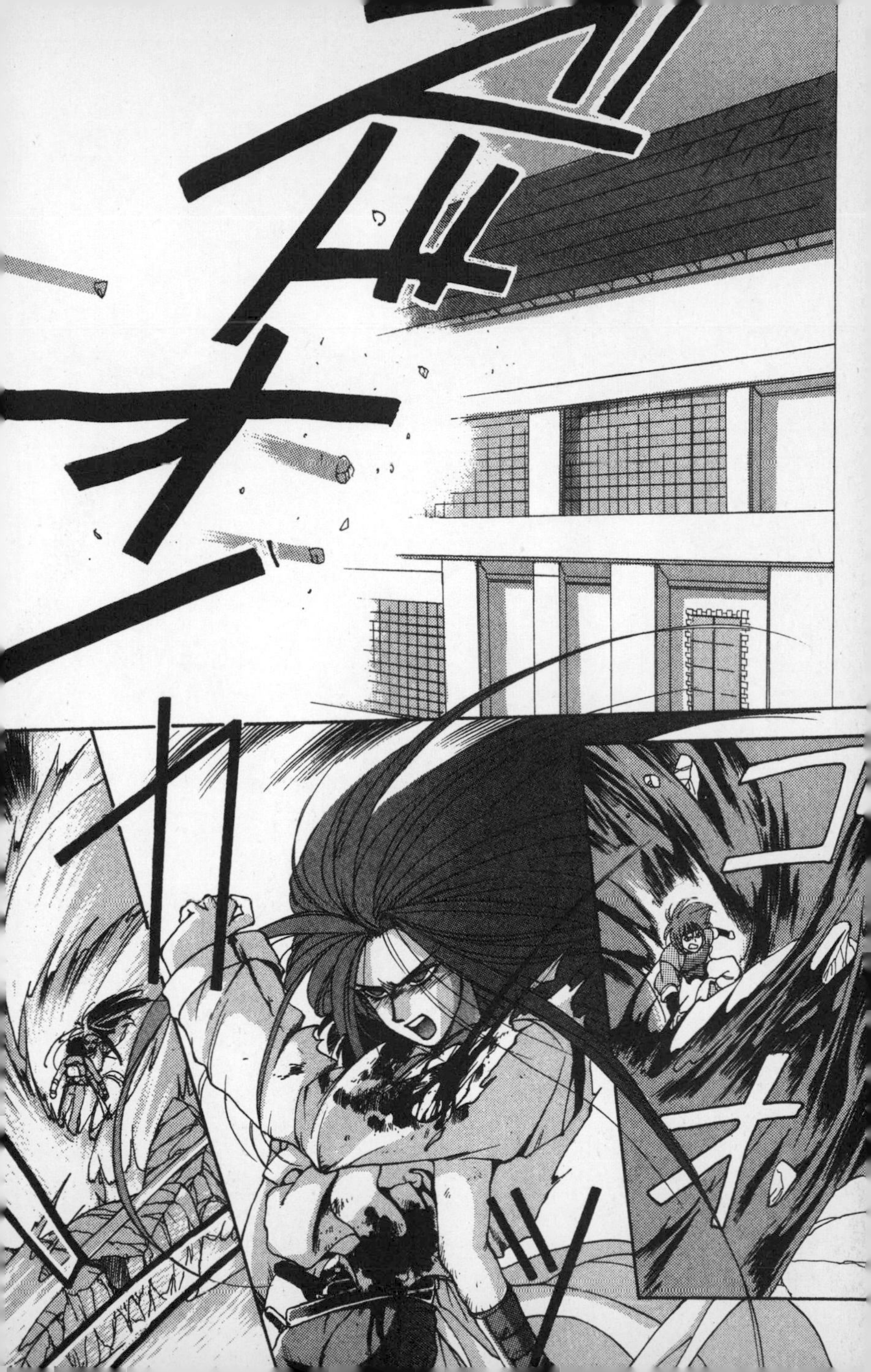

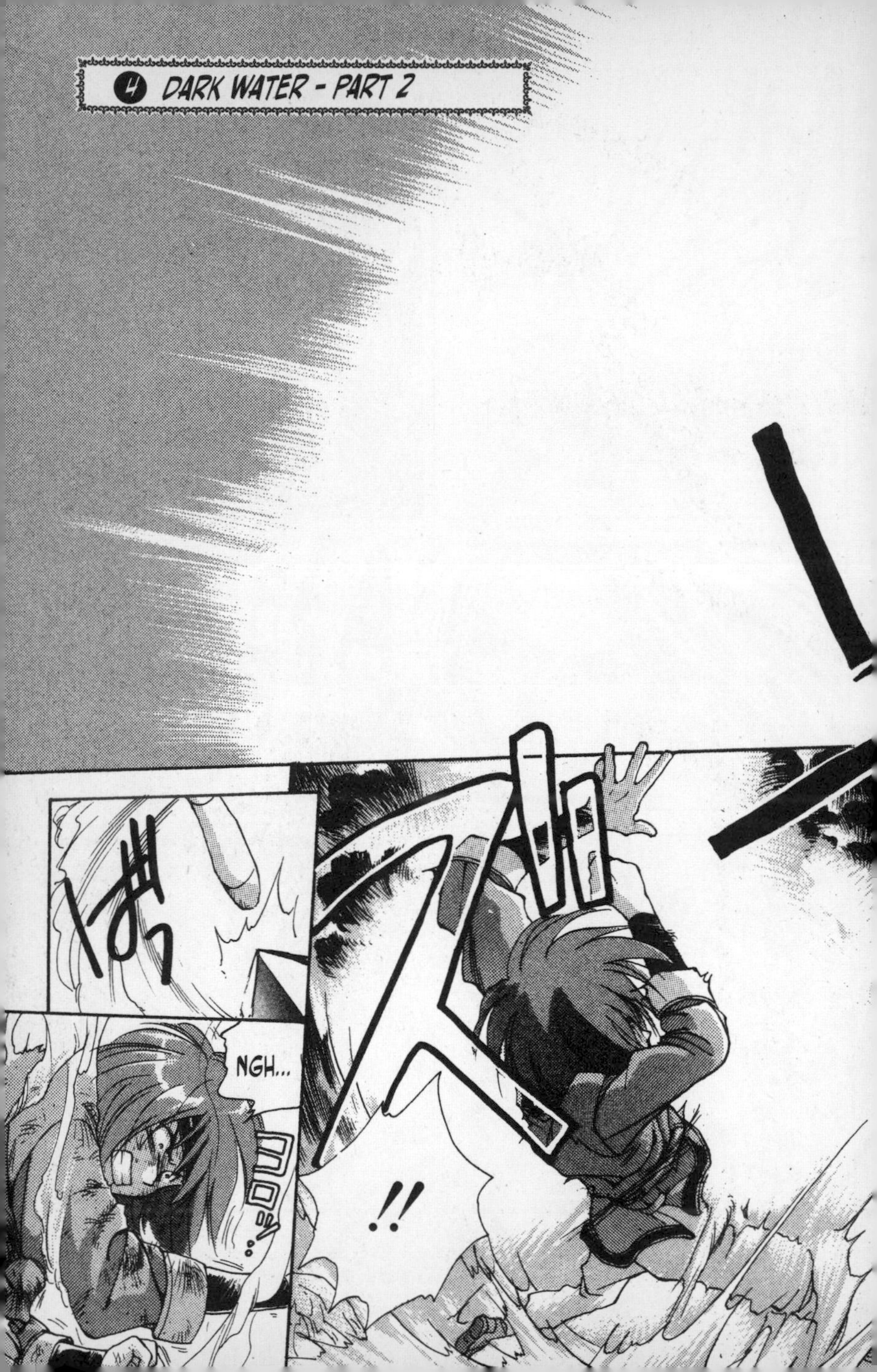
4 DARK WATER - PART 2
!!
NGH...

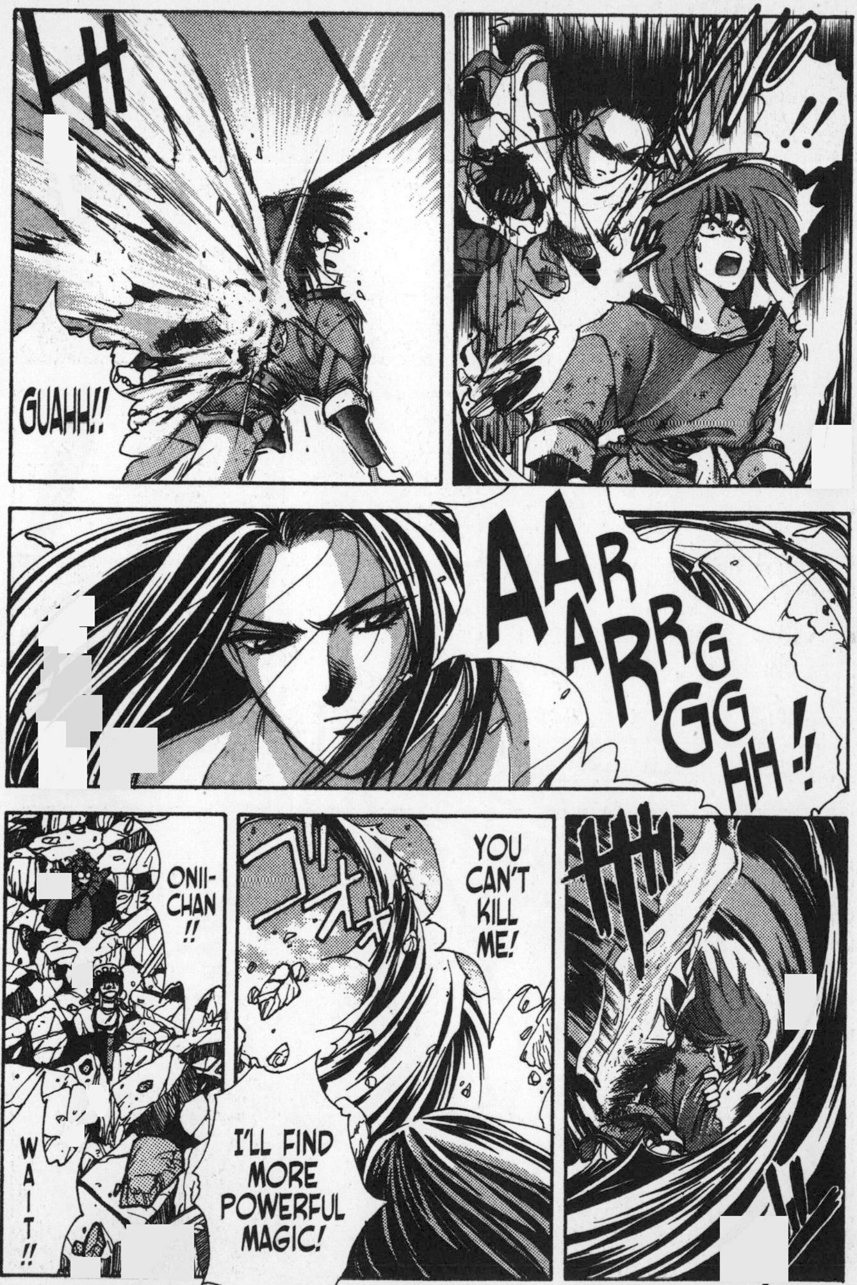
!!
GUAHH!!
AARARRGGGHH!!
YOU CAN'T KILL ME!
I'LL FIND MORE POWERFUL MAGIC!
ONII-CHAN!!
WAIT!!

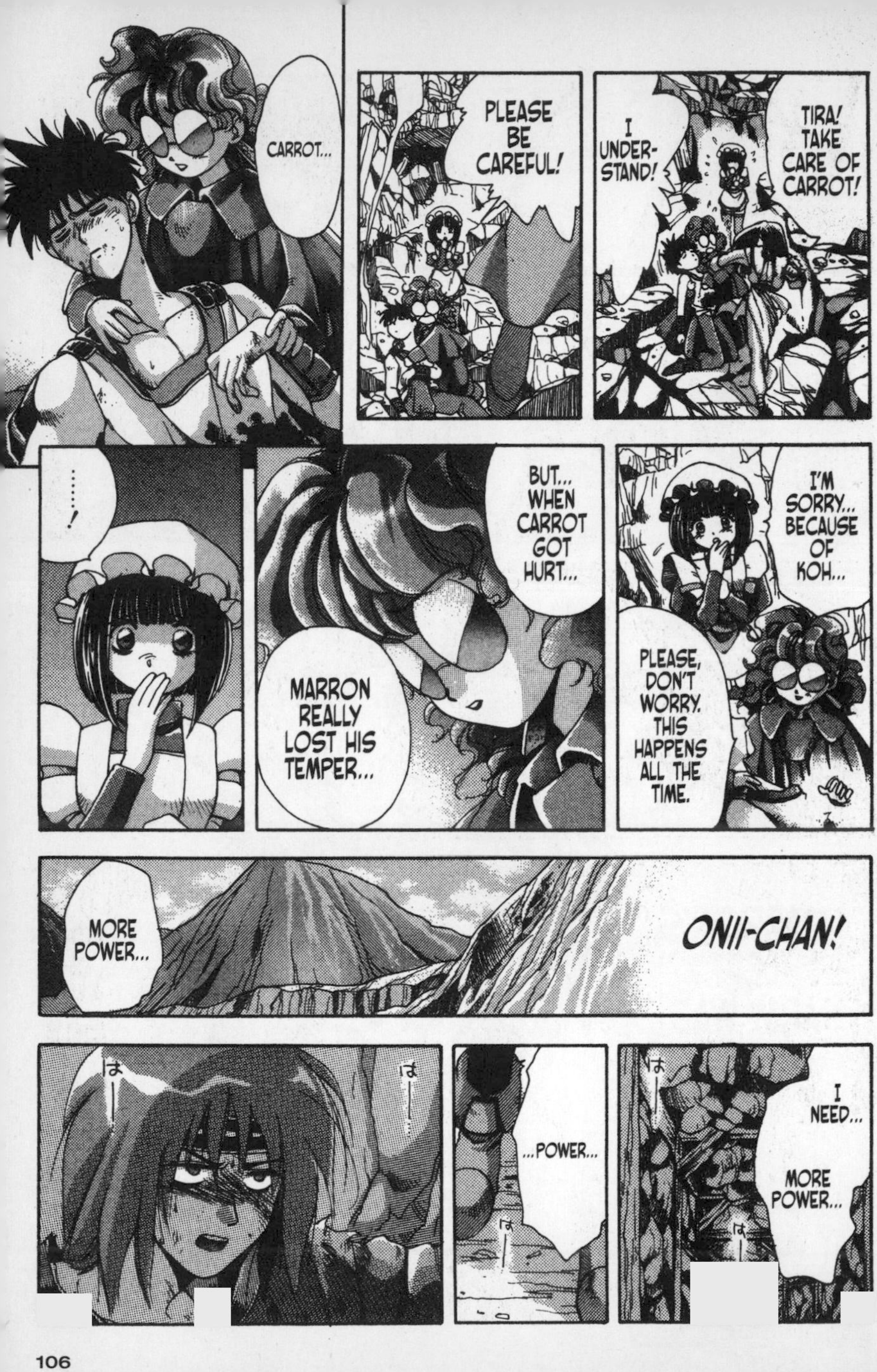
TIRA! TAKE CARE OF CARROT!
I UNDERSTAND!
PLEASE BE CAREFUL!
CARROT...
I'M SORRY... BECAUSE OF KOH...
PLEASE, DON'T WORRY. THIS HAPPENS ALL THE TIME.
BUT... WHEN CARROT GOT HURT...
MARRON REALLY LOST HIS TEMPER...
......!
ONII-CHAN!
MORE POWER...
はー
I NEED...
MORE POWER...
はー
はー
...POWER...
はー
はー
はー

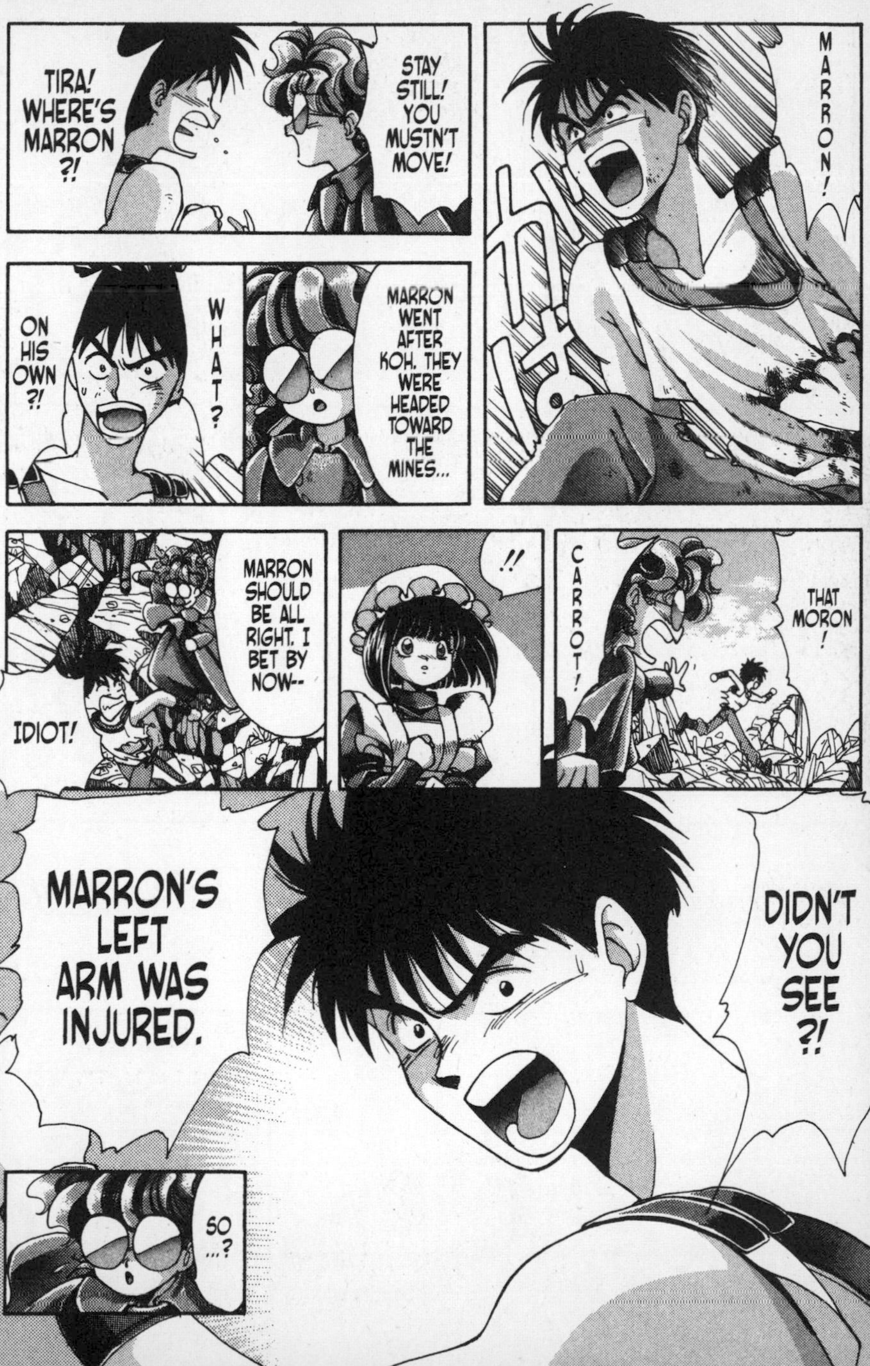
MARRON!
STAY STILL! YOU MUSTN'T MOVE!
TIRA! WHERE'S MARRON?!
MARRON WENT AFTER KOH. THEY WERE HEADED TOWARD THE MINES...
WHAT?
ON HIS OWN?!
THAT MORON!
CARROT!
!!
MARRON SHOULD BE ALL RIGHT. I BET BY NOW--
IDIOT!
DIDN'T YOU SEE?!
MARRON'S LEFT ARM WAS INJURED.
SO ...?

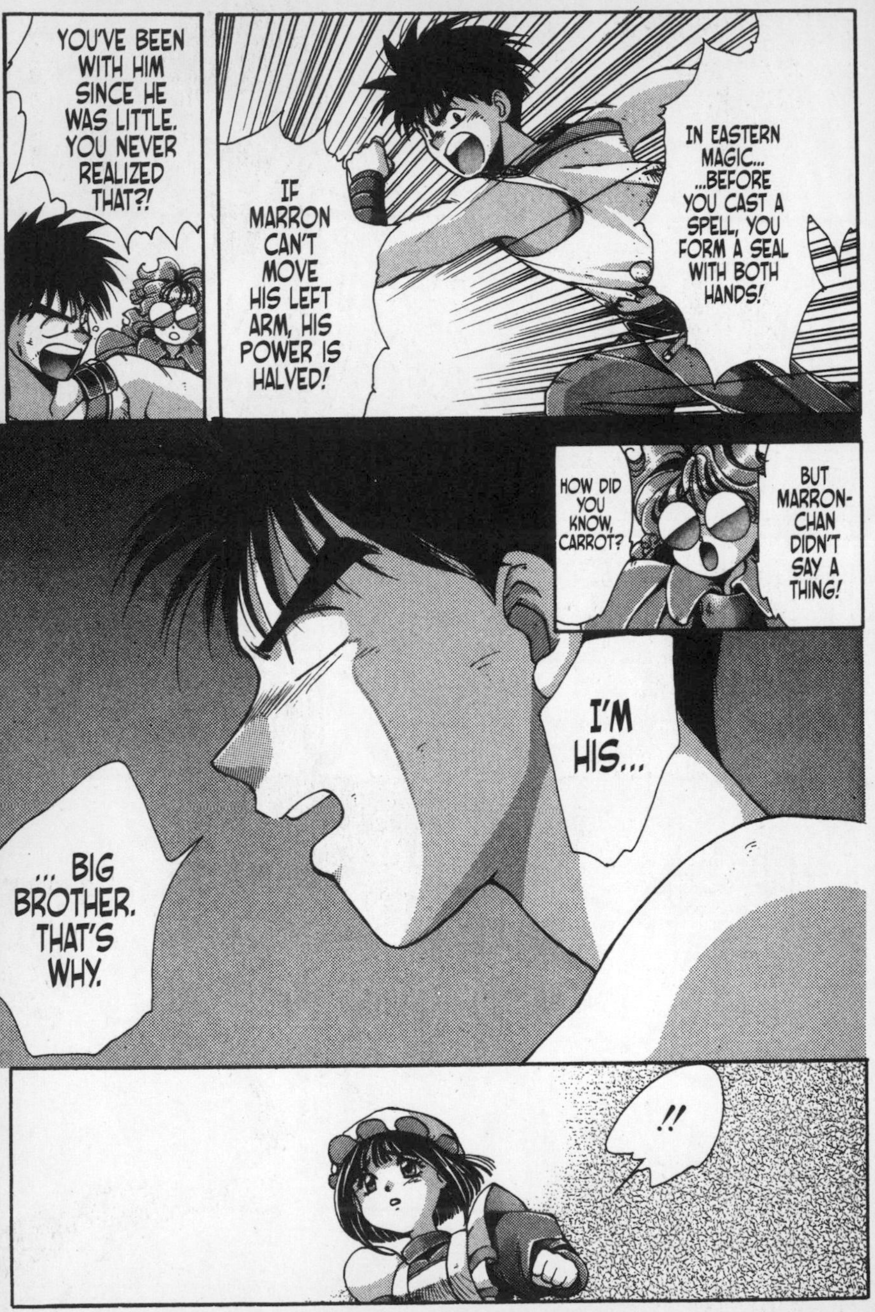
IN EASTERN MAGIC... ...BEFORE YOU CAST A SPELL, YOU FORM A SEAL WITH BOTH HANDS!
IF MARRON CAN'T MOVE HIS LEFT ARM, HIS POWER IS HALVED!
YOU'VE BEEN WITH HIM SINCE HE WAS LITTLE. YOU NEVER REALIZED THAT?!
BUT MARRON-CHAN DIDN'T SAY A THING!
HOW DID YOU KNOW, CARROT?
I'M HIS...
... BIG BROTHER. THAT'S WHY.
!!

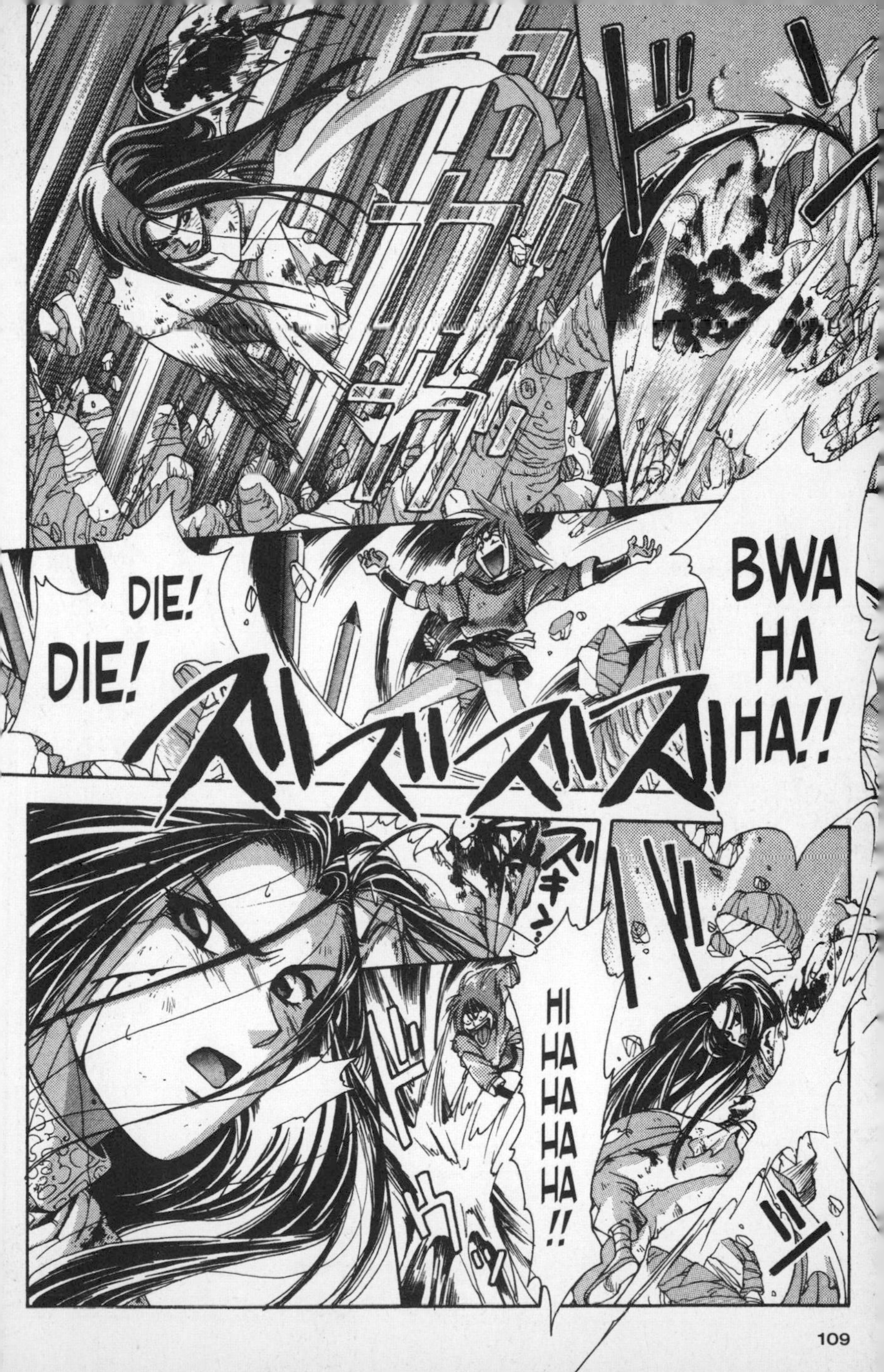
BWA HA HA HA!!
DIE!
DIE!
HI HA HA HA HA HA!!

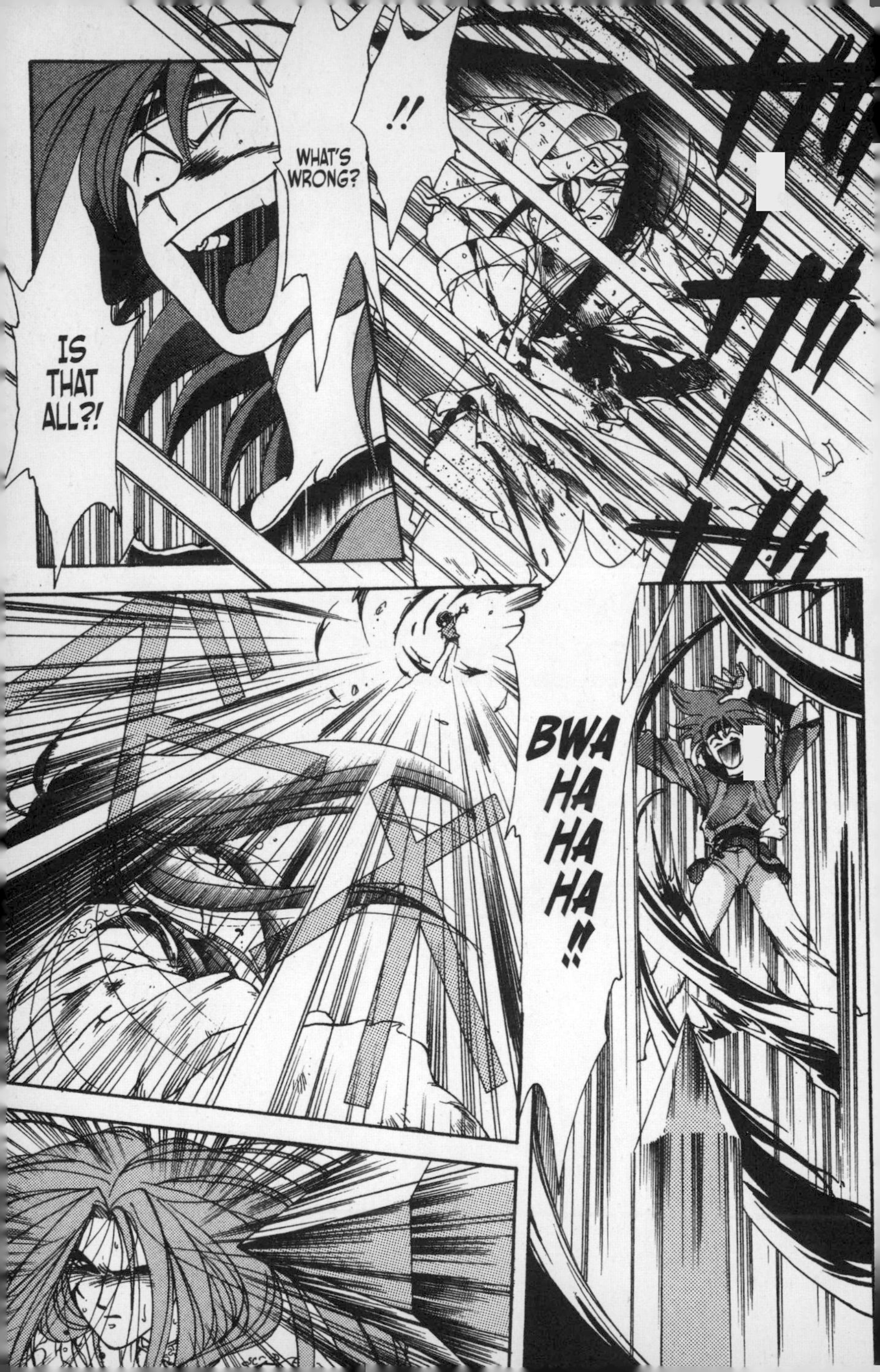
!!
WHAT'S WRONG?
IS THAT ALL?!
BWA HA HA HA HA!!

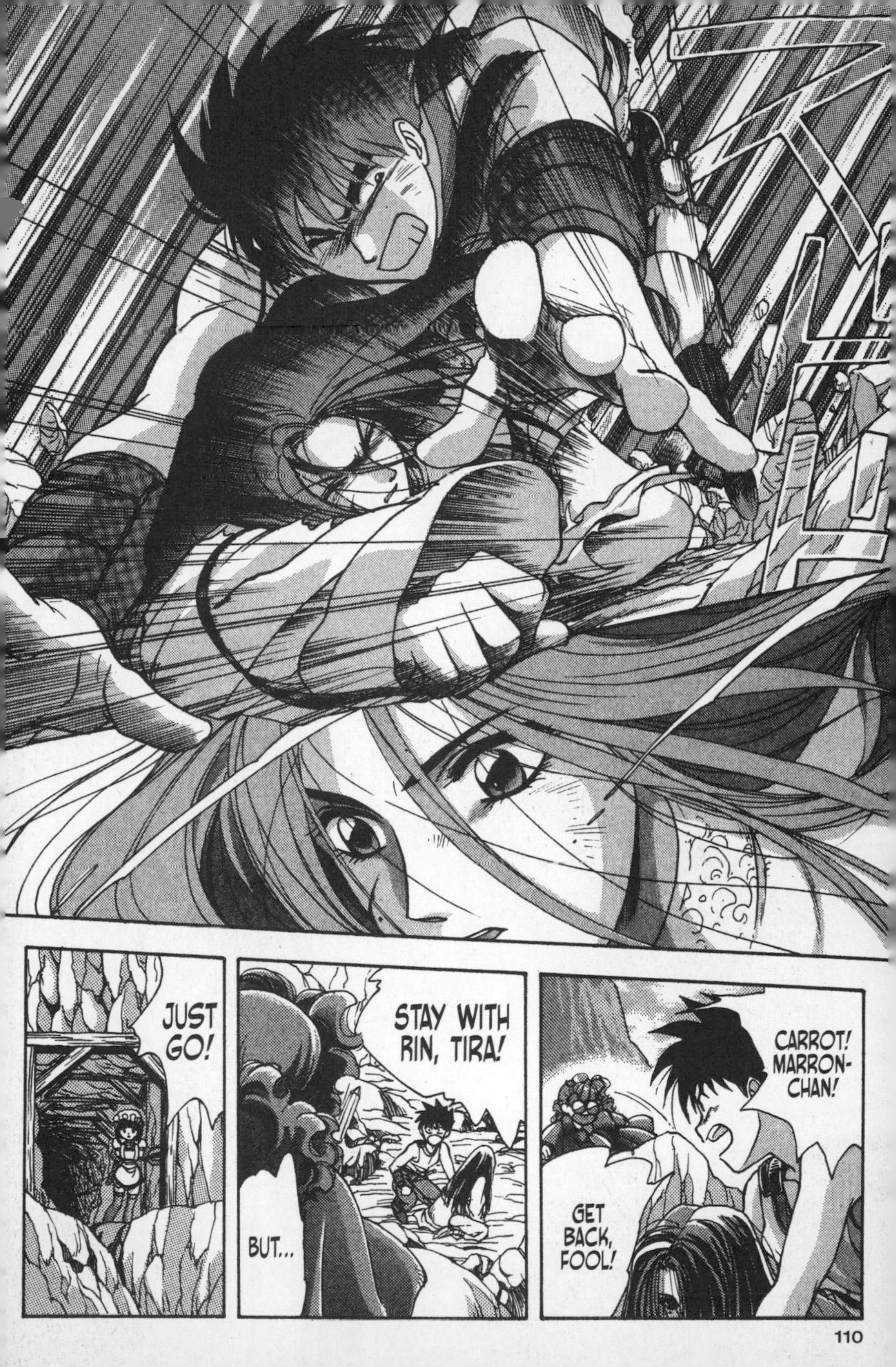
CARROT! MARRON-CHAN!
GET BACK, FOOL!
STAY WITH RIN, TIRA!
BUT...
JUST GO!

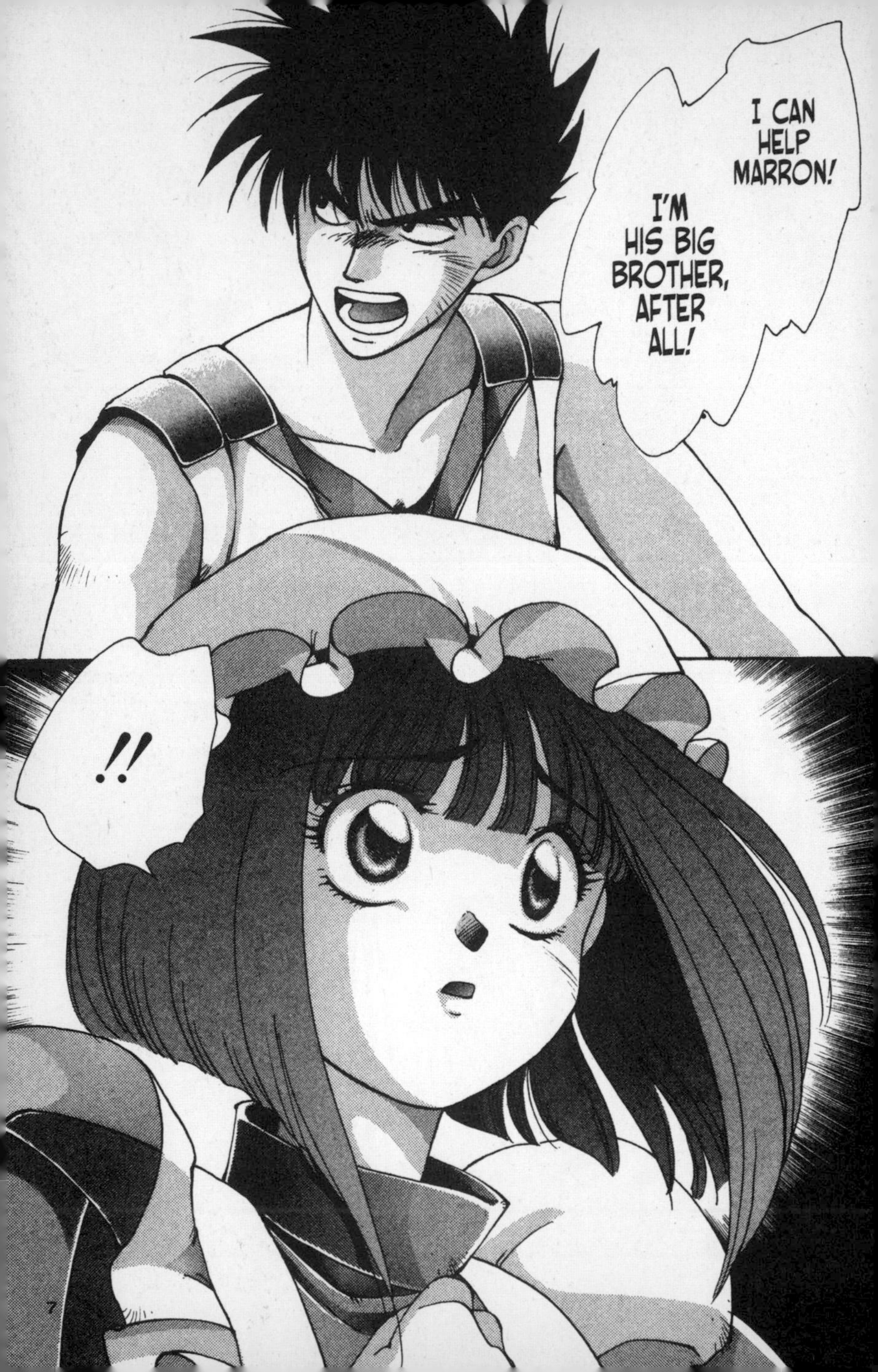
I CAN HELP MARRON!
I'M HIS BIG BROTHER, AFTER ALL!
!!

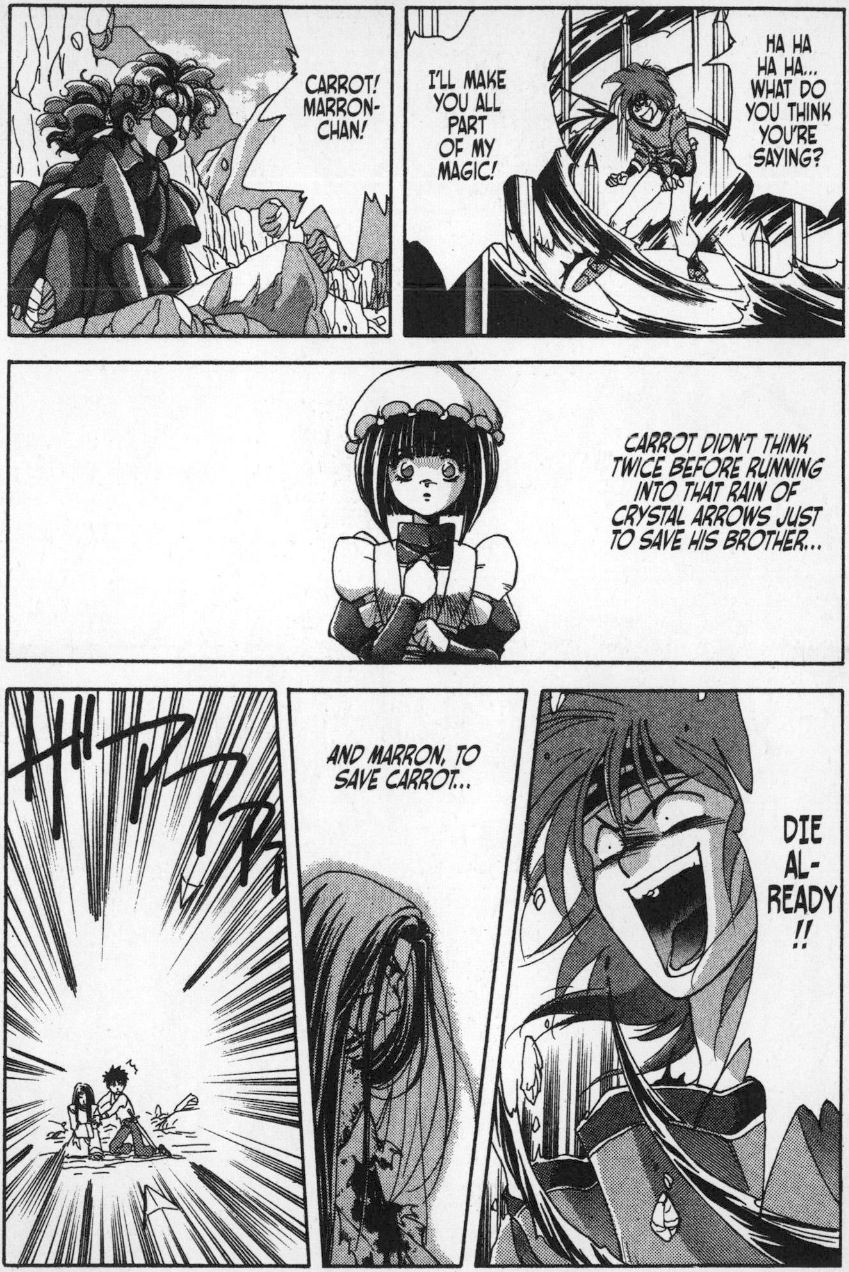
HA HA HA HA... WHAT DO YOU THINK YOU'RE SAYING?
I'LL MAKE YOU ALL PART OF MY MAGIC!
CARROT! MARRON-CHAN!
CARROT DIDN'T THINK TWICE BEFORE RUNNING INTO THAT RAIN OF CRYSTAL ARROWS JUST TO SAVE HIS BROTHER...
DIE AL-READY !!
AND MARRON, TO SAVE CARROT...

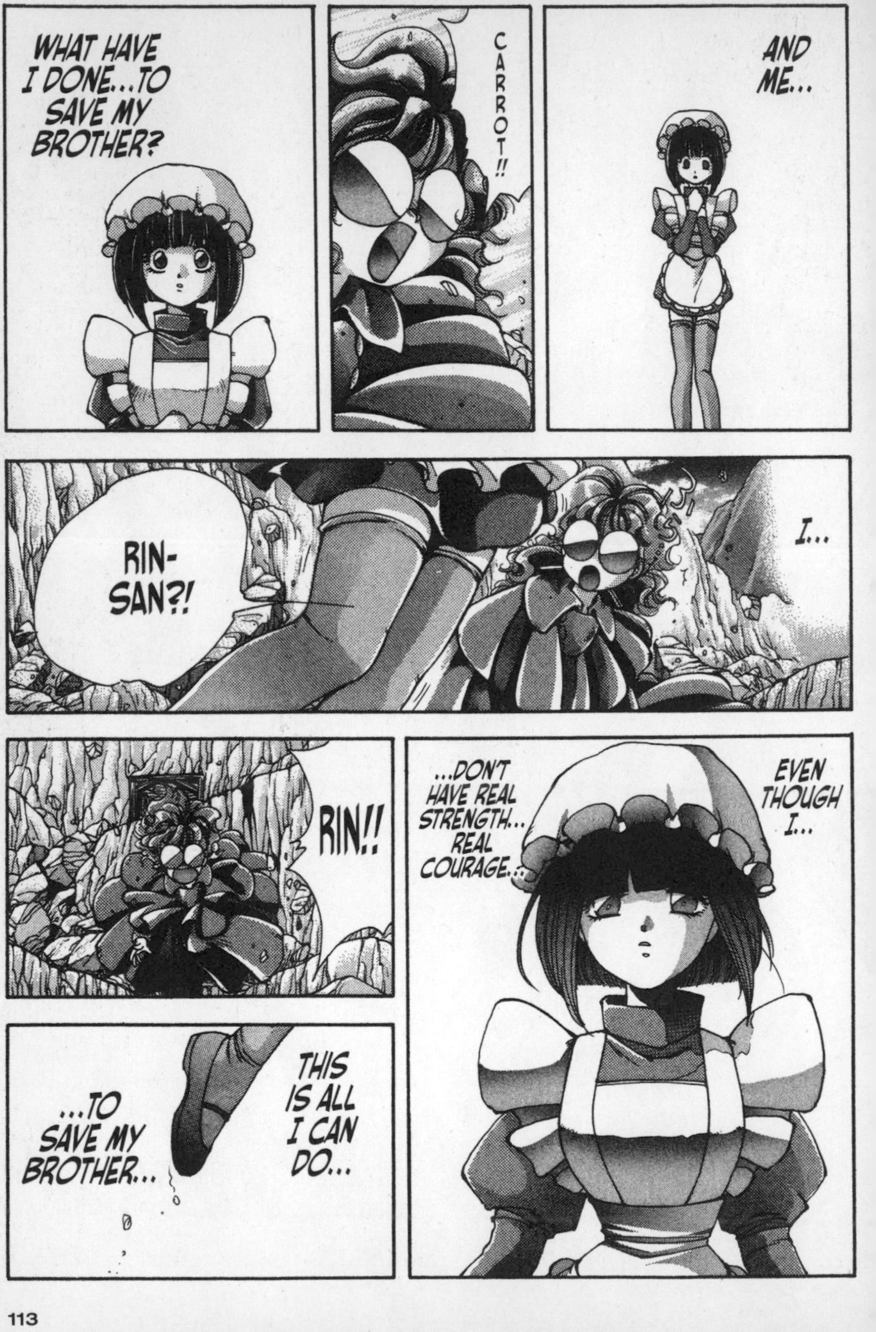
AND ME...
CARROT!!
WHAT HAVE I DONE...TO SAVE MY BROTHER?
I...
RIN-SAN?!
EVEN THOUGH I...
...DON'T HAVE REAL STRENGTH... REAL COURAGE...
RIN!!
THIS IS ALL I CAN DO...
...TO SAVE MY BROTHER...

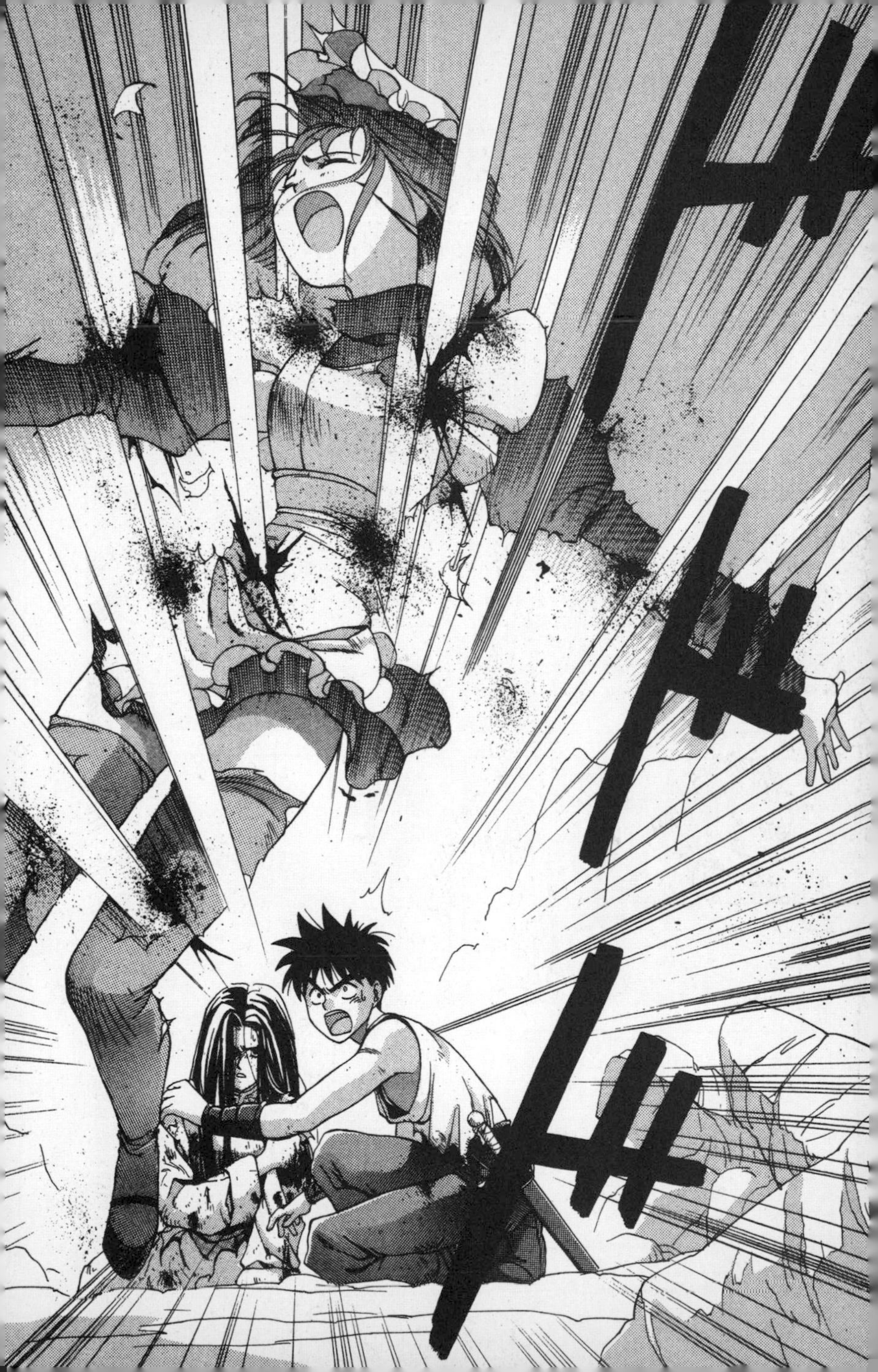

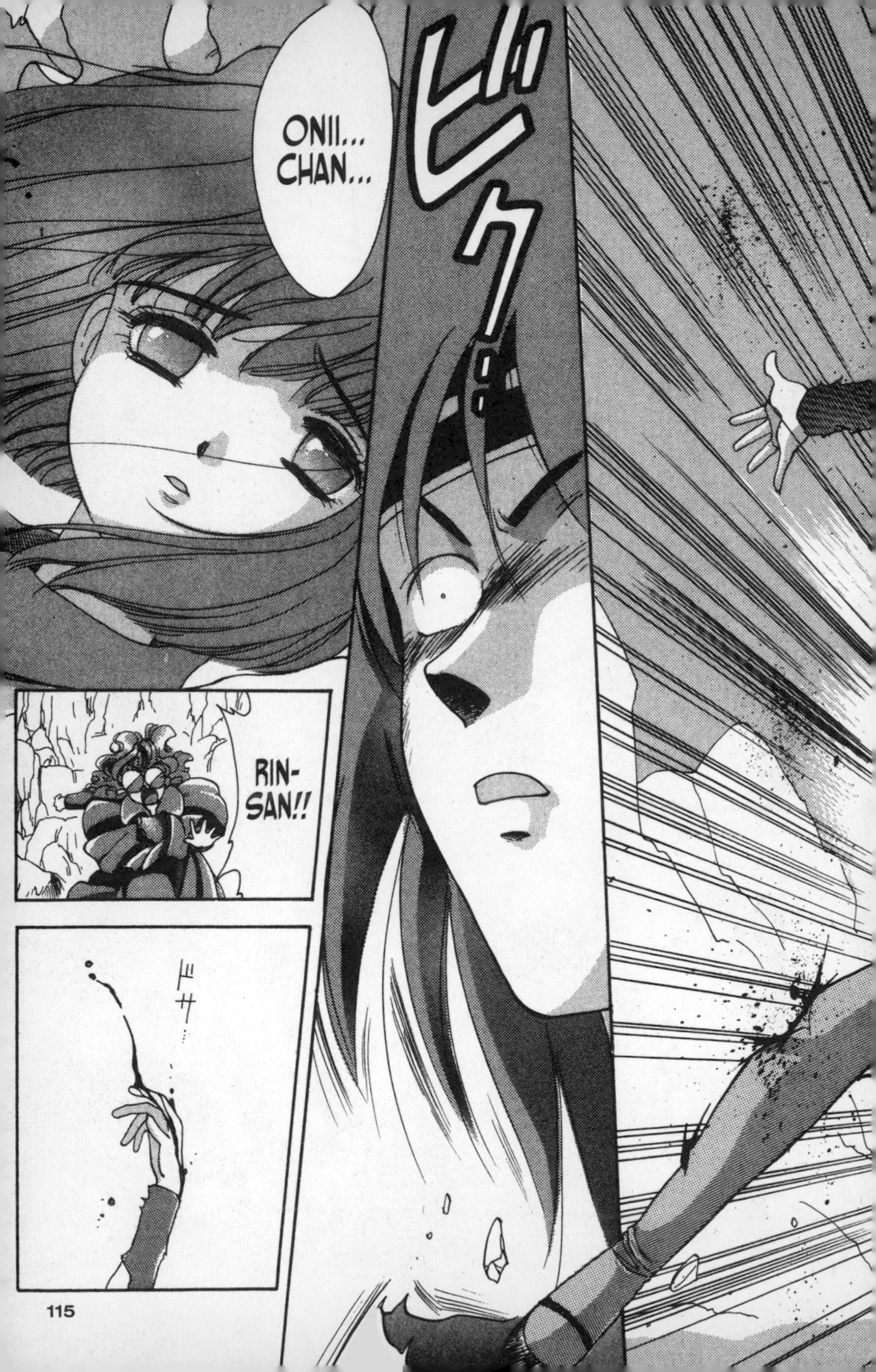
ビクッ!!
ONII... CHAN...
RIN-SAN!!
ドサ…

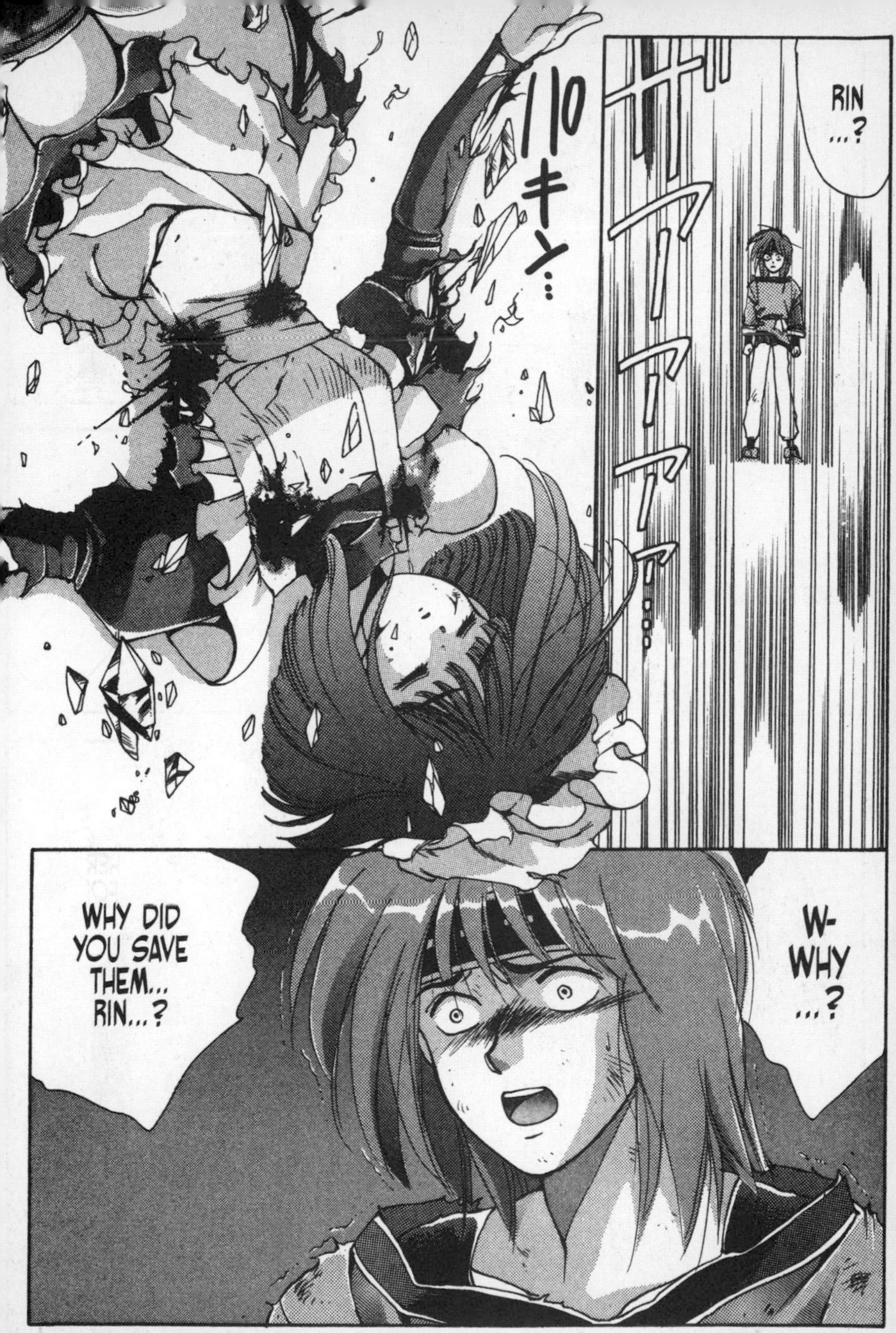
ザァァァァ…
RIN ...?
パキン…
W- WHY ...?
WHY DID YOU SAVE THEM... RIN...?

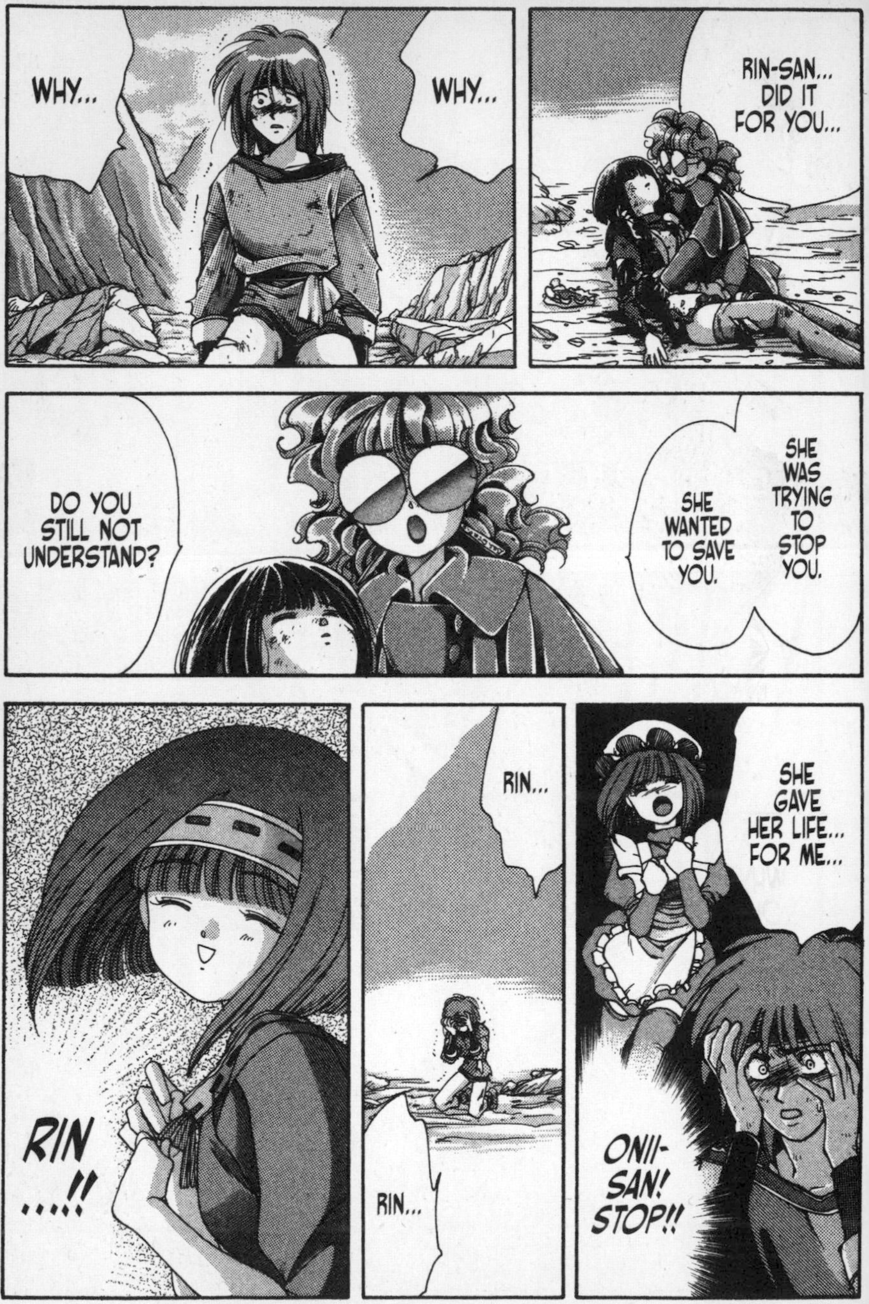
RIN-SAN... DID IT FOR YOU...
WHY...
WHY...
SHE WAS TRYING TO STOP YOU.
SHE WANTED TO SAVE YOU.
DO YOU STILL NOT UNDERSTAND?
SHE GAVE HER LIFE... FOR ME...
ONII-SAN! STOP!!
RIN...
RIN...
RIN ....!!

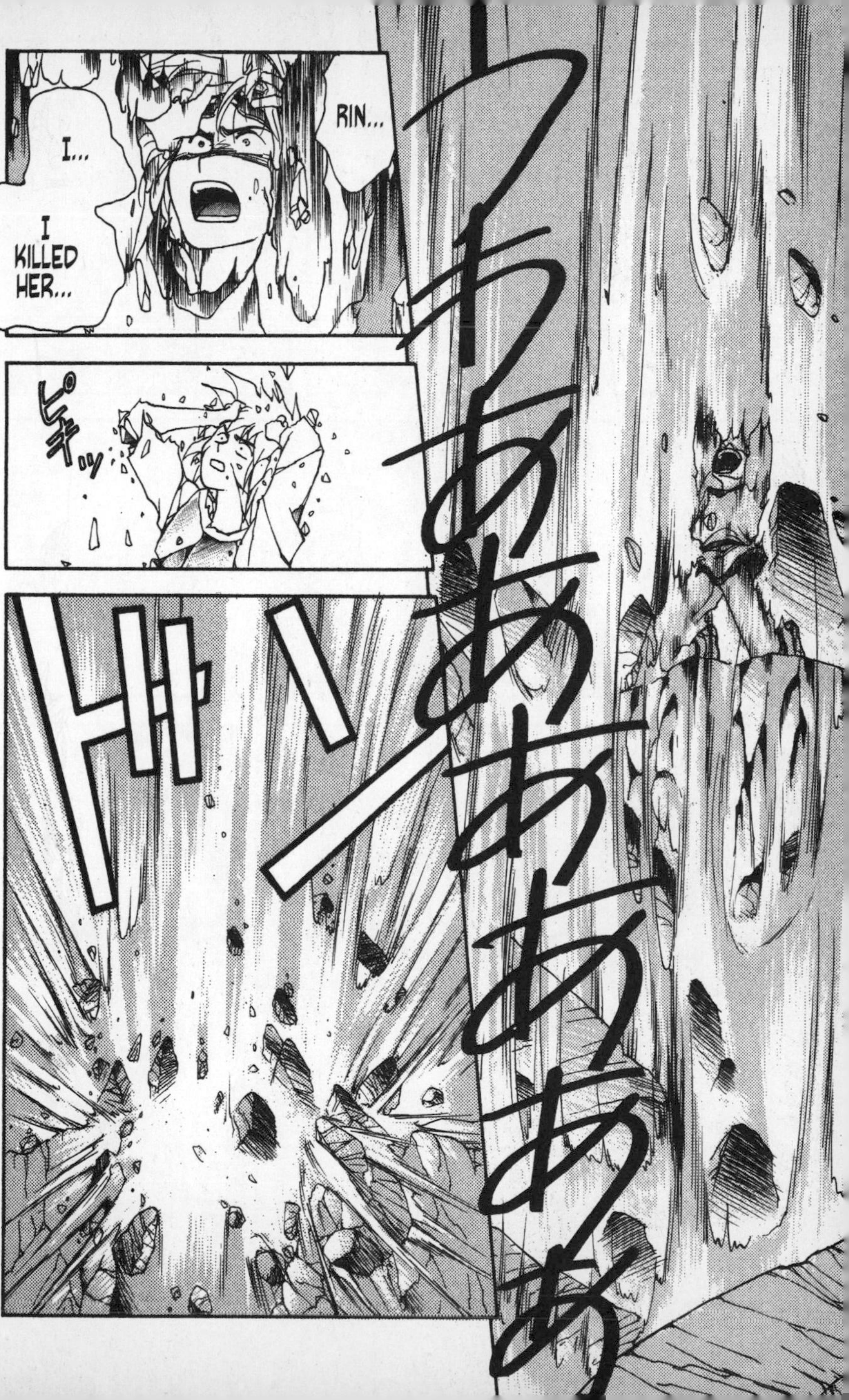
RIN...
I...
I KILLED HER...
ピキッ

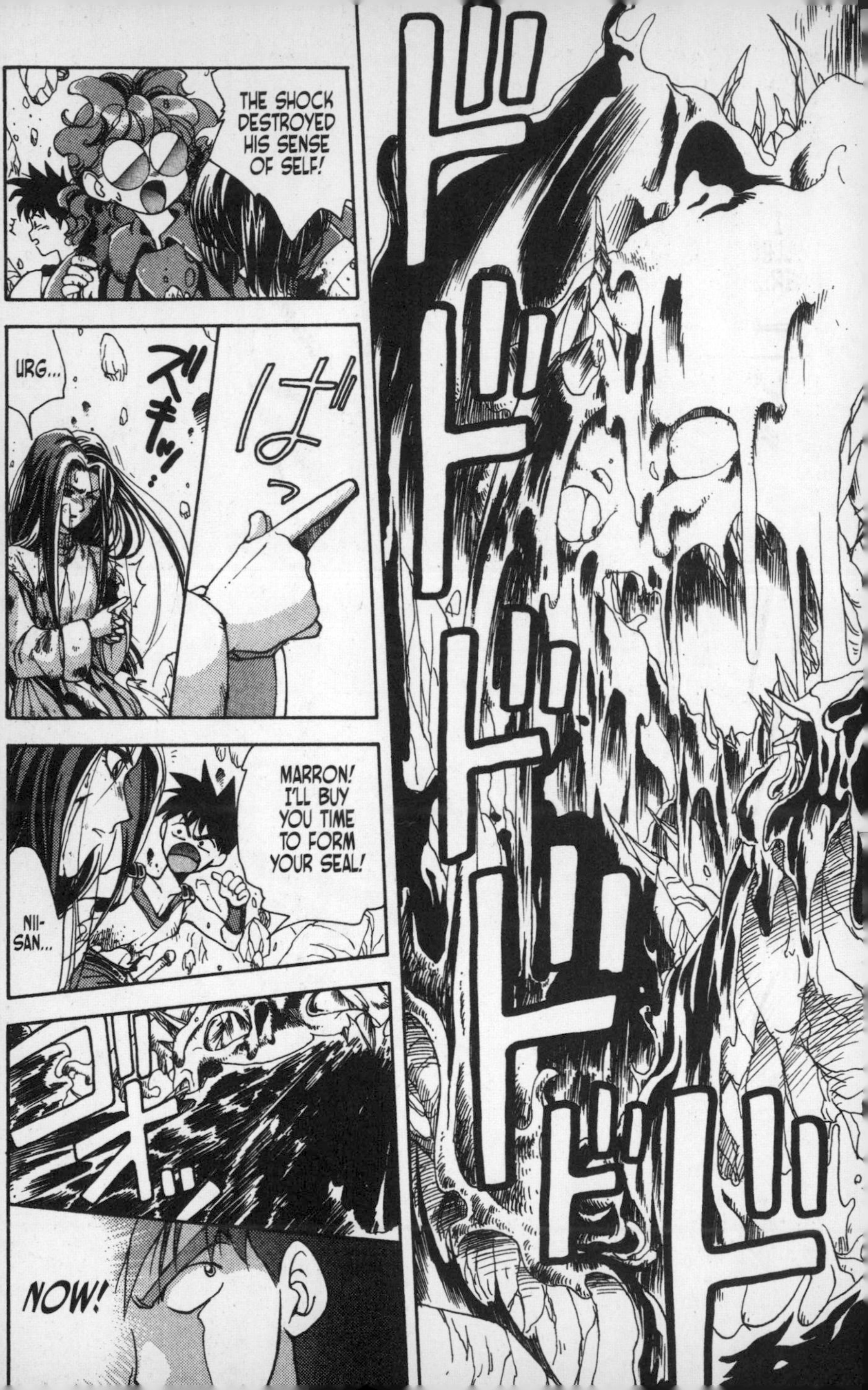
ドドドドドド
THE SHOCK DESTROYED HIS SENSE OF SELF!
ばっ
ズキッ!
URG...
MARRON! I'LL BUY YOU TIME TO FORM YOUR SEAL!
NII-SAN...
ゴォ
NOW!

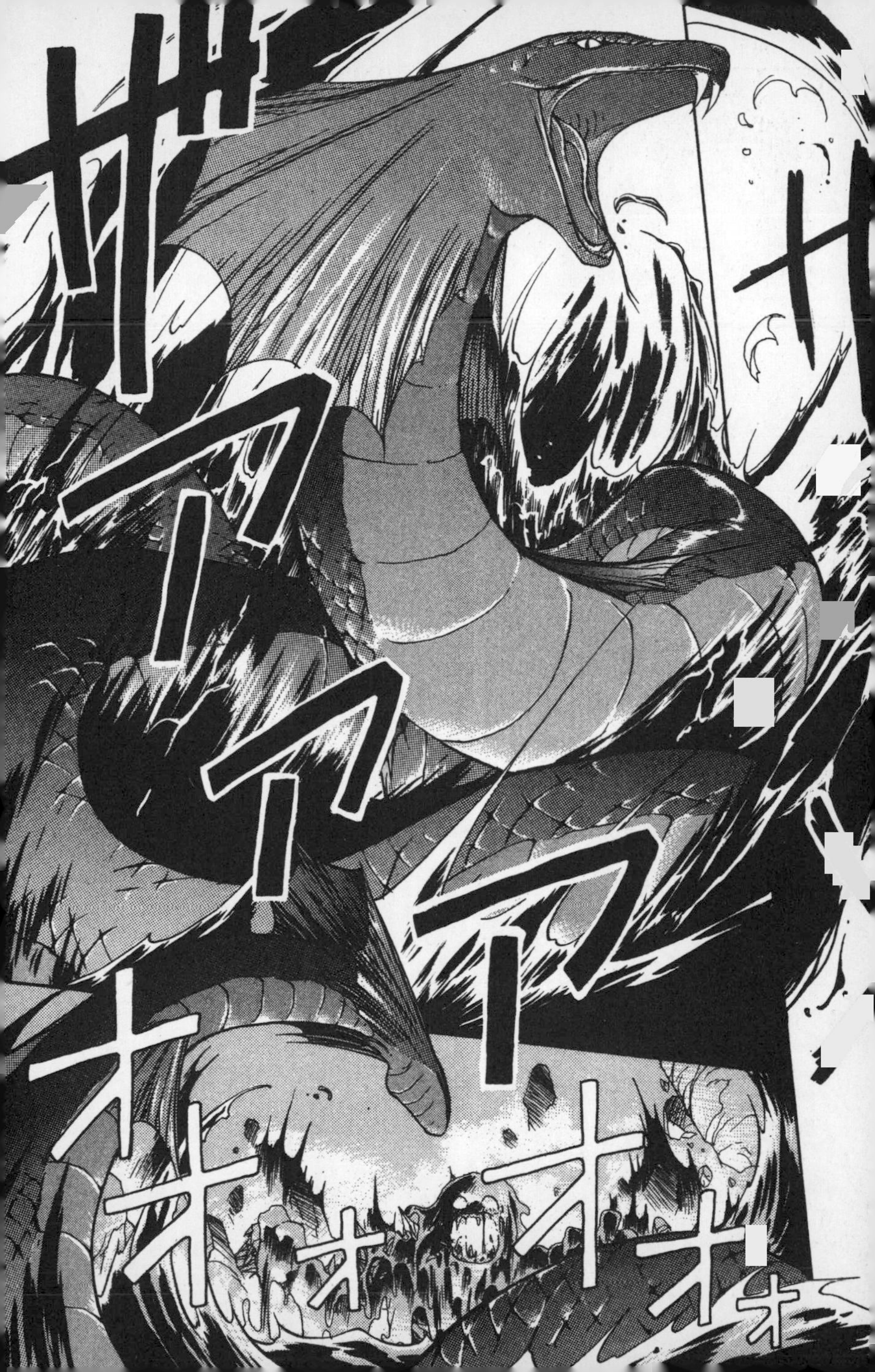
ガアアアオオオオォ

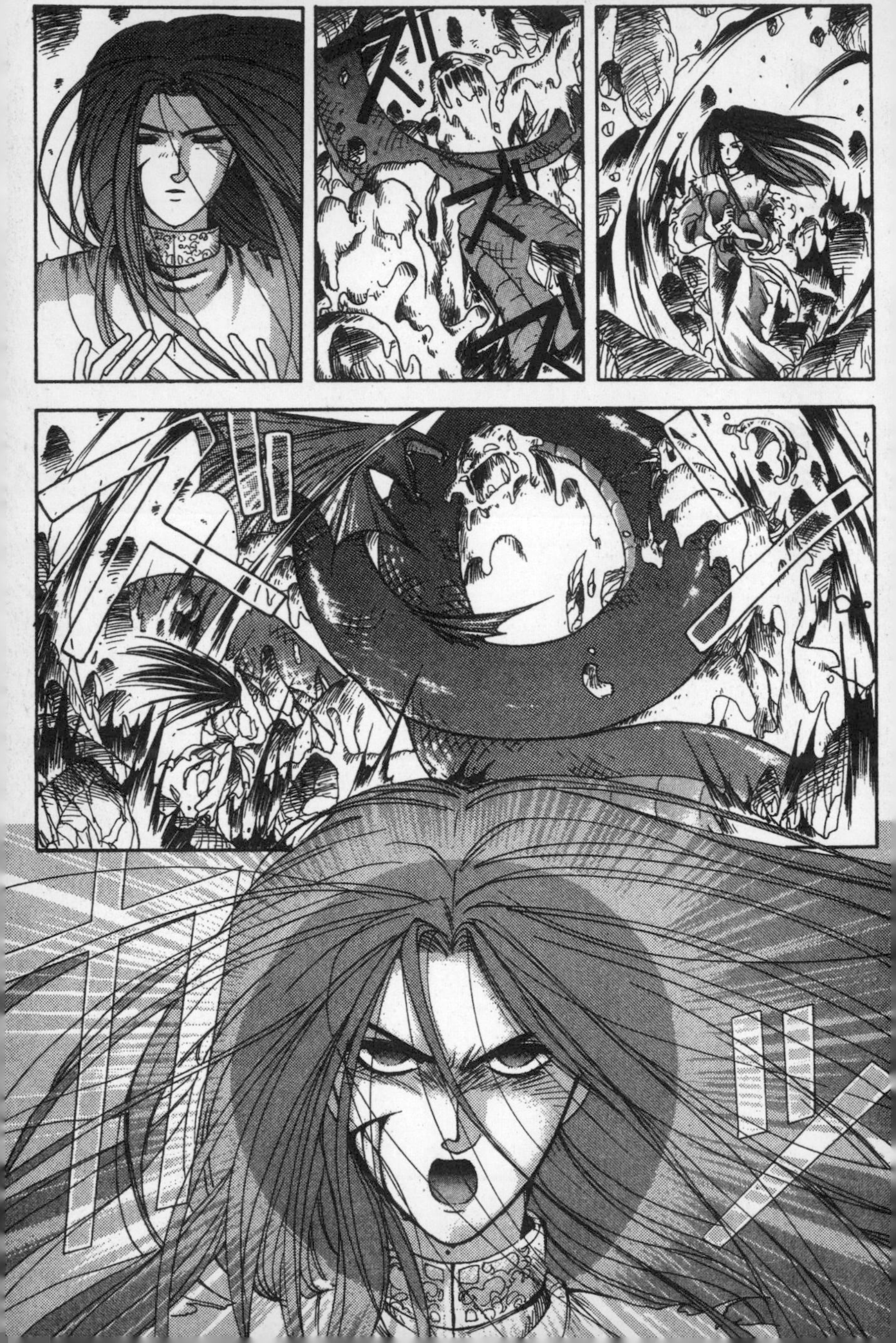
ズ
ズ
ズ

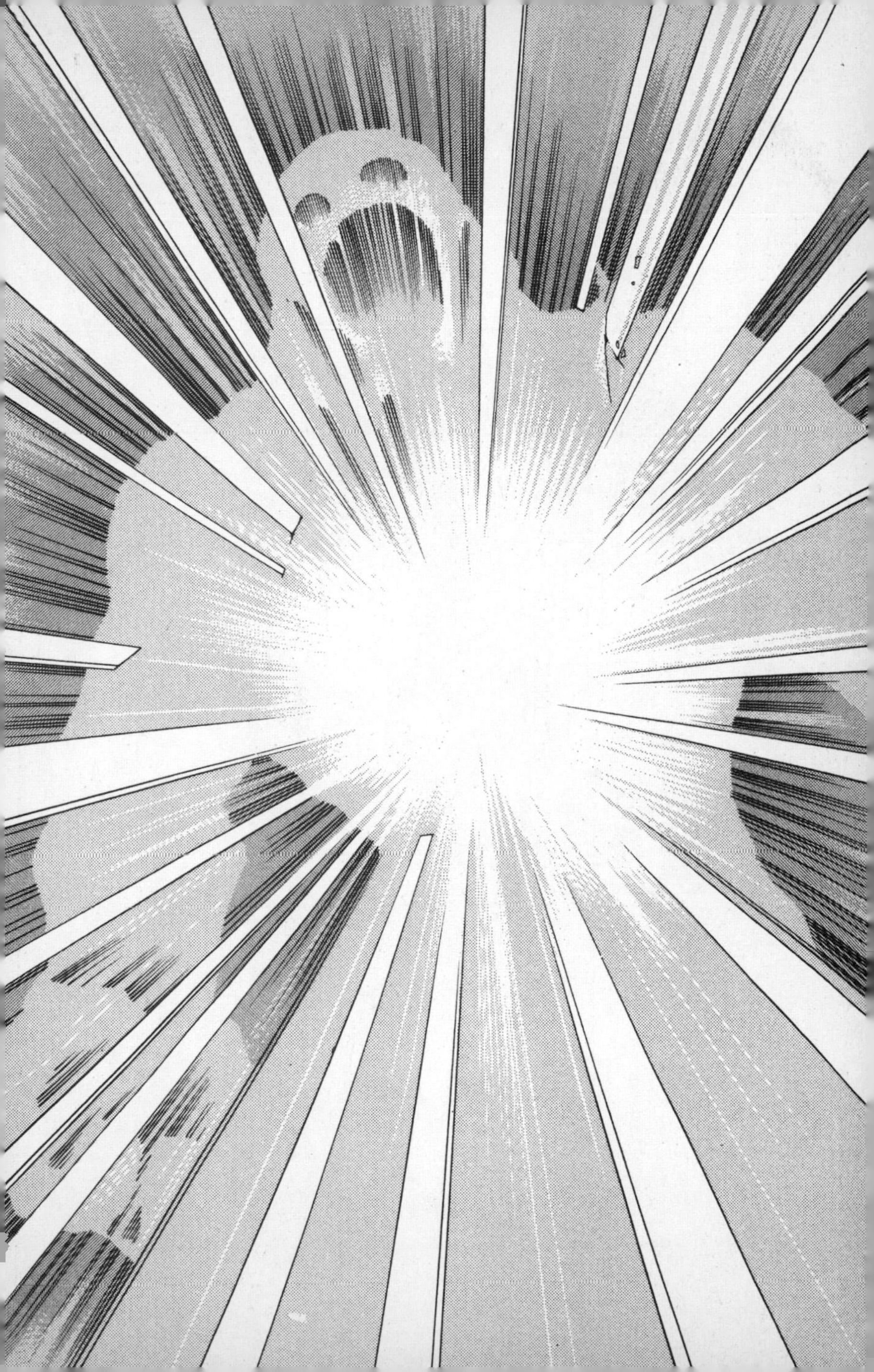

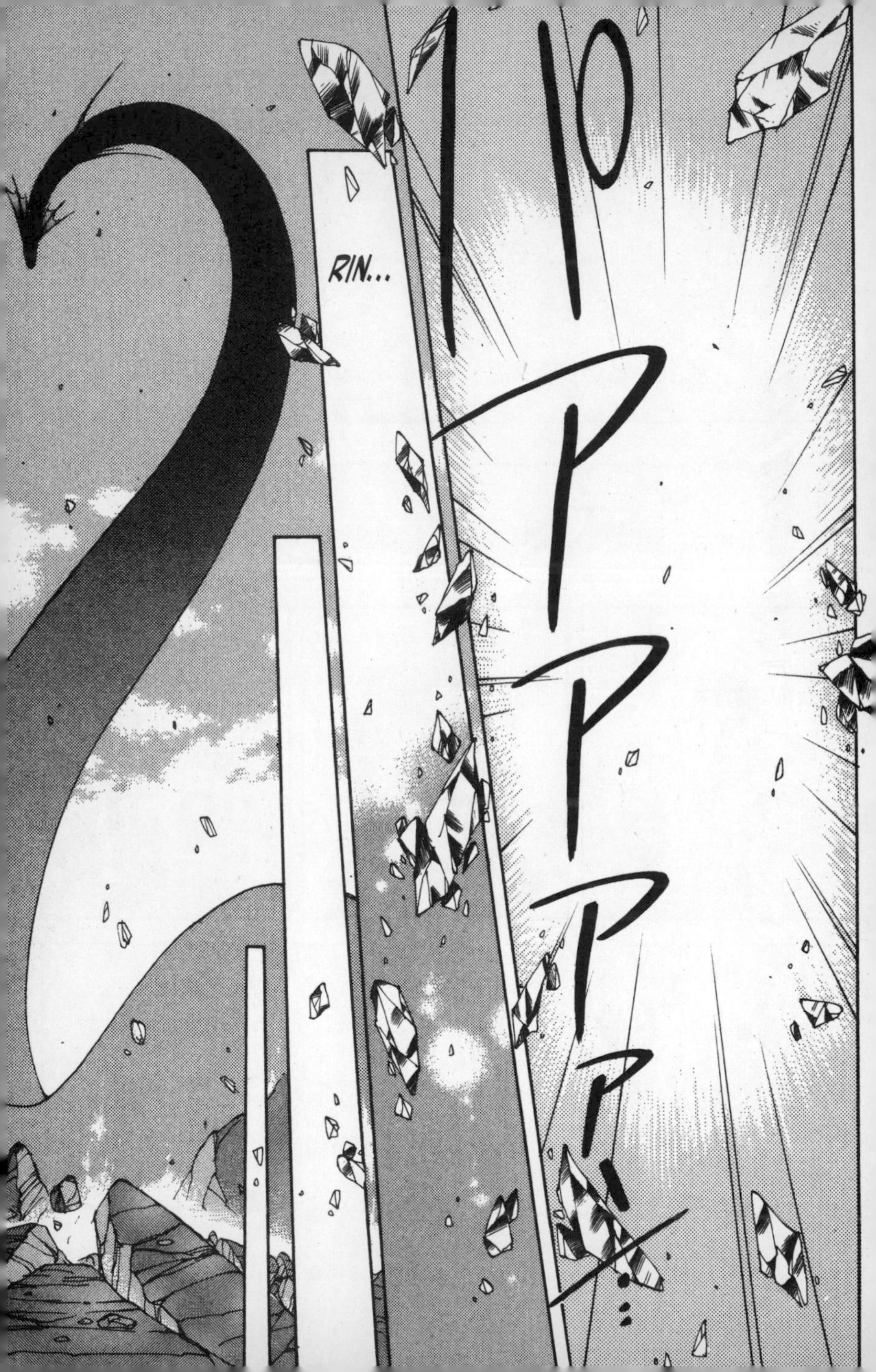
RIN...

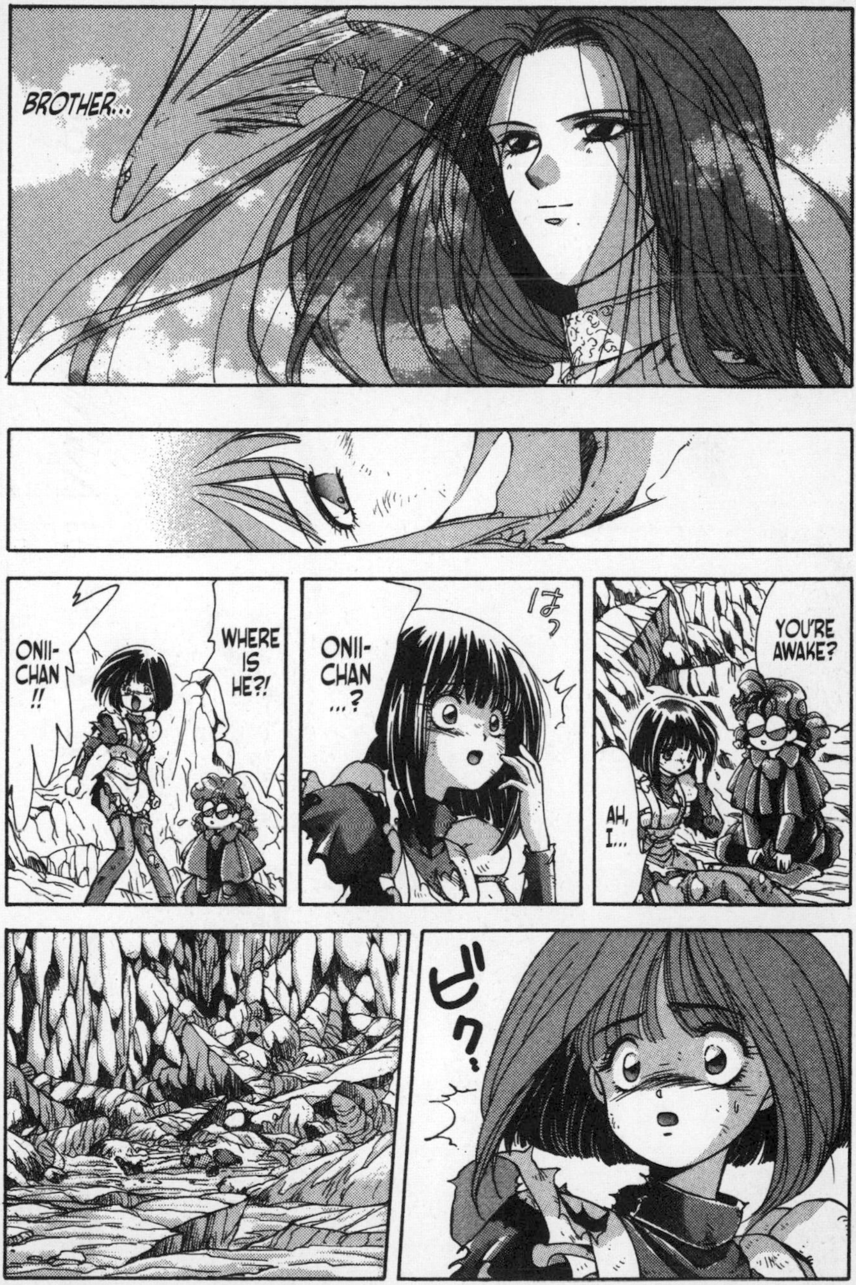
BROTHER...
YOU'RE AWAKE?
AH, I...
はっ
ONII-CHAN ...?
WHERE IS HE?!
ONII-CHAN !!
ビク

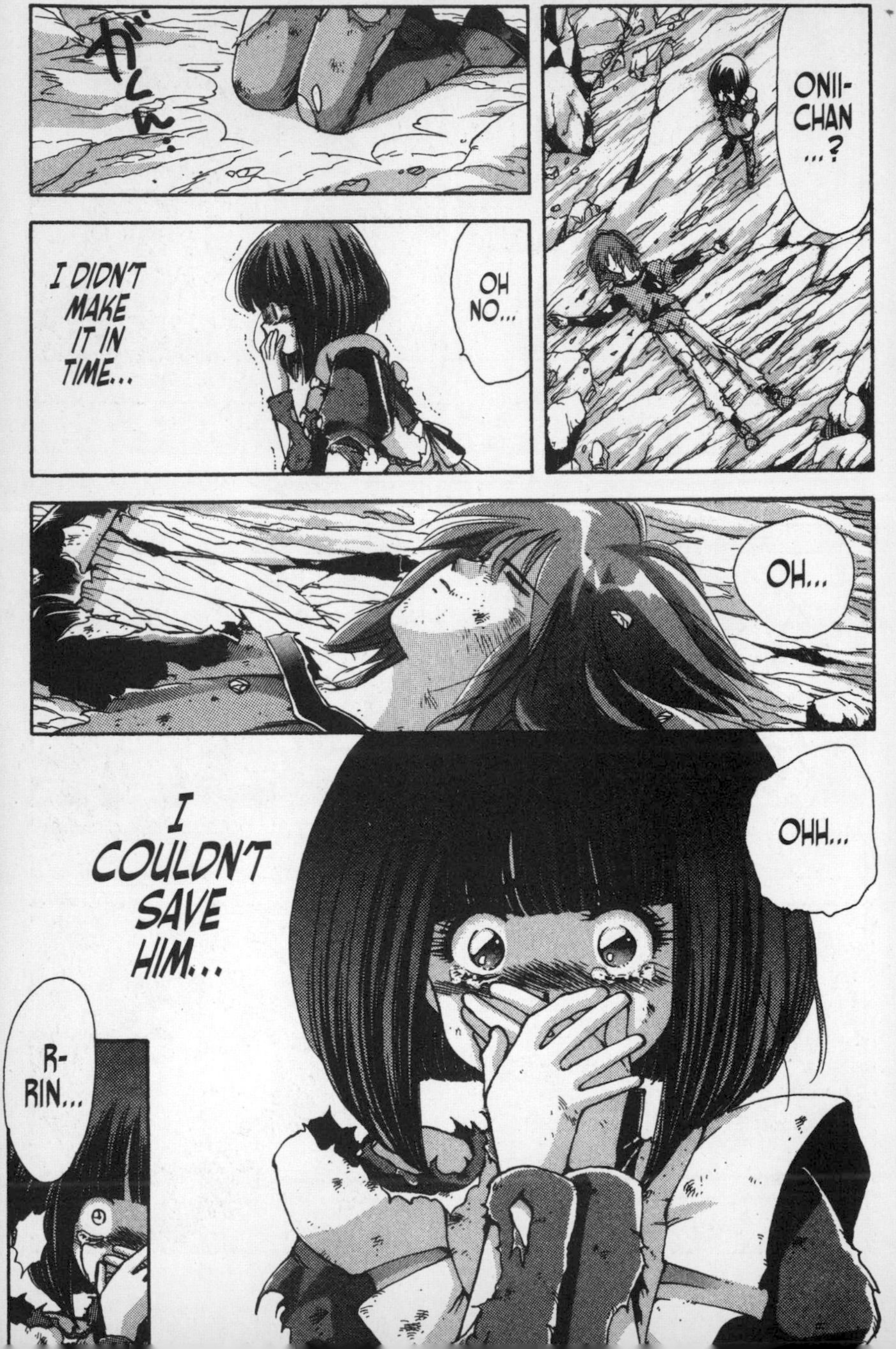
ONII-CHAN ...?
がしん..
OH NO...
I DIDN'T MAKE IT IN TIME...
OH...
OHH...
I COULDN'T SAVE HIM...
R-RIN...

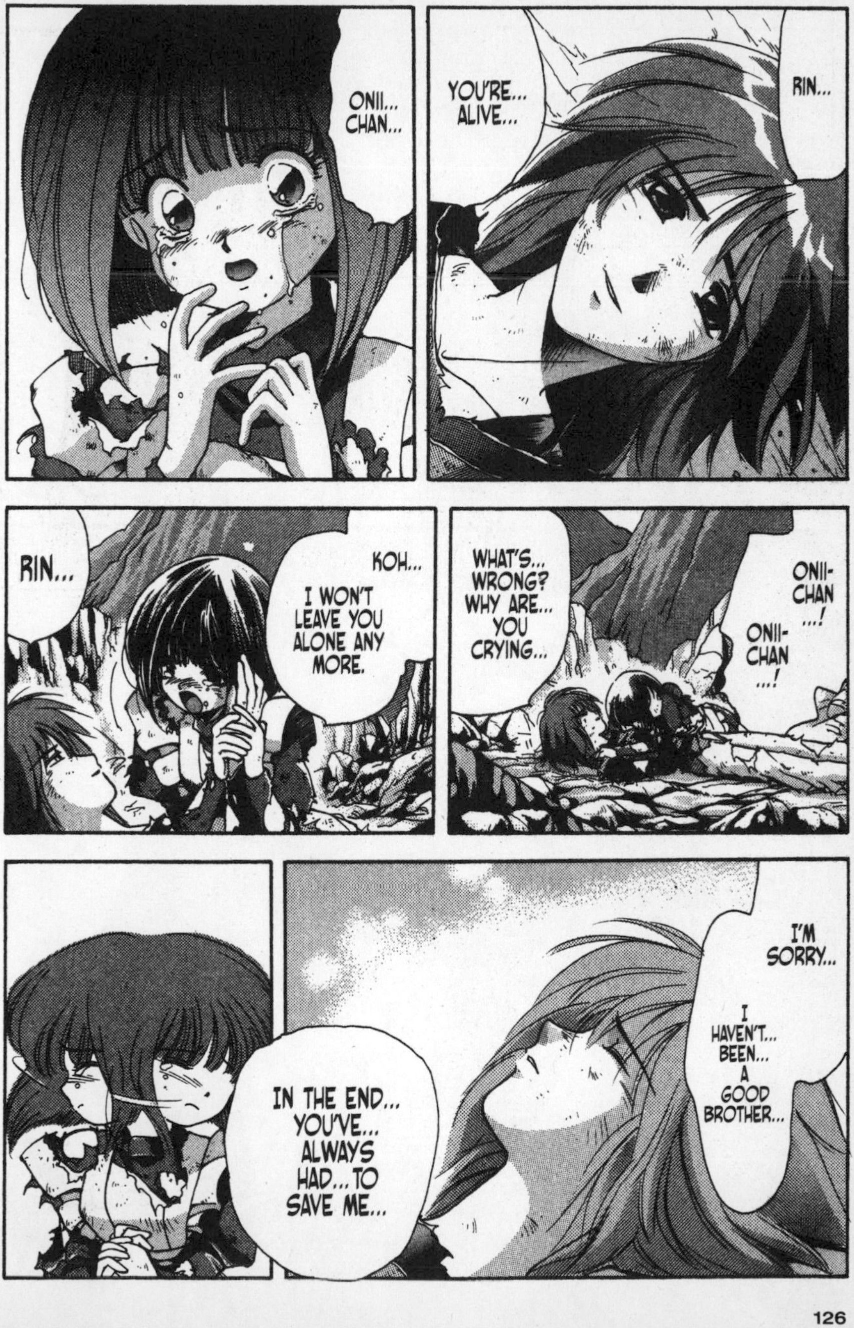
RIN...
YOU'RE... ALIVE...
ONII... CHAN...
ONII-CHAN ...!
ONII-CHAN ...!
WHAT'S... WRONG? WHY ARE... YOU CRYING...
KOH... I WON'T LEAVE YOU ALONE ANY MORE.
RIN...
I'M SORRY...
I HAVEN'T... BEEN... A GOOD BROTHER...
IN THE END... YOU'VE... ALWAYS HAD... TO SAVE ME...

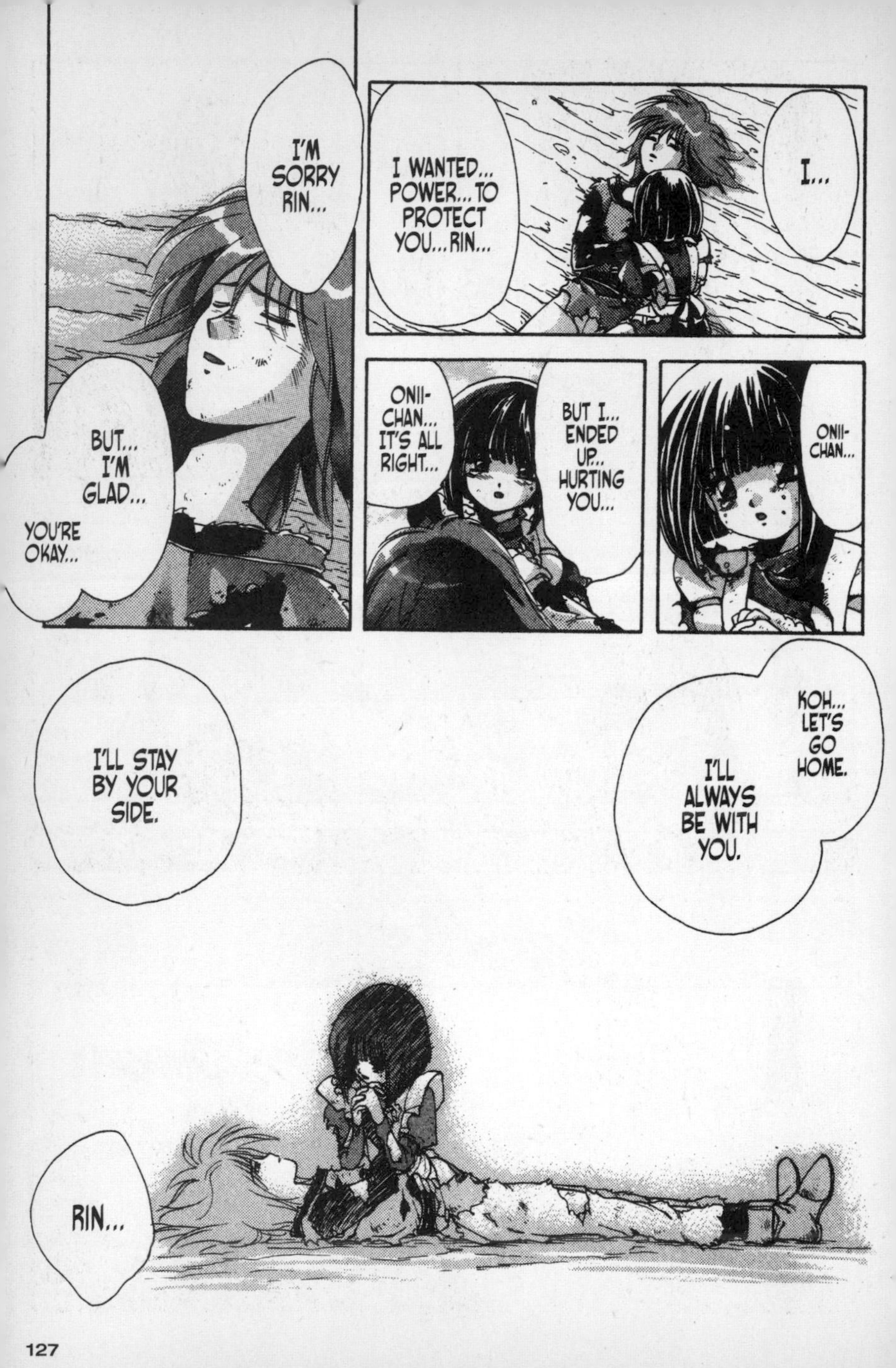
I...
I WANTED... POWER... TO PROTECT YOU... RIN...
ONII-CHAN...
BUT I... ENDED UP... HURTING YOU...
ONII-CHAN... IT'S ALL RIGHT...
I'M SORRY RIN...
BUT... I'M GLAD...
YOU'RE OKAY...
KOH... LET'S GO HOME.
I'LL ALWAYS BE WITH YOU.
I'LL STAY BY YOUR SIDE.
RIN...

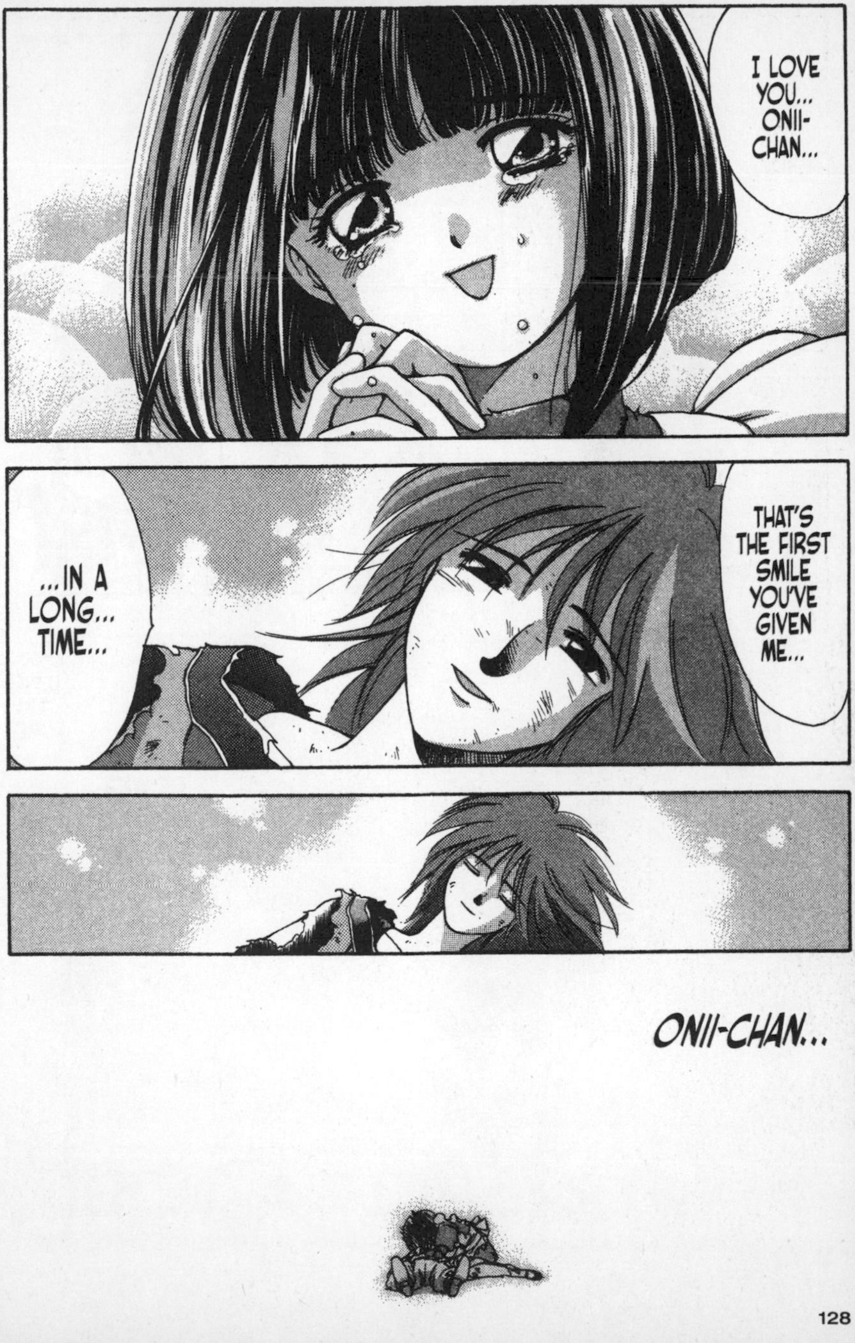
I LOVE YOU... ONII-CHAN...
THAT'S THE FIRST SMILE YOU'VE GIVEN ME...
...IN A LONG... TIME...
ONII-CHAN...

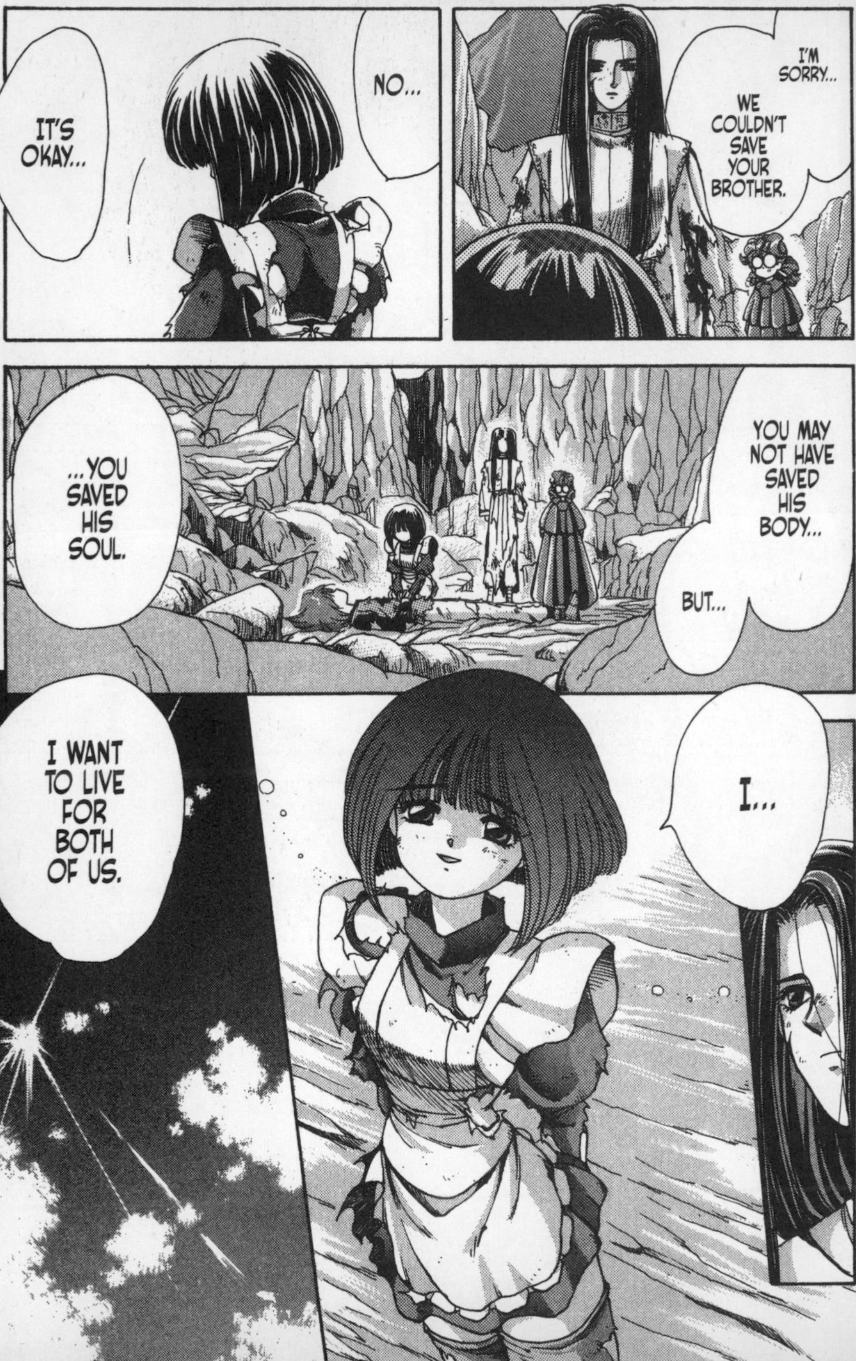
I'M SORRY...
WE COULDN'T SAVE YOUR BROTHER.
NO...
IT'S OKAY...
YOU MAY NOT HAVE SAVED HIS BODY...
BUT...
...YOU SAVED HIS SOUL.
I...
I WANT TO LIVE FOR BOTH OF US.

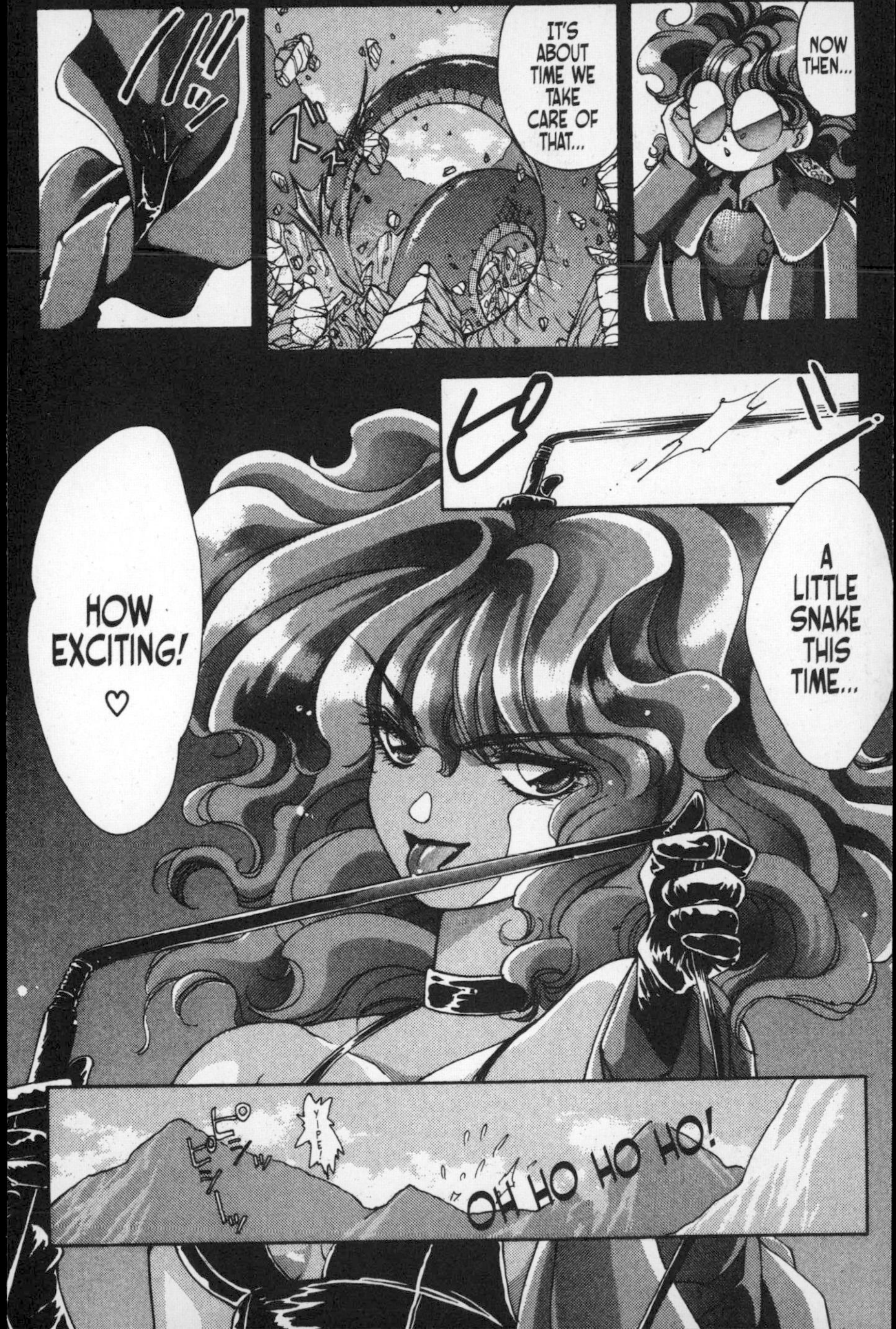
NOW THEN...
IT'S ABOUT TIME WE TAKE CARE OF THAT...
A LITTLE SNAKE THIS TIME...
HOW EXCITING! ♡
OH HO HO HO HO!
YIPE!

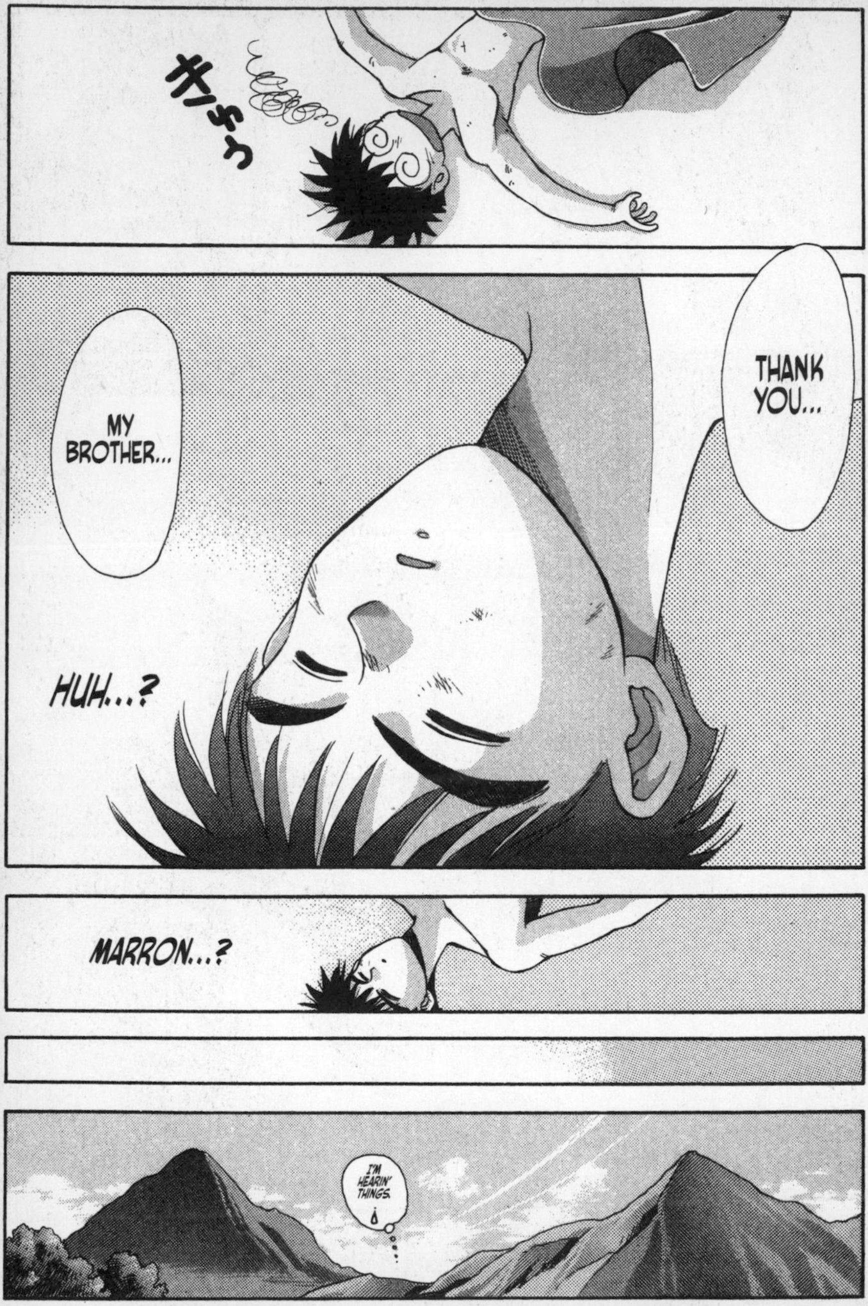
THANK YOU...
MY BROTHER...
HUH...?
MARRON...?
I'M HEARIN' THINGS.

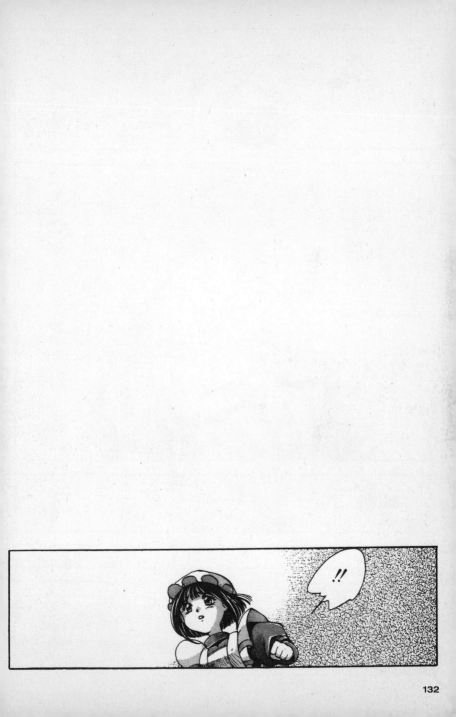

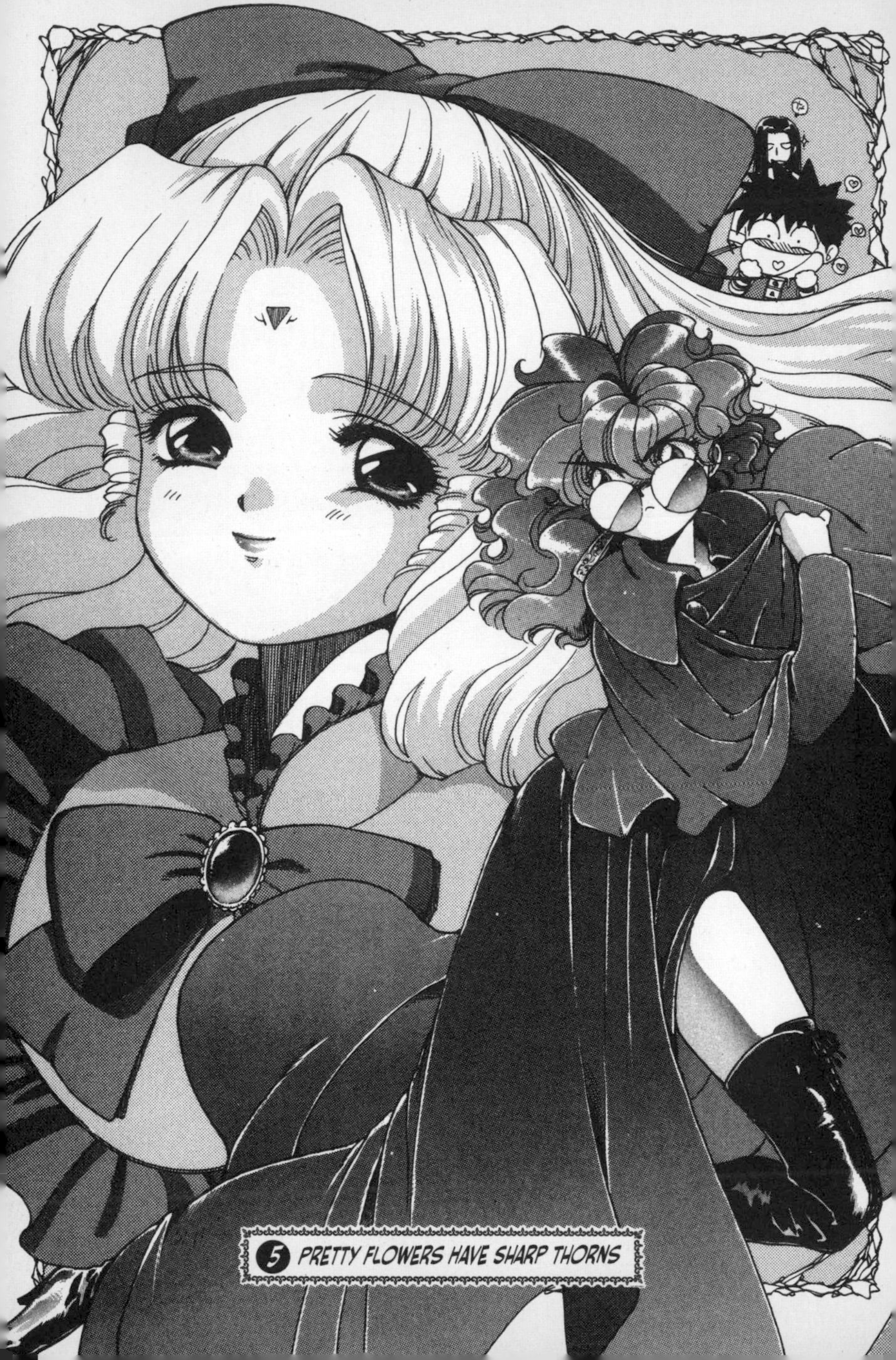
5 PRETTY FLOWERS HAVE SHARP THORNS

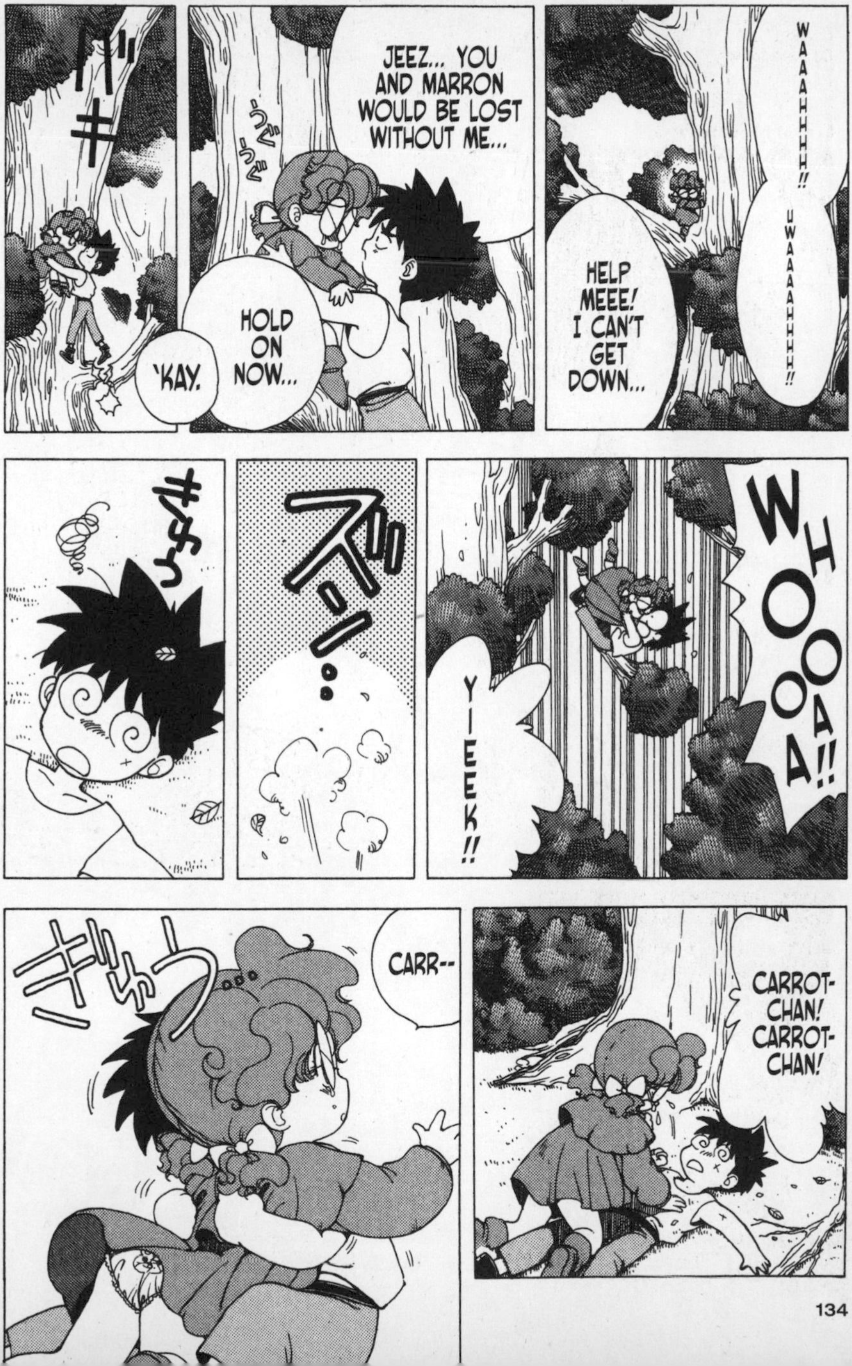
WAAAHHHH!!
UWAAAAAHHHH!!
HELP MEEE! I CAN'T GET DOWN...
JEEZ... YOU AND MARRON WOULD BE LOST WITHOUT ME...
うぐ うぐ
HOLD ON NOW...
'KAY.
バキ
WHOOOAA!!
YIEEK!!
ズーン..
きゅう
CARROT-CHAN! CARROT-CHAN!
CARR--
ぎゅう

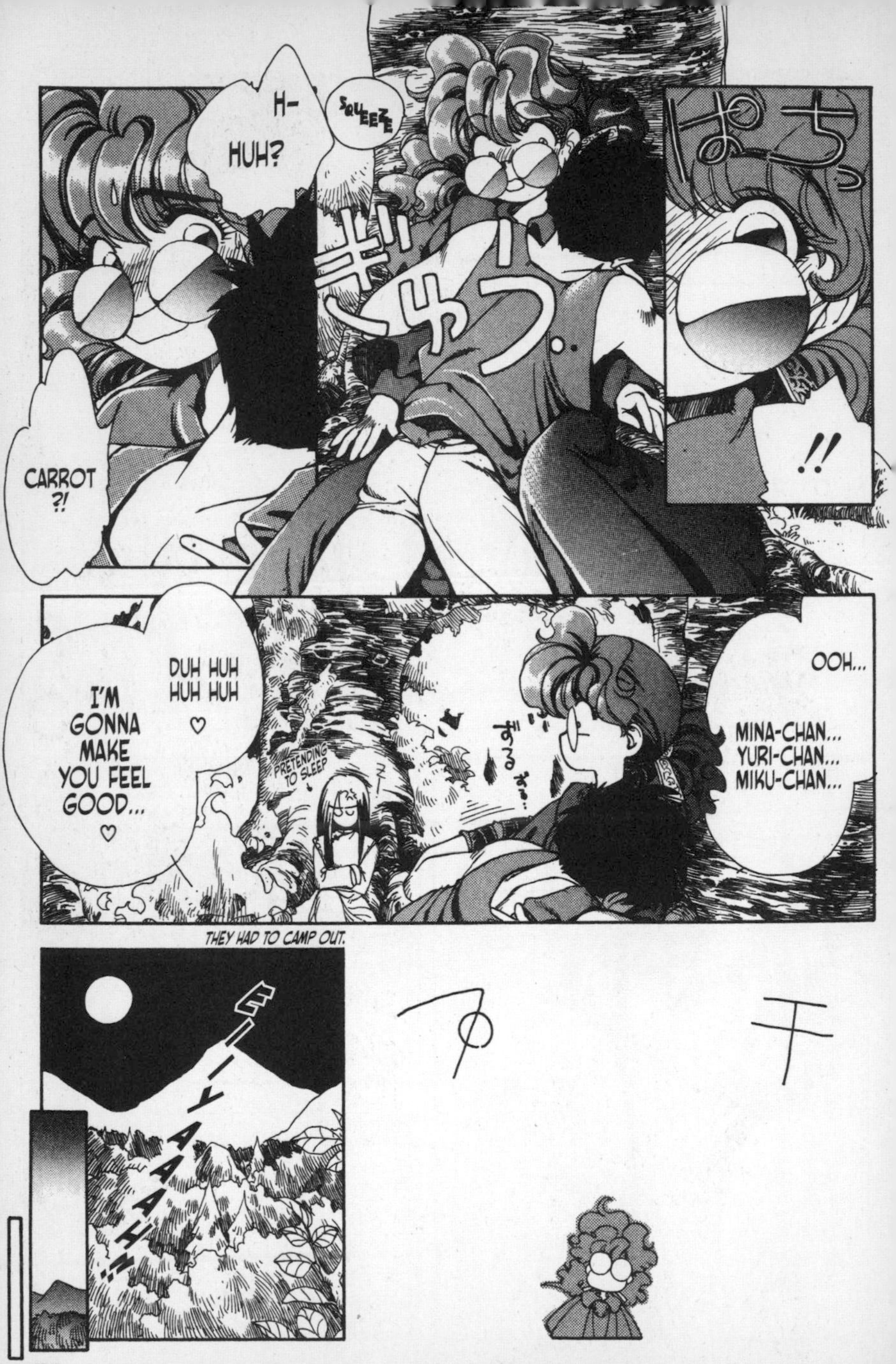
はっ
!!
SQUEEZE
ぎゅっ
H- HUH?
CARROT ?!
OOH... MINA-CHAN... YURI-CHAN... MIKU-CHAN...
ずるずる...
PRETENDING TO SLEEP
DUH HUH HUH HUH ♡
I'M GONNA MAKE YOU FEEL GOOD... ♡
THEY HAD TO CAMP OUT.
オチ
EIIYAAAAAH!!

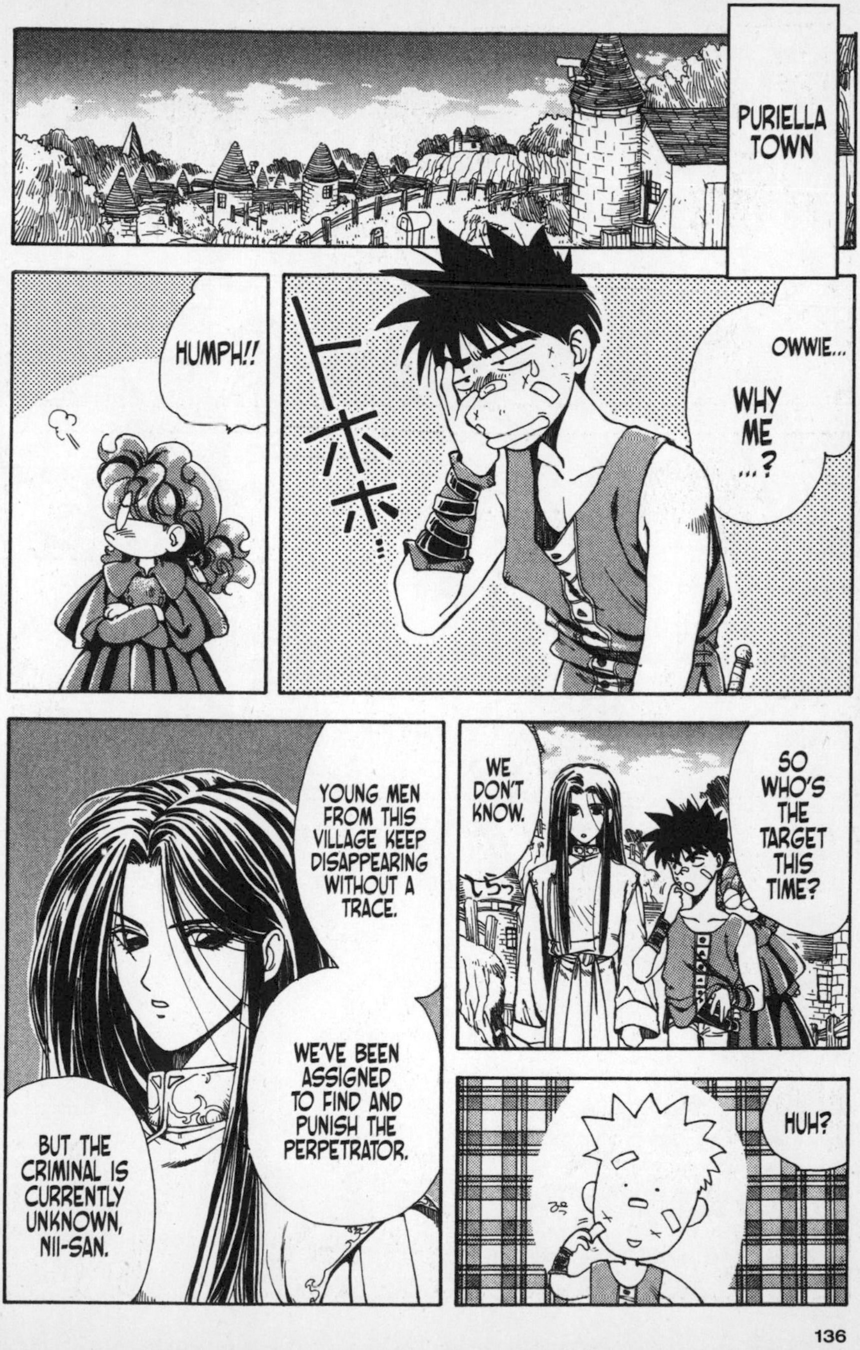
PURIELLA TOWN
OWWIE...
WHY ME ...?
トホホ...
HUMPH!!
SO WHO'S THE TARGET THIS TIME?
WE DON'T KNOW.
HUH?
YOUNG MEN FROM THIS VILLAGE KEEP DISAPPEARING WITHOUT A TRACE.
WE'VE BEEN ASSIGNED TO FIND AND PUNISH THE PERPETRATOR.
BUT THE CRIMINAL IS CURRENTLY UNKNOWN, NII-SAN.

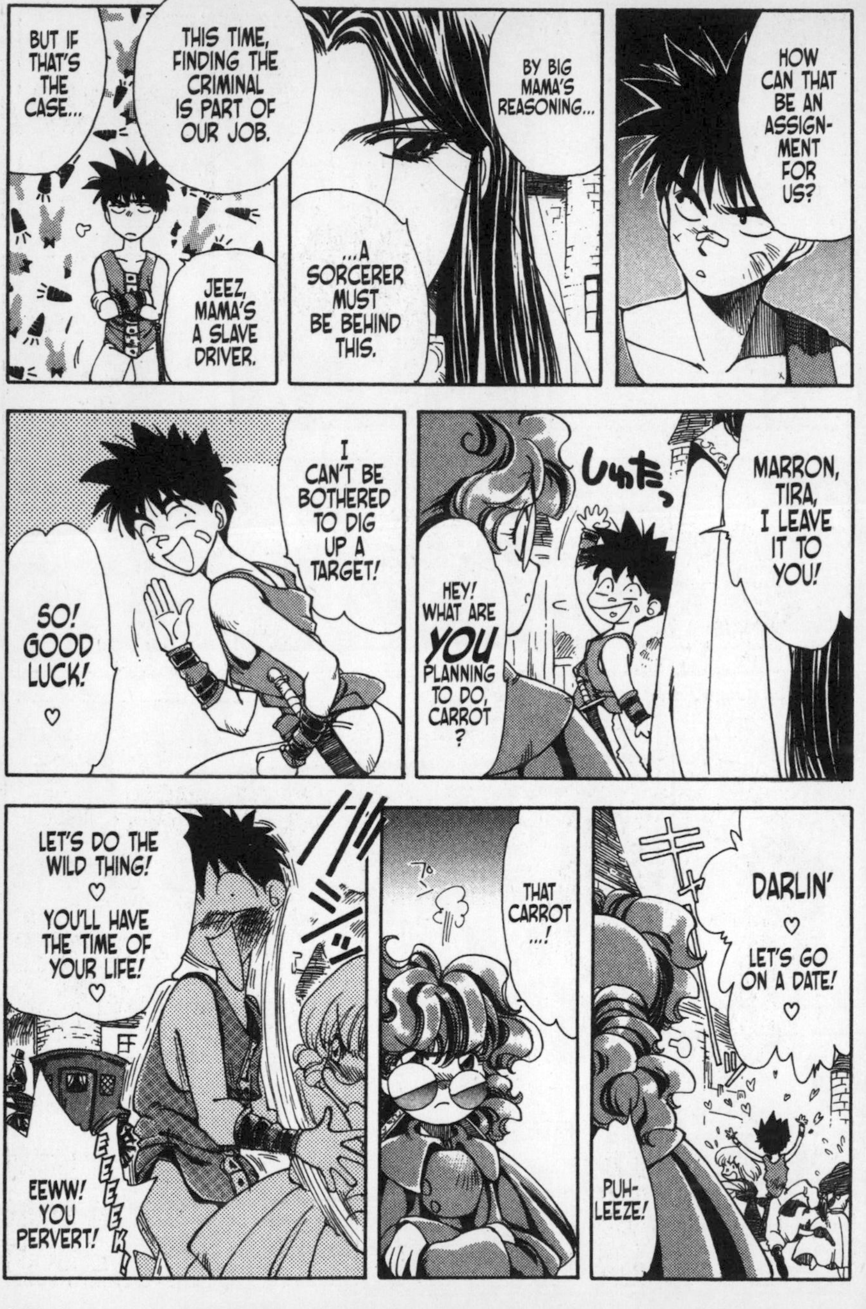
HOW CAN THAT BE AN ASSIGNMENT FOR US?
BY BIG MAMA'S REASONING...
...A SORCERER MUST BE BEHIND THIS.
THIS TIME, FINDING THE CRIMINAL IS PART OF OUR JOB.
BUT IF THAT'S THE CASE...
JEEZ, MAMA'S A SLAVE DRIVER.
MARRON, TIRA, I LEAVE IT TO YOU!
しゅたっ
HEY! WHAT ARE YOU PLANNING TO DO, CARROT?
I CAN'T BE BOTHERED TO DIG UP A TARGET!
SO! GOOD LUCK! ♡
DARLIN' ♡ LET'S GO ON A DATE! ♡
PUH-LEEZE!
THAT CARROT ...!
LET'S DO THE WILD THING! ♡
YOU'LL HAVE THE TIME OF YOUR LIFE! ♡
EEEEEK!
EEWW! YOU PERVERT!

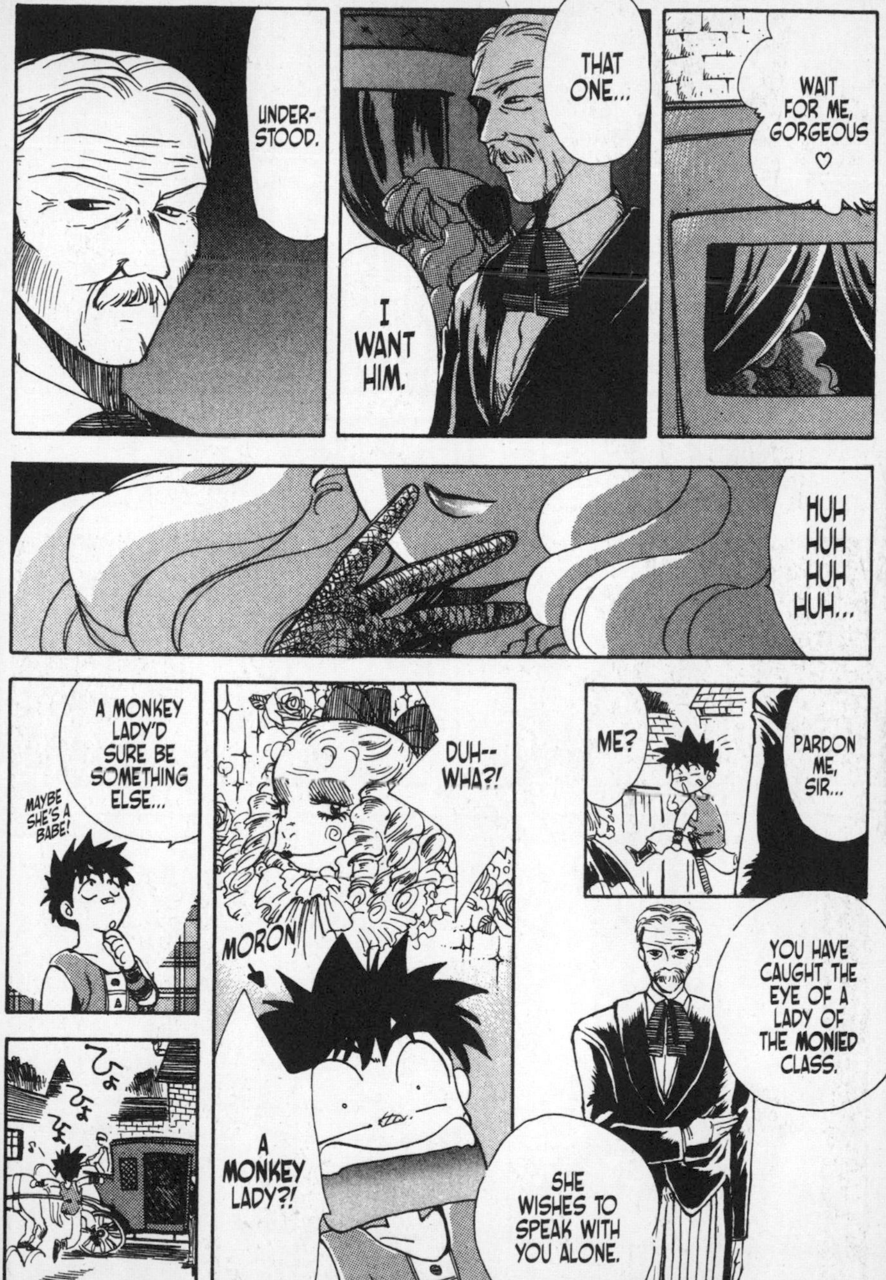
WAIT FOR ME, GORGEOUS ♡
THAT ONE...
I WANT HIM.
UNDER-STOOD.
HUH HUH HUH HUH...
PARDON ME, SIR...
ME?
YOU HAVE CAUGHT THE EYE OF A LADY OF THE MONIED CLASS.
SHE WISHES TO SPEAK WITH YOU ALONE.
DUH--WHA?!
MORON
A MONKEY LADY?!
A MONKEY LADY'D SURE BE SOMETHING ELSE...
MAYBE SHE'S A BABE!
ひょ ひょ ひょ

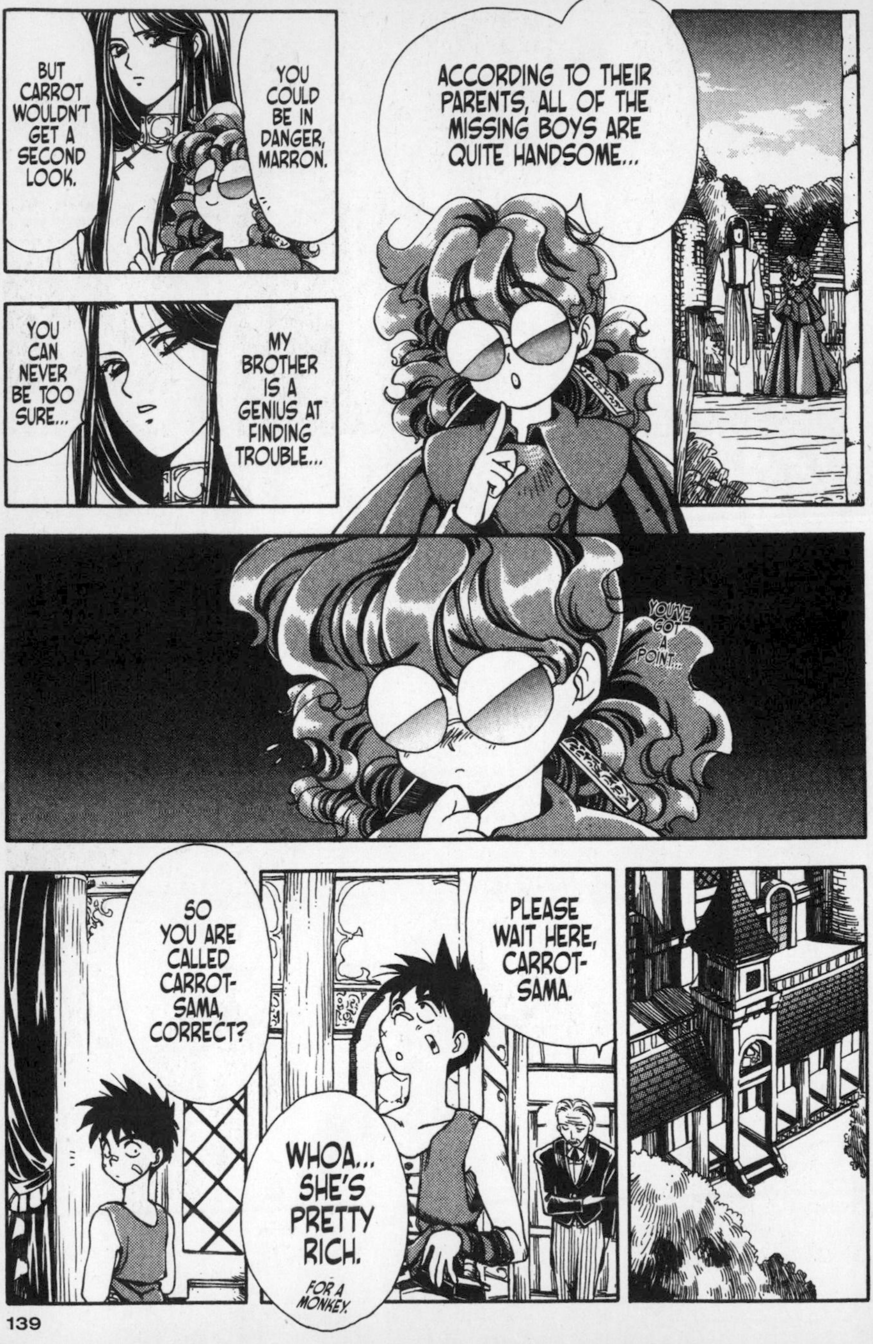
ACCORDING TO THEIR PARENTS, ALL OF THE MISSING BOYS ARE QUITE HANDSOME...
YOU COULD BE IN DANGER, MARRON.
BUT CARROT WOULDN'T GET A SECOND LOOK.
MY BROTHER IS A GENIUS AT FINDING TROUBLE...
YOU CAN NEVER BE TOO SURE...
YOU'VE GOT A POINT...
PLEASE WAIT HERE, CARROT-SAMA.
WHOA... SHE'S PRETTY RICH.
FOR A MONKEY.
SO YOU ARE CALLED CARROT-SAMA, CORRECT?

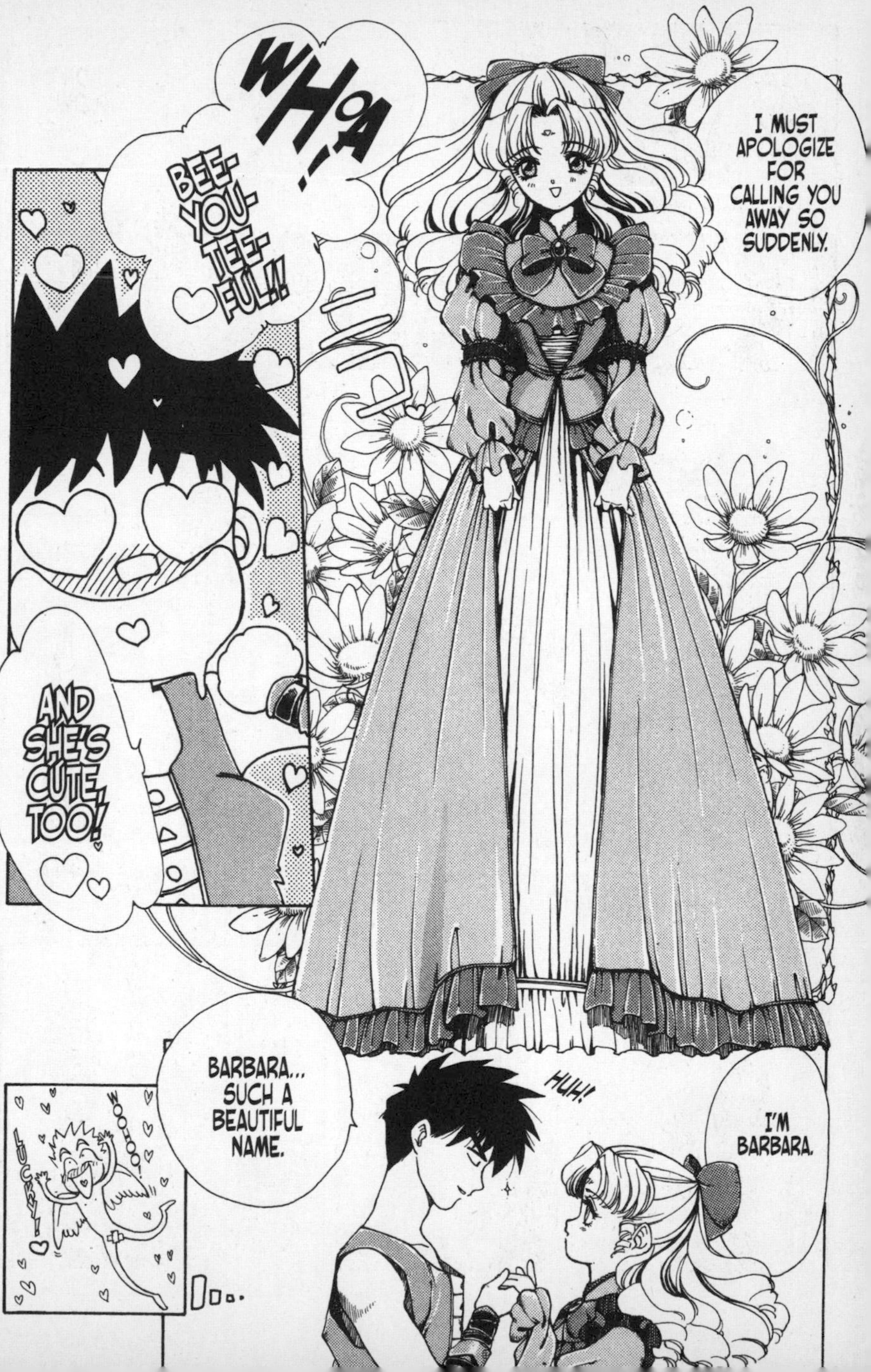
I MUST APOLOGIZE FOR CALLING YOU AWAY SO SUDDENLY.
WHOA!!
BEE-YOU-TEE-FUL!!
AND SHE'S CUTE, TOO!
I'M BARBARA.
HUH!
BARBARA... SUCH A BEAUTIFUL NAME.
WOO-HOO!
LUCKY!

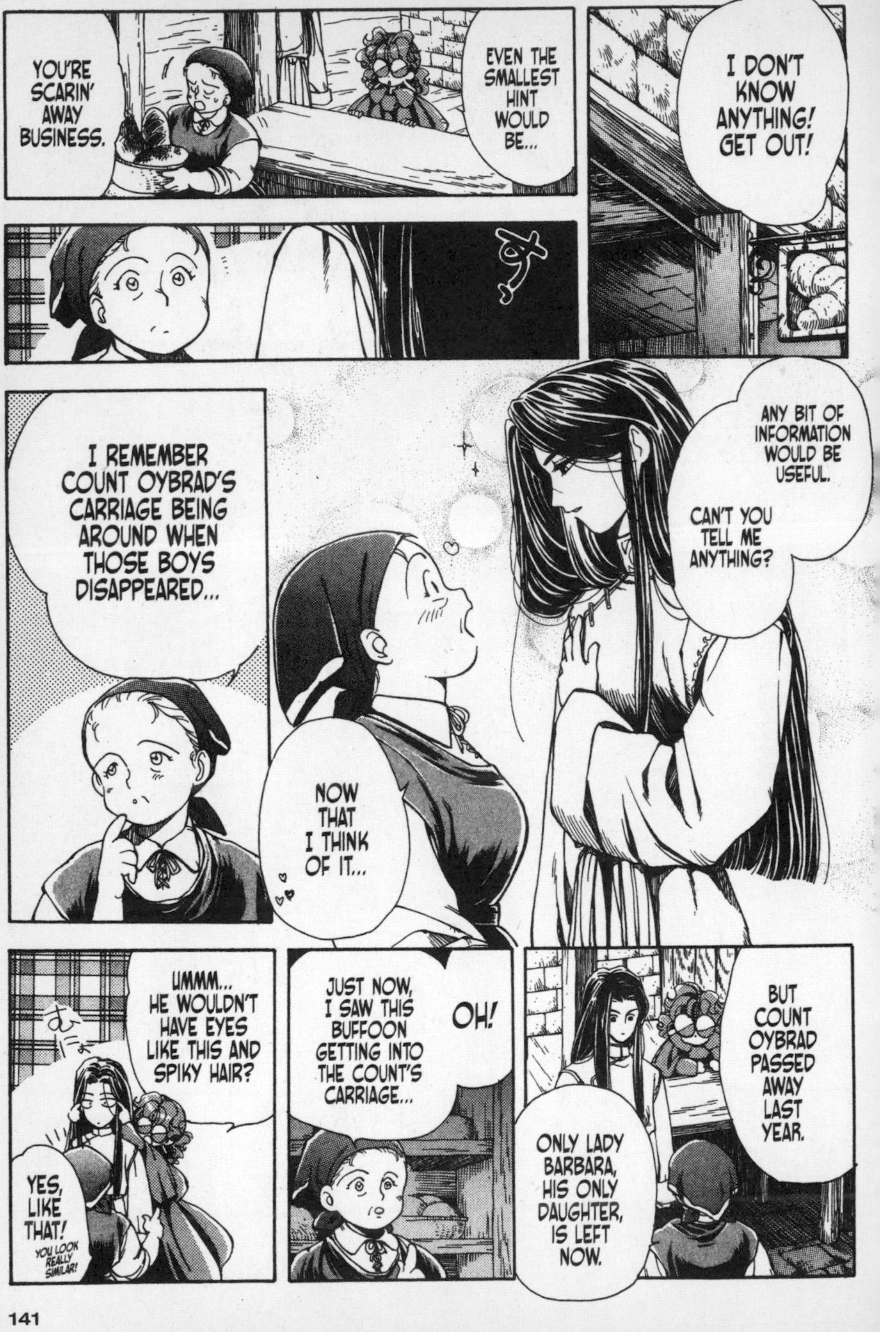
I DON'T KNOW ANYTHING! GET OUT!
EVEN THE SMALLEST HINT WOULD BE...
YOU'RE SCARIN' AWAY BUSINESS.
す
ANY BIT OF INFORMATION WOULD BE USEFUL.
CAN'T YOU TELL ME ANYTHING?
NOW THAT I THINK OF IT...
I REMEMBER COUNT OYBRAD'S CARRIAGE BEING AROUND WHEN THOSE BOYS DISAPPEARED...
BUT COUNT OYBRAD PASSED AWAY LAST YEAR.
ONLY LADY BARBARA, HIS ONLY DAUGHTER, IS LEFT NOW.
OH!
JUST NOW, I SAW THIS BUFFOON GETTING INTO THE COUNT'S CARRIAGE...
UMMM... HE WOULDN'T HAVE EYES LIKE THIS AND SPIKY HAIR?
YES, LIKE THAT!
YOU LOOK REALLY SIMILAR!

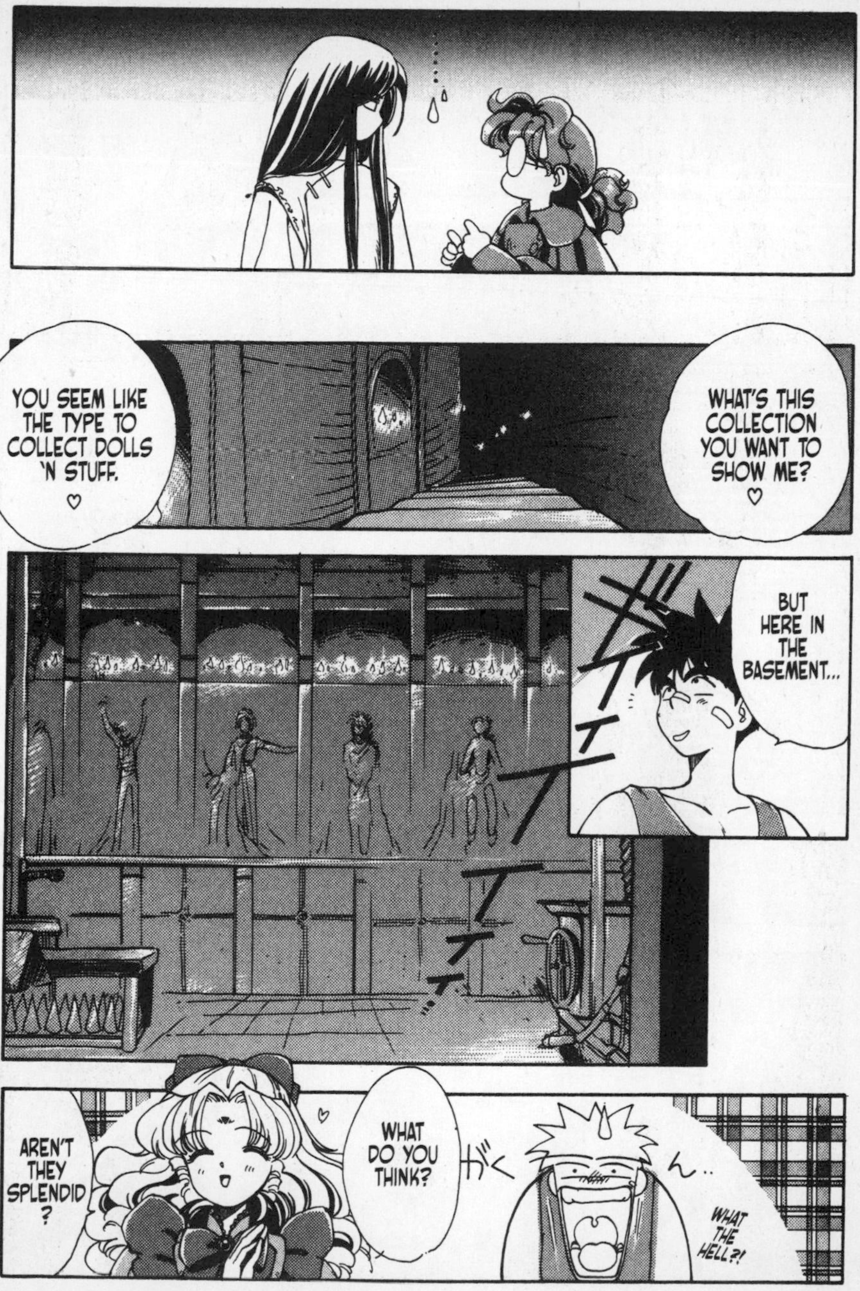
WHAT'S THIS COLLECTION YOU WANT TO SHOW ME? ♡
YOU SEEM LIKE THE TYPE TO COLLECT DOLLS 'N STUFF. ♡
BUT HERE IN THE BASEMENT...
WHAT THE HELL?!
ん..
がく
WHAT DO YOU THINK?
AREN'T THEY SPLENDID?

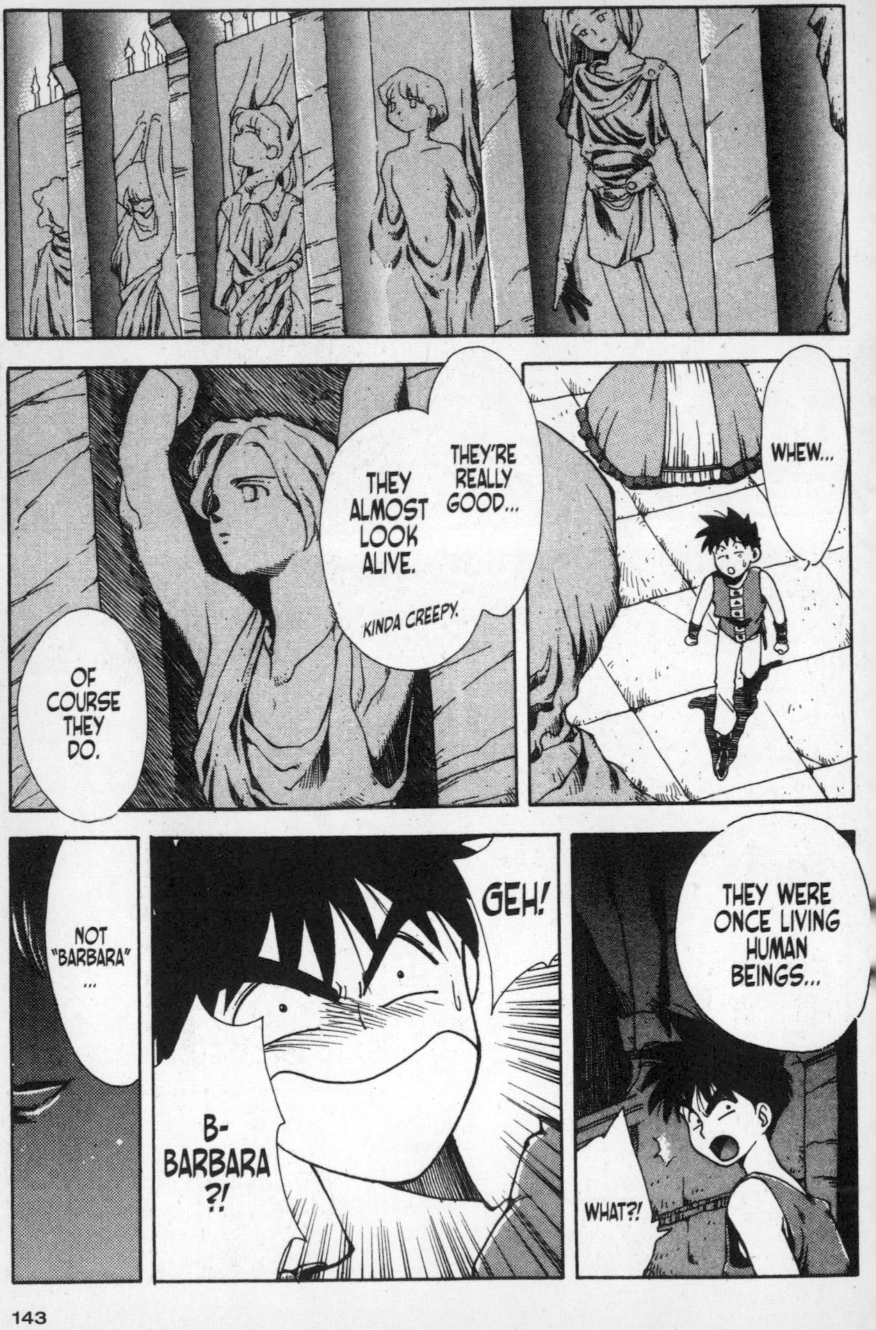
WHEW...
THEY'RE REALLY GOOD...
THEY ALMOST LOOK ALIVE.
KINDA CREEPY.
OF COURSE THEY DO.
THEY WERE ONCE LIVING HUMAN BEINGS...
WHAT?!
GEH!
B-BARBARA?!
NOT "BARBARA" ...

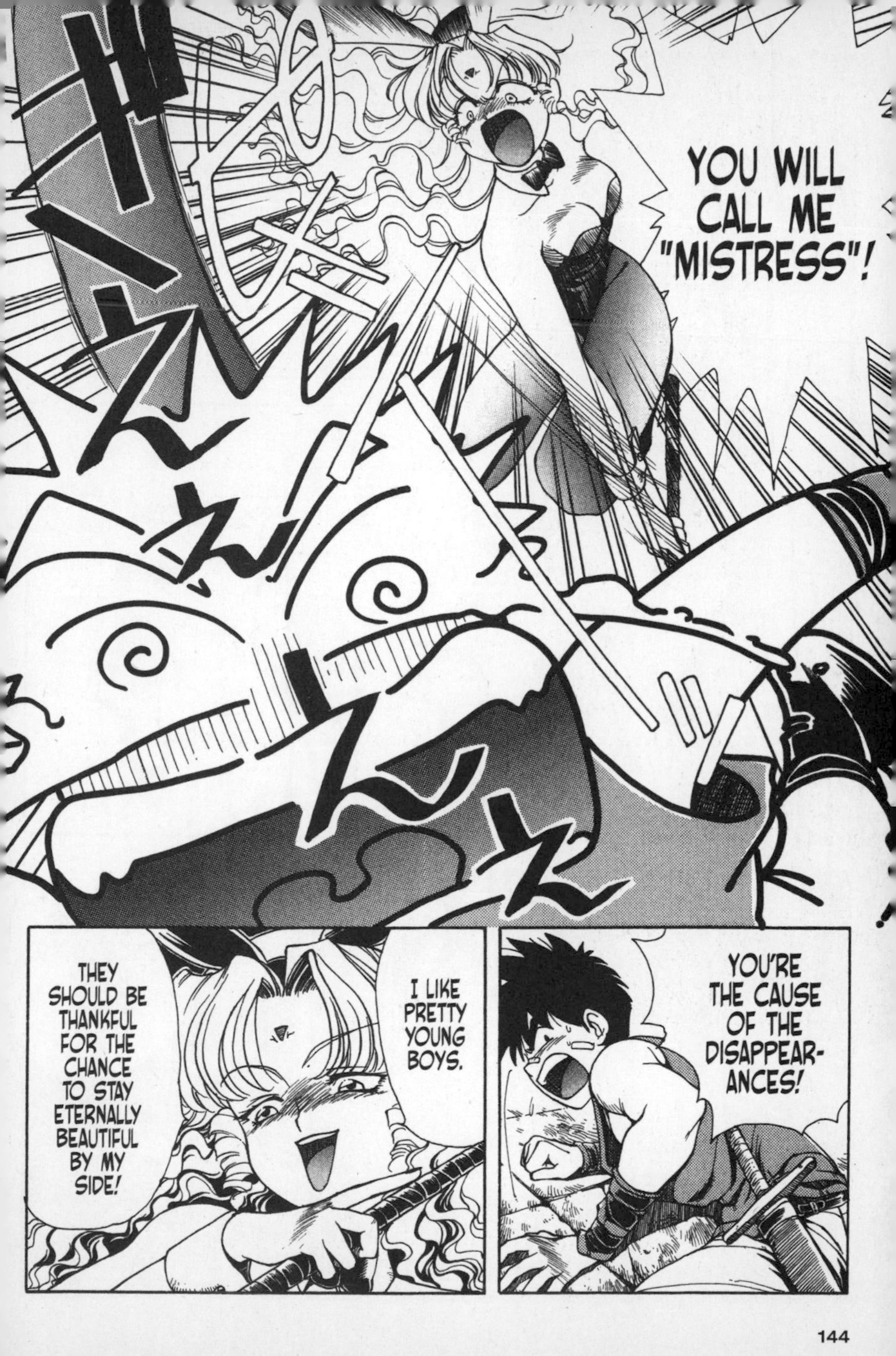
YOU WILL CALL ME "MISTRESS"!
YOU'RE THE CAUSE OF THE DISAPPEAR-ANCES!
I LIKE PRETTY YOUNG BOYS.
THEY SHOULD BE THANKFUL FOR THE CHANCE TO STAY ETERNALLY BEAUTIFUL BY MY SIDE!

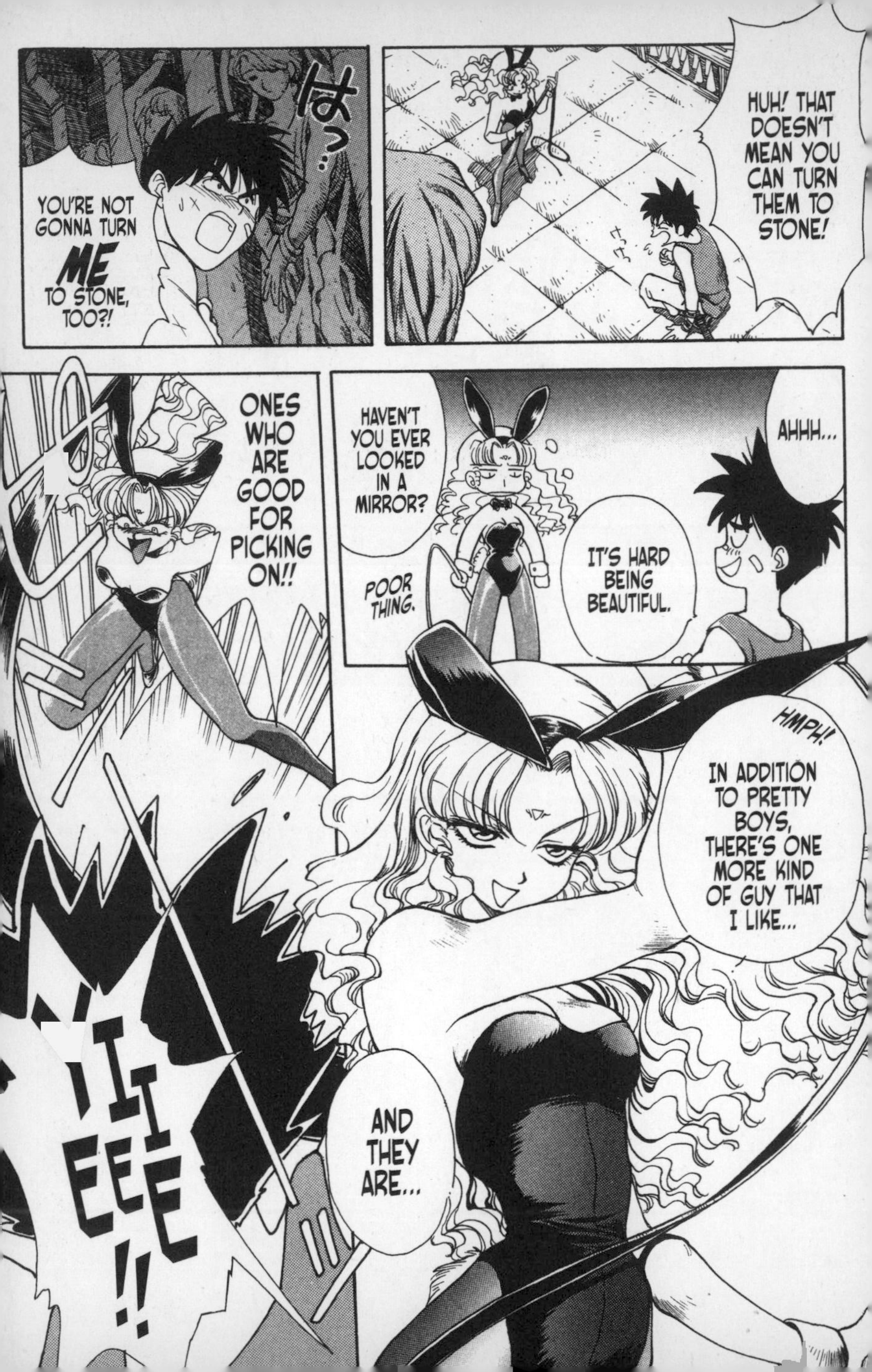
HUH! THAT DOESN'T MEAN YOU CAN TURN THEM TO STONE!
はっ…
YOU'RE NOT GONNA TURN ME TO STONE, TOO?!
AHHH...
IT'S HARD BEING BEAUTIFUL.
HAVEN'T YOU EVER LOOKED IN A MIRROR?
POOR THING.
HMPH!
IN ADDITION TO PRETTY BOYS, THERE'S ONE MORE KIND OF GUY THAT I LIKE...
AND THEY ARE...
ONES WHO ARE GOOD FOR PICKING ON!!
IIEEE!!

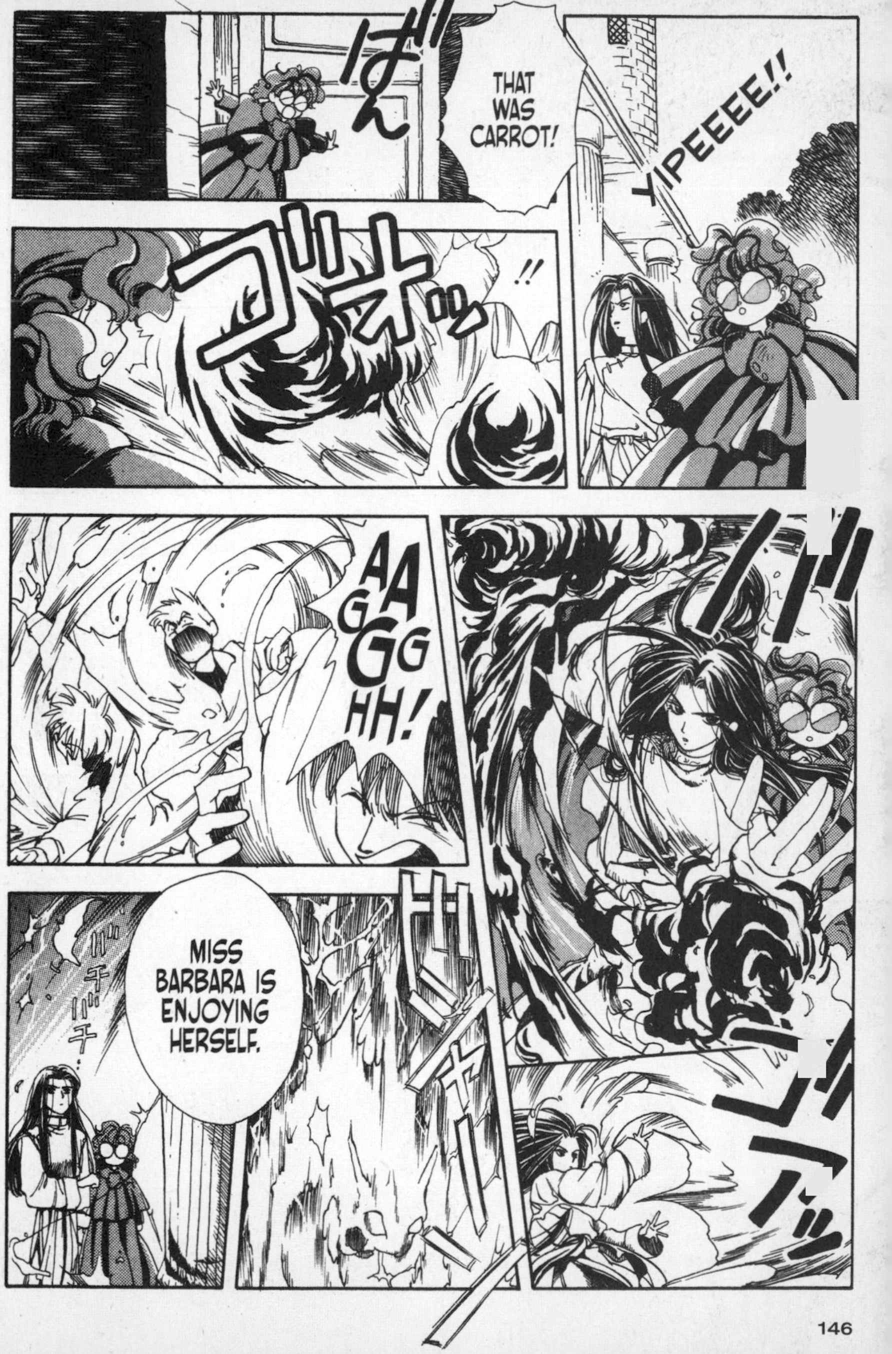
YIPEEEE!!
ばん
THAT WAS CARROT!
!!
AAGGGHH!
MISS BARBARA IS ENJOYING HERSELF.

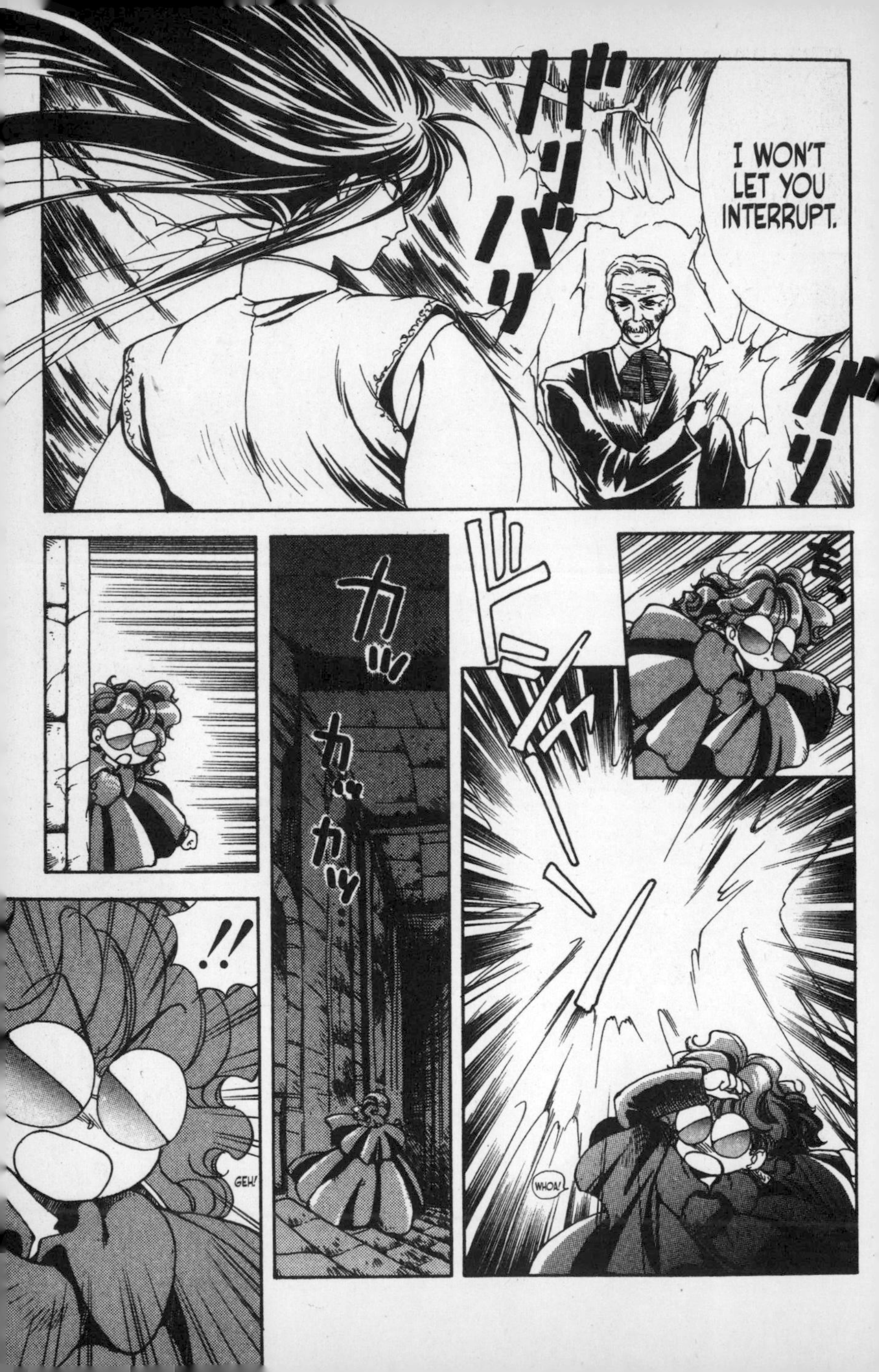
I WON'T LET YOU INTERRUPT.
WHOA!
!!
GEH!

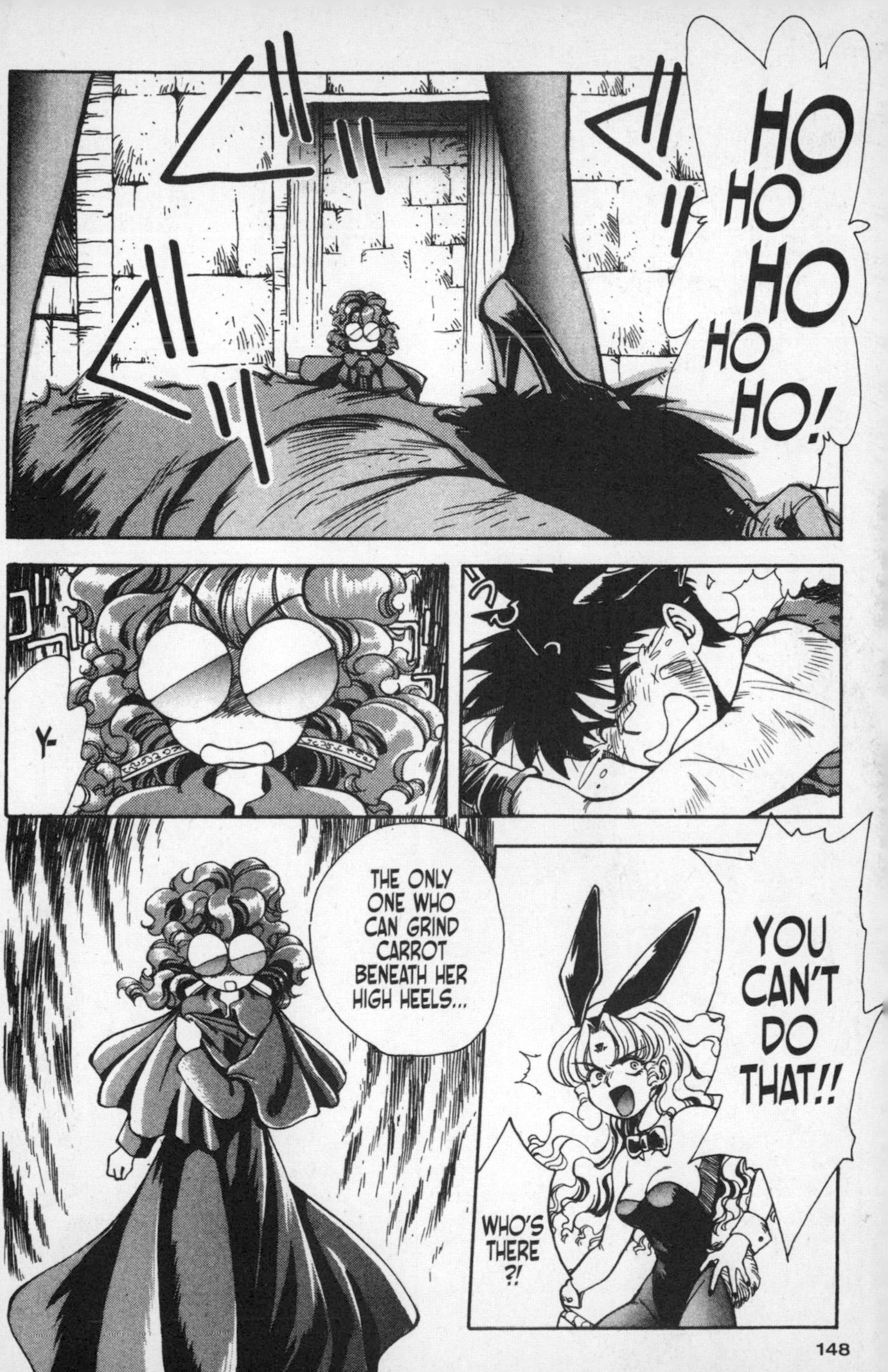
HO HO HO HO HO!
Y-
YOU CAN'T DO THAT!!
WHO'S THERE ?!
THE ONLY ONE WHO CAN GRIND CARROT BENEATH HER HIGH HEELS...

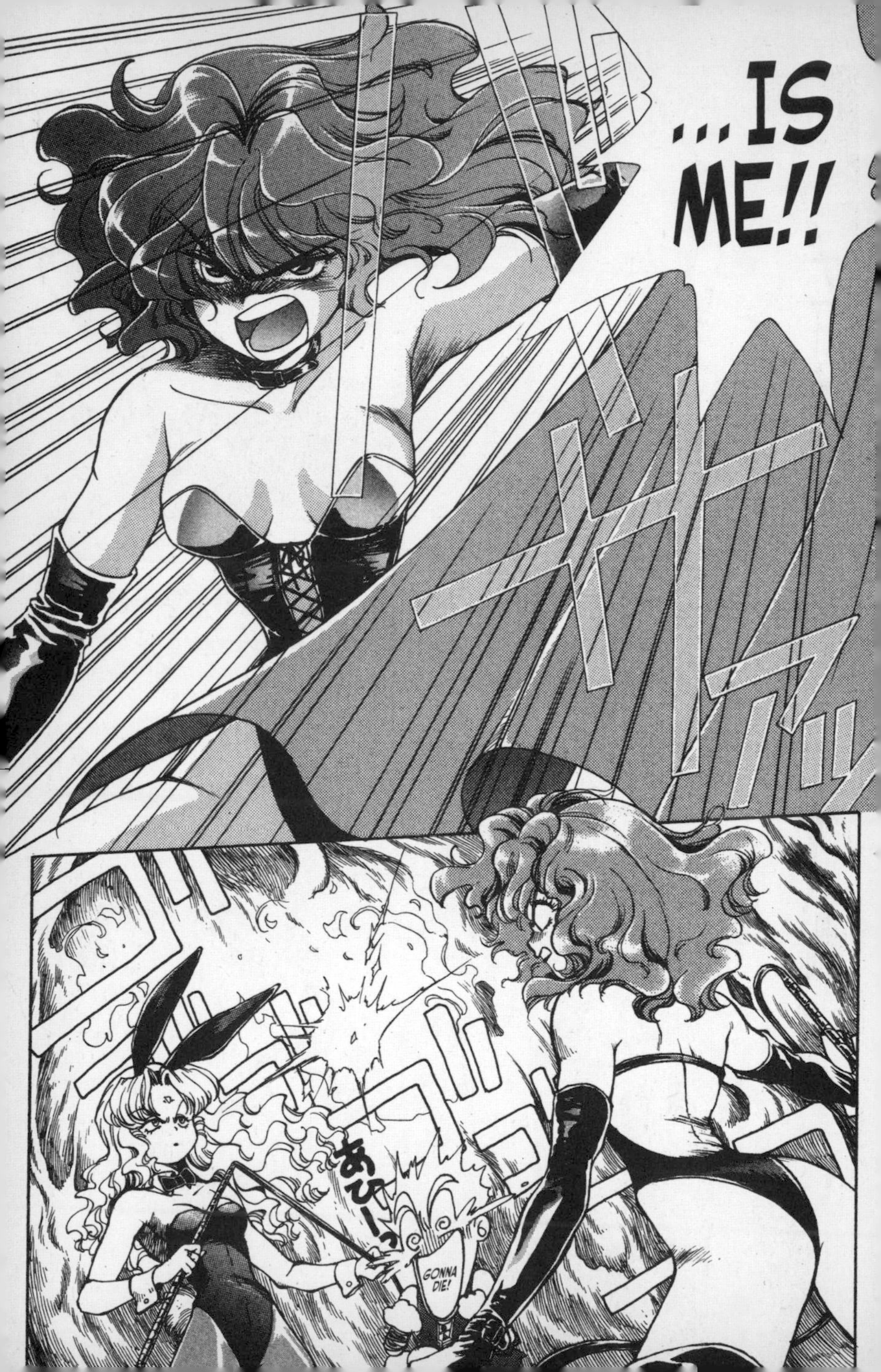
...IS ME!!
あひーっ
GONNA DIE!

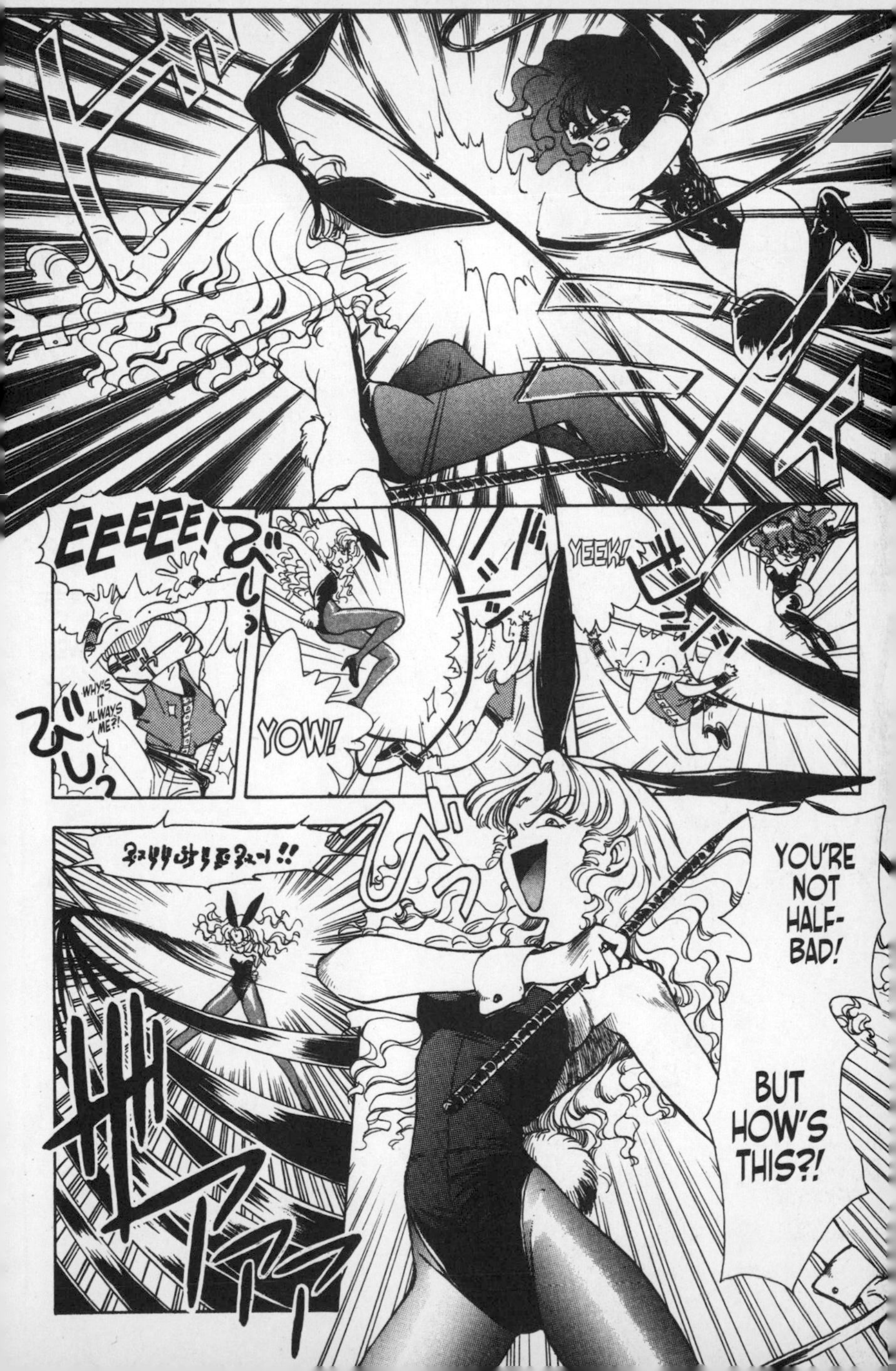
YEEK!
YOW!
EEEEEE!
WHY'S IT ALWAYS ME?!
YOU'RE NOT HALF-BAD!
BUT HOW'S THIS?!

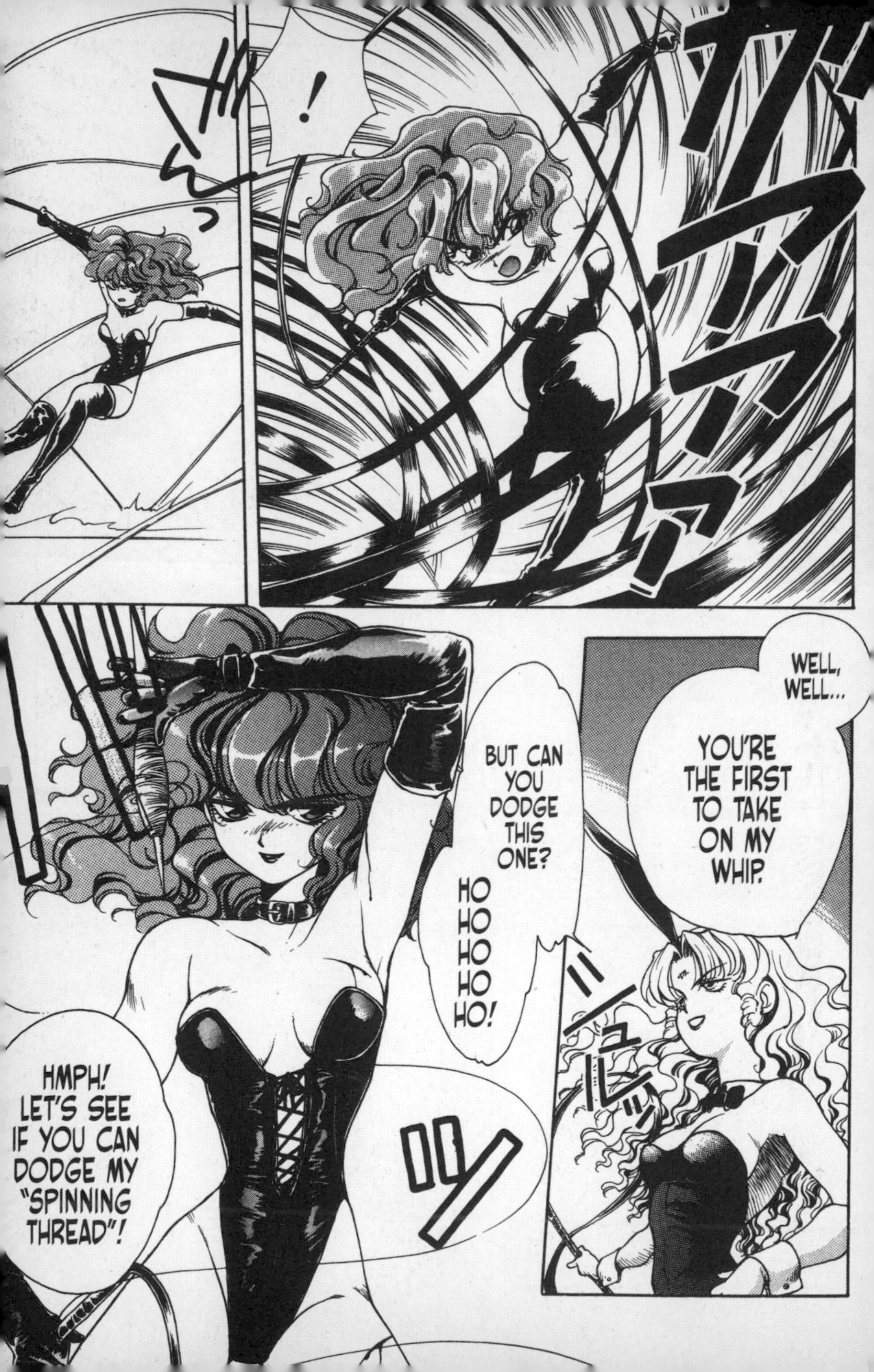
!
WELL, WELL...
YOU'RE THE FIRST TO TAKE ON MY WHIP.
BUT CAN YOU DODGE THIS ONE?
HO HO HO HO HO!
HMPH! LET'S SEE IF YOU CAN DODGE MY "SPINNING THREAD"!

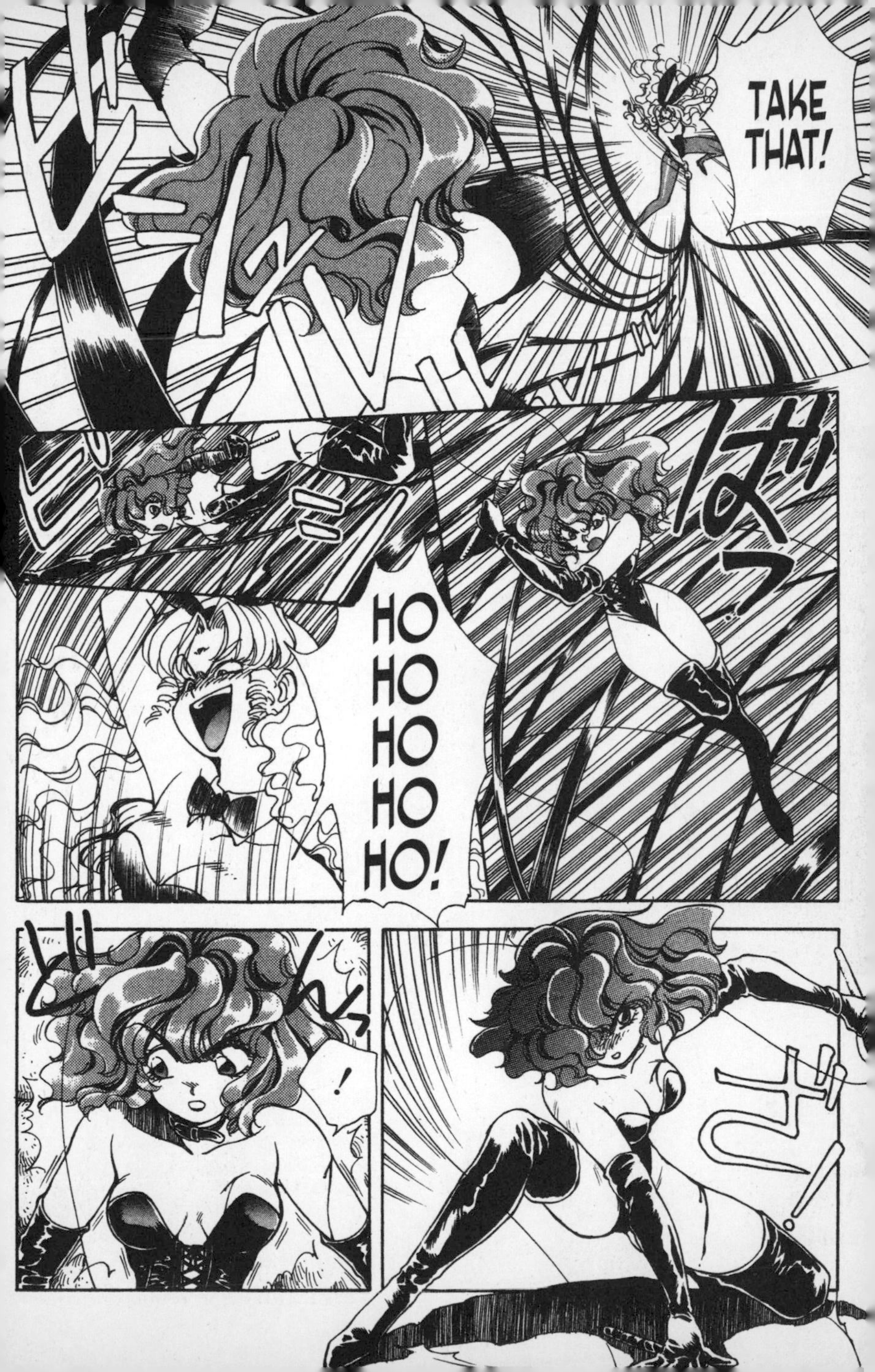
TAKE THAT!
HO HO HO HO HO!
!

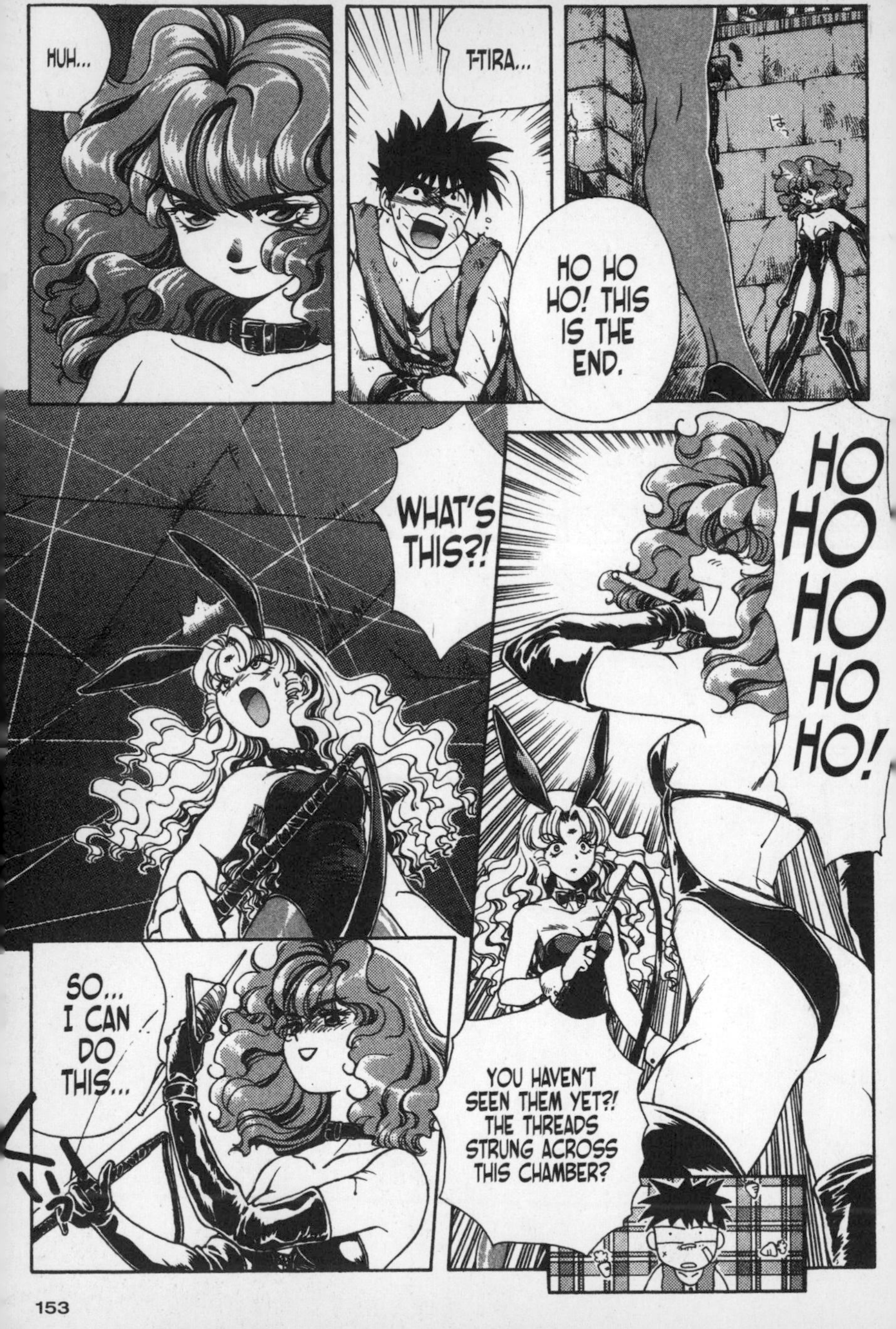
HO HO HO! THIS IS THE END.
T-TIRA...
HUH...
HO HO HO HO HO HO!
YOU HAVEN'T SEEN THEM YET?! THE THREADS STRUNG ACROSS THIS CHAMBER?
WHAT'S THIS?!
SO... I CAN DO THIS...

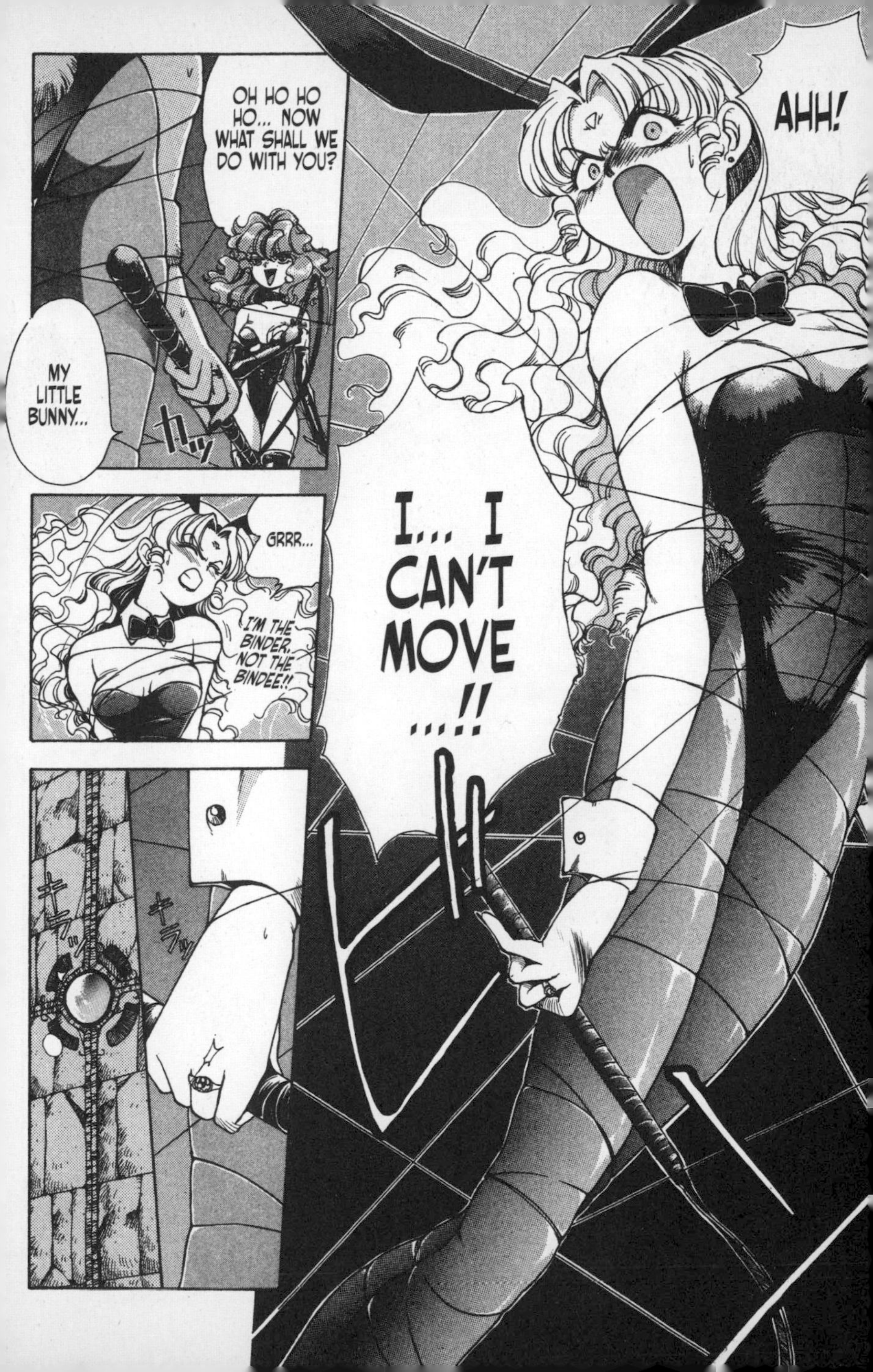

AHH!
I... I CAN'T MOVE ...!!
OH HO HO HO... NOW WHAT SHALL WE DO WITH YOU?
MY LITTLE BUNNY...
カッ
GRRR...
I'M THE BINDER, NOT THE BINDEE!!
キラッ
キラッ

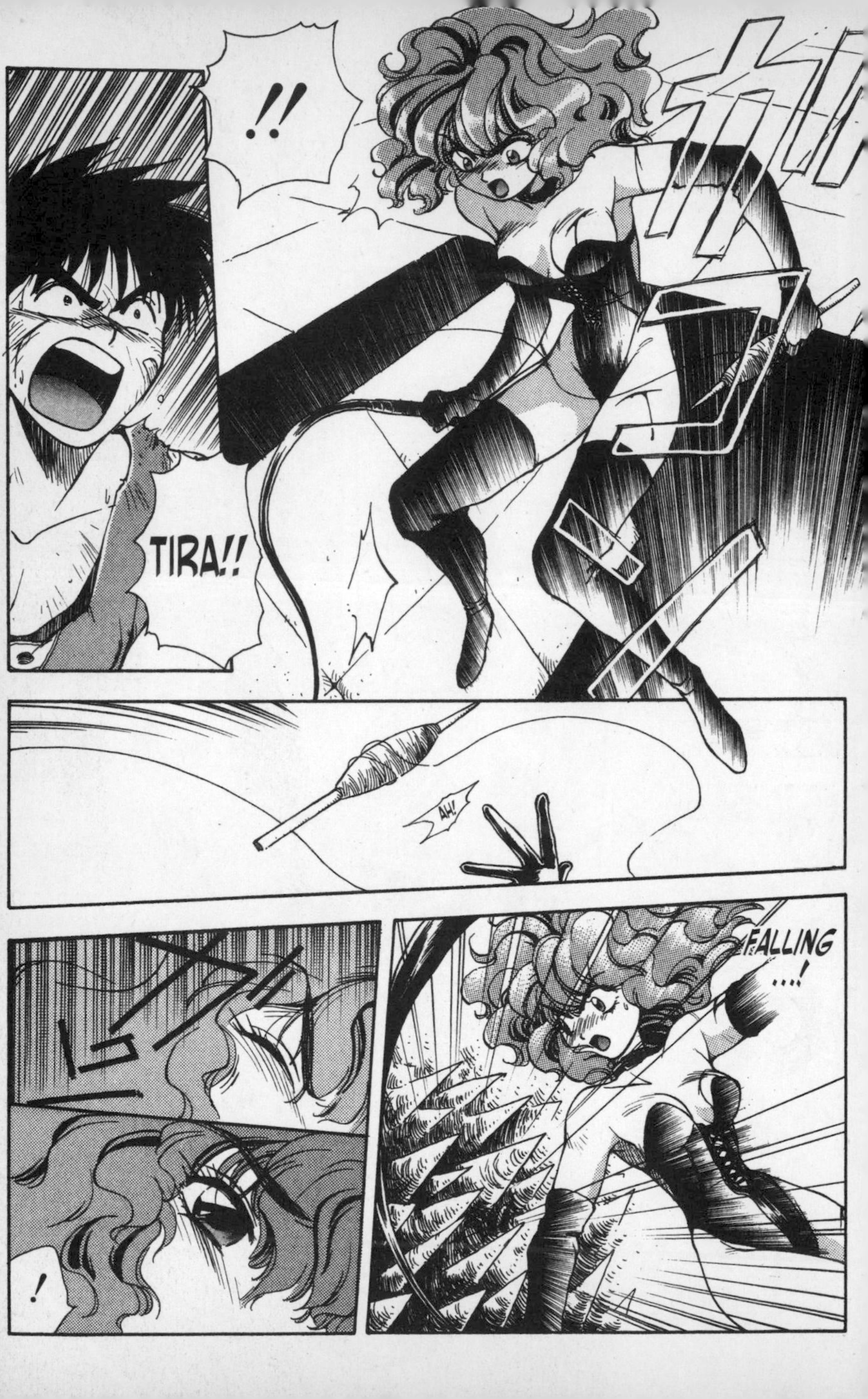
!!
TIRA!!
AH!
FALLING ...!
!

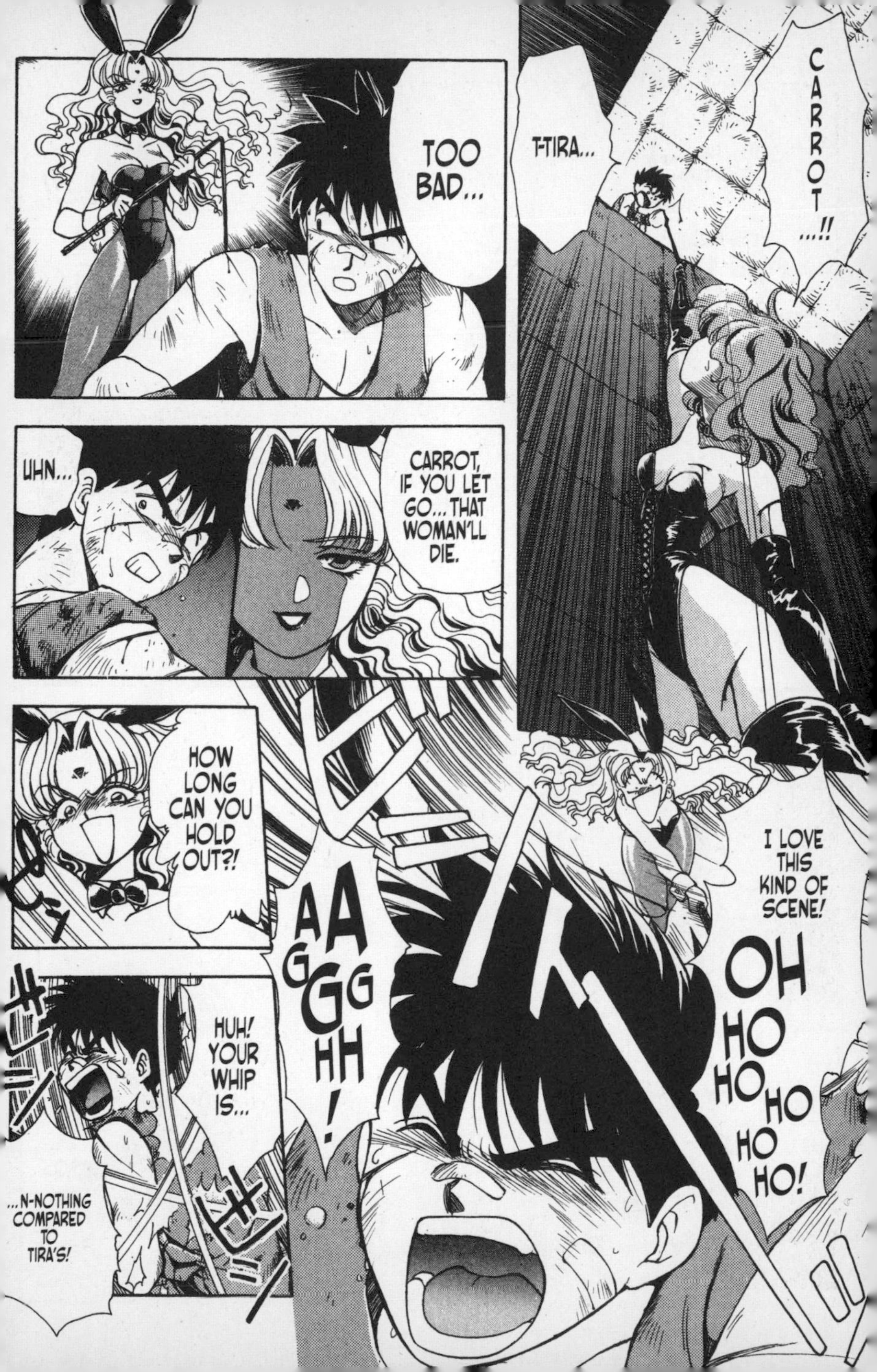

CARROT...!!
T-TIRA...
TOO BAD...
CARROT, IF YOU LET GO... THAT WOMAN'LL DIE.
UHN...
I LOVE THIS KIND OF SCENE!
OH HO HO HO HO HO HO!
AAGGGHH!
HOW LONG CAN YOU HOLD OUT?!
HUH! YOUR WHIP IS...
...N-NOTHING COMPARED TO TIRA'S!

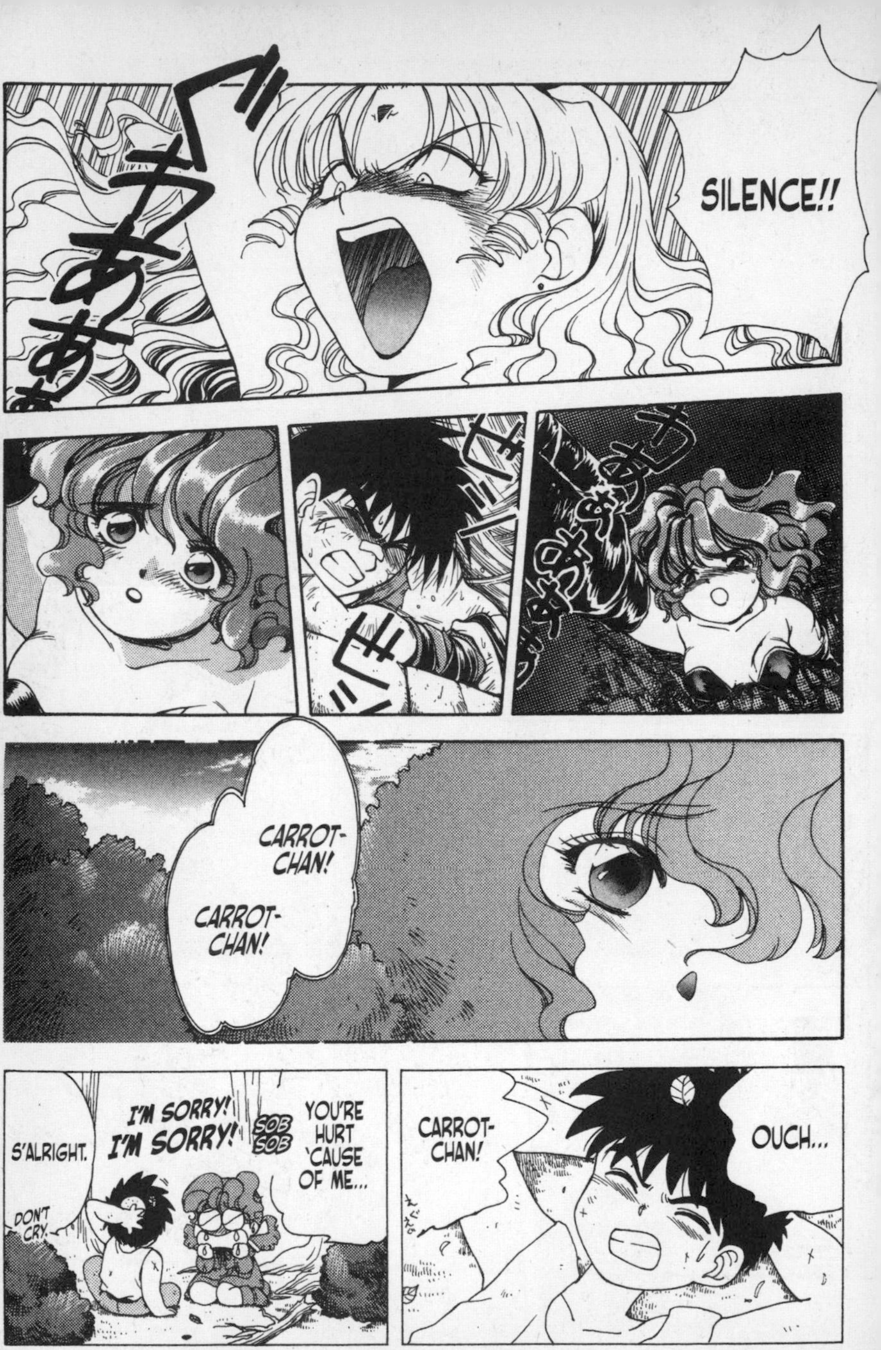
SILENCE!!
CARROT-CHAN!
CARROT-CHAN!
OUCH...
CARROT-CHAN!
YOU'RE HURT 'CAUSE OF ME...
SOB SOB
I'M SORRY! I'M SORRY!
S'ALRIGHT.
DON'T CRY.

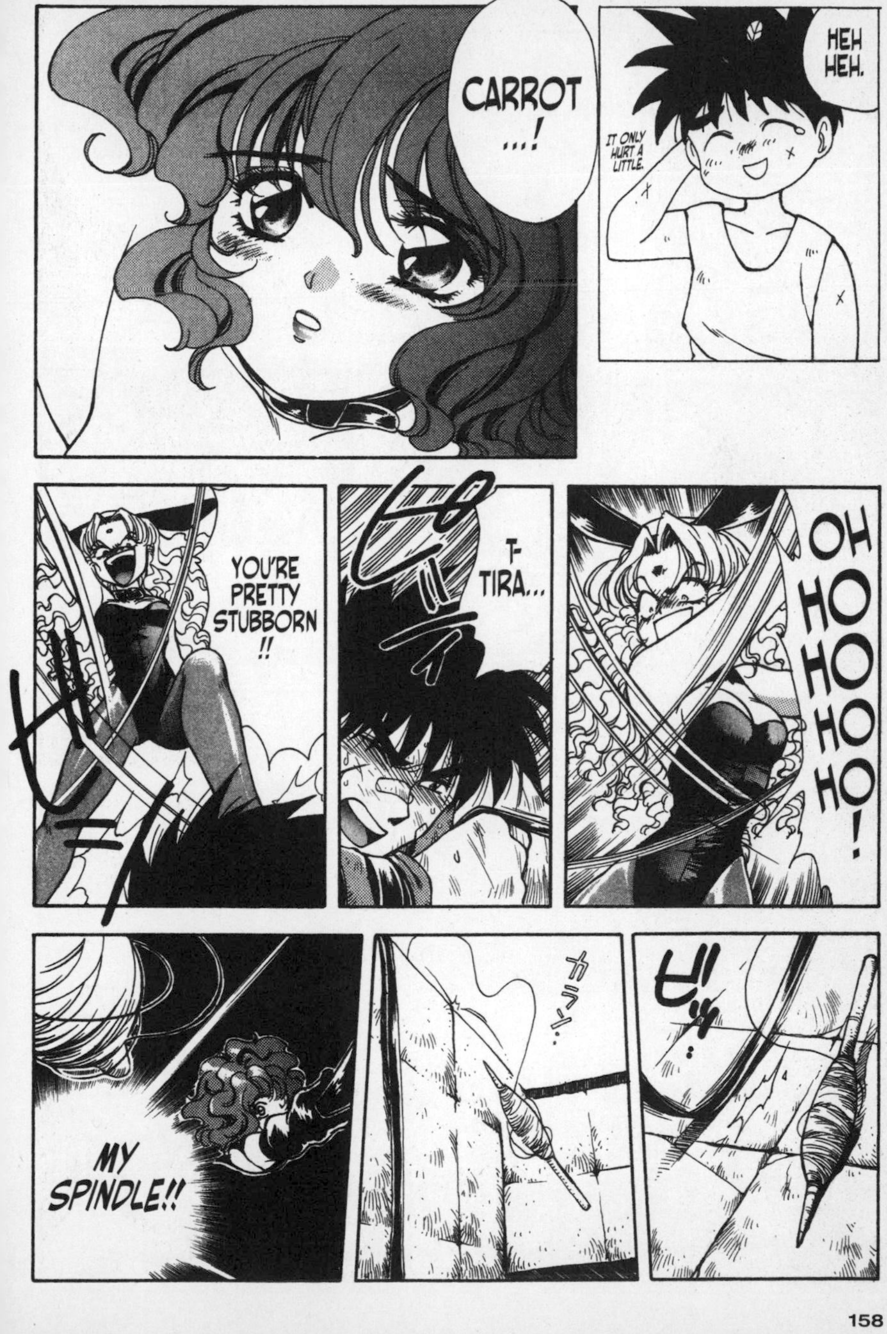
HEH HEH.
IT ONLY HURT A LITTLE.
CARROT ...!
OH HO HO HO HO HO!
T-TIRA...
YOU'RE PRETTY STUBBORN !!
MY SPINDLE!!

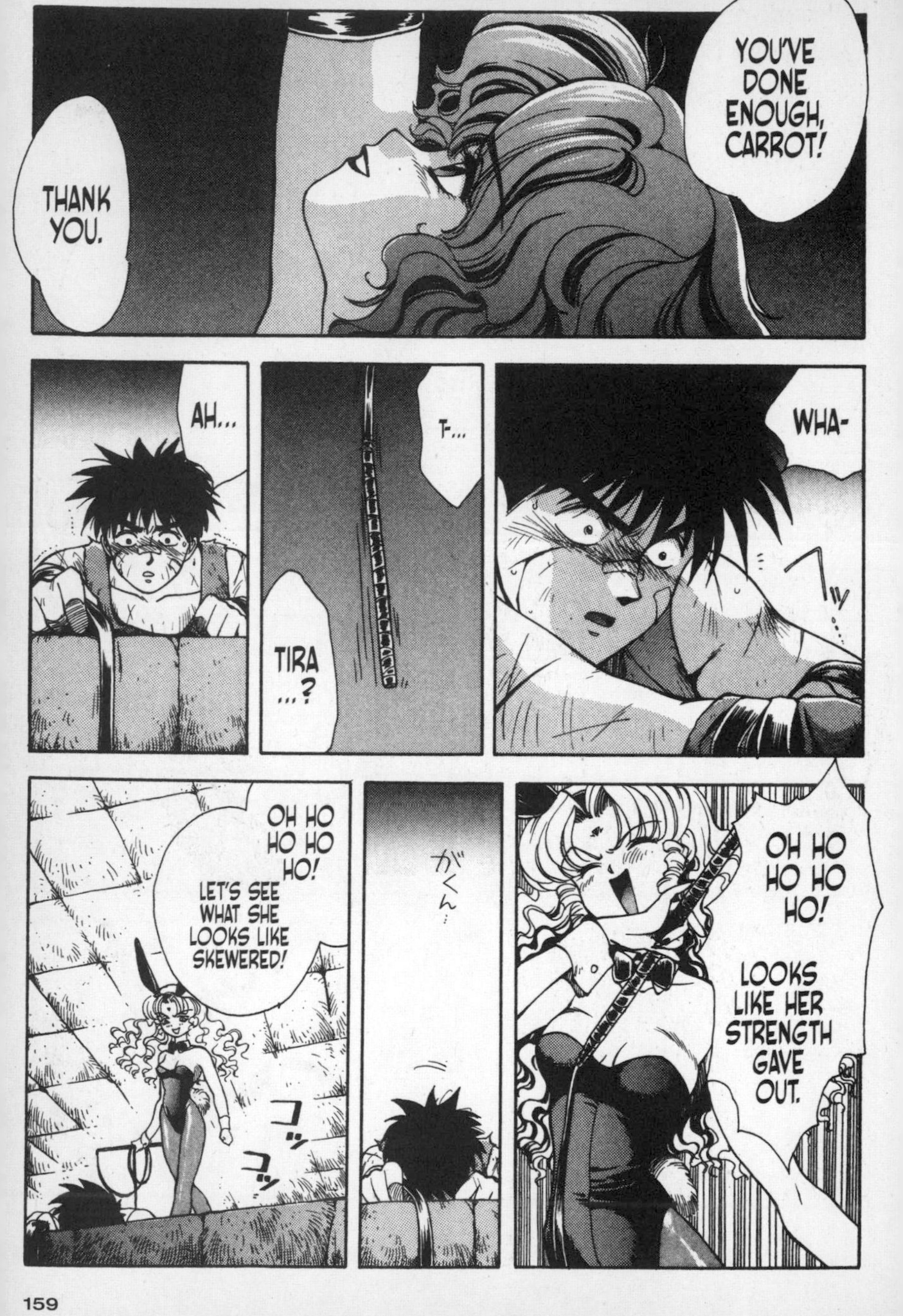
YOU'VE DONE ENOUGH, CARROT!
THANK YOU.
WHA-
ヘッ…
T-...
TIRA ...?
AH...
OH HO HO HO HO!
LOOKS LIKE HER STRENGTH GAVE OUT.
がくん…
OH HO HO HO HO! LET'S SEE WHAT SHE LOOKS LIKE SKEWERED!
コッ
コッ

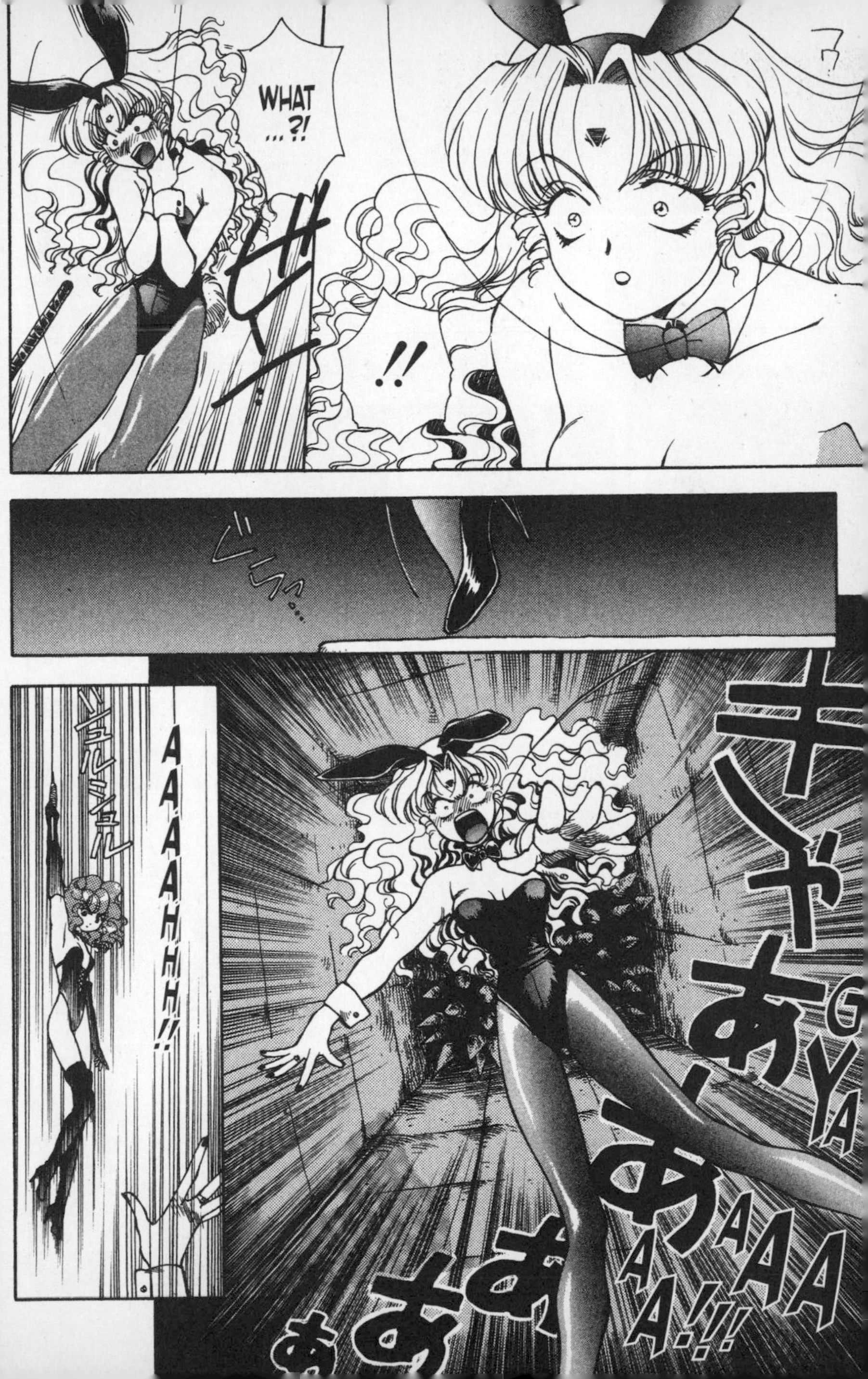
!!
WHAT ...?!
GYAAAAAAA!!!
AAAAAHHHH!!

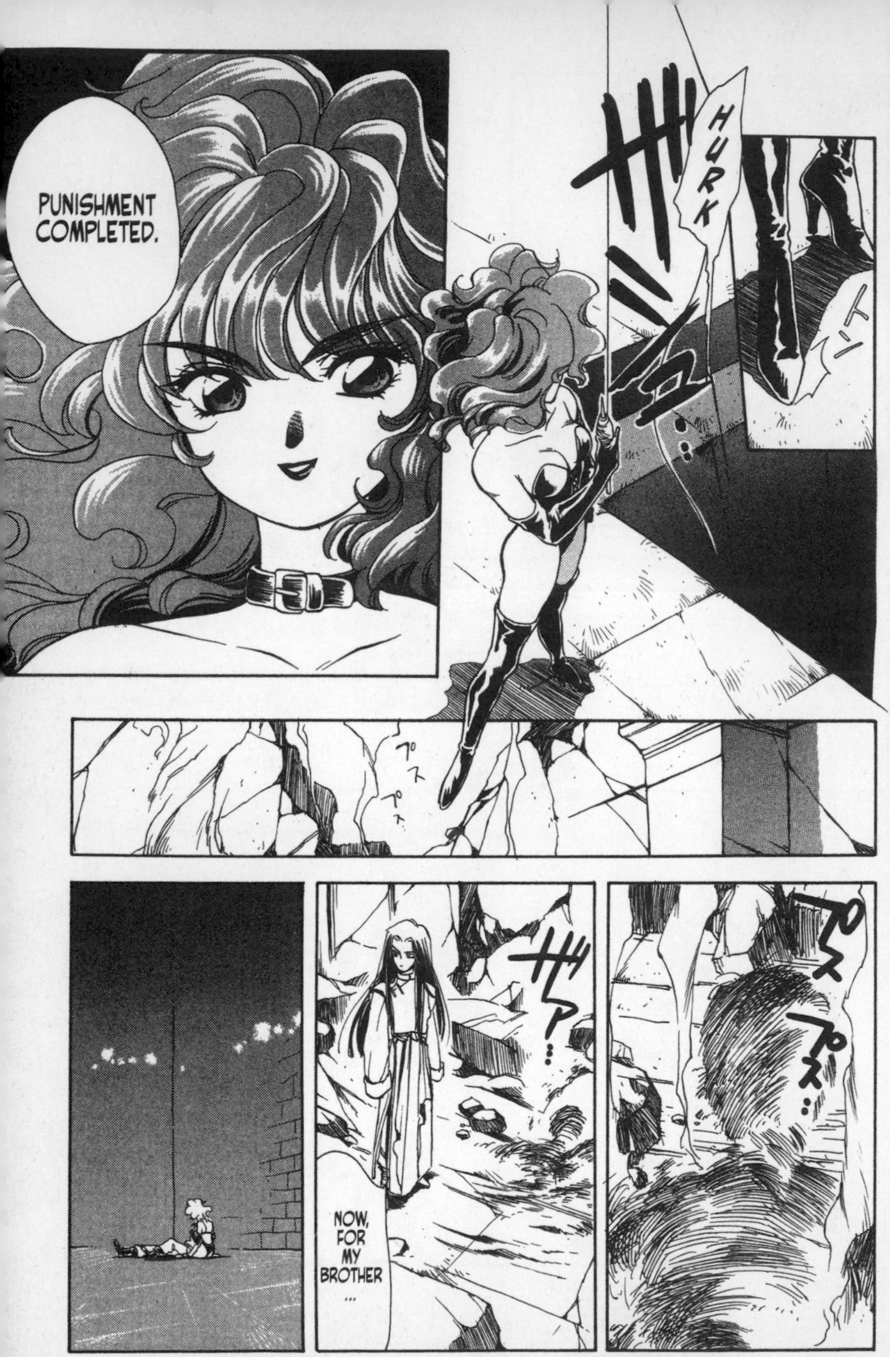
HURK
トン
PUNISHMENT COMPLETED.
プス プス…
プス プス…
ザァ…
NOW, FOR MY BROTHER ...

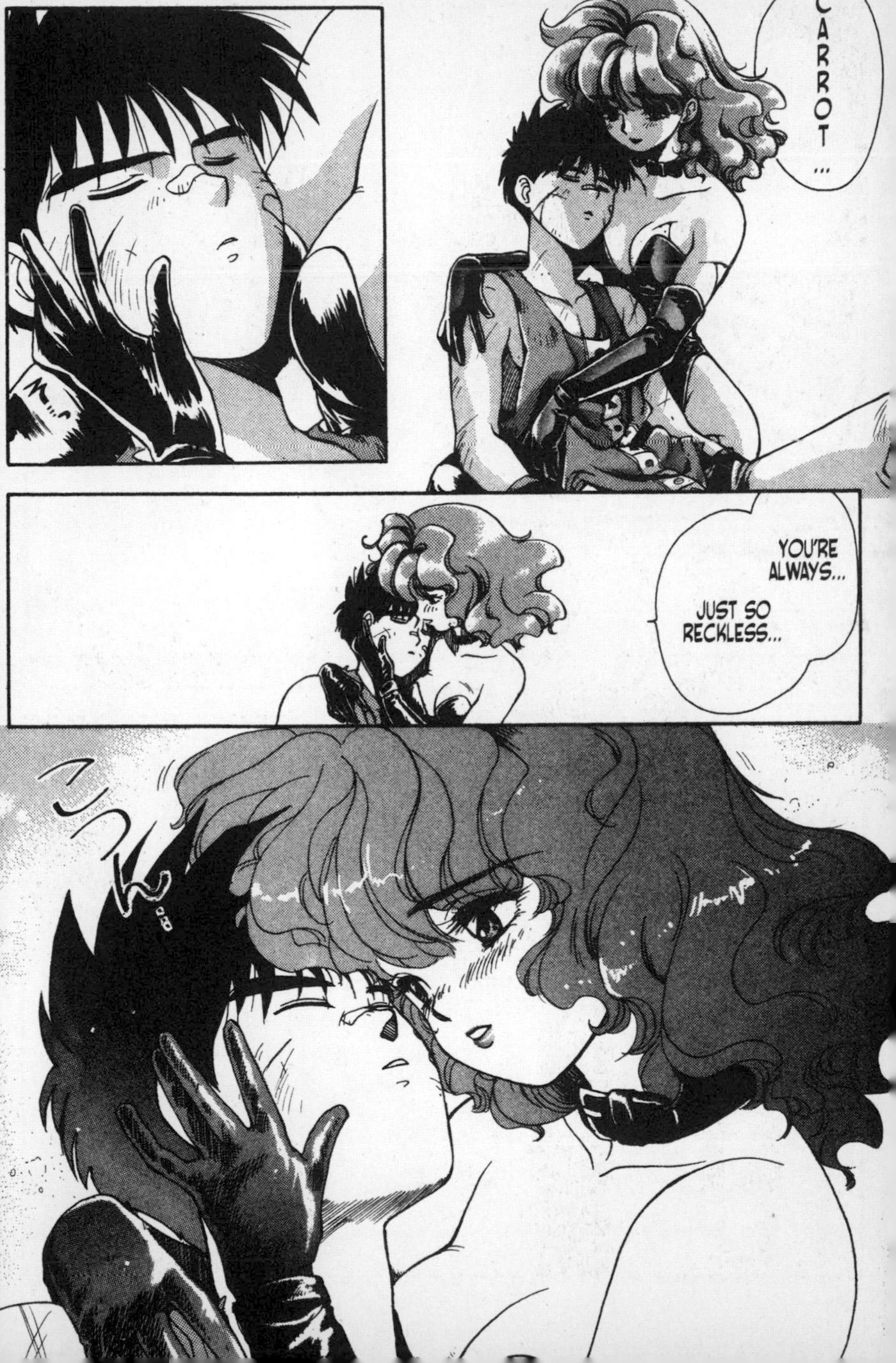
CARROT ...
YOU'RE ALWAYS...
JUST SO RECKLESS...
こつん

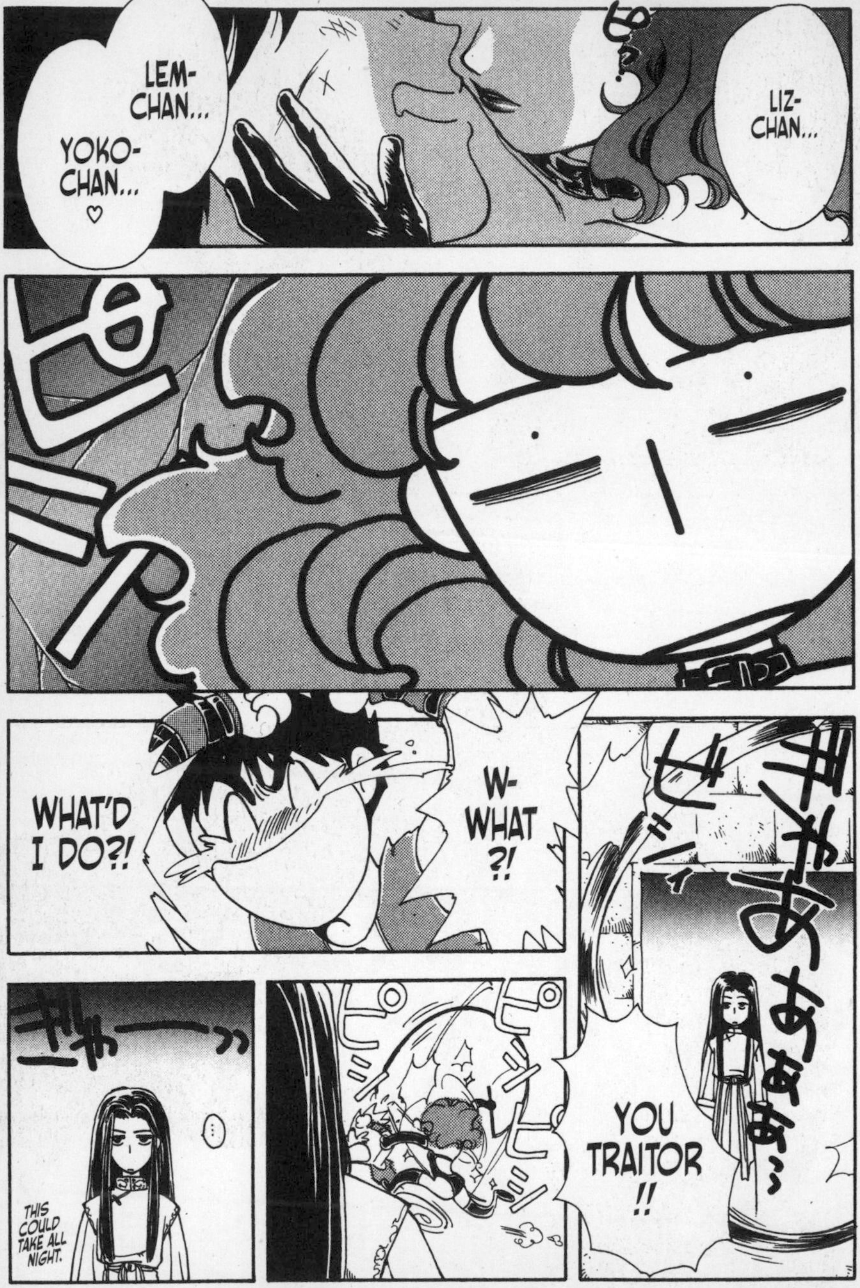
LIZ-CHAN...
LEM-CHAN... YOKO-CHAN... ♡
YOU TRAITOR!!
W-WHAT?!
WHAT'D I DO?!
...
THIS COULD TAKE ALL NIGHT.

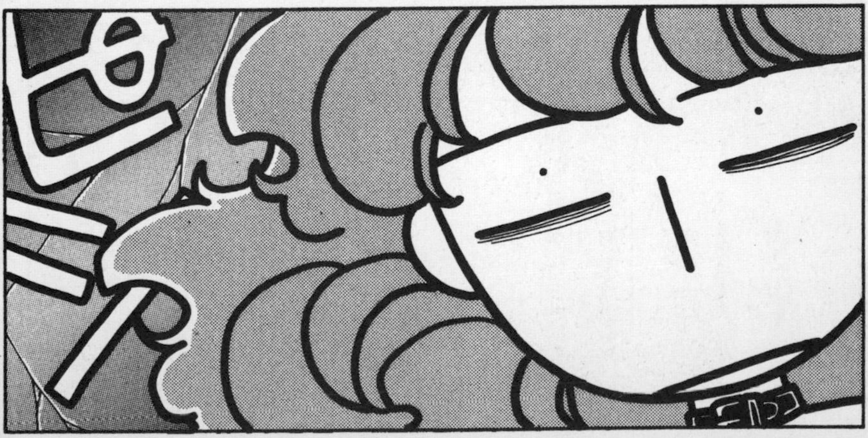
ピ

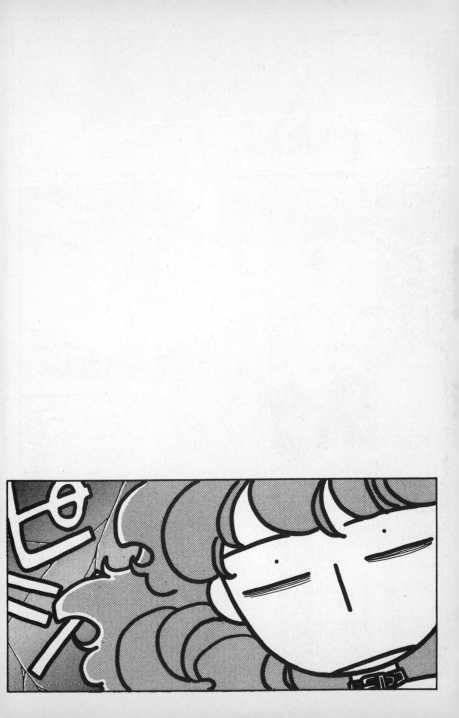

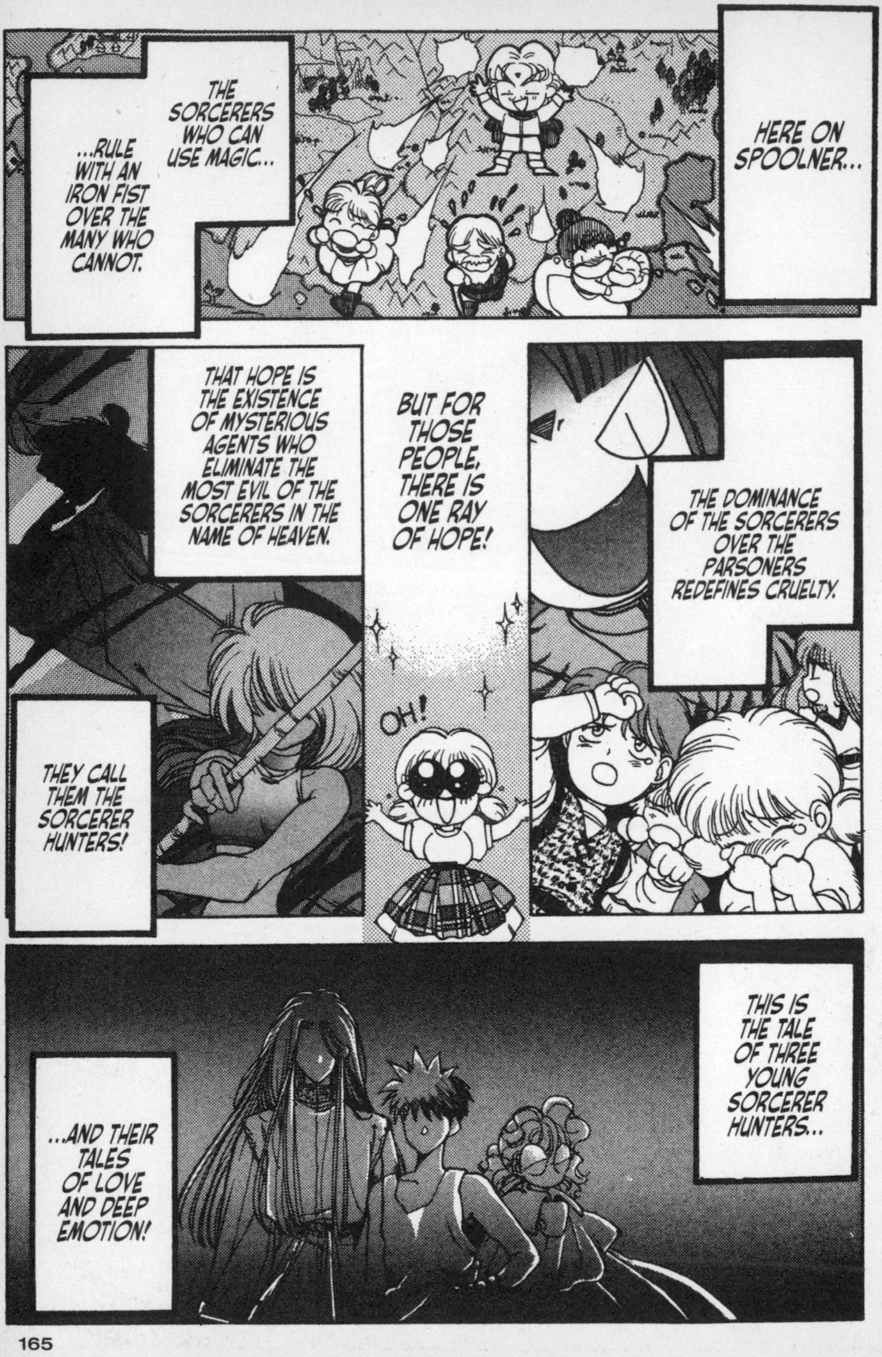
HERE ON SPOOLNER...
THE SORCERERS WHO CAN USE MAGIC...
...RULE WITH AN IRON FIST OVER THE MANY WHO CANNOT.
THE DOMINANCE OF THE SORCERERS OVER THE PARSONERS REDEFINES CRUELTY.
BUT FOR THOSE PEOPLE, THERE IS ONE RAY OF HOPE!
OH!
THAT HOPE IS THE EXISTENCE OF MYSTERIOUS AGENTS WHO ELIMINATE THE MOST EVIL OF THE SORCERERS IN THE NAME OF HEAVEN.
THEY CALL THEM THE SORCERER HUNTERS!
THIS IS THE TALE OF THREE YOUNG SORCERER HUNTERS...
...AND THEIR TALES OF LOVE AND DEEP EMOTION!

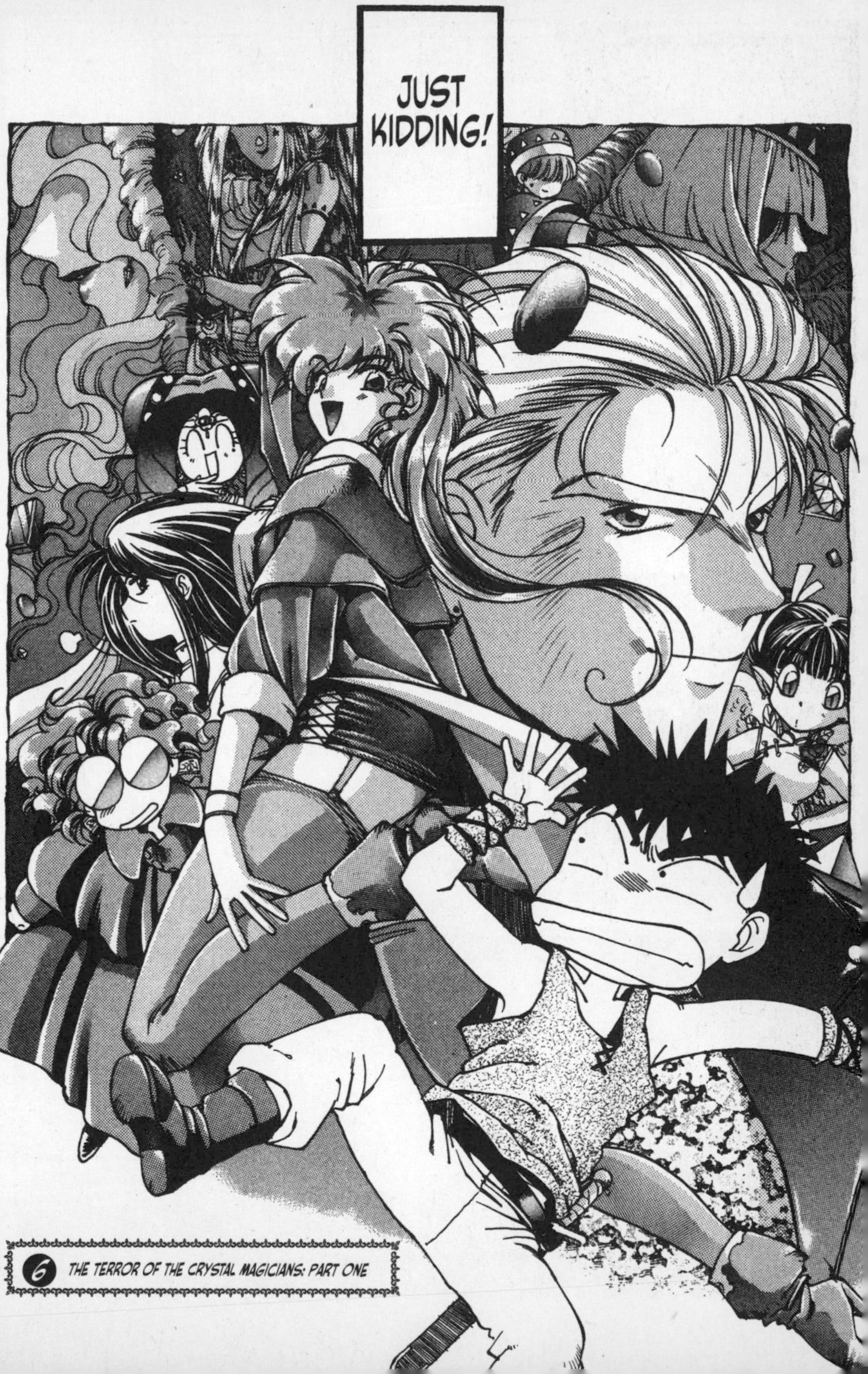
JUST KIDDING!
6 THE TERROR OF THE CRYSTAL MAGICIANS: PART ONE

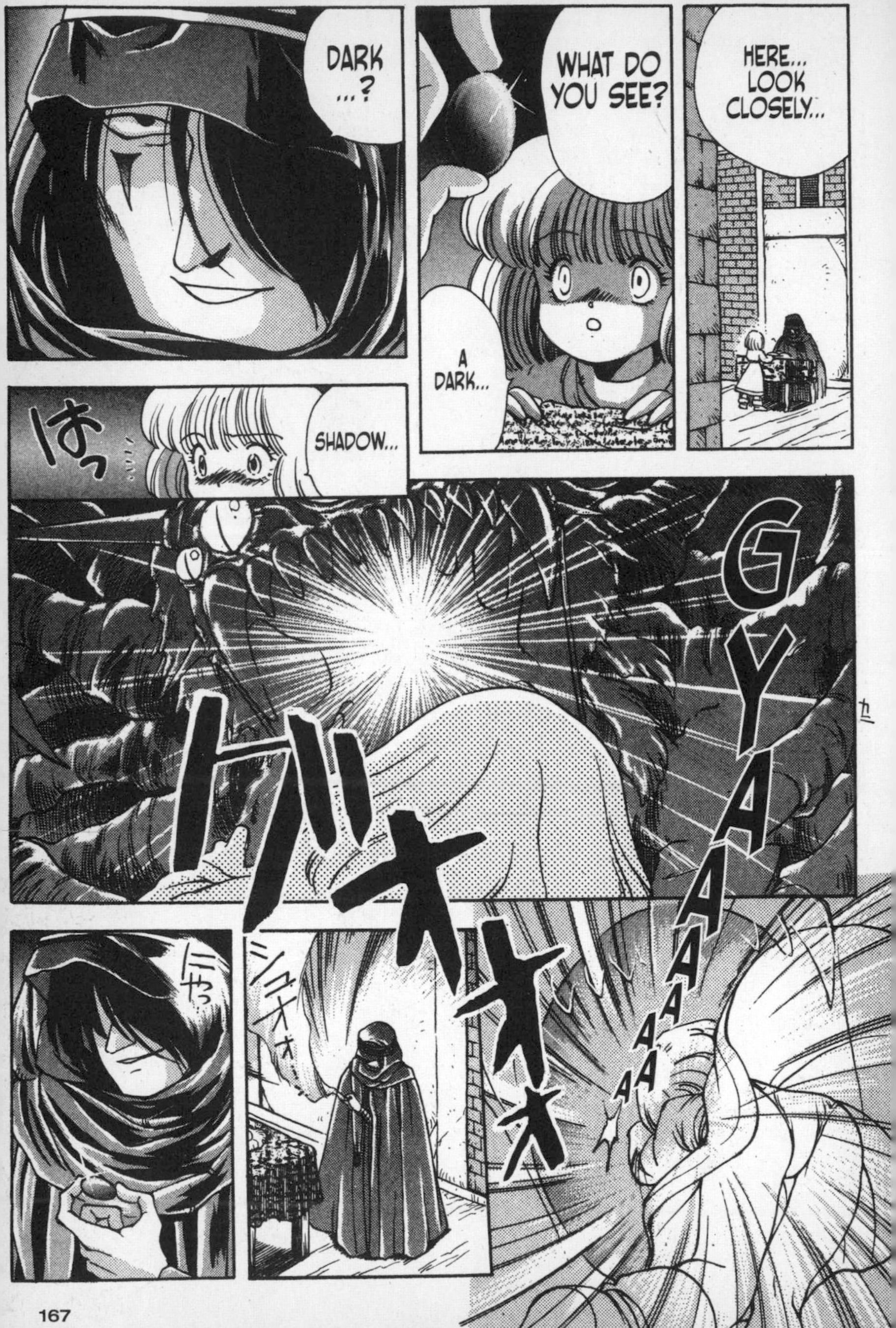
HERE... LOOK CLOSELY...
WHAT DO YOU SEE?
A DARK...
DARK ...?
はっ
SHADOW...
GYAAAAAAAAAA
にやっ

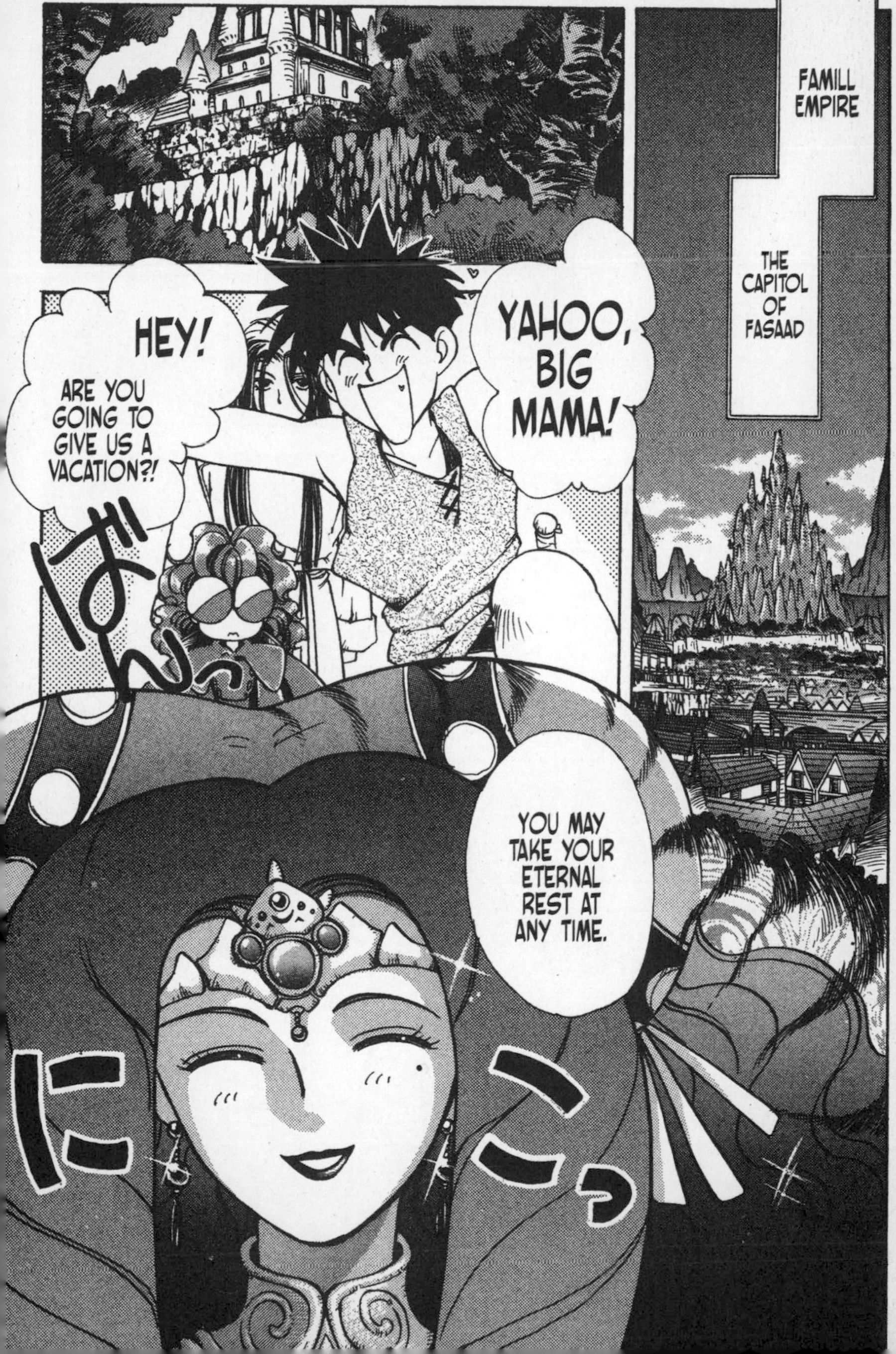
FAMILL EMPIRE
THE CAPITOL OF FASAAD
YAHOO, BIG MAMA!
HEY!
ARE YOU GOING TO GIVE US A VACATION?!
ばんっ
YOU MAY TAKE YOUR ETERNAL REST AT ANY TIME.
にこっ

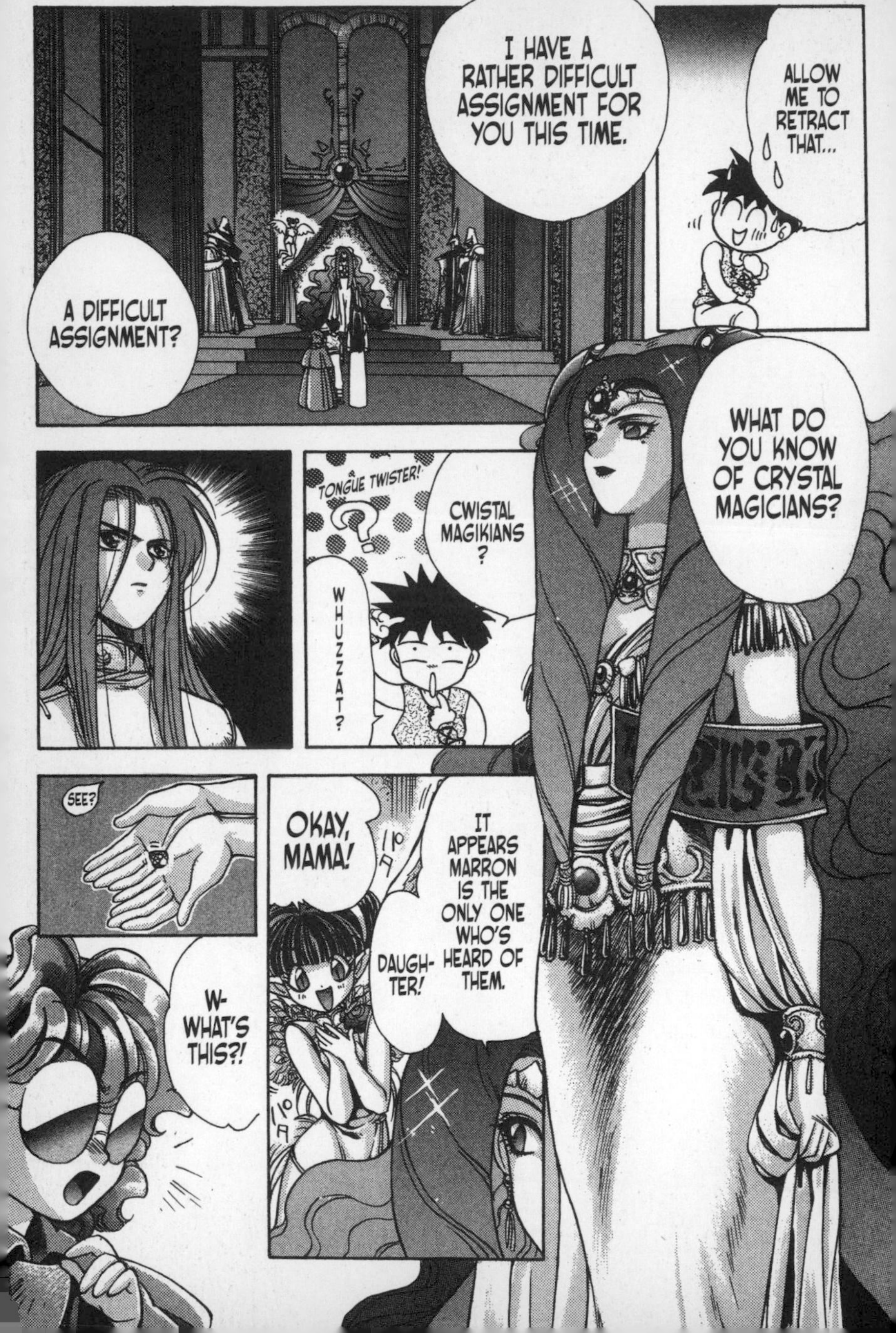
ALLOW ME TO RETRACT THAT...
I HAVE A RATHER DIFFICULT ASSIGNMENT FOR YOU THIS TIME.
A DIFFICULT ASSIGNMENT?
WHAT DO YOU KNOW OF CRYSTAL MAGICIANS?
TONGUE TWISTER!
CWISTAL MAGIKIANS?
WHUZZAT?
IT APPEARS MARRON IS THE ONLY ONE WHO'S HEARD OF THEM.
OKAY, MAMA!
DAUGH-TER!
SEE?
W-WHAT'S THIS?!

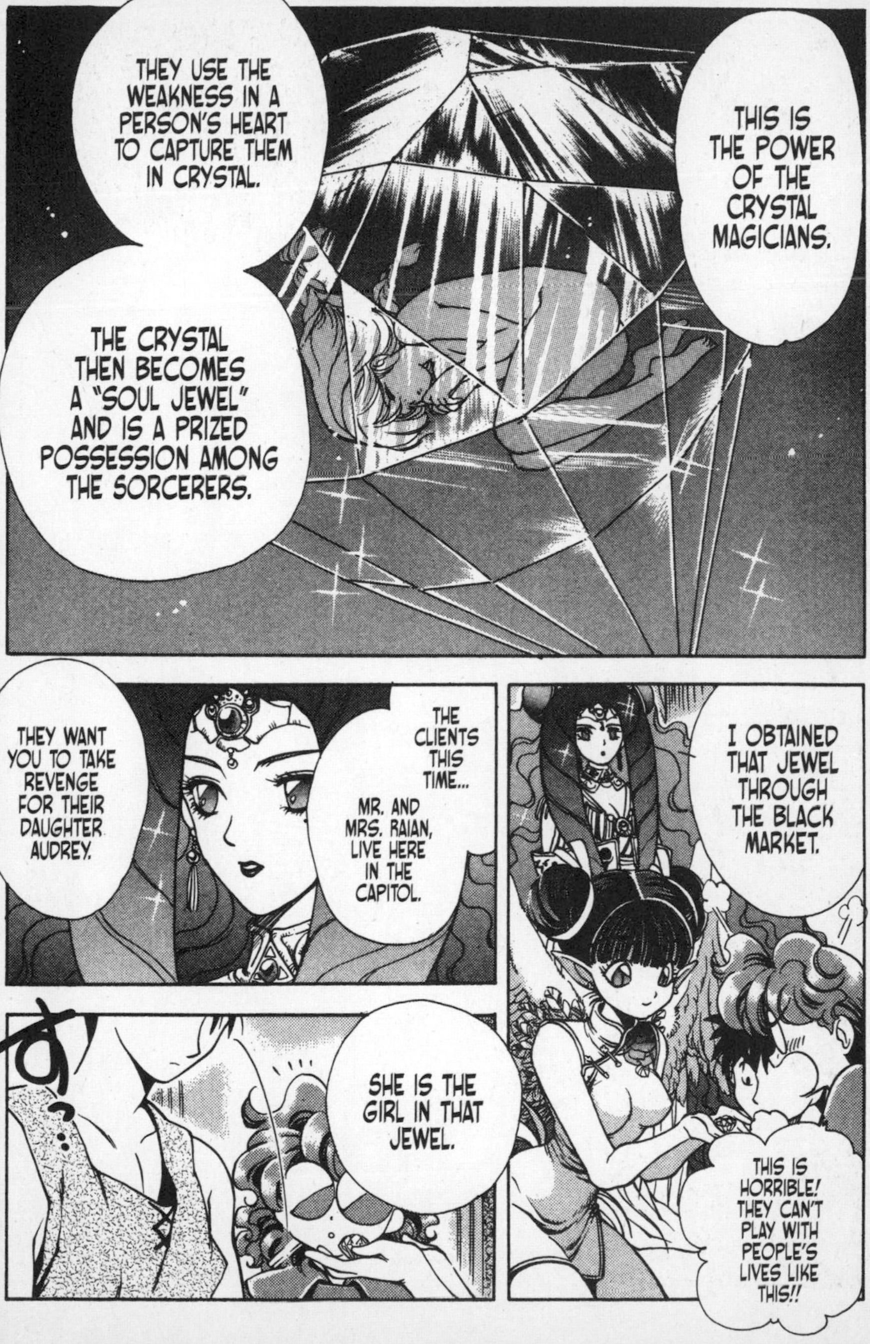
THIS IS THE POWER OF THE CRYSTAL MAGICIANS.
THEY USE THE WEAKNESS IN A PERSON'S HEART TO CAPTURE THEM IN CRYSTAL.
THE CRYSTAL THEN BECOMES A "SOUL JEWEL" AND IS A PRIZED POSSESSION AMONG THE SORCERERS.
I OBTAINED THAT JEWEL THROUGH THE BLACK MARKET.
THIS IS HORRIBLE! THEY CAN'T PLAY WITH PEOPLE'S LIVES LIKE THIS!!
THE CLIENTS THIS TIME...
MR. AND MRS. RAIAN, LIVE HERE IN THE CAPITOL.
THEY WANT YOU TO TAKE REVENGE FOR THEIR DAUGHTER AUDREY.
SHE IS THE GIRL IN THAT JEWEL.
すっ

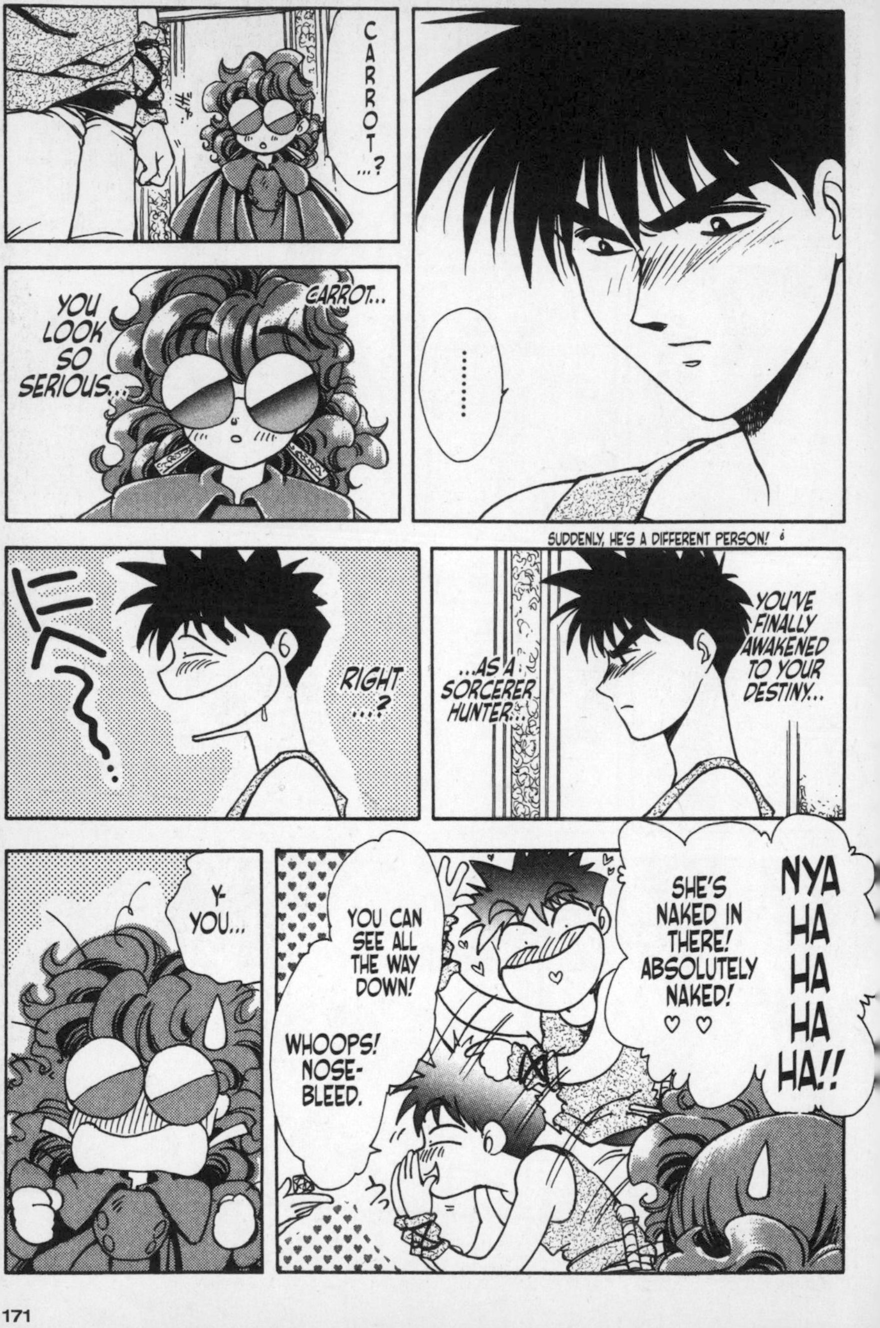
……
CARROT…?
CARROT…
YOU LOOK SO SERIOUS…
SUDDENLY, HE'S A DIFFERENT PERSON!
YOU'VE FINALLY AWAKENED TO YOUR DESTINY…
…AS A SORCERER HUNTER…
RIGHT…?
NYA HA HA HA HA HA!!
SHE'S NAKED IN THERE! ABSOLUTELY NAKED! ♡ ♡
YOU CAN SEE ALL THE WAY DOWN!
WHOOPS! NOSE-BLEED.
Y-YOU…

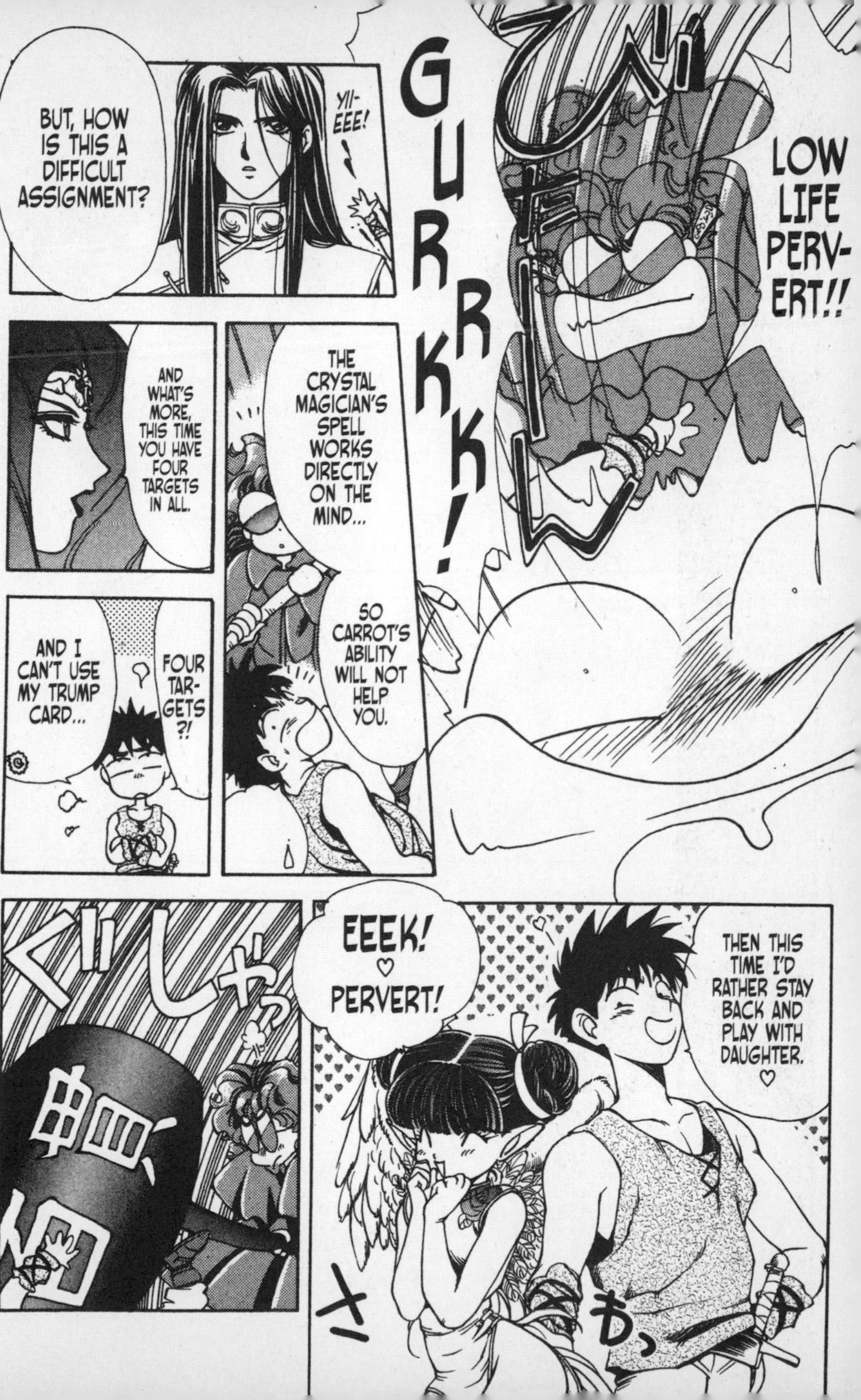
GURRKK!!
LOW LIFE PERV-ERT!!
BUT, HOW IS THIS A DIFFICULT ASSIGNMENT?
YII-EEE!
THE CRYSTAL MAGICIAN'S SPELL WORKS DIRECTLY ON THE MIND...
SO CARROT'S ABILITY WILL NOT HELP YOU.
AND WHAT'S MORE, THIS TIME YOU HAVE FOUR TARGETS IN ALL.
FOUR TAR-GETS?!
AND I CAN'T USE MY TRUMP CARD...
THEN THIS TIME I'D RATHER STAY BACK AND PLAY WITH DAUGHTER. ♡
EEEK! ♡ PERVERT!

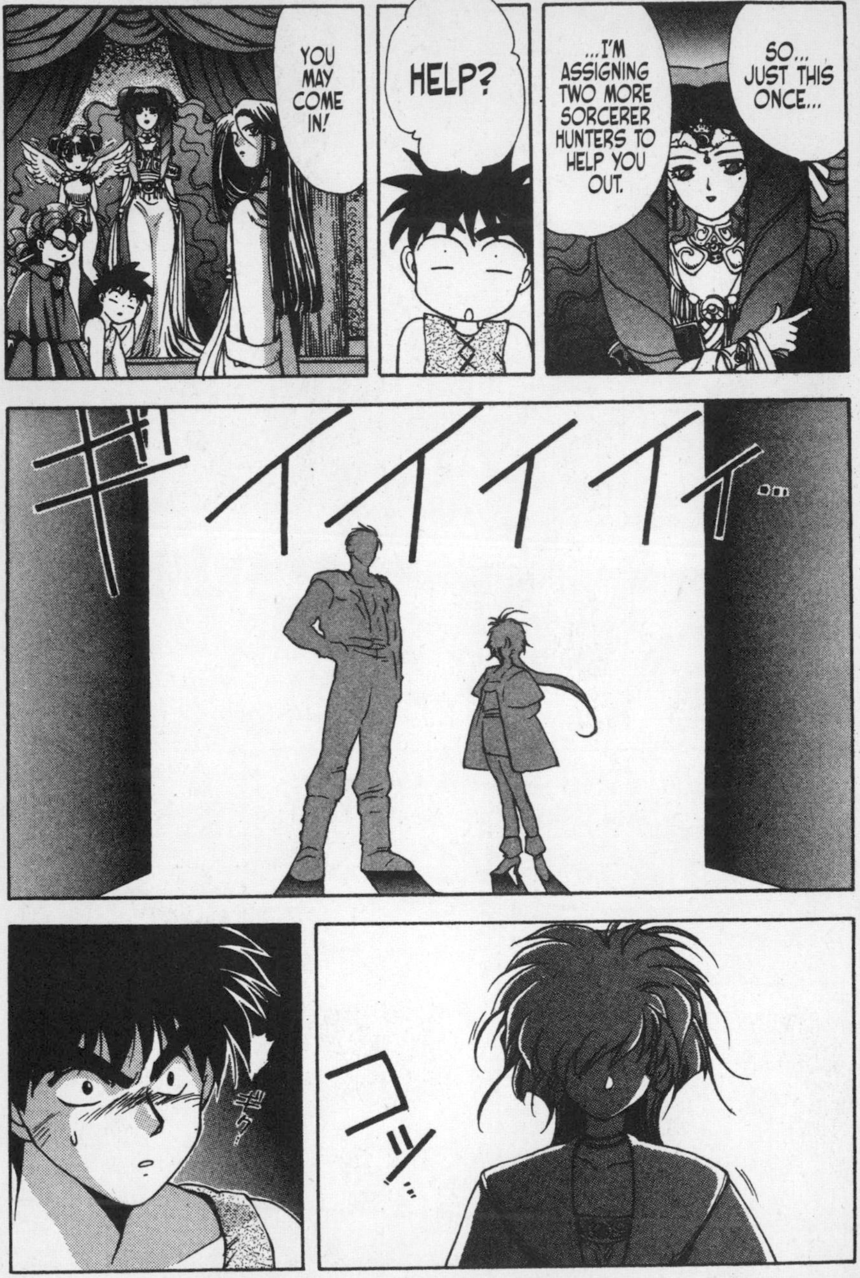
SO... JUST THIS ONCE...
...I'M ASSIGNING TWO MORE SORCERER HUNTERS TO HELP YOU OUT.
HELP?
YOU MAY COME IN!
ギイイイイイ
コッ

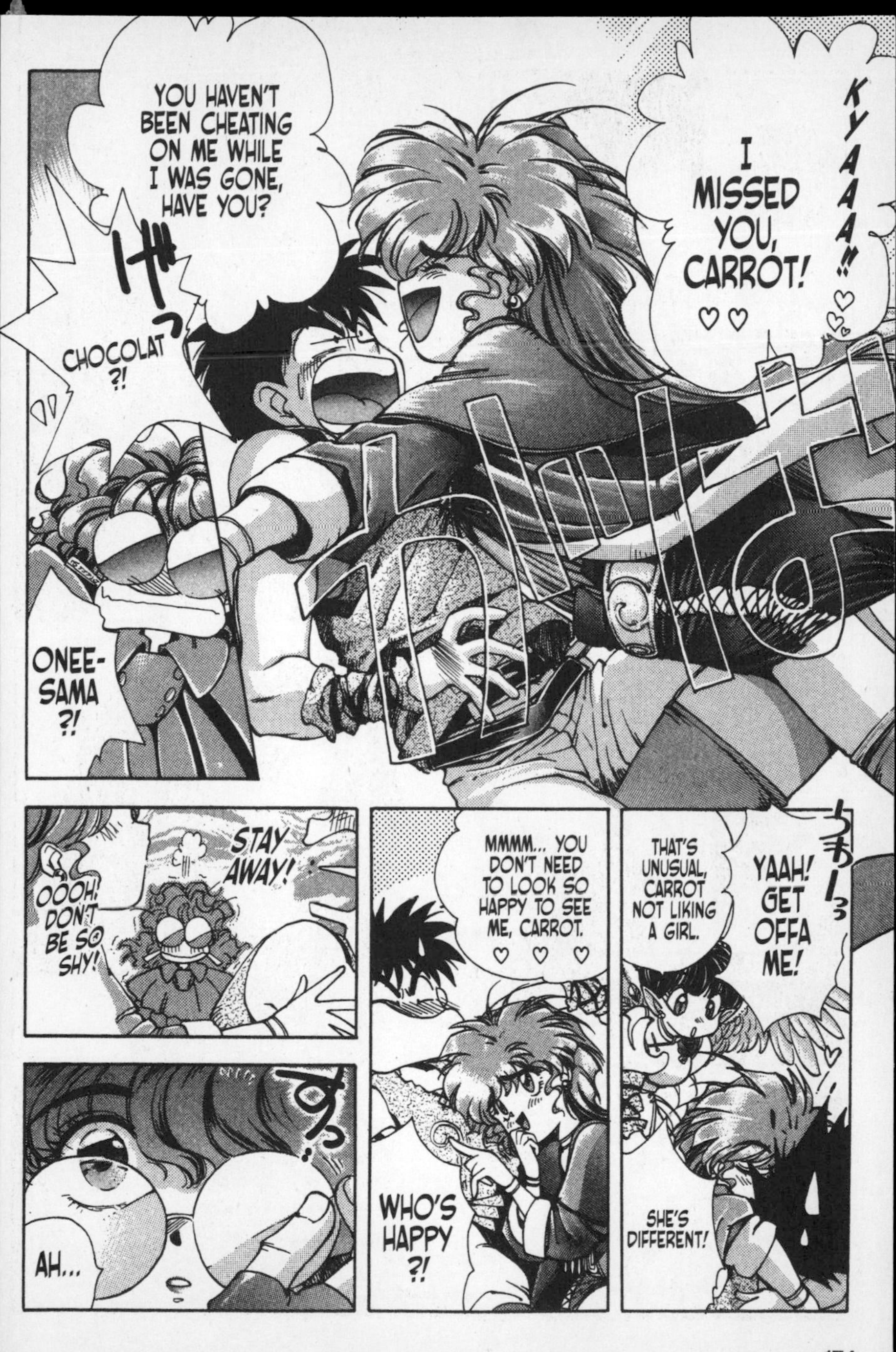
KYAAAA!!
I MISSED YOU, CARROT! ♡ ♡
YOU HAVEN'T BEEN CHEATING ON ME WHILE I WAS GONE, HAVE YOU?
CHOCOLAT?!
ONEE-SAMA?!
YAAH! GET OFFA ME!
THAT'S UNUSUAL, CARROT NOT LIKING A GIRL.
SHE'S DIFFERENT!
MMMM... YOU DON'T NEED TO LOOK SO HAPPY TO SEE ME, CARROT. ♡ ♡ ♡
WHO'S HAPPY?!
STAY AWAY!
OOOH! DON'T BE SO SHY!
AH...

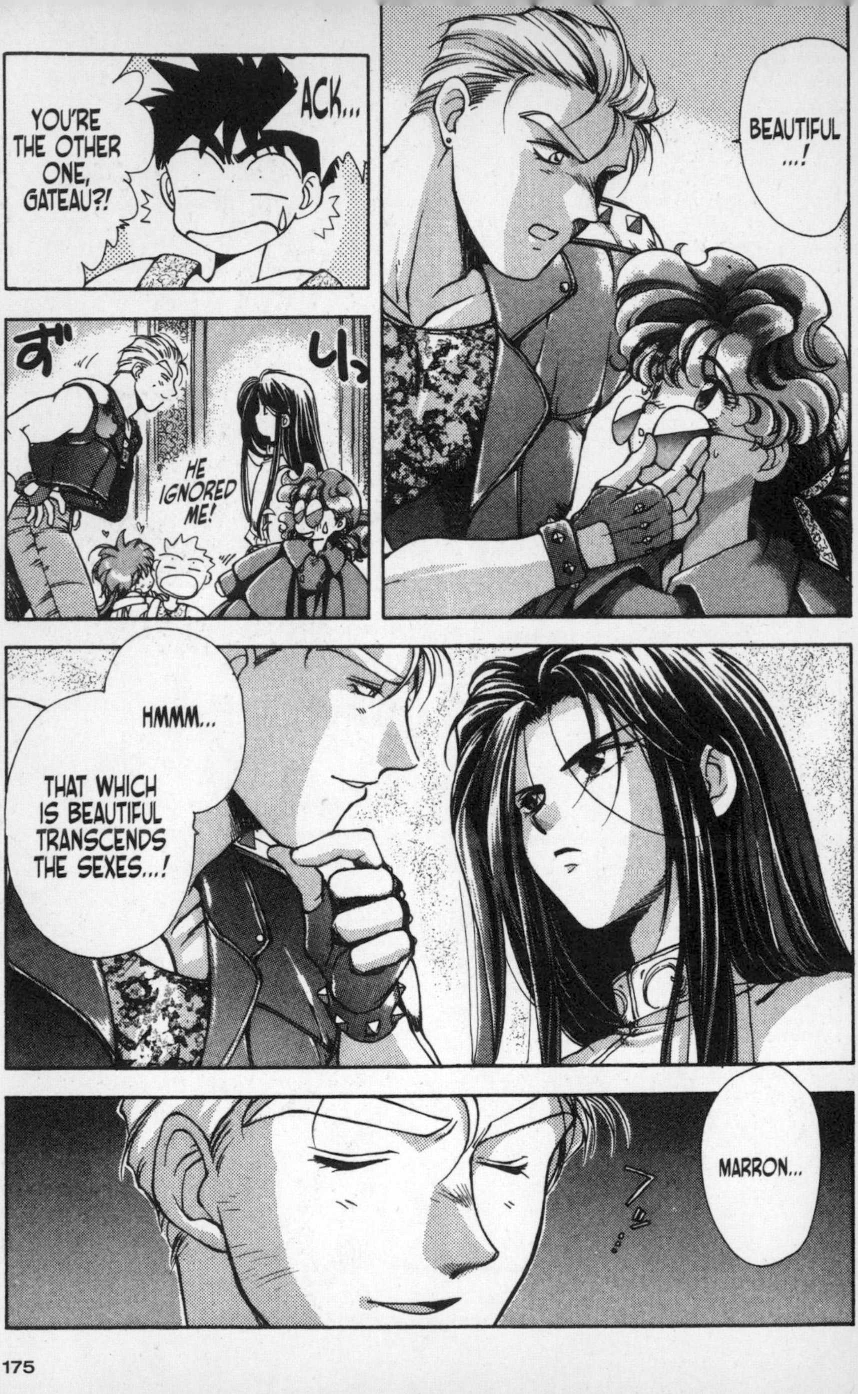
BEAUTIFUL ...!
YOU'RE THE OTHER ONE, GATEAU?!
ACK...
ず
りっ
HE IGNORED ME!
HMMM...
THAT WHICH IS BEAUTIFUL TRANSCENDS THE SEXES...!
MARRON...

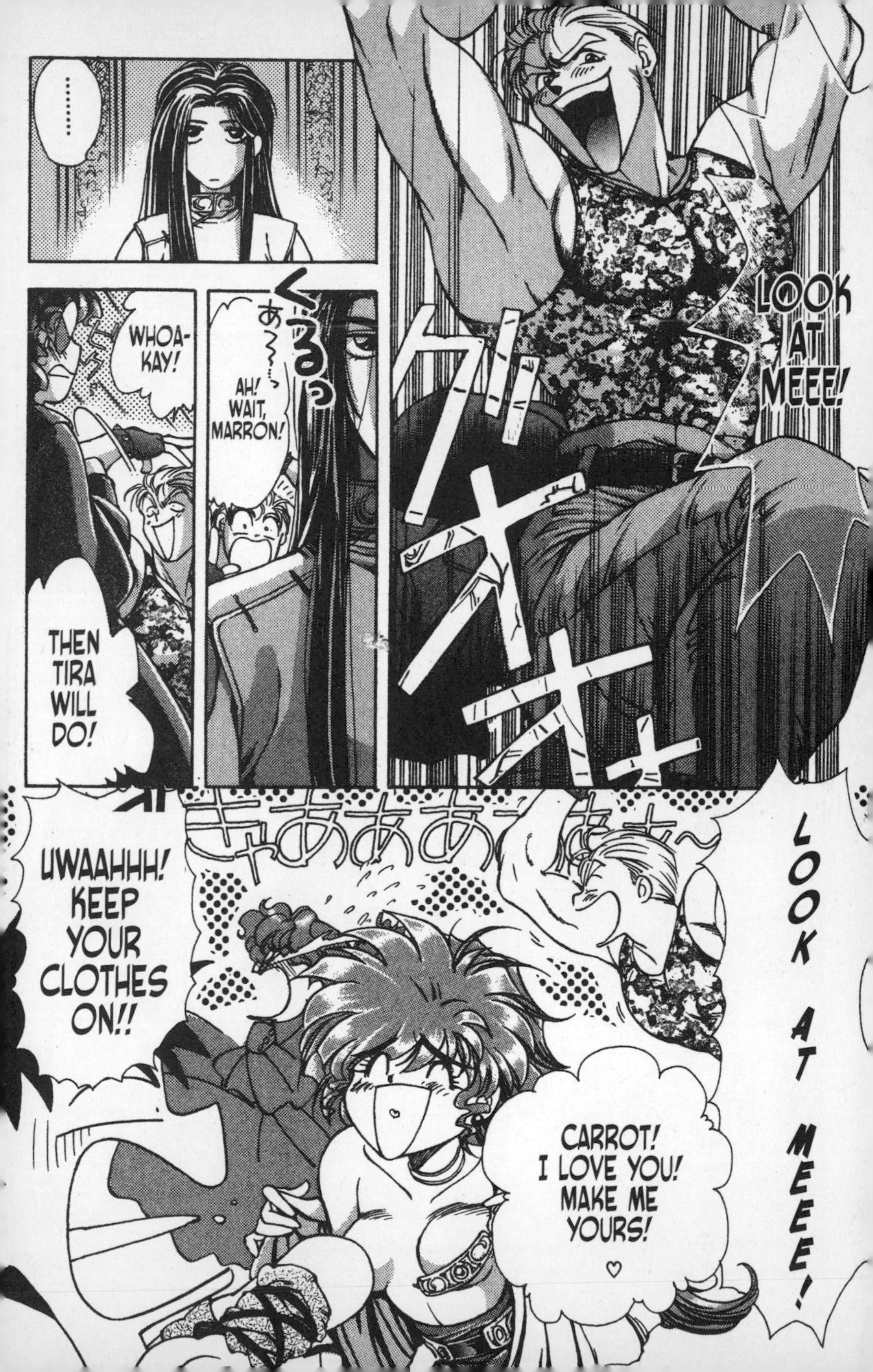
LOOK AT MEEE!
......
くるっ
あ〜〜
AH! WAIT, MARRON!
WHOA-KAY!
THEN TIRA WILL DO!
LOOK AT MEEE!
UWAAHHH! KEEP YOUR CLOTHES ON!!
CARROT! I LOVE YOU! MAKE ME YOURS! ♡

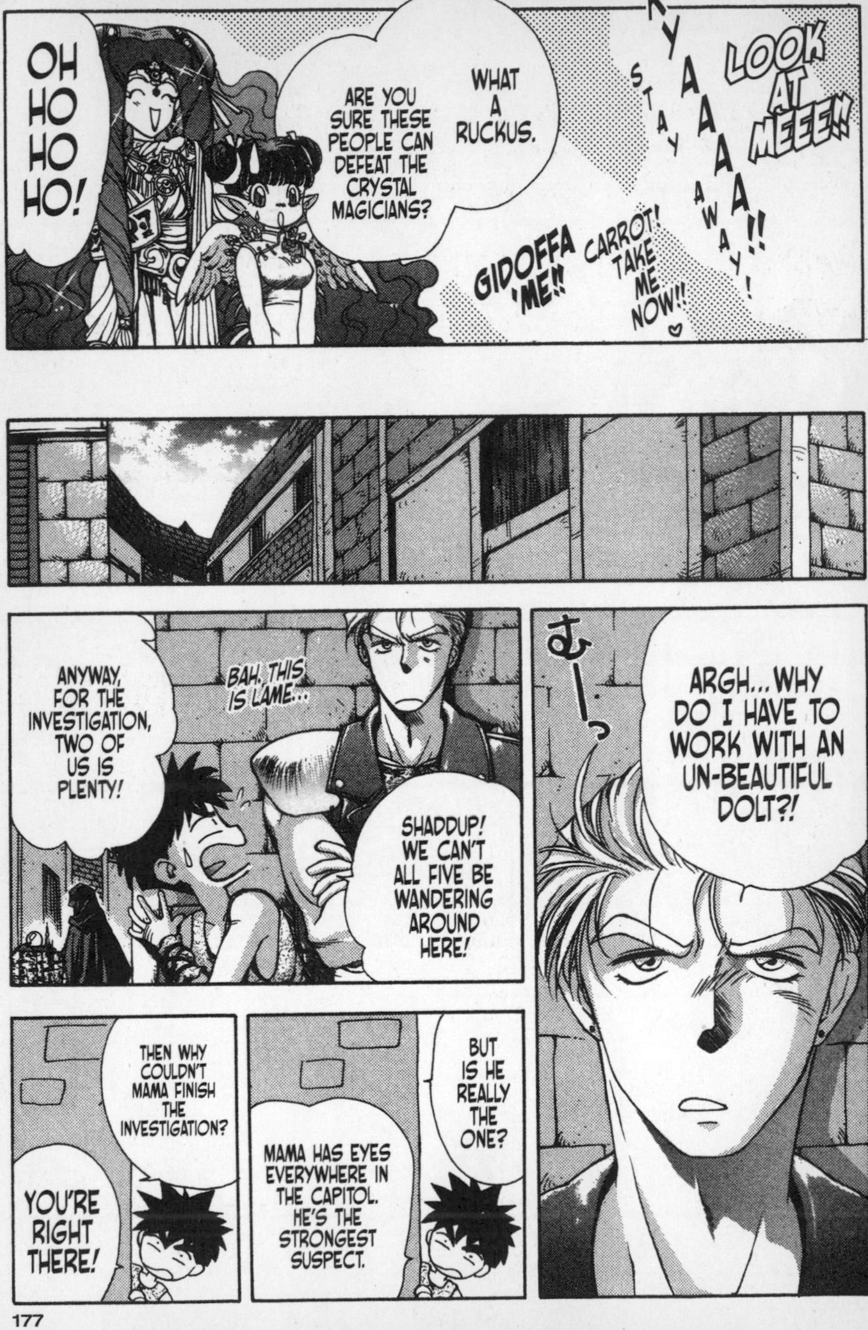
LOOK AT MEEE!!
KYAAAAAA!!
STAY AWAY!
CARROT! TAKE ME NOW!!
GIDOFFA 'ME!!
WHAT A RUCKUS.
ARE YOU SURE THESE PEOPLE CAN DEFEAT THE CRYSTAL MAGICIANS?
OH HO HO HO!
むーっ
ARGH...WHY DO I HAVE TO WORK WITH AN UN-BEAUTIFUL DOLT?!
BAH, THIS IS LAME...
ANYWAY, FOR THE INVESTIGATION, TWO OF US IS PLENTY!
SHADDUP! WE CAN'T ALL FIVE BE WANDERING AROUND HERE!
BUT IS HE REALLY THE ONE?
MAMA HAS EYES EVERYWHERE IN THE CAPITOL. HE'S THE STRONGEST SUSPECT.
THEN WHY COULDN'T MAMA FINISH THE INVESTIGATION?
YOU'RE RIGHT THERE!

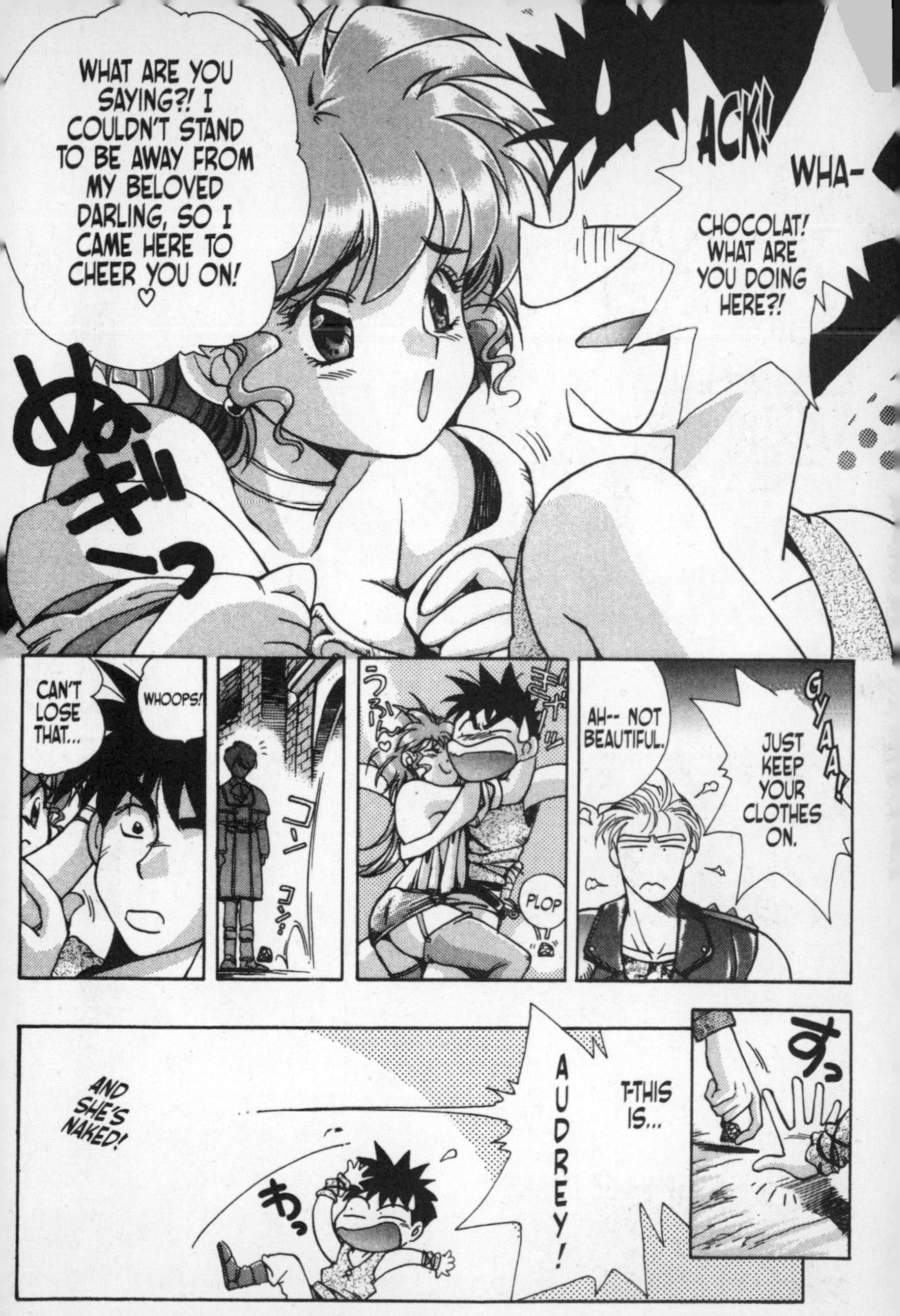
ACK!
WHA-
CHOCOLAT! WHAT ARE YOU DOING HERE?!
WHAT ARE YOU SAYING?! I COULDN'T STAND TO BE AWAY FROM MY BELOVED DARLING, SO I CAME HERE TO CHEER YOU ON! ♡
ぬぎーっ
GYAAA!
JUST KEEP YOUR CLOTHES ON.
AH-- NOT BEAUTIFUL.
PLOP
WHOOPS!
CAN'T LOSE THAT...
すっ
T-THIS IS...
AUDREY!
わっ
AND SHE'S NAKED!

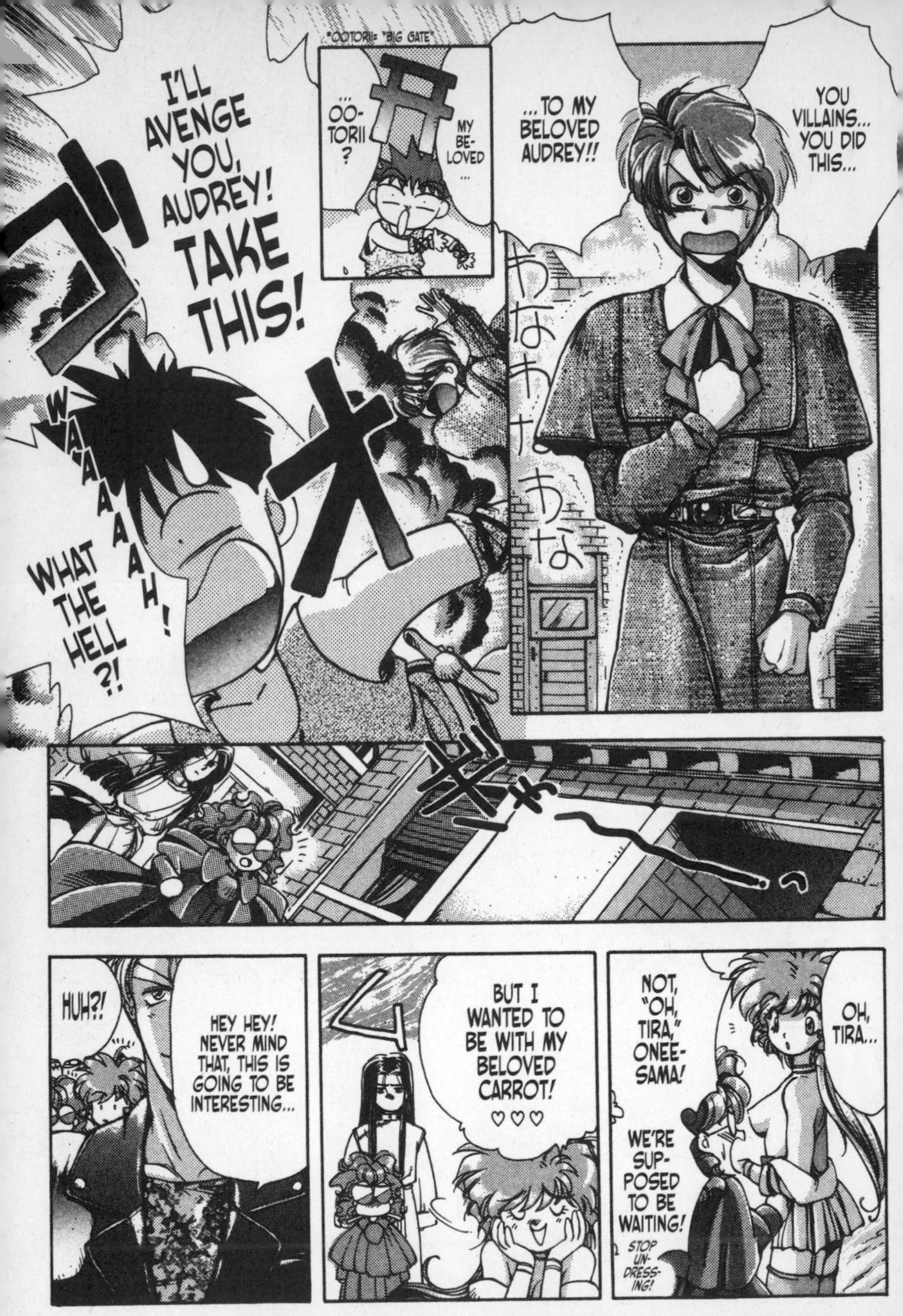
YOU VILLAINS... YOU DID THIS...
...TO MY BELOVED AUDREY!!
*OOTORII: "BIG GATE"
...OO-TORII?
MY BE-LOVED...
I'LL AVENGE YOU, AUDREY! TAKE THIS!
WAAAAAAAH!
WHAT THE HELL?!
OH, TIRA...
NOT, "OH, TIRA," ONEE-SAMA!
WE'RE SUP-POSED TO BE WAITING!
STOP UN-DRESS-ING!
BUT I WANTED TO BE WITH MY BELOVED CARROT! ♡♡♡
HUH?!
HEY HEY! NEVER MIND THAT, THIS IS GOING TO BE INTERESTING...

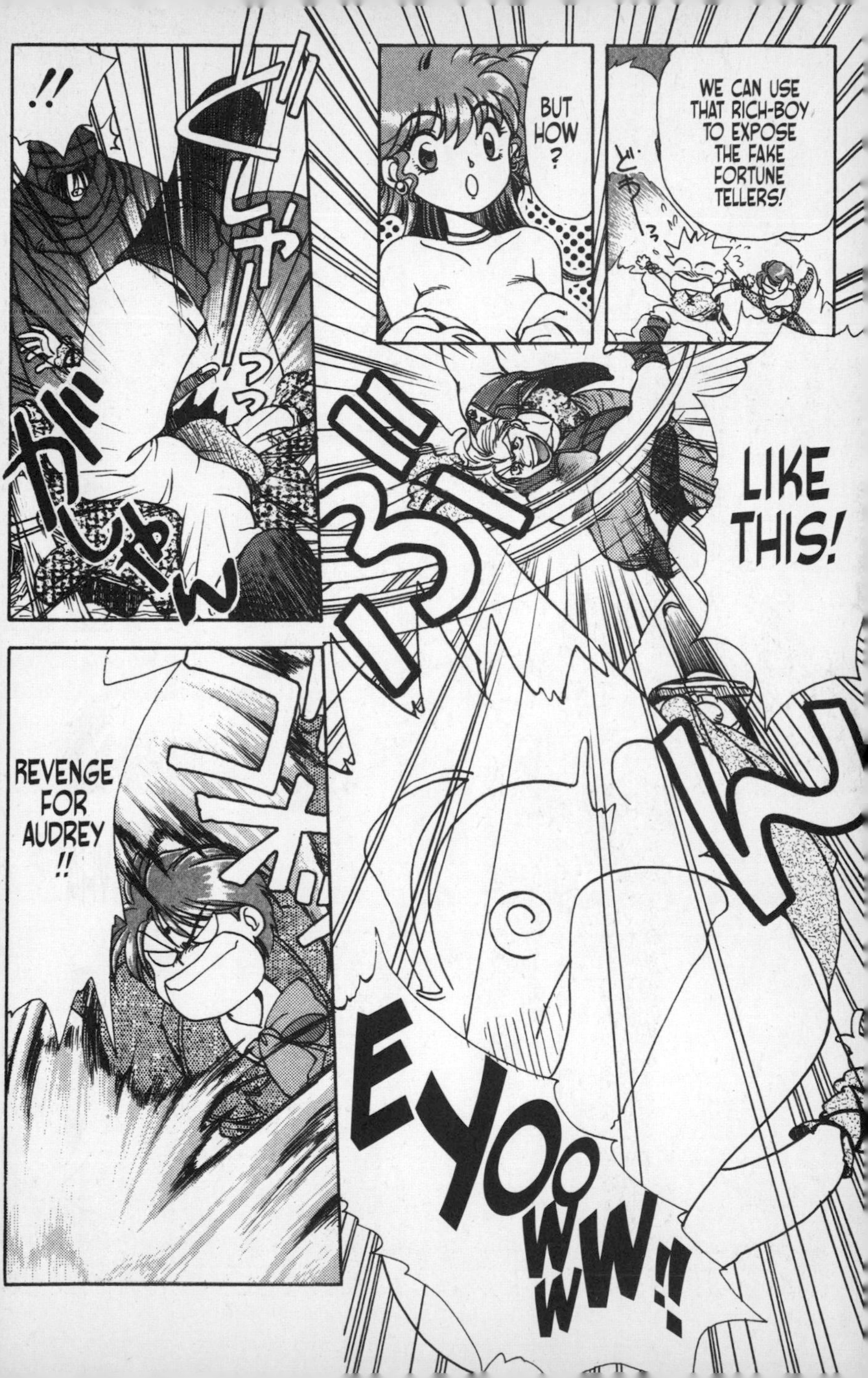
WE CAN USE THAT RICH-BOY TO EXPOSE THE FAKE FORTUNE TELLERS!
BUT HOW?
!!
LIKE THIS!
EYOOWWW!!
REVENGE FOR AUDREY!!

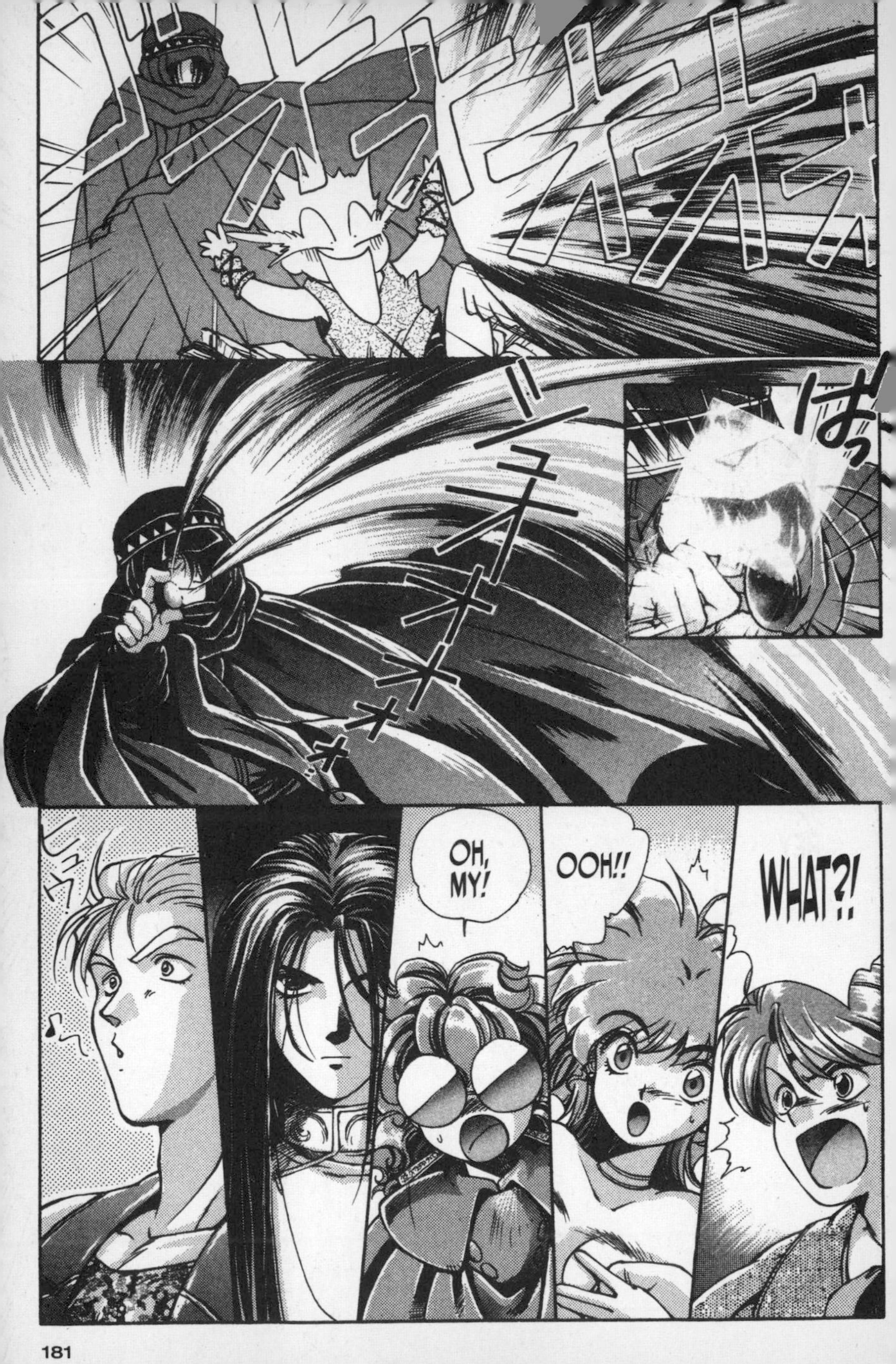
ぱっ
WHAT?!
OOH!!
OH, MY!

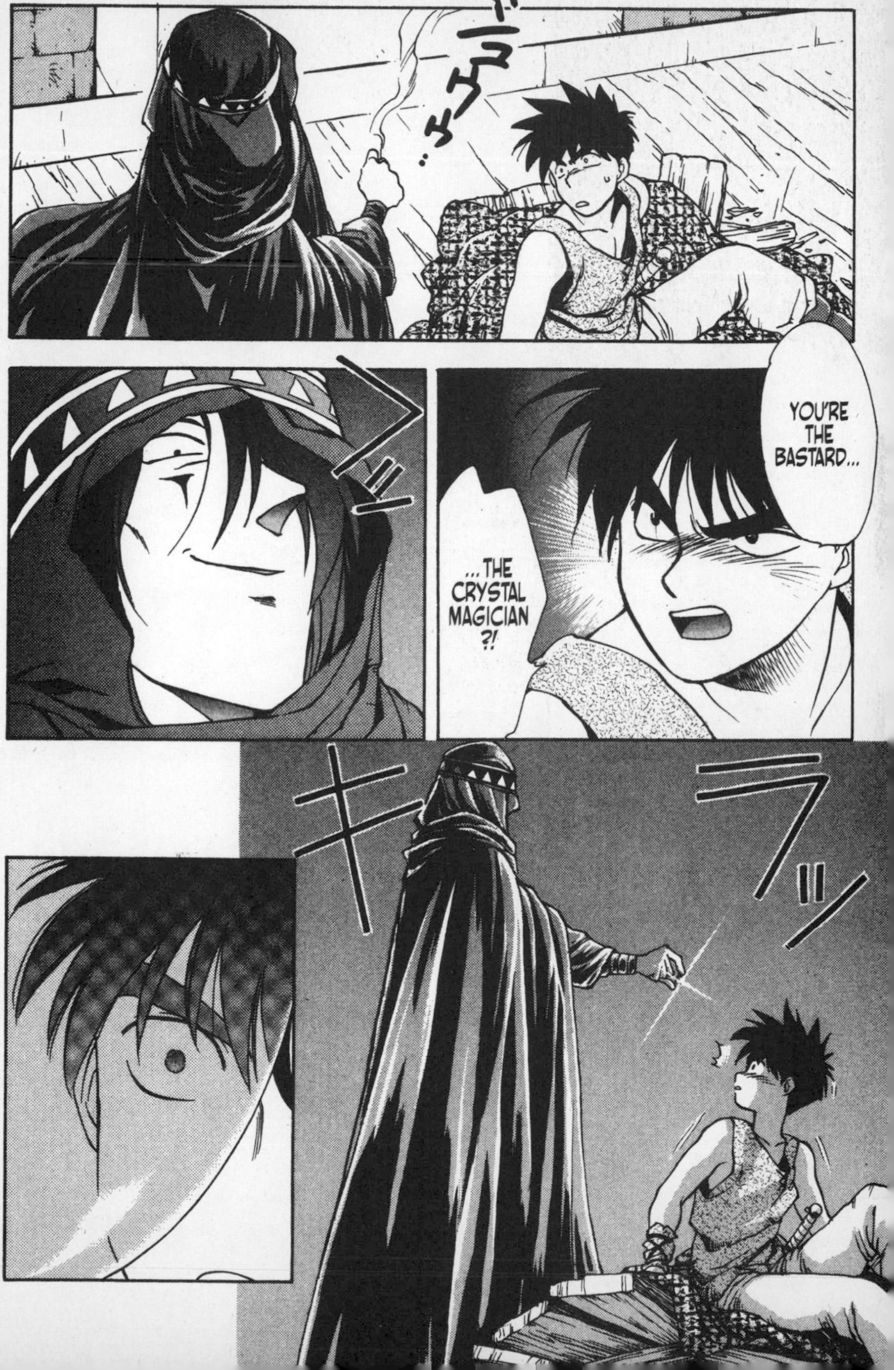
YOU'RE THE BASTARD...
...THE CRYSTAL MAGICIAN ?!
キラッ

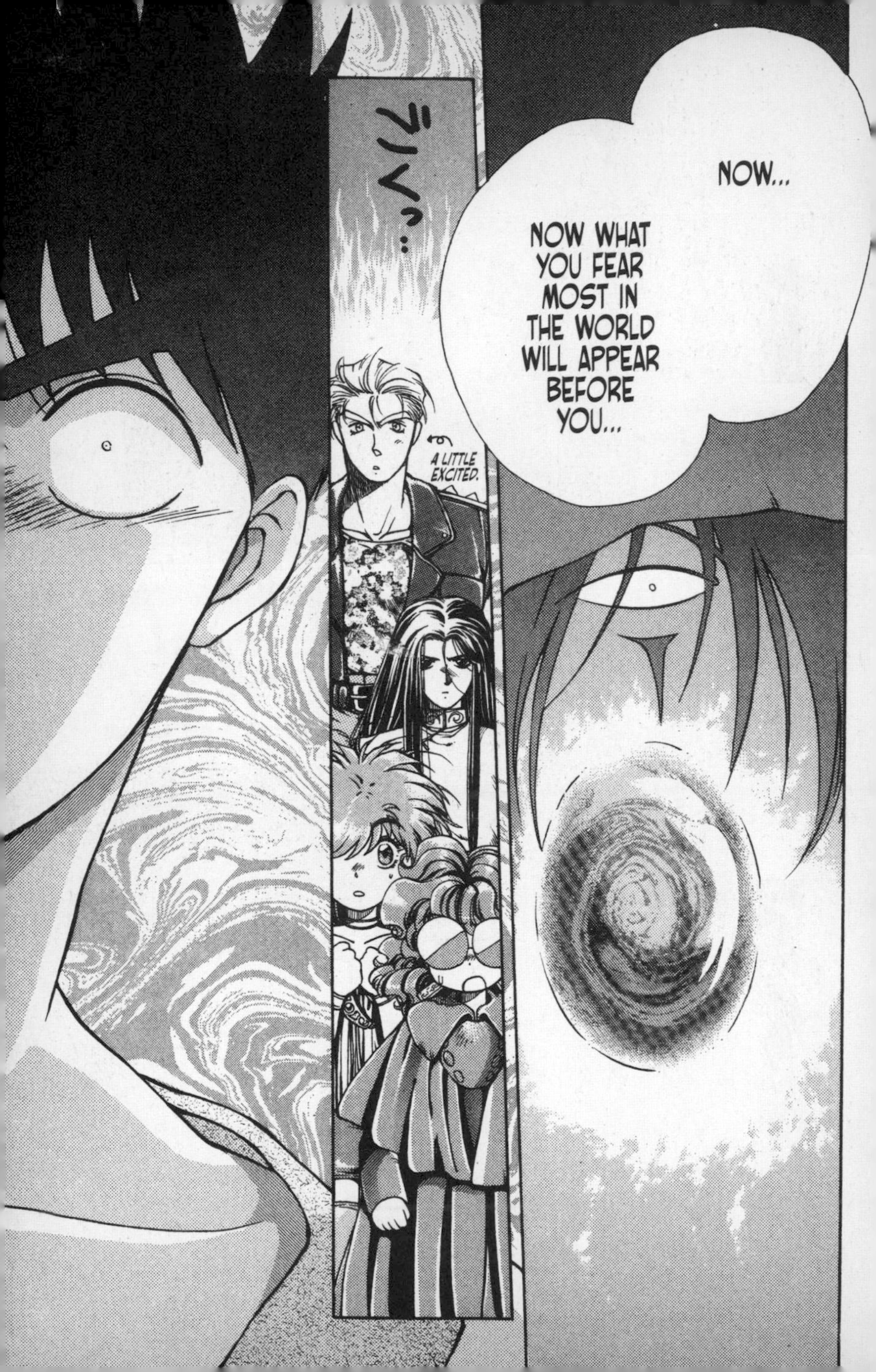
NOW...
NOW WHAT YOU FEAR MOST IN THE WORLD WILL APPEAR BEFORE YOU...
ゾくっ‥
A LITTLE EXCITED.

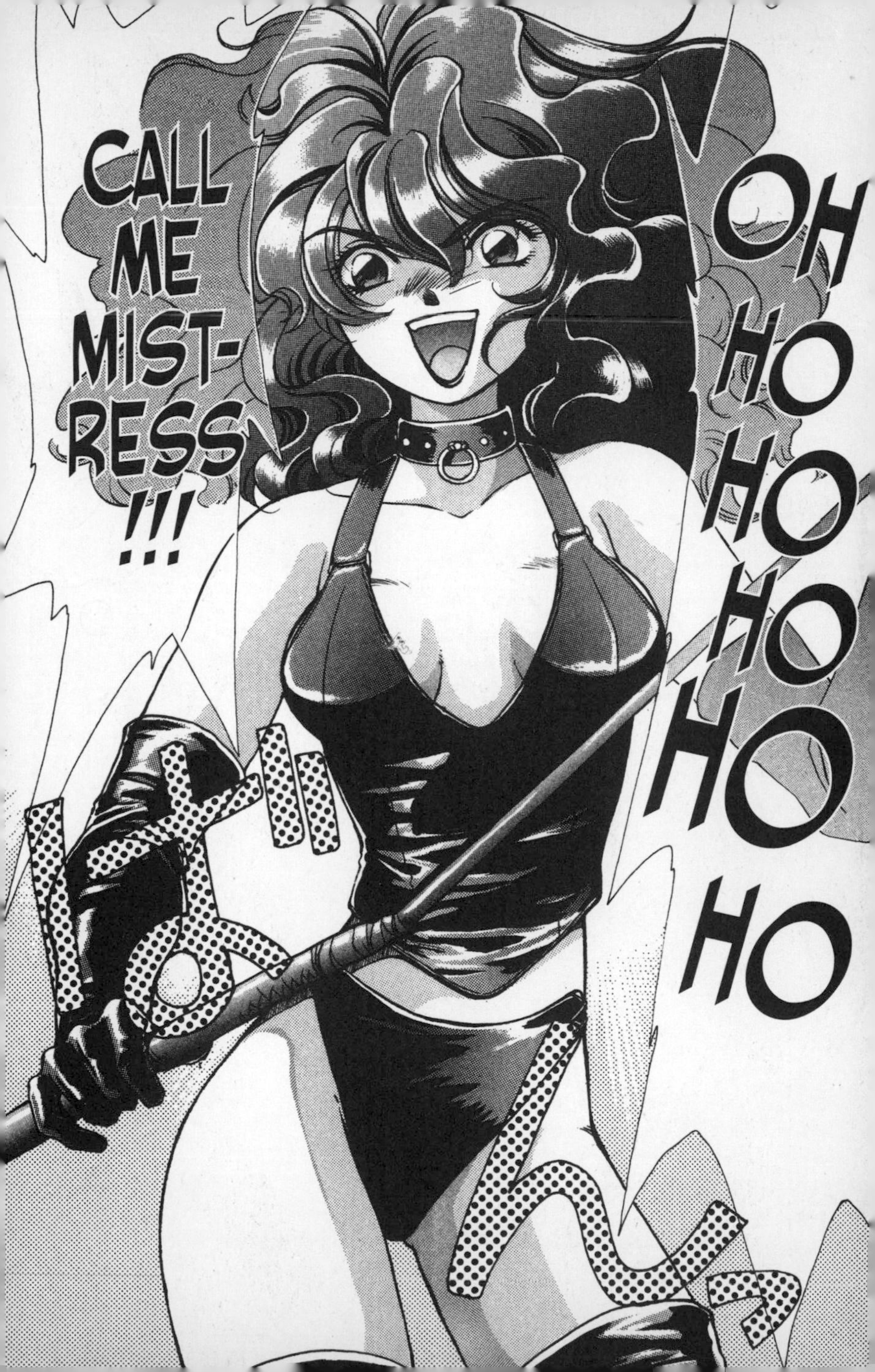
OH HO HO HO HO HO
CALL ME MIST-RESS!!!

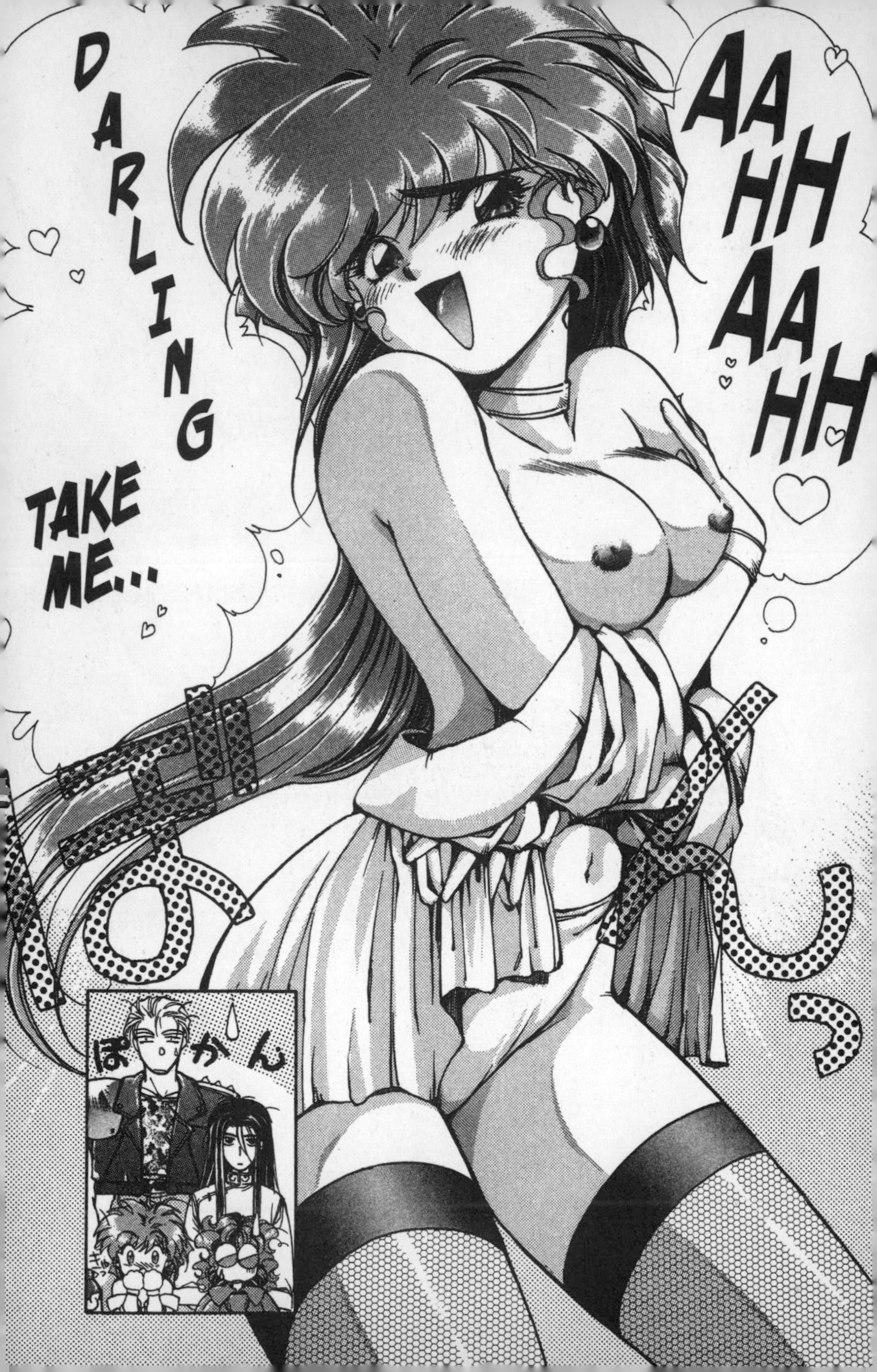
AAHHAAHH
DARLING
TAKE ME...
ぽかん

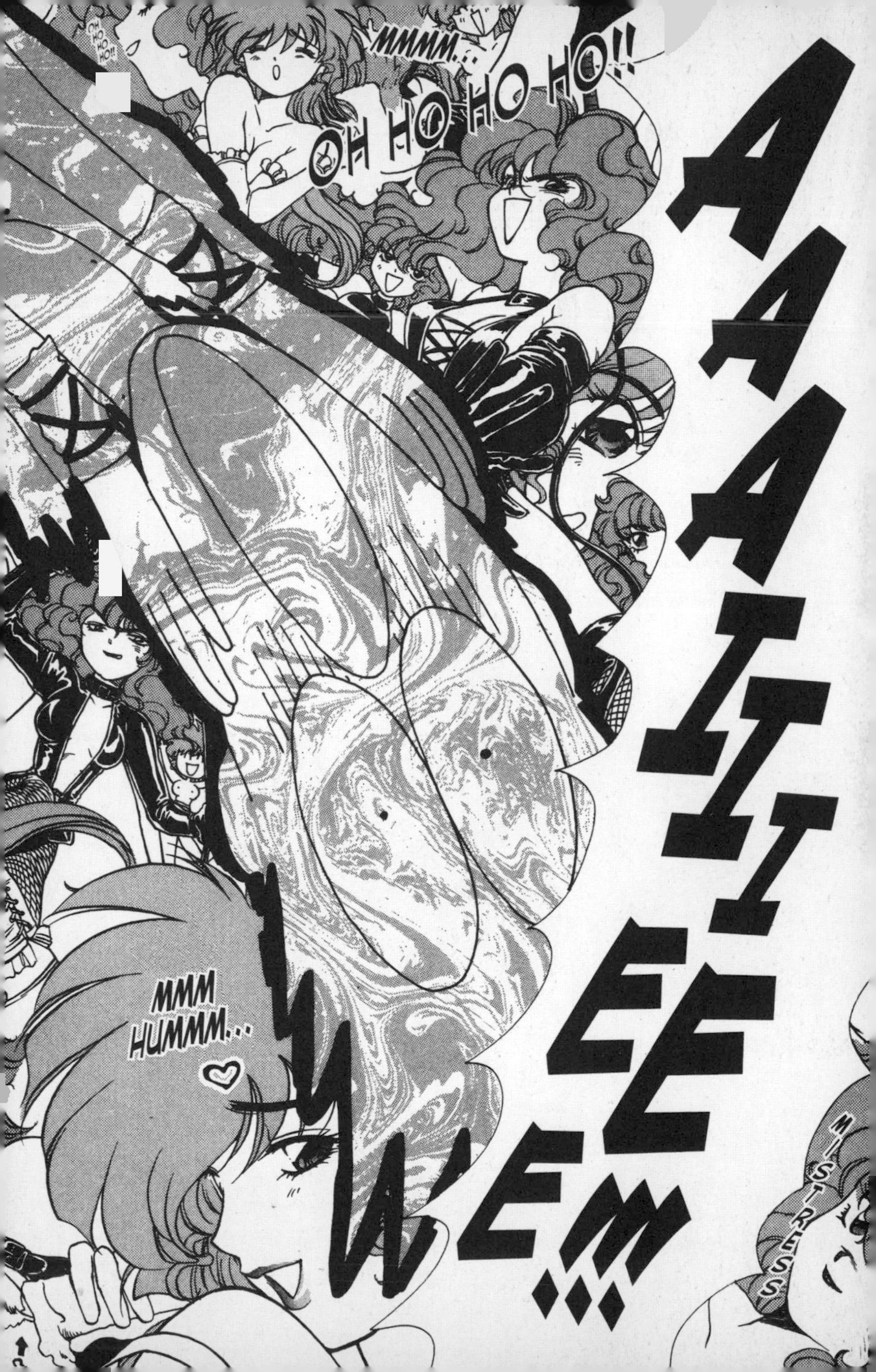

MMMM...
OH HO HO HO HO!!
OH HO HO HO!!
AAAIIIEEEEE!!!
MMM HUMMM...
MI-STRESS

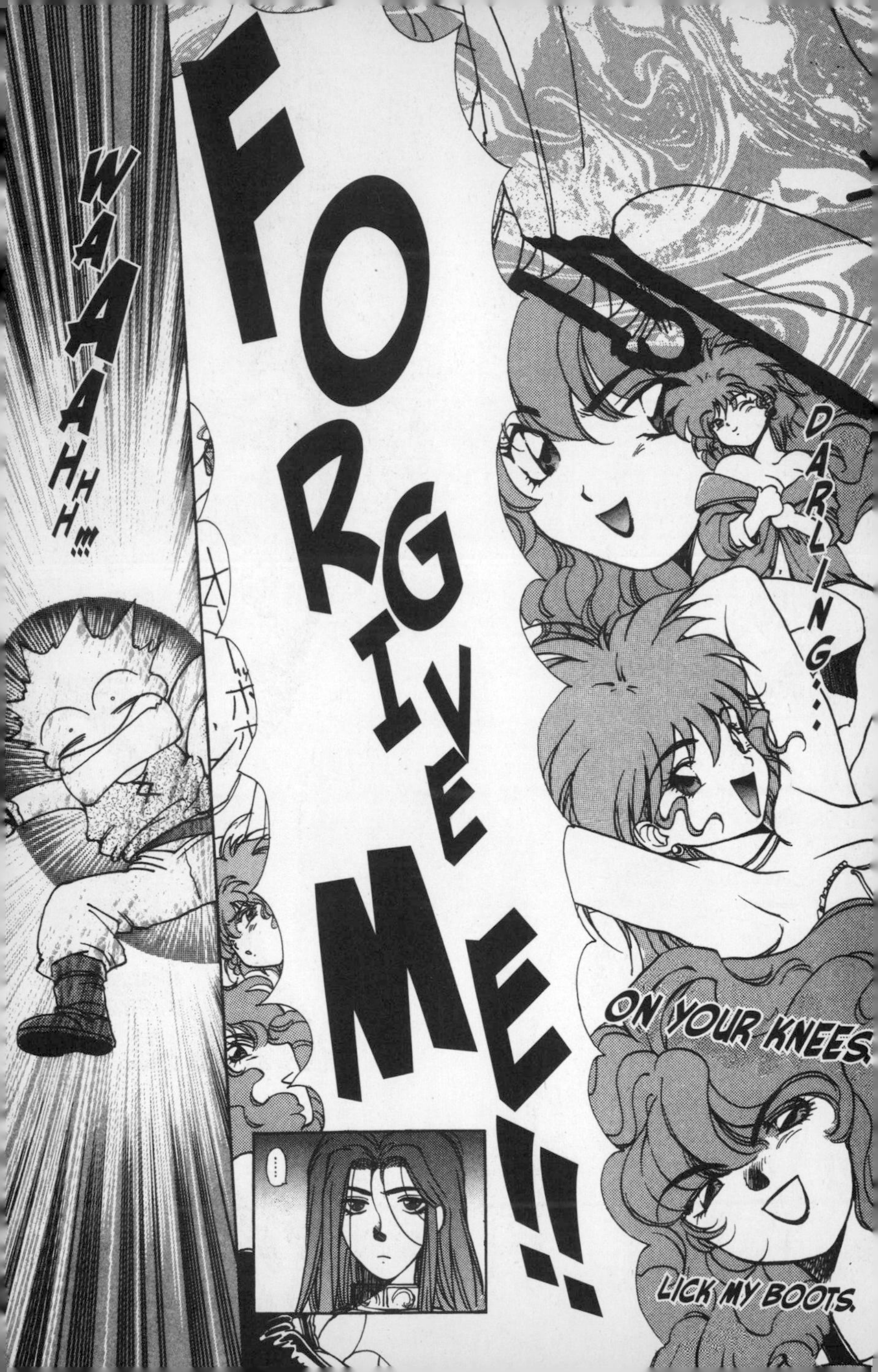
DARLING...
ON YOUR KNEES.
LICK MY BOOTS.
FORGIVE ME!!
....
WAAAAHHHH!!!

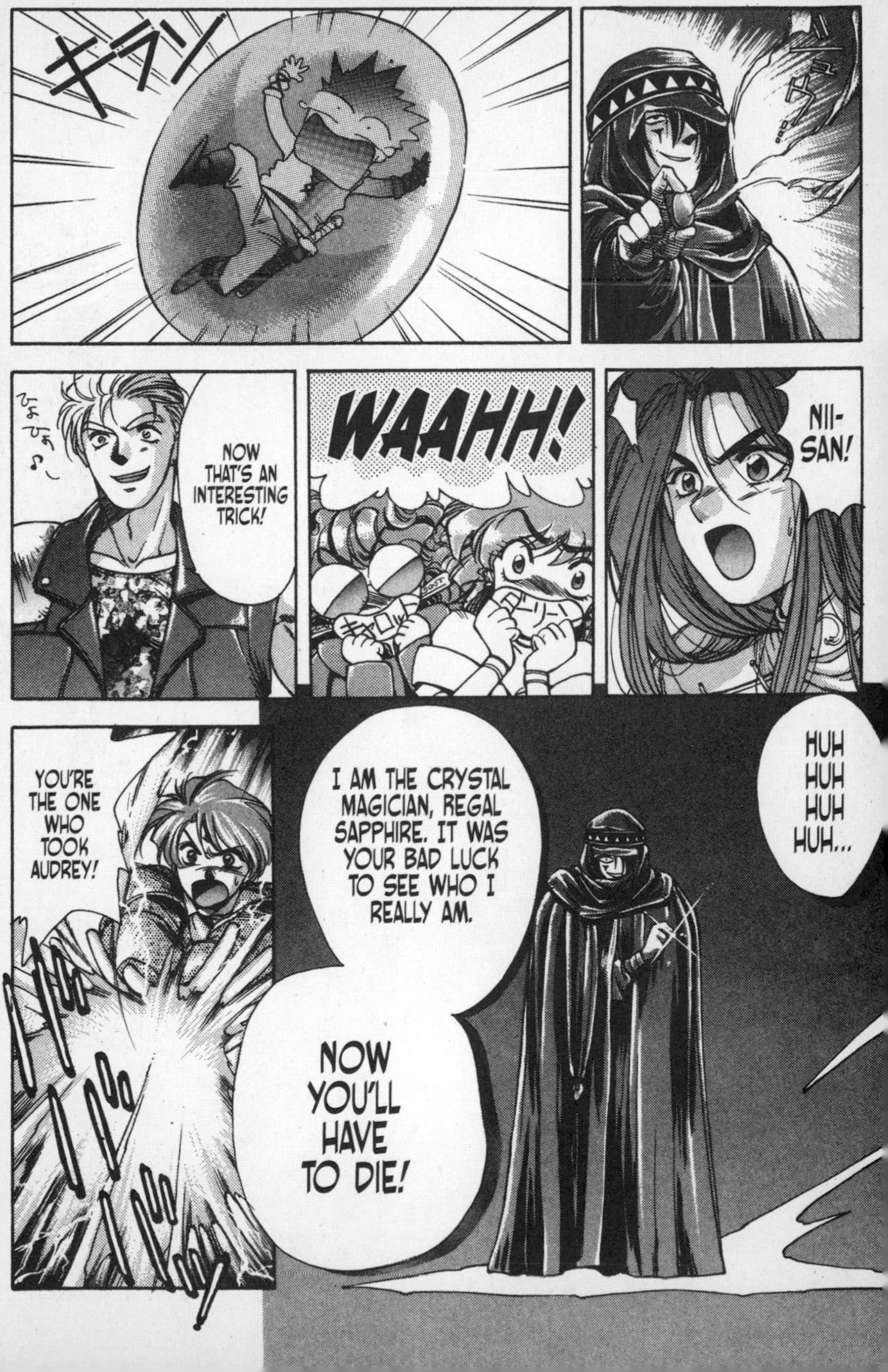
キラン
NII-SAN!
WAAHH!
NOW THAT'S AN INTERESTING TRICK!
HUH HUH HUH HUH...
I AM THE CRYSTAL MAGICIAN, REGAL SAPPHIRE. IT WAS YOUR BAD LUCK TO SEE WHO I REALLY AM.
NOW YOU'LL HAVE TO DIE!
YOU'RE THE ONE WHO TOOK AUDREY!

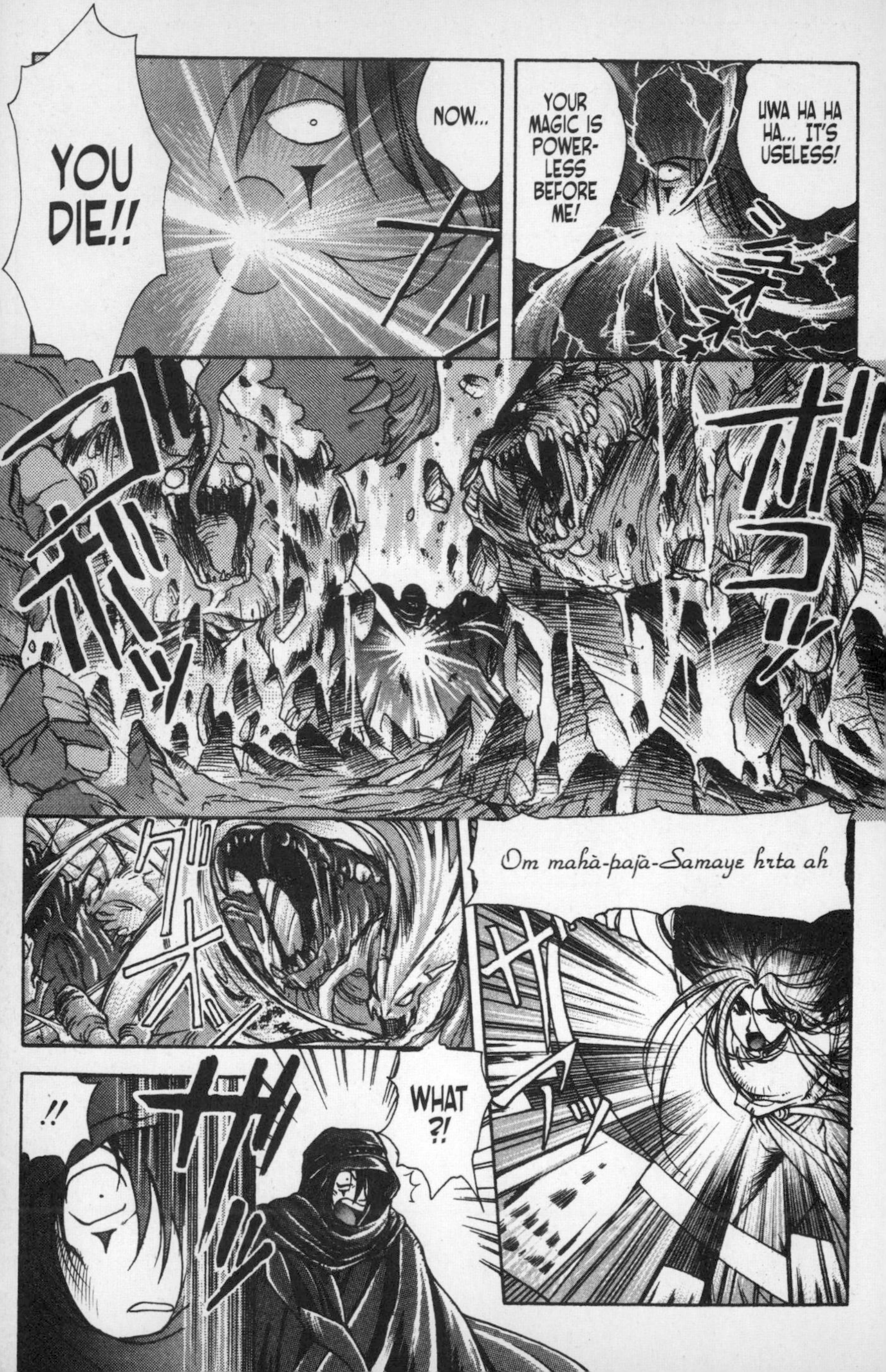
UWA HA HA HA... IT'S USELESS!
YOUR MAGIC IS POWER-LESS BEFORE ME!
NOW...
YOU DIE!!
Om mahà-pajà-Samaye hrta ah
WHAT ?!
!!

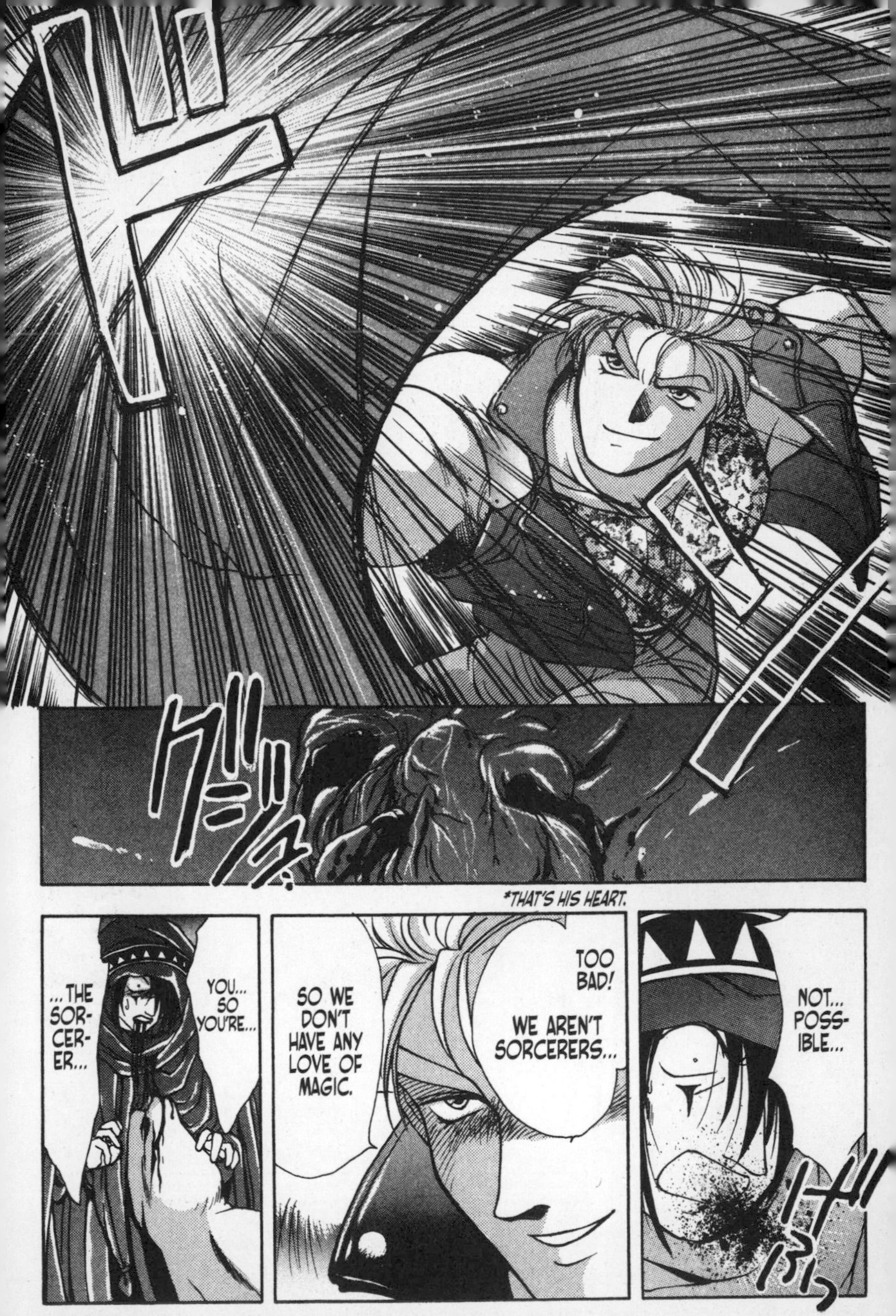
*THAT'S HIS HEART.
NOT... POSSIBLE...
TOO BAD!
WE AREN'T SORCERERS...
SO WE DON'T HAVE ANY LOVE OF MAGIC.
YOU... SO YOU'RE...
...THE SORCERER...

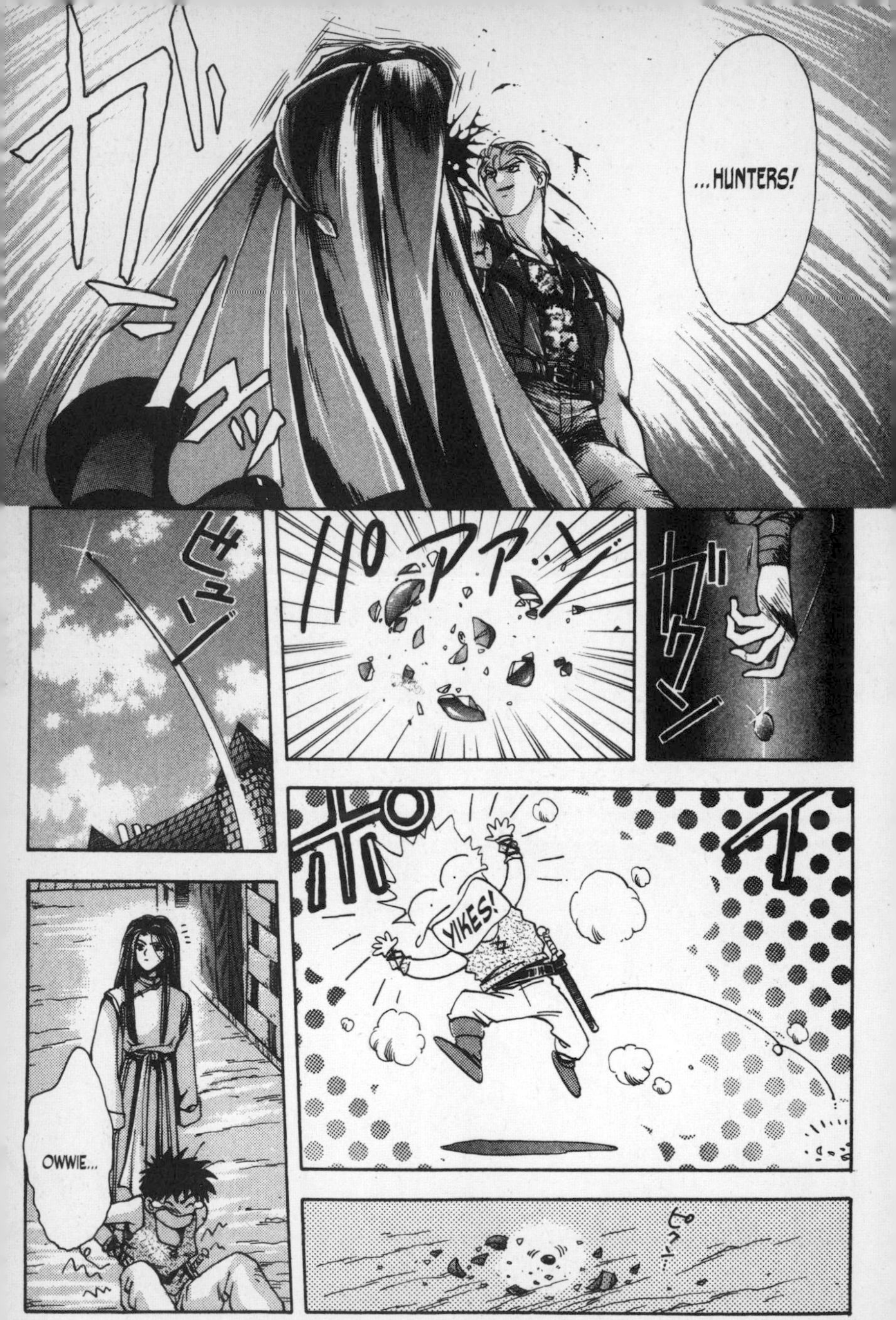
...HUNTERS!
YIKES!
OWWIE...

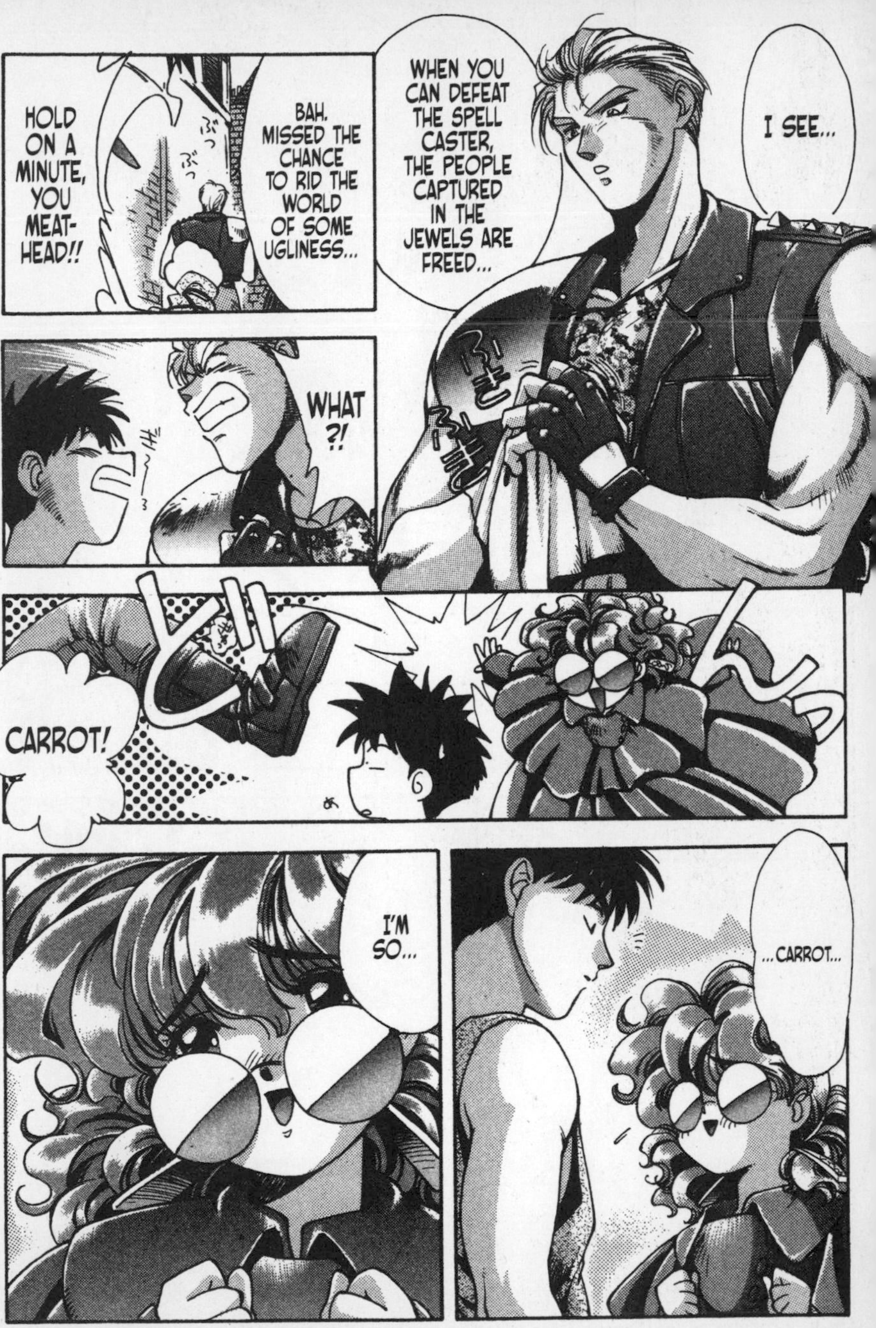
I SEE...
WHEN YOU CAN DEFEAT THE SPELL CASTER, THE PEOPLE CAPTURED IN THE JEWELS ARE FREED...
BAH. MISSED THE CHANCE TO RID THE WORLD OF SOME UGLINESS...
HOLD ON A MINUTE, YOU MEAT-HEAD!!
WHAT?!
CARROT!
...CARROT...
I'M SO...

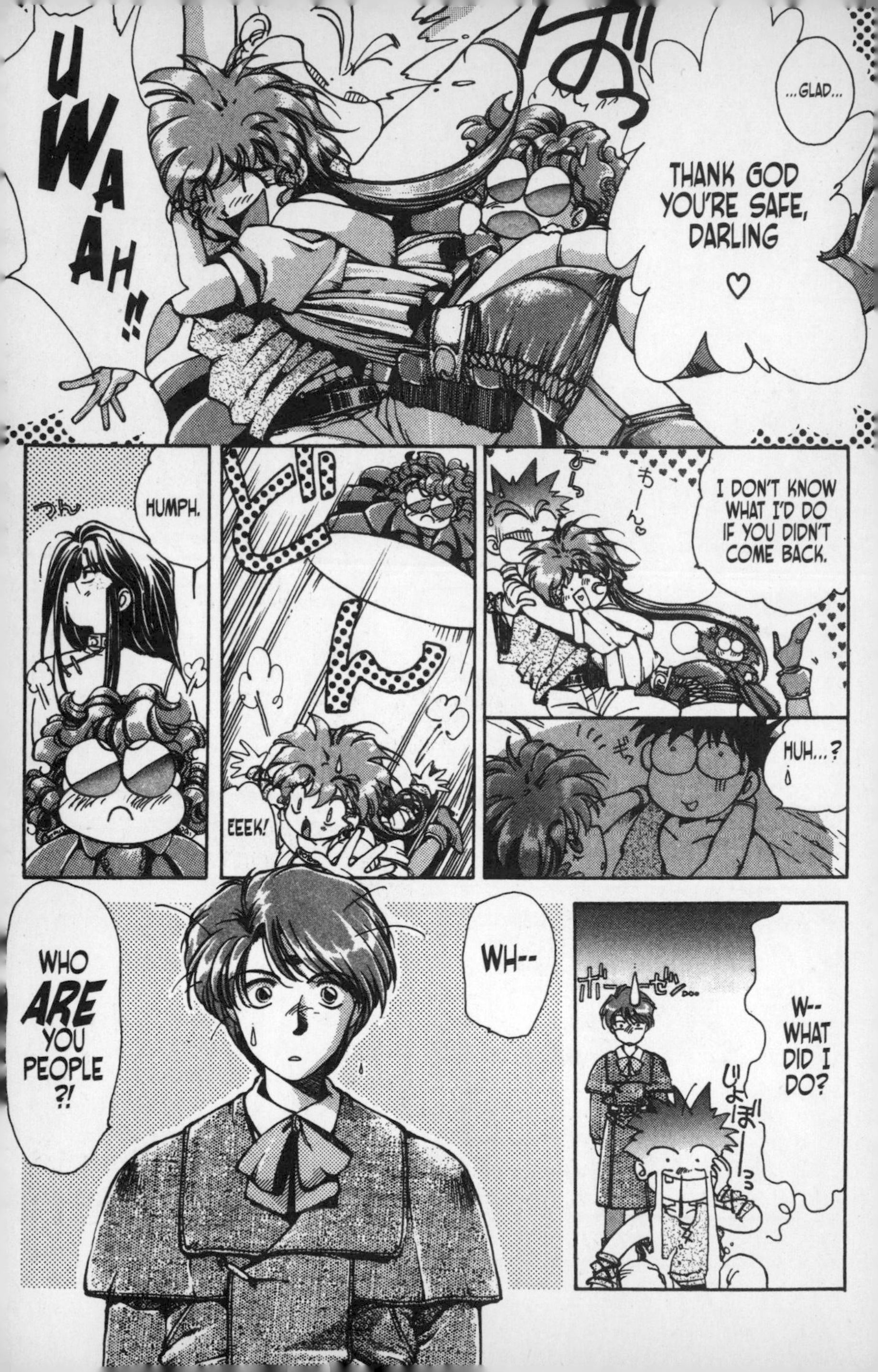

...GLAD...
THANK GOD YOU'RE SAFE, DARLING ♡
UWAAH!!
I DON'T KNOW WHAT I'D DO IF YOU DIDN'T COME BACK.
HUH...?
EEEK!
HUMPH.
つん
W-- WHAT DID I DO?
WH--
WHO ARE YOU PEOPLE ?!

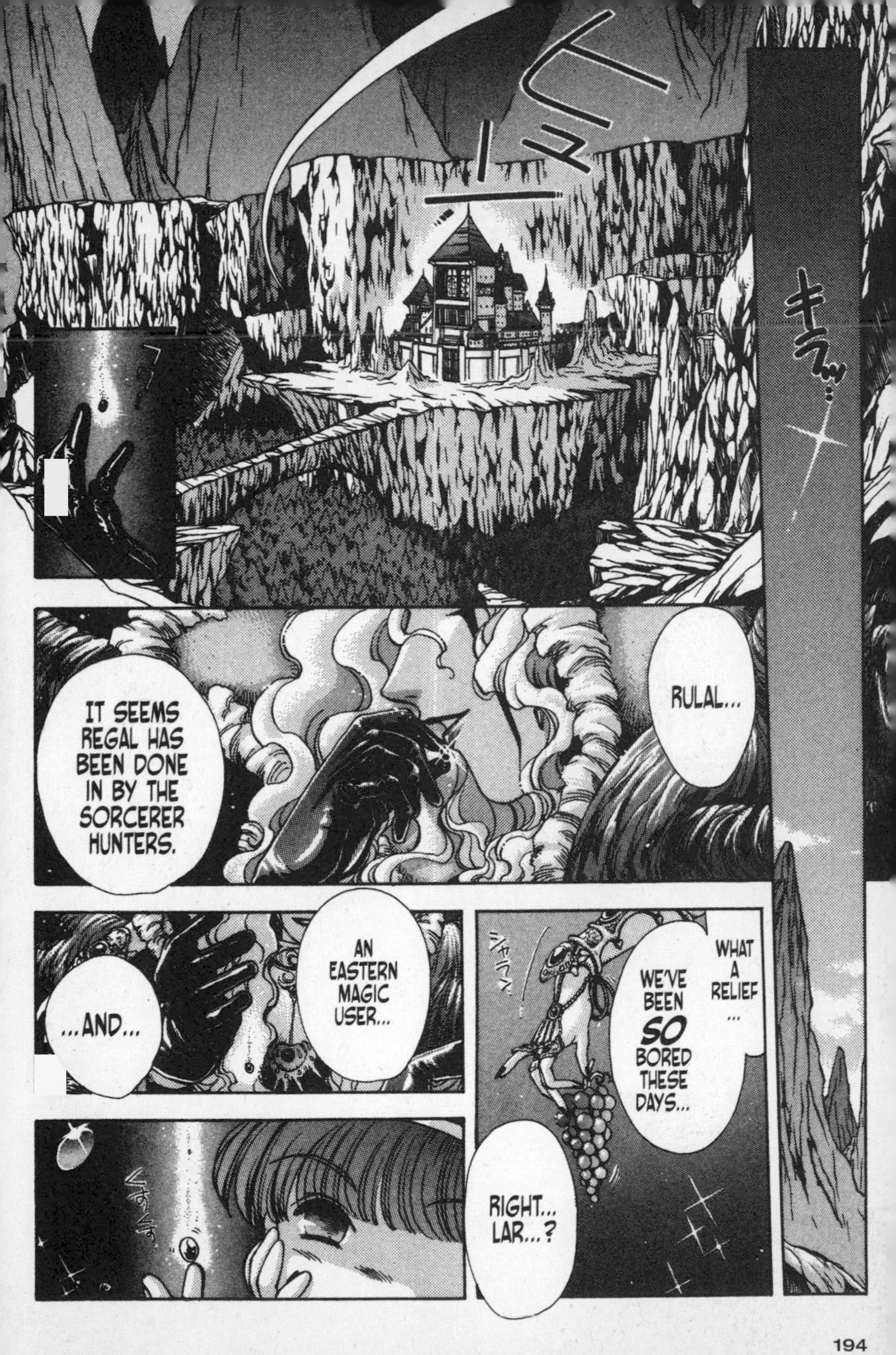
RULAL...
IT SEEMS REGAL HAS BEEN DONE IN BY THE SORCERER HUNTERS.
WHAT A RELIEF...
WE'VE BEEN SO BORED THESE DAYS...
AN EASTERN MAGIC USER...
...AND...
RIGHT... LAR...?

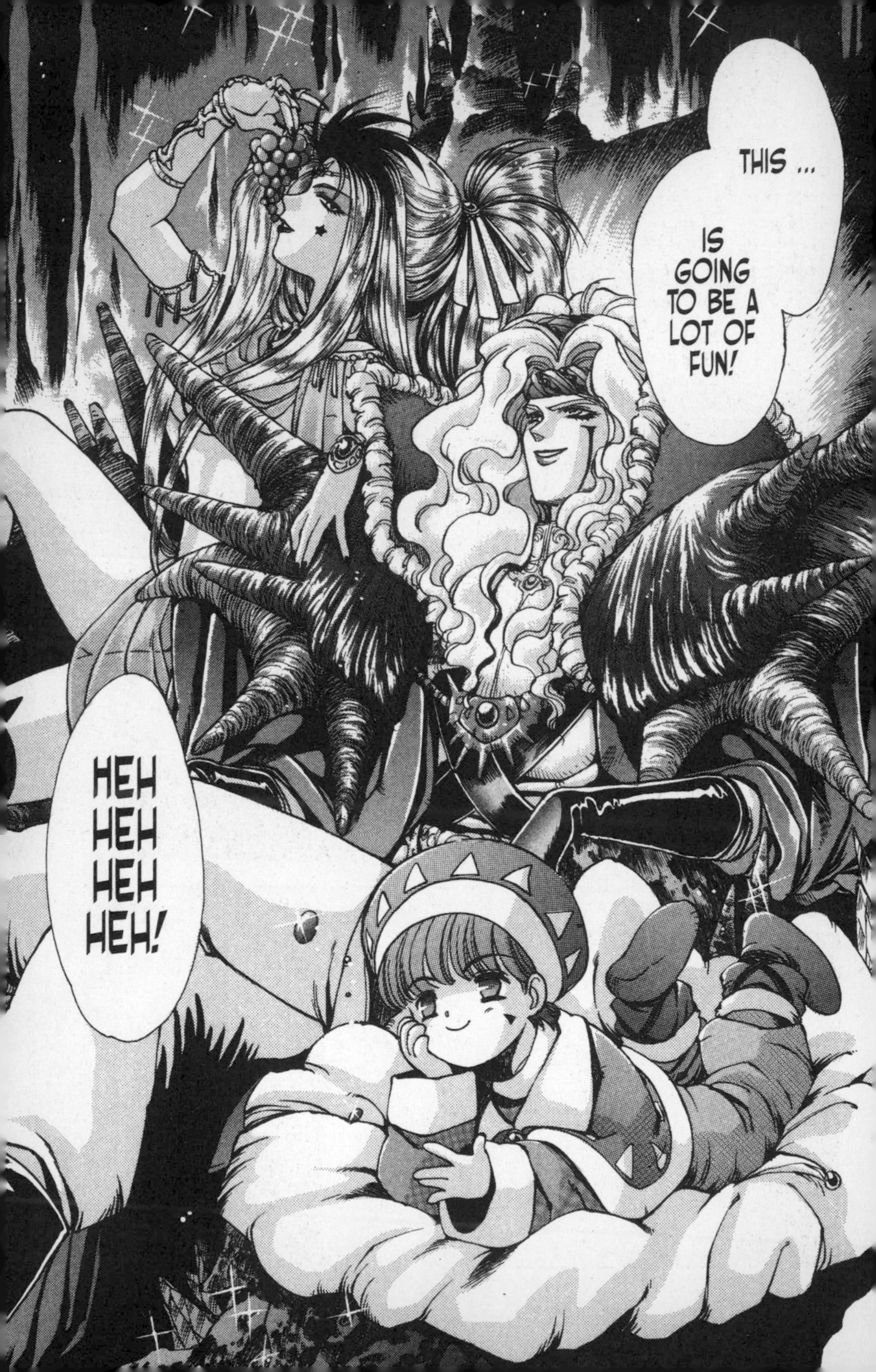
THIS ...
IS GOING TO BE A LOT OF FUN!
HEH HEH HEH HEH!

P R E V I E W

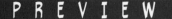

IN A WORLD WHERE MERCILESS SORCERERS ENSLAVE DEFENSELESS PARSONERS WITH THEIR EVIL ENCHANTMENTS, ONLY ONE MAN CAN END THE DARKNESS! WELL, ACTUALLY, THERE ARE THREE MEN AND TWO WOMEN. AND THOSE FIVE ARE KINDA HELPED BY A GODDESS, HER MAGICAL KNIGHTS, AND PAST GENERATIONS OF WARRIORS. BUT STILL, YOU GET THE POINT--THE ODDS ARE AGAINST JUSTICE IN THIS WICKED WIZARD WORLD, WHERE SOUL-STEALING SPELLCASTERS AND NEFARIOUS NECROMANCERS ARE OUT TO OPPRESS THE INNOCENT. EVEN A RELAXING DAY AT THE BEACH TURNS OUT TO BE NO PICNIC FOR OUR HEROES! THE EXCITEMENT CONTINUES IN *SORCERER HUNTERS* VOLUME 2!

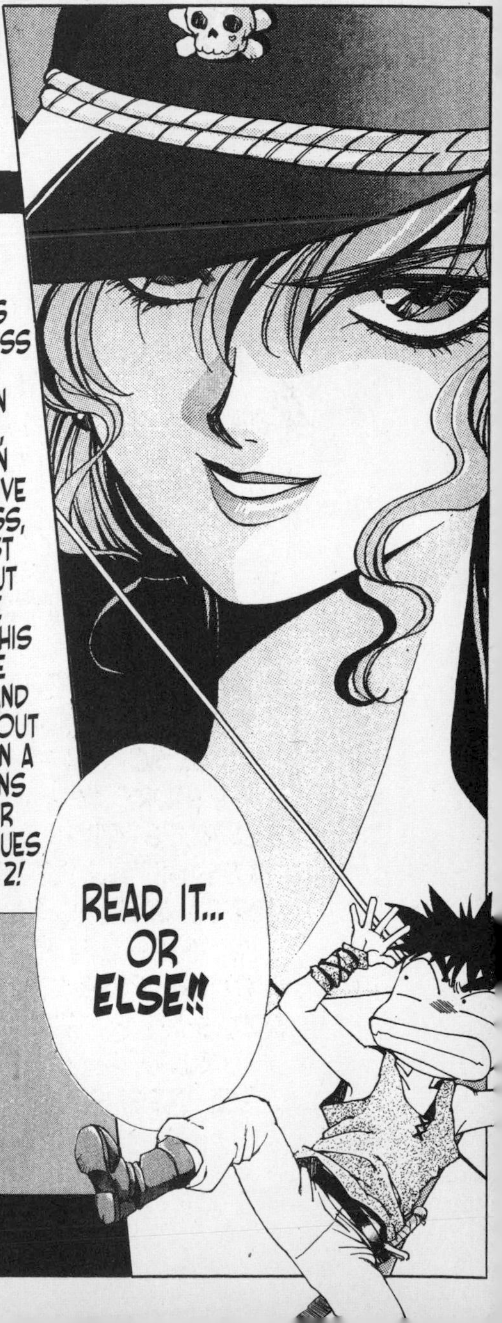
READ IT... OR ELSE!!

I'M HUNTING!

IN OTHER WORDS, I'M ALREADY, ALREADY, ALREADY, ALREADY TO THE THIRD! THE FIRST BOOK OF SORCERER HUNTERS IS ALREADY OUT! THIS MASTERPIECE IS THE JEWEL OF OUR SWEAT AND TEARS AND SNOT! (THAT'S DISGUSTING...) BUT STILL, I DON'T THINK I'VE HAD THIS MUCH FUN WORKING BEFORE! NO, I HAVEN'T! TIRA IS CUTE, AND MARRON IS BEAUTIFUL, AND, MORE THAN ANYTHING, CARROT'S PERVERTEDNESS IS FUN! GIRL-CRAZY, PERVERTED, UNFAITHFUL... THIS IS THE EPITOME OF WHAT MEN SHOULD BE! THERE ARE THOSE PURE-HEARTED SOULS AMONG THE READERS WHO WANT TO SEE CARROT NICELY PAIRED OFF WITH TIRA, BUT LET ME SAY UP FRONT THAT SATORU AKAHORI IS A BULLY FROM THE BOTTOM OF HIS HEART! ANYWAY, THERE ARE GOING TO BE MORE AND MORE CUTE GIRLS APPEARING IN THE STORY. WITH THESE MOUNTAINS OF SWEETIES, CARROT'S RETURN TO THE EVER-PRESENT TIRA JUST KEEPS GETTING PUT OFF. WHAT?! SATORU AKAHORI'S MARITAL RELATIONS ARE NOTHING LIKE THAT! JUST SO YOU KNOW...SPEAKING OF PRETTY GIRLS, THE GIRLS OMISHI DRAWS ARE JUST SO ADORABLE, AND THEIR BODIES ARE SO SEXY! I'M SO HAPPY I CAN'T STAND IT! ALL RIGHT, NOW I'LL HAVE TO KEEP HAVING CUTE GIRL GUEST STARS! ... AND SO AKAHORI BECOMES EMBROILED IN THE STORY.

JULY 1993 SATORU AKAHORI

AFTERWORD
あとがき

BONUS: SORCERER HUNTERS CHARACTERS GO TO SCHOOL!

OR SOMETHING LIKE THAT. RAY.OMISHI

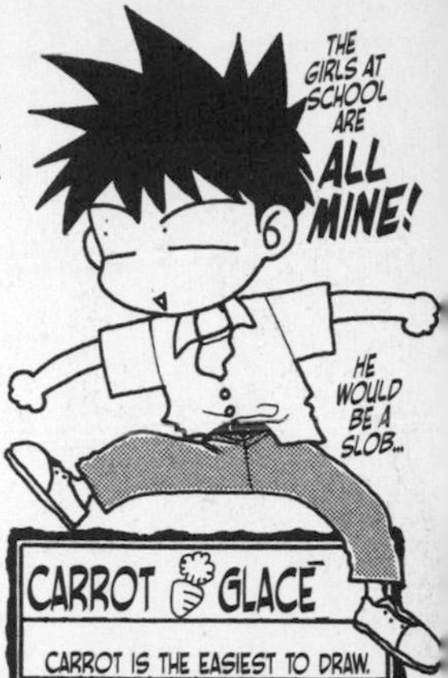
THE GIRLS AT SCHOOL ARE ALL MINE!
HE WOULD BE A SLOB...

HI THERE. I'M REI OMISHI, THE YOUNG ARTIST. I CAN'T BELIEVE THAT THIS IS MY FIRST COMIC, SO I'M A LITTLE BIT NERVOUS. THIS IS THE FIRST TIME I'VE DRAWN THE SAME CHARACTERS FOR SO LONG. THIS IS THE FIRST TIME I'VE BEEN BUSILY DRAWING COMICS MONTH AFTER MONTH. BEFORE, I HARDLY EVER FINISHED A STORY PROPERLY... THIS MUST BE BECAUSE OF HOW WONDERFUL MR. AKAHORI'S STORY IS. OMISHI JUST HAS SOOOO MUCH FUN DRAWING IT... ♡

SHE'S JUST LIKE ANOTHER READER...

CARROT GLACÉ

CARROT IS THE EASIEST TO DRAW. HE'S A TOTAL IDIOT, BUT THAT'S CUTE. THE BIG BROTHER WITH THE CONSTANTLY-CHANGING FACE... (IT'S NOT JUST CARROT I THINK...) BOO HOO!

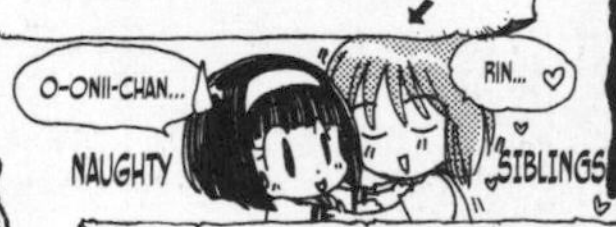
O-ONII-CHAN...
RIN... ♡
NAUGHTY
SIBLINGS

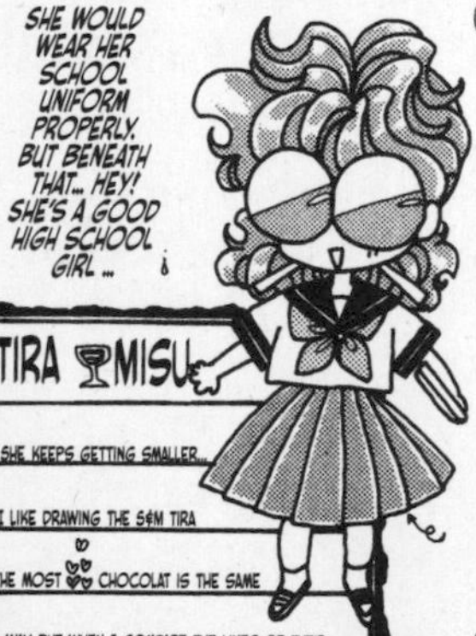
SHE WOULD WEAR HER SCHOOL UNIFORM PROPERLY. BUT BENEATH THAT... HEY! SHE'S A GOOD HIGH SCHOOL GIRL ...

THE FIRST THING I LOOK FORWARD TO WHEN I GET A NEW STORY IS THE GUEST CHARACTERS, ESPECIALLY SEEING WHAT KIND OF GIRL CHARACTERS THERE ARE! OUT OF THE ONES SO FAR, I LIKE RIN BEST. THE TWO OF THEM HAVE A KIND OF DANGEROUS RELATIONSHIP... I LIKED OLIVIA TOO. I LIKE STRONG-WILLED GIRLS!

TIRA MISU

SHE KEEPS GETTING SMALLER... I LIKE DRAWING THE S&M TIRA THE MOST. CHOCOLAT IS THE SAME WAY, BUT WHEN I COMPARE THE LINES OF THEIR FACES BEFORE AND AFTER THEY TRANSFORM, THEY'RE COMPLETELY DIFFERENT PEOPLE. BOO HOO HOO! EVEN THEIR BODY SHAPE CHANGES...I'VE BEEN TOLD BY A CAREFUL CRITIC. OMISHI TREADS HER OWN PATH...

MAYBE IT WOULD BE BETTER TO THINK OF IT AS SOME SORT OF TRANSFORMATION ITEM... TIRA'S S&M LOOK AND CHOCOLAT'S HAT... THEN ARE THEY TURNING INTO GROWNUPS? UMM, MAYBE NOT...

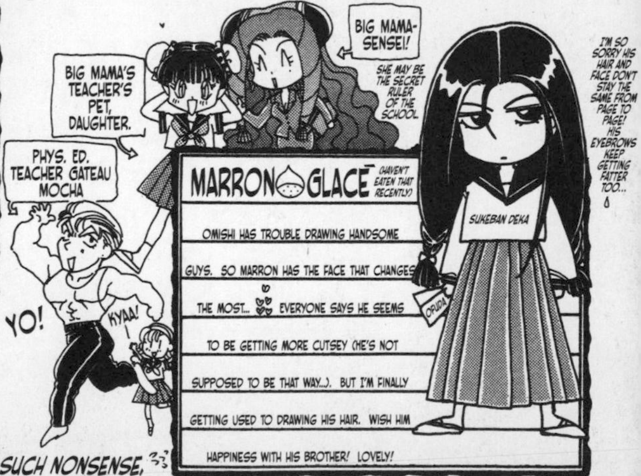
I'M SO SORRY HIS HAIR AND FACE DON'T STAY THE SAME FROM PAGE TO PAGE! HIS EYEBROWS KEEP GETTING FATTER TOO...
BIG MAMA-SENSEI!
SHE MAY BE THE SECRET RULER OF THE SCHOOL
BIG MAMA'S TEACHER'S PET, DAUGHTER.
PHYS. ED. TEACHER GATEAU MOCHA
YO!
KYAA!
SUKEBAN DEKA
OPUDA

MARRON GLACÉ (HAVEN'T EATEN THAT RECENTLY)

OMISHI HAS TROUBLE DRAWING HANDSOME GUYS. SO MARRON HAS THE FACE THAT CHANGES THE MOST... EVERYONE SAYS HE SEEMS TO BE GETTING MORE CUTSEY (HE'S NOT SUPPOSED TO BE THAT WAY...). BUT I'M FINALLY GETTING USED TO DRAWING HIS HAIR. WISH HIM HAPPINESS WITH HIS BROTHER! LOVELY!

I'M SORRY FOR WRITING SUCH NONSENSE, MR. AKAHORI!

THERE AREN'T ANY PEOPLE CALLED CRÈME BRULÉE, ARE THERE?

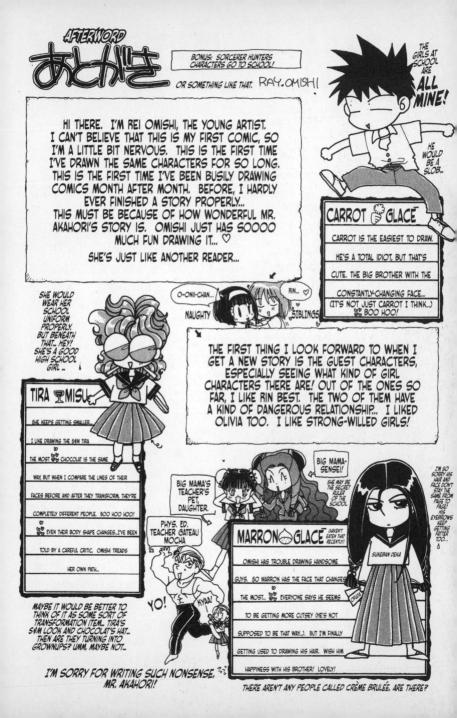

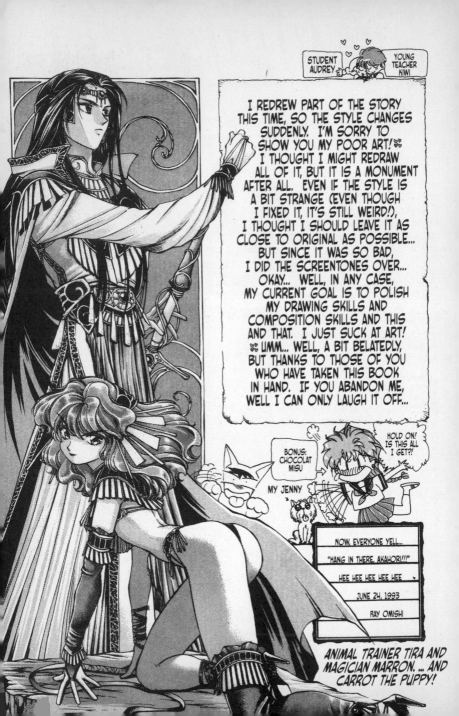

STUDENT AUDREY / YOUNG TEACHER KIWI

I REDREW PART OF THE STORY
THIS TIME, SO THE STYLE CHANGES
SUDDENLY. I'M SORRY TO
SHOW YOU MY POOR ART!
I THOUGHT I MIGHT REDRAW
ALL OF IT, BUT IT IS A MONUMENT
AFTER ALL. EVEN IF THE STYLE IS
A BIT STRANGE (EVEN THOUGH
I FIXED IT, IT'S STILL WEIRD!),
I THOUGHT I SHOULD LEAVE IT AS
CLOSE TO ORIGINAL AS POSSIBLE...
BUT SINCE IT WAS SO BAD,
I DID THE SCREENTONES OVER...
OKAY... WELL, IN ANY CASE,
MY CURRENT GOAL IS TO POLISH
MY DRAWING SKILLS AND
COMPOSITION SKILLS AND THIS
AND THAT. I JUST SUCK AT ART!
UMM... WELL, A BIT BELATEDLY,
BUT THANKS TO THOSE OF YOU
WHO HAVE TAKEN THIS BOOK
IN HAND. IF YOU ABANDON ME,
WELL I CAN ONLY LAUGH IT OFF...

BONUS: CHOCOLAT MISU

MY JENNY

HOLD ON! IS THIS ALL I GET?!

NOW, EVERYONE YELL...

"HANG IN THERE, AKAHORI!!!"

HEE HEE HEE HEE HEE

JUNE 24, 1993

RAY OMISHI

ANIMAL TRAINER TIRA AND
MAGICIAN MARRON. ... AND
CARROT THE PUPPY!

TOKYOPOP SHOP

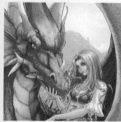
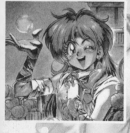

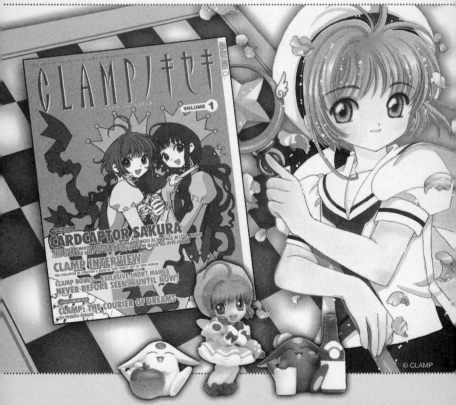

SOKORA REFUGEES™

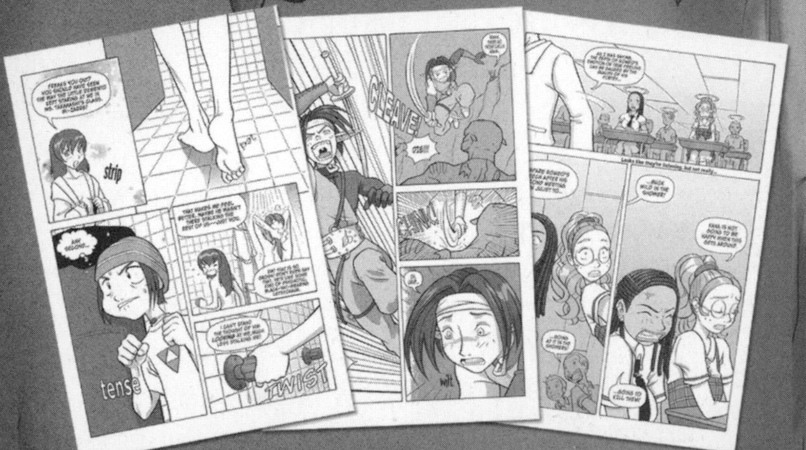

Kana thought life couldn't get any worse—behind on her schoolwork and out of luck with boys, she is also the only one of her friends who hasn't "blossomed." When she falls through a magical portal in the girls' shower, she's transported to the enchanted world of Sokora—wearing nothing but a small robe! Now, on top of landing in this mysterious setting, she finds that her body is beginning to go through some tremendous changes.

Preview the manga at:
www.TOKYOPOP.com/sokora

T
TEEN
AGE 13+

SOKORA REFUGEES

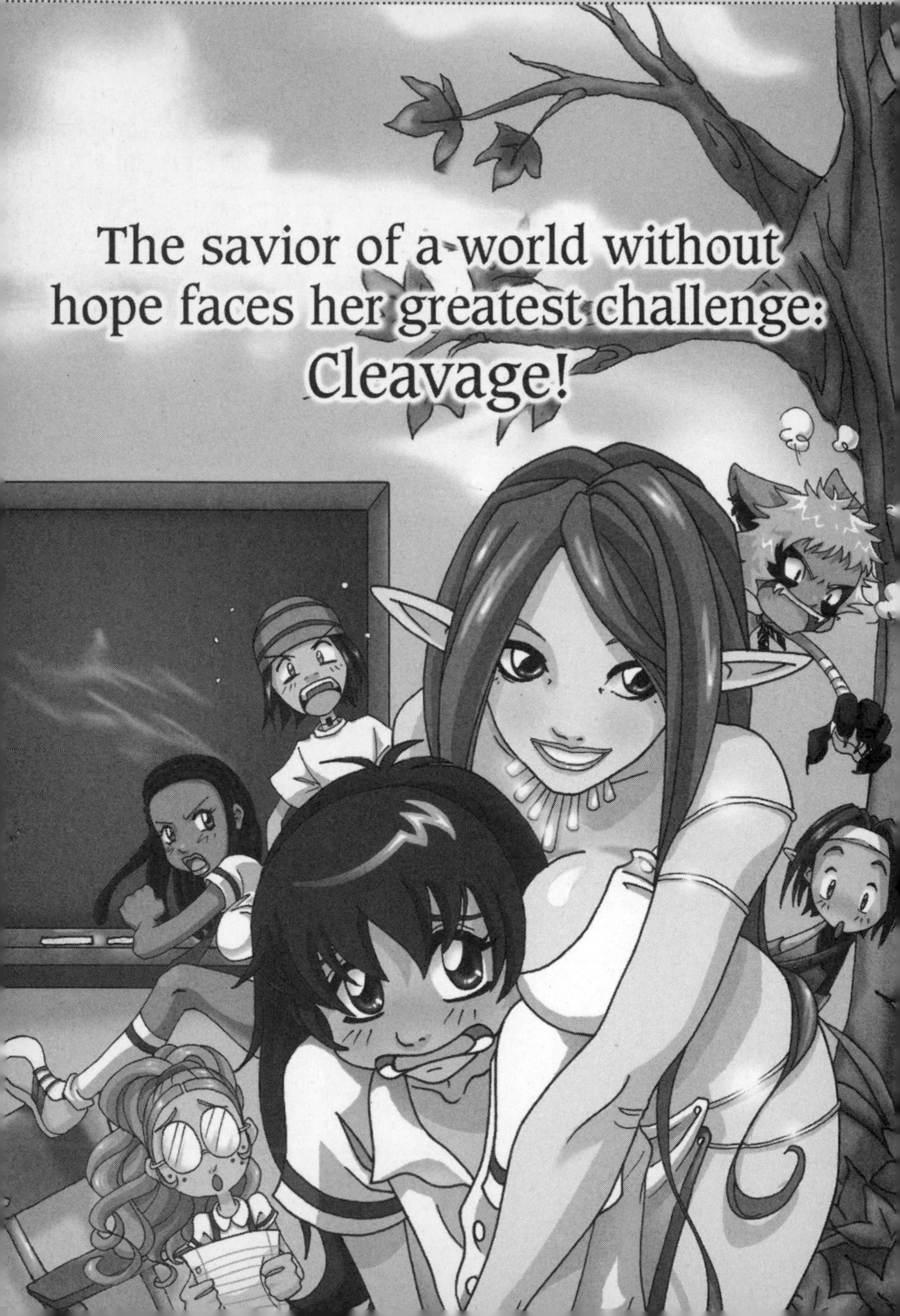
The savior of a world without hope faces her greatest challenge:
Cleavage!

EDITORS' PICKS

TOKYOPOP MANGA SUPPLEMENT

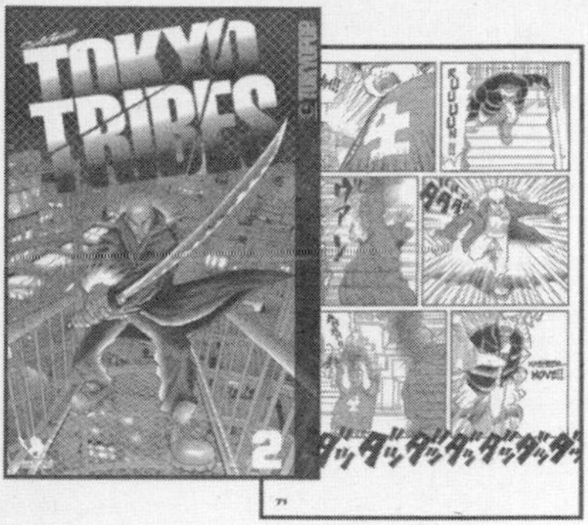
TOKYO TRIBES
2

BY SANTA INOUE

TOKYO TRIBES

Tokyo Tribes first hit Japanese audiences in the sleek pages of the ultra-hip skater fashion magazine *Boon.* Santa Inoue's hard-hitting tale of Tokyo street gangs battling it out in the concrete sprawl of Japan's capital raises the manga storytelling bar. Ornate with hip-hop trappings and packed with gangland grit, *Tokyo Tribes* paints a vivid, somewhat surreal vision of urban youth: rival gangs from various Tokyo barrios clash over turf, and when the heat between two of the tribes gets personal, a bitter rivalry explodes into all-out warfare.

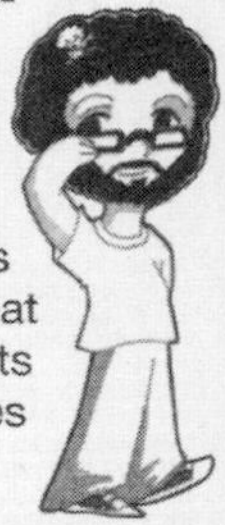

~Luis Reyes, Editor

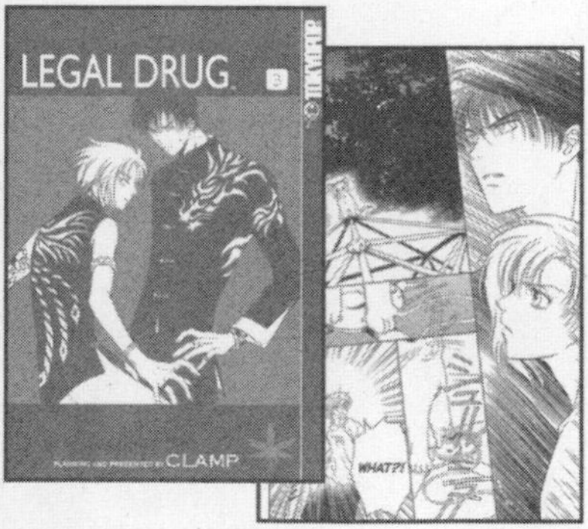
LEGAL DRUG
3
CLAMP
WHAT?!

BY CLAMP

LEGAL DRUG

CLAMP is the four-woman studio famous for creating much of the world's most popular manga. For the past 15 years they have produced such hits as the adorable *Cardcaptor Sakura,* the dark and brooding *Tokyo Babylon,* and the sci-fi romantic comedy *Chobits.* In *Legal Drug,* we meet Kazahaya and Rikuou, two ordinary pharmacists who moonlight as amateur sleuths for a mysterious boss. *Legal Drug* is a perfect dose of mystery, psychic powers and the kind of homoerotic tension for which CLAMP is renowned.

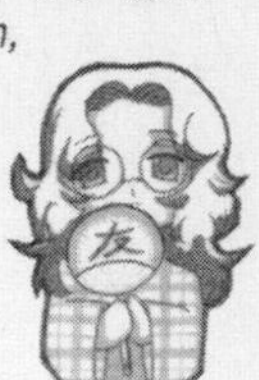

~Lillian Diaz-Przybyl, Jr. Editor

DOLL
4

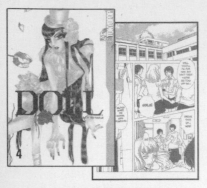

BY MITSUKAZU MIHARA

DOLL

Mitsukazu Mihara's haunting *Doll* uses beautiful androids to examine what it means to be truly human. While the characters in *Doll* are draped in the chic Gothic-Lolita fashions that made Mihara-sensei famous, the themes explored are more universal—all emotions and walks of life have their day in *Doll*. *Doll* begins as a series of 'one-shot' stories and gradually dovetails into an epic of emotion and intrigue. It's like the *Twilight Zone* meets *Blade Runner!*

~Rob Tokar, Senior Editor

PLANETES
VOLUME 01 MAKOTO YUKIMURA

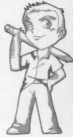

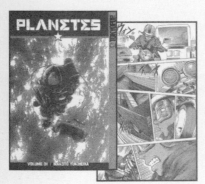

BY MAKOTO YUKIMURA

PLANETES

Makoto Yukimura's profoundly moving and graphically arresting *Planetes* posits a near future where mankind's colonization of space has begun. Young Hachimaki yearns to join this exciting new frontier. Instead, he cleans the glut of orbital junk mankind's initial foray into space produced. He works with Fee, a nicotine-addict beauty with an abrasive edge, and Yuri, a veteran spaceman with a tragic past in search of inner peace. *Planetes* combines the scope of Jules Verne (*Around the World in Eighty Days*) and Robert Heinlein (*Starship Troopers*) with the philosophical wonder of *2001: A Space Odyssey.*

~Luis Reyes, Editor

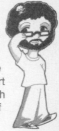

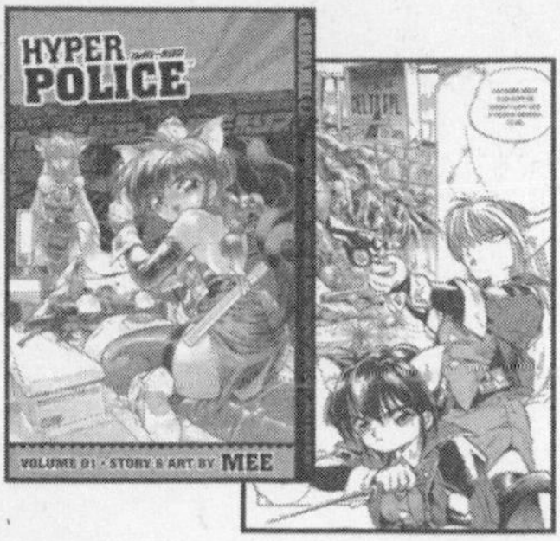
HYPER POLICE
VOLUME 01 · STORY & ART BY MEE

HYPER POLICE

BY MEE

In a future rife with crime, humans are an endangered species—and monsters have taken over! Natsuki is a cat girl who uses magical powers to enforce the law. However, her greatest threat doesn't come from the criminals. Her partner Sakura, a "nine-tailed" fox, plots to eat Natsuki and gobble up her magic! In this dog-eat-dog world, Natsuki fights to stay on top!

OT OLDER TEEN AGE 16+

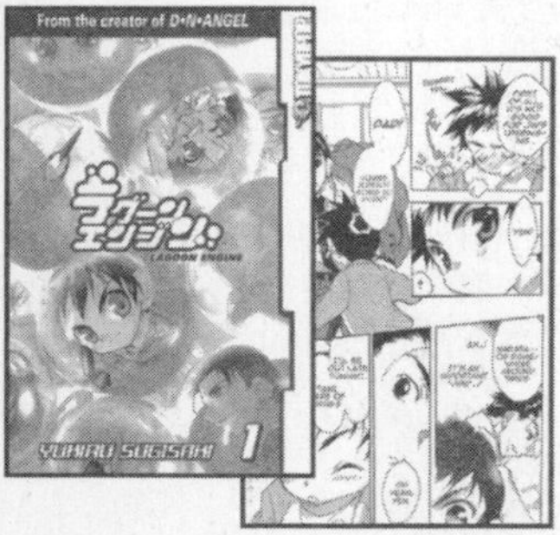
From the creator of D·N·ANGEL
YUKIRU SUGISAKI 1

LAGOON ENGINE

BY YUKIRU SUGISAKI

From the best-selling creator of *D·N·Angel!*

Yen and Jin are brothers in elementary school—and successors in the Ragun family craft. They are Gakushi, those who battle ghosts and evil spirits known as "Maga" by guessing their true name. As Yen and Jin train to join the family business, the two boys must keep their identities a secret...or risk death!

T TEEN AGE 13+

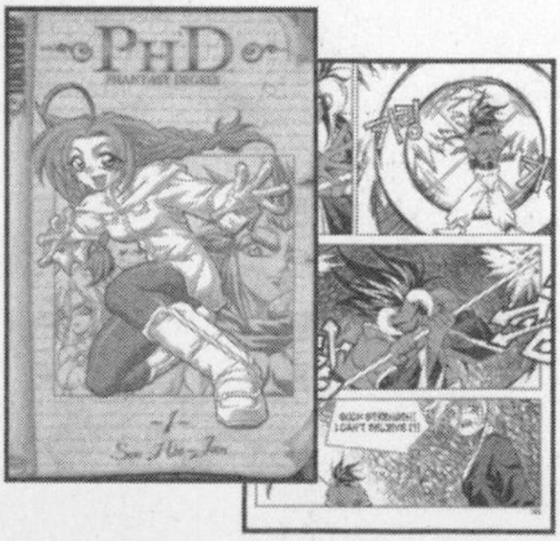
PHD

PHD: PHANTASY DEGREE

BY HEE-JOON SON

Sang is a fearlessly spunky young girl who is about to receive one hell of an education...at the Demon School Hades! She's on a mission to enroll into the monsters-only class. However, monster matriculation is not what is truly on her mind—she wants to acquire the fabled "King's Ring" from the fiancée of the chief commander of hell!

T TEEN AGE 13+

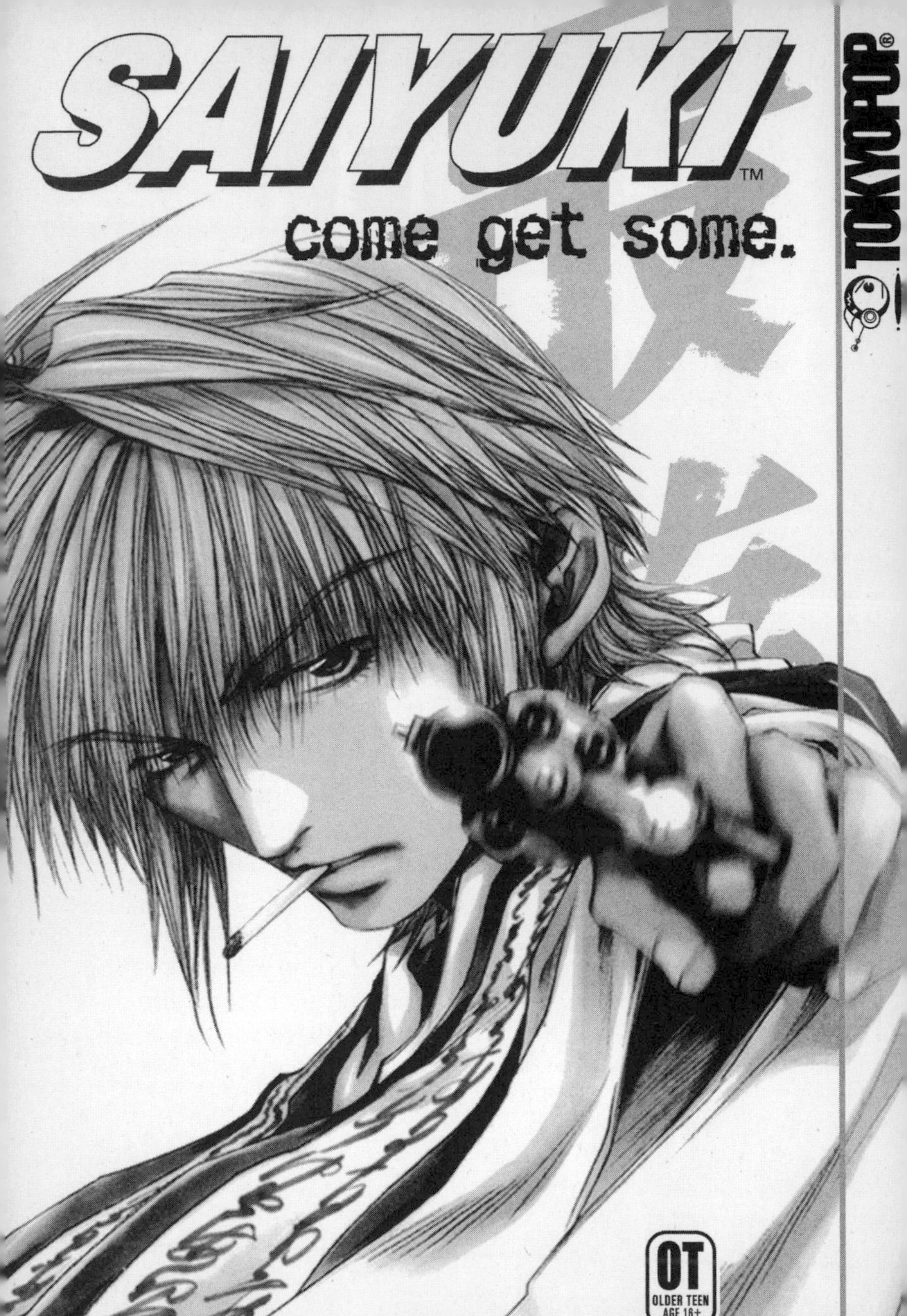
SAIYUKI™
come get some.
TOKYOPOP®
OT
OLDER TEEN
AGE 16+

STOP!

This is the back of the book.
You wouldn't want to spoil a great ending!

This book is printed "manga-style," in the authentic Japanese right-to-left format. Since none of the artwork has been flipped or altered, readers get to experience the story just as the creator intended. You've been asking for it, so TOKYOPOP® delivered: authentic, hot-off-the-press, and far more fun!

DIRECTIONS

If this is your first time reading manga-style, here's a quick guide to help you understand how it works.

It's easy... just start in the top right panel and follow the numbers. Have fun, and look for more 100% authentic manga from TOKYOPOP®!

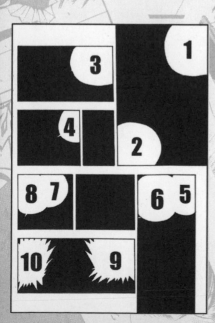

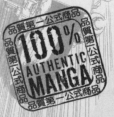